Eve1

MW01241899

Author's other works

Avenue Girls- Boulevard Girls- *Everybody has or knows someone like this,*

Ring Dancer's Destiny, *What would have happened if Guinevere and King Arthur never met?*

Baby Papers, *What's the use of waiting for Mr. Right if he's never going to come?*

Single Heart Single Love, *Can love change a hard, cold heart?*

Firebrand- (with literary partner Kathye Quick writing as P.K. Eden) *saving the world is serious business*

The Love Lesson- How *does a widow get rid of the one thing that could upset her true identity—her virginity.*

A Dream deferred, A Joy Achieved an anthology by Charisse Nesbit, featuring *Trial Basis* by Patt Mihailoff

Zane's Caramel Flava II - *Therapy (X-RATED)*

Zane's Chocolate Flava III – *The Night Game (X-RATED)*

Dedication

To my mother Leona

Special thanks to

Ms. Nathasha Brooks-Harris, who is not only an exceptional writer but one of the best editors ever.

Thelma Watkins, who is responsible for titling this current work and Darlene James, my literary cheerleaders,

My sister-in-law Deborah Freeman and my wonderful nephew Staff Sgt. George Martin Freeman,

My cousin Mary Meadows, whom I love with all my heart.

Kathye Quick a co-author of FIREBRAND, a wonderful generous friend and literary plotting superstar,

The Jazzy Jems Book Club: Stephanie, Sylvia, Portia, Donna, Mildred, Barbara and Alyce,

Selene Brady, a dynamic individual who not only *feeds* the soul and spirit but the belly as well, and is a person with an unquenchable thirst for learning and sharing.

Liberty States Fiction Writers - If you are looking to join a great group with a plethora of award winning and NY Times best-selling authors, this is the place and I count myself lucky to be in their company.

My husband George, who supports all of my accomplishments,

I also dedicate this novel to large and small **Book Clubs** everywhere because without them *I* and other writers would not be able to fulfill our love of writing.

To the living and loving God from whom all blessings flow and to whom I dedicate my spirit.

Introducing Artist, Alyce Faye-Jarrett

I am proud to be able to not only display a minute amount of the extraordinary artistic workmanship of a most talented local resident of New Jersey, but to give you an insight of her creativeness so boldly displayed within each of her pieces. Alyce is also an accomplished jewelry artiste of one-of-kind earrings, bracelets, Pins and necklaces. You've heard the saying *"you can't make a silk purse out of a sow's ear"* well I beg to differ. This is an artist who can take a crumpled piece of paper, a slice of ordinary window screen, scraps of bits of pieces of beads and glass and make a piece of art that will boggle the mind. Alyce is always on the go and her work can be seen at many tradeshows and fairs, including but not limited to the Annual and very popular *Newport Jazz and Capitol Jazz Festivals, Gallery D'Estee in Chicago, The curates art show in Harlem New York and the Princeton Gallery in New Jersey.*

Alyce hosts an annual *by invitation-only* display and sale of her creations in December where visitors from all over the United States come to enjoy an afternoon of viewing and purchasing with great food and libation.

Please visit *alycefayeoriginals.com* to view her art and to contact and follow her on twitter.

While these pictures are not associated with actual story content, it is my pleasure and honor to have been granted permission to display some of her incredible work in this short story collection.

CONTENTS

Emotional Corruption
Something Sweet
Hard Lesson
When the Music Fades
Never too old Never too
Hip Hop Terror Young
What a Man
Crash Course
Mirror Images and Broken Vows
The most unlikely Man
Campus Stripper
The Fairest Gentleman
Substitute Mom
Drop out to Graduate
High on the Down Low
Tee for Two
The Drummond House Legend
Fleeing Lies
Stolen Money Reclaimed Heart
Alone and Destitute

Acknowledgements for When the Music Fades

Martin Taylor, Bucky Pizzarelli, Clayton-Hamilton Jazz orchestra, Chick Corea, Norah Jones, Nancy Wilson, Diana Krall, Abby Lincoln, *Alicia Keys, Rihanna, John Legend, All others are gratefully acknowledged*

This is a work of fiction, Names, Characters, places and incidents are the products of the author's imagination or are used fictitiously. Any resemblance to actual events, locales or persons, living or dead is entirely coincidental.

Title ID: **6555939**

ISBN-13: **978-1537531793**

EMOTIONAL CORRUPTION

Gail had always been civically minded. In High school she was on the junior political debate team and in her second year of college she knew she wanted to major in political journalism. With the help of several of her family members was able to attend college full time and as long as she continued to excel they did what they could to help her through. Gail knew the only way she could pay them back was to do a good job, succeed and make them proud.

~*~

She had interned for a while and gotten several jobs right out of college but all they did was whet her appetite for something more substantial and more permanent. Finally she started freelancing for a local newspaper doing small articles and features, hoping it would be the stepping into the big time at the Virginia Tribune.

One morning the central desk editor called her into his office and told her he had a lead on a story that every journalist on every newspaper in Virginia and the surrounding area was chomping at the bit for.

"Gail, I want you to get out to *BOTTOM BAY*, Reed Jackson is campaigning and it seems he's got the whole town in an uproar." He'd said.

"Isn't he the one who…"

"The very one, now go on get out of here and get me a story."

Every politician makes promises, and over the years Gail had heard more than her share. She also knew that many rarely come through so she was hoping one way or another this story would help jumpstart a permanent career for her where she would someday be journalistic household name.

~*~

Everyone knew how for more than seventy years the poorest of the poor had been relegated to a small community along the flood line on the Virginia coast called *Bottom Bay Cove*. They had been given housing that was little more than shacks and over the years built into unstable but slight better livable conditions. They had been given little on the way amenities that other towns received and were clandestinely warned not to venture or stay too long into the town area where the more prosperous folk lived.

Over the years people lived, died and passed on their piddling plots of land and homes on *Bottom Bay* to their children and grandchildren with nothing more to show for their efforts but a gorgeous sunrise and sunset, and short sandy shell strewn beach.

Because there was little work and virtually no commerce, the people settled into a type of quiet desperation and as time went on the homes fell into disrepair and the general feeling was that of total hopelessness.

It wasn't until a newly elected town council began to act on what they had been whispering about for the past few years that made people sit up and take notice. *Bottom Bay* was prime waterfront property. All *they* had to do was find a way to displace the current inhabitants without making it look like they were stealing. It wasn't long before homes were being bought up and houses were becoming boarded up eyesores, much to chagrin of the remaining locals who were still trying to hold on to and maintain their properties as best they could. They began to protest and refused any and all offers, which were minimal at best. Even low level pressures from thugs were resisted, and the police began to get involved, but with nowhere near the level of support that they should have shown. Finally they demanded that a representative come to hear their side.

Reed Jackson leaped at the chance, not only because he felt he had everything in the bag but because he was a limelight junkie. He took up the challenge for a meeting and called for an open air town meeting where he intended to lay out his plan for development.

The locals met him with shouts of anger as they pointed to the tractors and bulldozers down at the far end of the beach.

~*~

Gail arrived at the cove just before noon. The crowd was thick with local people and of course a few reporters.

She edged her way toward the loud, deep voice booming over the sound of bulldozers that were leveling some vacated shacks and *Mom and Pop* stores a few hundred yards away.

"You hear that sound?" the baritone voice said, "It's the sound of progress. It's the sound of the future,"

Gail stepped up front and looked at the charismatic councilman who stood before his constituents, jacket-less in his crisp white shirt with the sleeves rolled up. She snickered to herself. There must have been some kind of handbook that all politicians read on how to look like *regular folks*.

She noticed that he was better looking than the average *up and coming* campaigner which she knew gave him an edge with younger voters—not to mention the women. His velvet brown eyes were sexy with sleek black brows and lashes that looked like the belonged on a porcelain doll.

She noticed that city police and what looked like private security was keeping picketing objectors far enough away so that even their chants couldn't be heard above the roar of Reed's many and obviously paid supporters.

After a lull in his speech, questions about the expulsion and relocation of the indigenous people began to pop up. His answers were quick, well thought out and smooth as ice melting on a hot plate.

"Excuse me, Mr. Jackson; is it true that you refused to meet with Cal Emerson to discuss the rebuilding process because he opposes your views?" Gail asked over the chorus of other reporters.

His dark eyes swung down to her and had she been less confident and hungry for an exclusive, she would have wilted under his intense gaze.

"And you are?" He said with a grin that was charmingly lethal.

"Gail Fray— South Virginia Herald," she said.

"Well Miss Fray, I think you should review your facts. I have tried to contact my opponent's camp on several occasions but have as yet to receive a call back—next question." He said looking at another reporter, one who was doing more flattering than asking pertinent questions. With one quick glance by him Gail had been dismissed and she didn't like it.

He spent another few minutes mingling with the crowd with his bodyguard—a big fellow with a frown and shoulders that were as wide as a couch, then made the symbolic gesture of shoveling the first bit of dirt where ground was to be broken for the new project.

After the meeting which left the locals irritated and disgruntled, Reed was surrounded by throngs of his personal, staff, well-wishers and general hanger-on's as he walked back to his limousine. A tall burly staff member held out his suit jacket which he slid into easily, smiled, waved to the disenchanted crowd once more then got into the waiting limousine.

Gail caught up just as the driver entered the car, started the motor and began to edge slowly away.

"Mr. Jackson!" She yelled at the tinted window, "Is there anything you want to say to the public about your ties with the Garlucci family?"

The car stopped and the window rolled silently down a scant inch. She looked passed his eyes in time to see a pair of lithe bare legs crossed at the ankles in high stiletto heels.

"Miss, Fray…" he said in a low irritated tone, "I don't think it's wise to spew outrageous and I am sure unfounded allegations about me or my campaign."

"Well I…" But he cut her off.

"If you want an exclusive, you'll have to stand in line like everybody else."

"I'm not like everybody else," Gail said with a sarcastic grin.

"Neither am I," he said as the window slid noiselessly up and the car continued on.

Gail was furious, but intrigued. There *was* a story there—she could smell it and she was damn sure going to get it.

For the next three weeks Gail was relentless in calling Reed's office trying to get an interview, but only got every excuse from *he was in a meeting* to *he is not available*.

It didn't take her long to get the picture that it appeared that he was exclusively unavailable to her. By the second week her editor was in an uproar.

"What's going on Gail? Reed Jackson's interviews have been appearing in every newspaper, tabloid and penny saver except ours" he yelled, "Either you get me an exclusive or you are out."

Was he for real? Was she about to lose her job? She had no choice, she had to step up her game and get that story. She strategized her next move and felt that it might be a good idea to get an interview with Reed's opponent, Cal Emerson and then work her way back to Reed.

Cal Emerson was the dark horse-underdog who surprised everyone when he was the first black man elected to head the HUD Virginia Land Rejuvenation program. From everything that she'd heard and read about him, he seemed dedicated and on the up and up and for the people. But as with most men with political aspirations, looking good and lying was synonymous in the arena of getting what you want. She hesitated calling him, not sure if she was ready for another round of disappointments and promised callbacks that might never come, but she had to try.

To her pleasant surprise, Cal's secretary told Gail to come over anytime and that he would be happy to grant her an interview. She prepared her questions carefully, not wanting to alienate or antagonize, but she wanted to make it clear about what she was doing and why she was doing it.

Cal Emerson's office was across town in a shoddy building with furniture that could use some *Endust* or even better, replacing. There were three people working in the front when she arrived who were professional and polite. His secretary—a woman in her fifties and as round as a biscuit, greeted Gail warmly and promptly showed her into Cal Emerson's office.

That's not a good sign, she thought, *a politician who was not too busy to see me? Hmmm?*

He stood up when she entered.

"Thank you for seeing me Mr. Emerson." Gail said after showing him her press credentials.

Cal was a tall, thick legged, heavily muscled man with piercing hazel eyes. His hair was cut short ending neatly at his collar and his clothes, although rumpled were of good cut and quality.

"You can call me Mr. Emerson in print, in here call me Cal," he said extending his slender but strong hand.

She shook it and he gestured to a chair opposite his battered desk. She extracted a small recorder from her purse and looked at him.

"Do you mind?" she asked.

"Not at all, I have nothing to hide."

Gail smiled and started asking routine background questions about his place of birth, family and friends. After a few minutes he interrupted her.

"I'm sure you're not interested in my family, my family tree or what I ate for dinner last night Ms. Fray so why not just cut to the chase."

Gail knew there was no need to beat around the bush so she came right out with it.

"I'm interested—well, the people are interested in knowing your views on the new project over at *Bottom Bay Cove*."

"It's no secret how I feel about that. I'm sure you've read all about it in other papers or seen my limited interviews." he said trying to contain a derisive grin.

It was true; it seemed the media enjoyed the loud, verbose image of Reed Jackson while giving his opponent only the barest attention and stingy and minimal interviews.

Cal began telling her why he thought Reed was all wrong—not only for the project, but for the office he *currently* held. Then enthusiastically went on to tell her what *his* plan was for the Bottom Bay area if he was elected to the post.

"Conserve and rebuild," he said with pride. "But for the people *already* living there not for yuppies and investors with deep pockets who think they can own the waterway view."

"But you have to admit, that in today's market it is prime real estate?" Gail said.

"They didn't seem to think so seventy years ago when they moved black people out of the local areas and into that area and out of their view. They gave them that land Ms. Fray, when it was nothing more than an eyesore where people dumped garbage and nobody wanted it. Now developers think it's okay for them to come in and own the beach side sunshine? I don't think so"

"It's happening all over." Gail offered.

"Well it's time somebody stopped it. It's time that black people get to enjoy some of what everybody else does just because they have money."

"What if they *want* to sell?"

"Then they should have proper representation so that they don't get cheated like so many have and get a fair price for their property."

She was impressed and mentally agreed with him, but she needed to get his take on what his opponent was about. She looked down at her notes.

"The preliminary outline that Reed Jackson presented to the town council was geared toward bringing in millions of dollars in tax revenue and new jobs. Even you can't argue that it would help immensely," she said.

It was hard for him to control his distaste when she mentioned Reed's name but she saw him fight to hold himself in professional check.

"My illustrious opponent is in it for the money and by that I mean *big* money for himself."

"And you have facts to support this?" She said pushing the recorder closer to him.

"I do." His eyes held a glint of smiling self-assuredness.

"Care to elaborate?"

"I would think that would be your job Ms. Fray. After all, isn't that what you do—find out what you can from who you can?"

She caught his sarcasm and supposed his press secretary had told him she'd been unable to get an interview with Reed, after all that was *her* job.

"I will admit Mr. Jackson's been a little reluctant to see me, but I'm hoping to wear him down."

"There's nothing like keeping hope alive, good luck." He said.

They talked a little more about the project, then before she knew it he was coaxing out *her* personal life.

"My! My!" she said with a nervous laugh, "You should hang out a shingle the way you can get people to talk."

"I minored in Psychology. I'm studying for my second doctorate now."

"Impressive." she said admiringly. She asked a few more questions and made a few more notes, then put her things away and stood up.

"Well Mr. Emerson, I think I have everything for now. I appreciate you seeing me."

"Feel free to call any time you need an exclusive, I'm sure I can pull something out of my bag of tricks for you."

"And don't think I won't. You aren't the only one with aspirations and thanks again for seeing me."
She was almost at the door when he called out.

"Oh Ms. Fray,"
She turned to face him.

"There's a gala at the governor's home Friday evening— very black tie and everyone who is anyone will be there. Who knows, you might be able to get a good lead on a story out of it."

"Oh?"

"Of course it is *invitation only* and I find myself without an escort."

"Are you asking me out?" She could hardly believe it."

"It's not a date per se, more like getting you in with the movers and the shakers; that is what you want isn't it?"

"I'm not much for political balls especially where everyone is swinging their *preverbal* balls if you get my meaning?" She said.

He gave her a mock pained grin. "Would it help if I told you Reed Jackson is going to be there?"
She perked. "What time should I be ready?"

"I'll pick you up at seven sharp." he grinned.

Gail's editor was elated when she told him about the invitation and even allowed her to put her new evening outfit on expense.

"Just get me a lead story Gail," he said chewing the back end of his pen.

~*~

Cal was right on time Friday evening and looked like a dream in his tuxedo and highly polished evening shoes and when she saw him Gail could feel her heart take an unaccustomed leap.

"A rose for a beautiful rose," he said handing her the long stemmed thorn-less flower in the limousine.

She could see he was impressed with her simple black sheath with matching glittery seed pearls along the bodice and down the front. Her hair was swept up, curled into tight ringlets and her make-up was flawless thanks to *Shurlene* at the MAC counter at Macy's.

The sit-down dinner for the hundred or so people was expensive and elegant, and just as Cal had promised, all of the most influential people in city were there, including two mayors, three film superstars and a host of sports legends as well. But to her utter disappointment Reed was nowhere to be found.

After dinner there was dancing in the glass domed solarium and as she danced with Cal she almost forgot the reason she was there. It felt good to be in a man's strong arms and she had just relaxed and settled her cheek against his when...

"May I cut in?"

She knew that voice, it was Reed. She felt Cal tense and hold her tighter. Gail stepped away and looked from one to the other and saw a challenge that could easily get out of hand.

Cal gave him a lopsided grin and let go of her.

"Of course—that is if the lady doesn't mind," he said with a smile that held thinly veiled murderous tendencies.

Reed looked at her and she couldn't say no. This opportunity could pave the way to her dream job.

"Well one dance can't hurt," she said turning to Cal but he was already walking away.

Reed took instant control of the moment and pulled her smoothly and tightly to him. She was sure and hoped no one noticed that he deliberately moved his leg between hers so that his thin wiry thigh rested neatly and close against her pubis. His moves were slight but purposeful. He held her too close and she tried to disengage herself gracefully, but he held her firmly.

"So, Ms. Fray what has my almost worthy adversary been saying about me?" he pushed in against her as if to make a point.

"Nothing that everyone else isn't already saying."

"Oh? And what's that?"

"If you want to know you'll just have to grant me a small amount of your time to find out—say Monday about noon?" She said smoothly.

Every politician wants to know what the other knows, and they all thought they knew how to make the media work for them and Reed was no exception. But she knew a thing or two herself and she was going to work the moment for all it was worth.

"I'll tell you what," he said evenly, "I'm taking *LADY LUCK*–that's my yacht, out for a spin around the *Bottoms* tomorrow, why don't you come along."
Gail wasn't prepared for that. "Sorry, I'm off tomorrow and I have plans."

"You're a journalist Ms. Fray, you're never off. If you want that exclusive tomorrow is the only time I can give you. Think about it. We set sail at 11AM sharp."
He leaned in close to her ear, his breath hot and seductive. "Bring a bathing suit!" he whispered.

~*~

Gail was up all night wondering if she should take Reed up on his offer or if she should *demand* another time. *Why am I hesitating?* Not only was her job on the line, but this interview could land her the lead story on the front page and possibly the position at the paper she coveted.

At 10:59 the next morning she was at the only dock near the *Bottom Bay* pier. It was brand new because Reed had it built; *So everybody can use it*, she remembered reading in an article. But consequently, no one owned a boat except him.

"Right on time!" she heard him call out from the top of the massive catamaran. "Here let me give you a hand."   He hoisted her on board and nodded to the thin, wrinkled old man standing by a tethered rope. The man unhitched it and in a moment she heard the gentle sound of the engine turning as the yacht backed away from the pier.

A quarter of an hour later after he'd offered her a mimosa and brie topped with caviar she looked around for others.

"I thought you said *we* were sailing…"

"*We* are—you and me."

The boat glided on the water noiselessly and the sky shone beautifully against the back drop of the mid-morning horizon. When they stopped at the far side of the coastline, there was nothing but high, dense sea grass and marsh brush. The water was slapping gently against the side of the boat and Gail saw Reed get up and began to take off his light weight jacket and shirt.

"Did you bring your suit?" He asked continuing to disrobe.

"No I didn't," she said keenly. She had no intention of swimming; she was here for a story and turned to get her notepad and pen from her bag. When next she looked up, Reed was standing three feet away from her, perched on the low ledge of the boat—totally naked. She wanted to look away but her eyes were glued to his hard body and his other rather impressive attribute.

"What's the matter, tax dollars not paying enough to buy you a bathing suit?" she said trying to be glib and not show how at unease she was.

"I never wear one when I'm alone if I can help it—or if in the company of a beautiful woman." He winked then dove into the water, slicing through it neatly as he disappeared into its depths.

Gail waited a few minutes and when he hadn't surfaced she panicked and ran to the rail.

"Mr. Jackson!" She yelled leaning over the railing, but there was no answer and no movement except the slow lazy eddy of the water. "Reed!" she called louder this time.

A second later she felt a hand reach up and snag her jacket as she was pulled into the water.

Down into the murky depths, she went, but she could feel him holding her as he swam back to the surface. She was never in any real danger but she came up sputtering and blowing like a fish out of water.

Her clothes seemed to shrink against her body as his arms curled around her and pulled her into him as they treaded water.

Suddenly Reed was kissing her deeply and she would forever wonder what happened to her just then. *Was it was the chill of the cool water? The warm noon day sun? Or the secret hypnotic call of water nymphs of legend told in every fantasy book she'd ever read* as she kissed him back. His lips enslaved her as they kicked frantically to stay afloat.

A moment later he was pushing her up the boat ladder, following behind then without a word pulled her below deck to the main cabin where he began stripping off her wet clothes.

"Can't have you catching your death the first day on my boat, what would people say?" he said huskily.
Nothing seemed real and everything she had come to do left her head as he kissed her again then worked his tongue over her naked body.

Reed Jackson was no choir boy and could have done any sex club justice as he laid her face down and pulled her up onto all fours and began his tongue dance all over her bottom, front and everything in between. The pleasure of it was maddening and it was totally wrong. Gail was completely overtaken by the seduction and to her embarrassment, let him have his way.

His tongue pleasuring lasted endlessly making a lie out of the old tale of what black men *never* do. He did things to her she had never let anyone do and with his hypnotic voice urged her do things she'd never done and teased decadent words from her that she had never said to anyone.

Reed liked to be ridden so she rode him wildly as he pinched and sucked her nipples, he put one finger then two in her mouth and she sucked on them like a lollipop. She felt another orgasm coming, she had come so many times during his tonguing that she didn't feel she had any juice left, but once again it was racing through her like a rocket. He began bucking wildly up into her, and she couldn't remember if he had put on a condom, but there was no worry because as soon as he reached his peak he pulled out and pulled her face down to meet the hot streams of stickiness, but much his irritation she turned away so most of it hit her shoulder and beyond. Finally her breathing slowed and she was exhausted and did what she thought only men did, *she* fell asleep.

~*~

The uneasy feeling of someone staring awakened her. Reed was seated on the bed opposite her, bathed, shaved, wearing a pair of neatly pressed khaki's and a sailor blue cashmere sweater.

"I guess I'm ready to be interviewed now," he said taking a swig from the fluted glass he was holding.
She asked for the bathroom where she showered and dressed feeling ashamed and wondering if she'd paid a dear price for story she was about to get.

When she got home, there were two messages on her answering machine, one from her editor the other from Cal.
"Hey Gail, look I know this is weird, but I haven't been able to stop thinking about you and was wondering if you might join me for dinner tonight." He left a call back number and all she could so was stare at the phone for a long time.

She stripped off her still slightly damp clothes and went to the shower and scrubbed herself raw. Wrapped in a terrycloth robe she went to her laptop to configure her story. Reed hadn't given her much and completely denied any ties with the organized crime faction that was slowly and quietly infiltrating the *Bottom Bay* area. She didn't call Cal that night, she didn't think it would be fair to see him with the memory of his opponent's touch was still on her.

The next day her editor was mildly mollified but not overly enthusiastic over the story and told her she'd have to do better. Reed didn't call her after that day on the boat and she was grateful because she had no idea what she'd say to him.

Two weeks later she drove up to Melling, a town about fifty or so miles away to meet up with Kerra Stoler an old college friend. She was in town on business and Gail agreed to meet her to catch up on old times for a few hours. They met at a quaint little seafood restaurant overlooking a large, tree lined lake. Kerra was exactly the same as she was in college only more beautiful and dressed a lot better. They laughed, drank and joked about their old dorm days. Before they knew it, it was almost one a.m.

"Gail this has been a blast but I have an early flight so I'd better get back to the hotel and get some shut-eye," she said going for the check which Gail had been unsuccessful in grabbing away from her.

"I ain't no *po ass* ya know," Gail said jokingly.

"I didn't say you were, but I get to write it off as a business expense," Kerra winked and signed the receipt

They were outside the restaurant having a last little chat before saying their good-byes when they heard a commotion going on in the nearby parking lot. A man was trying to separate two women who were in the throes of the best hair pulling fight Gail had seen since covering the WW SMACKDOWN at Madison Square Garden the year before. One woman was exceptionally and unfairly tall and had the drop on the shorter woman. There was something familiar about the man who was trying to avoid wayward punches being thrown as he tried to separate them. Recognition hit her like a plank in the face and Gail walked over to them and smiled.

"Well good evening Mr. Jackson. Care to give a statement?" she said extracting her mini recorder from her purse and pushing it up to his face.

~*~

Gail called Reed's office the next morning to see if he wanted to offer her an exclusive on the *girl-fight* she'd witnessed but after several more calls and getting only his voicemail she left a final message and told him she would be sending in the story as soon as she finished with the editing—just in case he wanted to make a statement.

Cal called again a few days later and this time Gail accepted his invitation to dinner. She couldn't believe how at

15

ease she was with him. Everything about him was perfect. He had great visions about what he wanted to do with the new project and was positive that he could make a difference. The only thing that marred her evening was when Reed stopped by the table, along with the short, beautiful women who had been in the fight.

"Good Evening Cal, "he said pointedly ignoring Gail. Cal nodded.

"I hope you've ordered the *shrimp fra-diavilo*, they say it's wonderful." his smile was slick with hidden sarcasm. Finally, he dragged his eyes over to Gail.

"Hello Ms. Fray. I hope you enjoyed yourself the other day; we should do it again sometime. Have a good evening." A flush of mortified warmth crept up Gail's legs.

"What did he mean?" Cal asked.

She hesitated before telling him the truth that she had been invited on Reed's boat for an interview.

"Show off!" Cal laughed dismissing the incident and focused his attention back on her.

That night when Cal kissed her at her door her heart did so many flip-flops she thought would have to go to the emergency room for an EKG.

~*~

They say *you should never cross the devil or politicians because they both wallow in the same fiery muck* and can do you a lot of damage. She had given Reed a call leaving a message on his voicemail. *"I'm giving you one last opportunity before I send in my story in case you wish to surprise me with a statement."* He hadn't returned her call, but made a statement alright; one that smacked Gail right between the eyes.

It was four a.m. the next morning and someone was literally leaning on her doorbell. Sleepily, she got up and padded to the door and looked through the peephole. It was Cal and there was fire in his eyes.

"Cal what are you doing here at this…" she said opening the door and he literally pushed his way in.

"So what was all this Gail huh? A way to get into my camp and find out my plans so you can give them to your lover?"

"What? What are talking about Cal? What lover?"

"Oh you're good—real good. I'd expect this from someone like him, but not you."
Gail was confused, tired and exasperated.

"Not from me what? What have I done?"
Suddenly his eyes lowered as he shook his head. "Gail, from the first moment I saw you I knew you were special and I was thinking that things might grow into something good between us."

"I felt that too Cal. These last few days have been wonderful," she said going to him. But he took a step back, almost as though it burned him to be near her.

"I should have known better. You media sluts are all alike. All you want is a story and you don't give a damn how you get it," he said moving to her.

Had he just called her a slut? "Now just you wait a minute Cal..." But he cut her off.

"Why don't we just do what you do best and get your exclusive the only way you seem to know how." He began tugging at the tie to her robe, snatching it open, revealing her skimpy sleeping apparel.

"Cal, are you crazy? What's wrong with you?" She said slapping at his hands.

"Oh I guess I'm not good enough. I don't have a boat; I don't have enough charisma and or enough ostentatious panache for you. Is that it? But hey now that I know what you like maybe I can give it to you just he did, I know *I* can handle that."
He was pulling her toward him. But this time she pushed him away hard.

"What the hell is the matter with you?" she admonished.

"Oh perhaps you need a little visual stimulation." He snatched a thin, square case from his breast pocket and extracted the silver toned disk. Striding to her DVD player he pressed the button and inserted it. In moments Gail was horrified as she saw herself-her *naked s*elf, moving back and forth against Reed's tongue. Ice filled her veins and words gurgled incoherently in her throat.

"Cal please… I can explain…"

"Yeah well that…" he pointed to the screen, "is explanation enough." And he turned and left, slamming the door behind him.

~*~

Gail was in hell. Everything was all wrong. Reed had taped them and then sent it to Cal and she knew it was because she had told him she was going to send in the story about his being mixed up in a *girl fight* in Melling that night. It was all too clear, Reed had drawn a line in the sand and there was no way she was prepared to step over it. She also knew that any feelings Cal had for her were crushed the second he viewed that video and she knew there was no way he could forgive her or ever get him back.

Days passed and she finally sent in the story about Reed, after all what harm could he do to her now? He countered by holding an exclusive with a rival paper along with the shorter of the two girls in the fight Gail had witnessed, announcing that they were engaged and everything else written about him was a result of misinformation and a ruse to defame him. Furthermore he said that the fight story that had been reported by *Gail Frey* was an incompetent fabrication of the truth. "*We had just finished out engagement dinner and going back to my car when a former mental patient attacked us for no reason at all.*" Reed had said to the paper and a number of interviews and daytime television shows.

Of course, the *former mental patient* in question could not be found to corroborate the facts as he said them.

Gail seethed, she knew his story wasn't true but his charisma and gift of gab had everyone enthralled and believing every word he said. She became a laughing stock and her editor was madder than she'd ever seen him.

"I'm sorry Gail, but we have to let you go."

So there she was with no job, no integrity, loss of respect and at that moment no self-esteem.

~*~

Things were heating up on the land rejuvenation project and it looked like Reed was going to get his way. Every speech he made sounded as though he was *for* the people who lived on *BOTTOM BAY COVE* when in fact he was cheating them out of their land for a pittance so that he could sell it to developers for millions. Gail read that he was attending dinners, parties and other elaborate events hosted by Anthony Garlucci and his crime family. His staff however, always made it sound as though he was only going to tell them in nicest way possible that their donations was not needed in his world. Everyone knew it wasn't true but no one could prove a thing. The biggest insult was when Gail received an expensive, engraved invitation to his engagement party—to be held on his boat the *LUCKY LADY*. A little handwritten note at the bottom said, *would love to get you wet all over again!*

She tore it into small pieces and threw it in the trash. Gail was so depressed and could do nothing more than become one with the half gallon container *of Edy's praline crunch ice-cream* and try to forget everything that had happened over the past few weeks. On more than one occasion she thought about calling Cal but every time she got up the nerve, she knew there was no point. *He would never forgive me no more than I can forgive myself,* she thought.

~*~

She was well into the Praline crunch and deeply involved in an old movie on TCM one evening when her doorbell rang. It was late and her heart leapt because she thought it might be Cal. She put down the container of ice cream and literally ran to the door and snatched it open.

A stunningly beautiful woman with legs that went on until the day *after* forever stood in front of her.

"Ms. Fray, I think I have something you want,"

Without invitation she brushed passed Gail in a hail of expensive perfume and stood in the middle of her living room.

"And who are you?" Gail asked puzzled.

"Maybe if I bunch up my fists you'll remember." Recognition hit Gail in the face like a freight train; she was the tall woman fighting with the short woman who was now Reed's fiancée'.

The tall woman's amazing smile softened into a wide grin as she held out her large delicate hand.

"Jordana Mason."

"Okay Miss Mason, won't you have a seat?" Gail offered after shaking her hand.

She sat and the slit in her skirt spread, revealing more of her gorgeous gams.

"First things first; here's a little gift for you," She said as she pulled a few discs from her large *Hermes* shoulder bag and handed them to Gail. She saw the titles written in Reed's own hand with her name on them.

"These are the tapes of you on his boat. Reed was going to post them on the internet—for a fee of course..." Jordana said with a brilliant smile, "But he can't because these are the only copies and here is the only tape." She handed Gail a video.

"Oh Miss Mason. Thank you... but... how and most importantly why?" She asked through impending tears.

"Honey, do you think men get anywhere without the help of a woman? When I met Reed he was a down and out law student who couldn't pass the bar. I took it for him and passed with flying colors."

"Oh my, But..."

She held up a finger to stop her from talking.

"I've been through a lot with him and there's no way I'm going to let him just push me aside for some light-skinned, half-ass mini skank who will enjoy everything I helped him get. He may not want me, but neither one of them will be getting a damned thing when I'm through."

"But how...."

Again she hushed Gail up.

"You want your job back don't you?"

Gail nodded.

"Well, these ought to help." She pulled out what looked like two ledger books.

Gail took them and opened one and saw entry after entry of large sums of money that had been given to Reed by the Garlucci family as well as other shady supporters and set up in several Off Shore accounts

"Oh my God!" Gail squealed with delight."

Jordana got up and straightened her skirt.

Gail set the incriminating evidence down on the table and leapt to her feet and grabbed Jordana and hugged her tight.

"How can I ever thank you?"

"Don't mention it and if all that fails you can always use this."

She opened her purse and extracted an expired driver's license and handed it to Gail. She looked at the picture of the handsome mustached man. She looked up at Jordana with puzzlement. Jordana pointed a long polished fingernail to the name. *JORDAN MAYSON.* Gail was in shock.

"You mean?"

"That's right honey and with money I got out of Reed's safe I'll be able to complete the rest of the operation he promised me five years ago."

This was too much. Gail knew she had the world back in her hands.

"Can I offer you a drink Ms. Mason?"

"Perhaps another time," and she strode to the door with more grace than a cat-walk model. She had her hand on the knob then turned back to Gail.

"Oh yes, I understand that Reed sent a copy of that tape to your friend—what's his name Cal-something-or-other? Well don't worry I left a message on his machine and told him that Reed used a date rape drug on you and that he'd done it to lots of women before and that none of what he saw on the tape was your fault."

Gail went to her and this time reached up and kissed *Jordana/Jordan* right on the lips and thanked her.

"Girl, you know I don't roll your way anymore." Then she smiled and sashayed down the hallway.

Almost as if timed, just as she closed the door, her phone began to ring. She answered it, it was Cal.

"Gail, I need to see you. I want to see you."

"Come Cal, come now." She said breathlessly.

~*~

Gail wanted to give her editor at the paper another chance so she took her scoop to him first telling him that if he didn't want it then she would be offering it up for grabs. After reading her article and looking at the evidence, he was more than happy to not only use the article but give her the position of top feature reporter with a substantial raise as well.

The second the story broke, Reed skipped town, the Garlucci's hot on his heels. She knew it wouldn't be long before they would catch up with him and demand their money back or else. She turned the books over to the Prosecutor's office and destroyed the incriminating tapes of herself with Reed.

Gail never told Cal the truth about date rape drug that *Jordana* had leaked to him, she figured there was just some things better left the way they were.

Life was back to normal and she was enjoying her relationship with Cal. He was a good, decent and honest man.

He invited her to Chicago to meet his family and it was easy to see where all the love came from and took to them immediately. Typically they all began to tease her about him finding *the right one* and was looking forward to an announcement.

~*~

Now with Reed was out of the picture, people really began to listen to Cal and with a mix of private and individual donations he received substantial and *honest* backing for the new *BAY* project and the rebuilding had begun.

The People of *BOTTOM BAY COVE* finally got what they deserved and worked so hard for and were satisfied that their homes wouldn't be sacrificed in the name of *palatial holdings for the rich* and they would continue to enjoy their familial surrounding for years to come.

New life had come into a dismal and dying area that brought in new and fair proposals for the area. Small enterprises were welcome as long as they employed locals and agree to invest funds so that local mom and pop stores and kiosks were able to thrive.

Cal was so proud of his accomplishments but he knew they still had a long way to go. He was able to purchase a plot to build his own home—*big enough for two or more* he said with a wink and mischievous smile.

In the end the people of BOTTOM BAY got what they *wanted* and Gail got what she *needed*, a great job and a good man in her life.

Something Sweet

I always thought I was completely informed of the homeless situation that was so prevalent in New York where I'd lived most of my life. But I was not ready for the level of desperation I'd seen after I'd arrived in Canada. I'd always thought of this particular country as being a little bit cleaner, a little more elite and that Canadians would be totally un-accepting of situations that would appear to degrade the integrity of their homeland. I couldn't have been more wrong. The sorrow of the homeless plight was just as prevalent here as in any other urban city.

I moved to Canada in April of 2015 after suffering a failed marriage and several casual relationships—the last being so abusive that I barely got away with my life. Although the man who'd nearly killed me stole nearly everything I owned including my brand new car, thankfully he was unable to get at my savings and checking accounts. When he called a few days later and threatened me again if I didn't give him thousands of my hard earned dollars, I withdrew it all the next day, and left the country.

I had found a small, but nice apartment in a Toronto and immediately began looking for a job at a bakery or restaurant where I could show off my pastry chef skills. An advertisement for the *Sweets Expo* at the *Metro Toronto Convention Center* caught my eye and I couldn't wait to go. It was wonderful. The annual premier gala celebrated sweets of all kinds, but chocolate was main ingredient of almost everything. The entire building was filled with chocolate and candy manufacturers from around the globe were marketing their latest confections and new innovative candy and pastry making devices. I knew right then what I had to do. I was going into business of my own.

As a minority, it was a little easier to get a loan here than in the states, but you had to have a good marketing plan and little of your own capital. The loan officer worked out the details and I got the money and she even gave me the name of a realtor that helped first-time business owners. I met with him a week later and he showed me several properties, but none of them were quite right. Finally, there was a tiny storefront at the edge of town and it's just like the old saying; *when it's right you know it*. It was off the beaten path but I could see the possibilities so I took it.

I spent endless hours in secondhand shops and culinary auctions to get used blenders, mixers, molds and other materials I needed. Within three months *THE SWEET BOX* opened and I almost lost my shirt.

That first week, I had three customers and I hadn't seen them since. I gave out free samples and even made up little boxes with business cards and gave them to almost every shop on the main drag—nothing. I was beginning to regret my decision on the location and my bank account was racing towards empty-ville.

One morning as I walked toward the front door of my small confectionery emporium, I saw a policeman rousing the homeless man huddled in my doorway. This was nothing new, I had shooed the man away a few times myself—after I'd given him some change or some chocolate confection from my shop of course. I had come to know the unwanted visitor as *the insult joker*, because he had a way of turning his affronts into something funny. His blue eyes were full of mirth but with a hidden sadness.

Usually it was white police officers that roused him with bored non-commitment. *Come on old man; move along,*" they'd say and usher him up and away from my establishment doorway. This time however, the officer was tall, with dark skin and from where I stood, had a butt tighter than an old maid's facelift. Not to mention that those glorious buns were encased in a pair of pants that had a crease sharp enough to cut one of my three pound chocolate slabs.

I didn't care for the way this particular officer was yelling at the old guy nor the way he threatened him with his nightstick.

"Hey!" I yelled and ran over when I saw him threaten to bring the club down. The officer stopped midair.

"Don't you dare hit him!" I went to the man and glanced down to make sure he was all right.

"And you are?" The officer said.

"Saljon' Bronte." I thought the made-up French name sounded exotic and fit my shop.

"Yeah, if you hit me I'll sue you so bad your great grandchildren will be in debt." The old man interjected.
I glared at him to stay out of this.

"Well Miss Bronte…" The officer said. "We have orders. He's an eyesore to the city and can't lay around anywhere he wants."
The man was struggling to stand up and his arthritic knees cracked as he straightened. "You hear that sonny? That's what it sounds like when you're cold, old and try to get it up."

Inwardly I cringed; I knew he was crossing over into dangerous territory when I saw the officer's face tighten with controlled rage and not appreciating his humor.

"I ought to run you in." He sneered.

"Oh yeah?" the old man continued. "I bet you couldn't run a chicken into a coop."
I wanted to laugh but I didn't dare.

"That's it! We're done you old drunk, I'm taking you in—turn around."

"Okay, but I didn't know you were *that* kind of guy," the old coot said and made an effeminate gesture with his finger and I almost busted out laughing when I saw the officer's face nearly pop with indignation. He pulled the old man around roughly, and I stepped between them.

"Look, you can't take him," I said.

"Stay out this. He's a menace. Look at him, he's unkempt, he's obviously a drunk and he has no visible means of support, He's going to the precinct."

"He has a job Officer…" I glanced at his name plate. "Officer Montrose."

"Doing what?" he asked with an unconvinced sneer.

"Well, he sweeps up and gets rid of the trash," I was thinking as quickly as I could.

"Oh yeah well what's his name?" he asked suspiciously.

The man stared at him, the mirth gone from his face. "You know my name," the old man said.

For a moment their eyes locked and I could see the officer chewing the inside of his cheek, then he turned and stared down at me, his dark eyes blazing.

"Lady, I'm just doing my job. We get twenty calls a day about riff-raff like him loitering in front of respectable businesses like your…" He looked up at my sign, "…*SWEET BOX.*"

"He wasn't loitering, he was sort of…waiting," I corrected him. I knew that he knew it was a lie, and he sighed and shook his head as he stepped away from the shadowy doorway and into the sunlit street and looked directly at the older man.

"It looks like today is your luck day."
The man stood straight as he could and adjusted his tattered coat.

"Some things never change," the Officer said glancing at the man, then at me before turning and walking away.
I couldn't help but take in the richness of his skin which was the same color as my double mocha soufflé drops and his eyes that had the hue of the rich coffee bean sugar patties.

I looked at the old man. Now that the cop was gone, I figured I'd just send him on his way. No such luck.

"Where's the broom?" he said with an impish smile.
I groaned, unlocked the door and that's how I met Mosely—or as he later told me, *Mose-to-my friends*-Collins.

~*~

I'll never forget the morning before Valentine's Day. It was dismal and damp with the threat of rain looming on the horizon. I'd had a few customers before lunch but nothing since and I felt like I should just close up and go home, but decided if nothing happened within the hour I would do just that. I sat behind the counter reading a trade magazine when the little bell over the door sounded. The man who entered was chubby, red cheeked and his sparse comb-over had wisps of brown and gray hairs sticking out all over his head.

"Okay here's what I need…" he began.

No good morning, no hello—nothing. But he wanted buy and I couldn't afford to be insulted by his insensitivity. He didn't even bother looking in my refrigerated showcase or the display of fancy petit fours that were neatly arranged under a large clear glass dome.

"I want one hundred forty boxes of your best assortment—say eight to a box." He was looking around, "And make up about ten platters of those little cake things." He pointed to the petit fours.

"Yes sir, anything else?" My heart was beating fast. This was the biggest order I'd had since I opened.

"Do you have anything with a liquid filling?"

"Why yes, I have milk or dark chocolate with anisette or delicate almond liquor and of course crème de menthe, whichever you prefer. And we have pastries filled with strawberry or cherry filling."

"Good! I need six dozen of each, mix them up and I'll need a chocolate mousse cake with raspberry filling if you can—say for about ten people or so."

I almost swooned with happiness as I wrote his order down rapidly. I was reaching for my calculator and asked… "And how will you be paying?" I said hoping he would say cash because I didn't have an account with the usual credit companies yet.

He took out an alligator bound check book and I groaned inwardly. *What if it wasn't good? What if I got stiffed?* I caught his eye as he looked at me. Then he put the check book away and pulled out his wallet.

"I'll leave a three-hundred dollar deposit and we'll square the rest when you deliver it tomorrow, no later than 11 a.m."

He handed me his business card and the cash. *AMBROSE IMPORTS—Dexter Ambrose Owner and CEO,* then left the store in a hurry. .

I was thrilled, my first big customer. Then realization hit me. If I was going to fill his order I would have to work all night long. What had I been thinking? But necessity is the mother of invention so I closed the store for an hour and went to Crestwood University where I could look at the message board and hopefully find a student willing to work at least part of the night to help me.

"Whatcha lookin' for?" A voice behind me asked.

The boy was about 5'9, thin as a rail and as black as an onyx stone. His name was Maxwell Odile and he was a first year student from Nigeria. He lived with his mother and four siblings in a shabby part of town and said he would do *anything t*o get some money. After admonishing him about the dangers of that particular statement, I introduced myself and told him I would need him from about five to ten o'clock that night and I could pay fifty dollars.

"No problem!" he said.

I was immediately ashamed of the paltry amount but it was all I could afford at the moment.

I didn't go right back to the shop—since I didn't have that many customers anyway and went shopping for the things I would need to complete the order.

Maxwell was waiting at the front door of the store precisely at the time I'd indicated and ran to help me when he saw me struggling with bags and cumbersome boxes.

Inside after explaining the basics I began my tasks with concentration and zeal borne of desperation. I couldn't have made a better choice with Max, he was strong, a fast learner and followed directions easily. Some things were easier than others and I got them out of the way first. There were a few mishaps which I boxed and set aside for Maxwell to take home to his family later.

"Man these are really something Miz B. You could be an artist or something,"

I beamed at the compliment and told him to keep working.

It was close to eleven and I was a little more than half done and Maxwell offered to help the rest of the night, but I paid him seventy-five dollars instead of the fifty I originally offered and with the box of lopsided but expertly decorated goodies and made him go home. "You're a student, you need your rest."

Finally at two-thirty in the morning and with my confections all beautifully decorated and packed, I was ready for my Valentine's Day delivery. I was dog tired and went home to get a few hours' sleep.

My alarm sounded and I hit the snooze button twice before I finally got up. Still tired I noticed I wasn't late but I would have to hurry if I intended to make my delivery on time.

I got to my store and found Mose waiting for me along with a group of people—mostly men, waiting.

"Bout time you got here, these men need some candy and cake for their valentines, where you been anyway?"

I didn't have time for him right then and even though I had a trip to make I couldn't turn away money, after all that is why I was in business. I opened up and went behind the counter and began to take the orders, all the while glancing at the clock. Mose had gotten a cloth and was wiping down the glass cases. After I had served the last customer I went to the back storeroom to get the boxes, trays and gaily colored organza bags, from the refrigerator. I was tying them up and putting them on a cart and just as I was about to wheel it out when I heard voices out front. I hurried out, parking the cart by the glass case and I couldn't believe what I was seeing.

Mose was behind the counter with a pencil stuck behind his ear and one in his hand taking down orders from a man who was rattling off his request, behind him was at least five other people and more looked like they were coming in.

There was no way I was going to make the delivery on time and I as frantic, after this was my first really big order and first impressions can make or break a business.
I boxed and bagged up orders while Mose rang them up. It was 9:20 and I thought I had better call Mr. Ambrose and tell him I would be late, when suddenly Maxwell Odile entered the store.

"Hey there Miss B, I was wondering if you would be needin' any help today?"
He looked at the customers perusing the confectionary cases, "But it looks like you be needin' help right now," he said.

"Well… " I began.
Mose, was bagging up coconut clusters and glanced over at the cart.

"Is that a delivery or a pick-up?" he asked.

"Delivery." I said looking forlornly at the clock.

"Then you better get on it. Me and lil man right here got this."
I stared at him a full minute.

"Go on, everything will be okay, I promise I will watch him like a hawk."
And who is going to watch you? I wondered.

"Look, anybody ordering that much chocolate must be in great need, so go on we'll take care of these customers."

This was my first big order, *but could I throw caution to the wind and trust two people I hardly knew?* Mose leaned over to me. "You gave me a chance, so why not take a chance?" I decided that was what I was going to do, if they robbed me blind then it was what I deserved and I'd know to never trust anyone again.

"Okay…" I said, "It's across town, I'll be back in an hour."

"Take route fifteen, traffic is lighter," Maxwell said. I packed up the battered van that I'd gotten a good deal on, mostly because it needed more work than I could afford and off I went.

~*~

Ambrose Imports was an impressive office building that held several other large businesses. I went to the receptionist with my wheeled cart and told her I was making a delivery. A moment later someone came to escort me to Mr. Ambrose's suites. I expected to leave them with the very attractive and efficient looking administrative assistant but when I arrived, Mr. Ambrose himself came out and examined the boxes.

"Excellent! The Cala Lilly is a nice touch," he said examining one of the boxes.

"It's marzipan and edible, that's why its wrapped," I said proudly.

"Looks fine. And the cake?" I handed him the box and he opened it, and then looked at me. "This is exquisite work, you're an artiste." I blushed at the compliment, thanked him and handed him the $400 plus balance bill. He looked at it, then at me. I'd given it a 15% mark-up as most businesses do and I gulped thinking the price was too high. He went into his office and returned a moment later and handed me a folded official check.

"If you need the cash right away, take it to my accounting office on the fifth floor." I folded the check and put it in my purse. "No need Mr. Ambrose…" I said taking his extended hand.

I left the building feeling like I was floating on air. Singing with joy, I drove to the bank to deposit the check. As I unfolded it I saw that it was made out in the amount of $1,500. It had to be mistake. It was way more than the balance, and if it was a tip, what a gratuity. A little post-it note attached read: *You need to get acquainted with your self-worth, your packaging alone is worth the money."*

I smiled all the way back to the shop. As I drove up, I saw people entering and exiting the store. Parking the van, I jumped out and huried inside. Men and women were laughing as Mose rang up orders and telling joke after joke. *"Yeah…"* he said, *"that girl was so fat she used hoola hoops to keep her socks up."*

"Whoa! Miz B, check it out," Max said holding a try of chocolate covered strawberries; "These people want Valentine's day sweets and they want it now."

Things calmed down at 1 O'clock, but rallied again after three.

"Wow, what a day." I said to Max when there was another lull. "It's a good thing you came by when you did."

"I came back to see if I could make another $50.00. I think we did well especially with the old dude cracking them up.
"

It was a good day's work and while I knew it was because it was Valentine's Day, I was able to bank over thirty six hundred dollars, but I knew I couldn't expect that on a normal work day or week for that matter.

I was way wrong. Thanks to Mr. Ambrose, my business began to build consistently as he steered customers to the *Sweet Box.* I hired Mose part-time at first but within a few weeks he was full-time and Maxwell came whenever he could.

By the end of the third year I was a premier chocolatier with an exclusive clientele. I'd been written up in several papers and some of my recipes were included in some of the most renowned Pastry chef cookbooks.

~*~

One evening after closing as I was putting some finishing touches on chocolate raspberry tarts for a wedding, Mose came in back and hung up his apron.

"So…" he began.

"Yes?" I said not looking up from my painstaking project putting edible gold leaf paint on filigree pattern.

"So I guess you heard that old sayin' "

"Which one?"

The one about *all work and no play*… you know that one don't you?"

"I don 't have time to play."

"Well girlie you best make time, before you know it you'll be old and doddie like me."
I smiled."Are you asking me for a date Mose?"

"Hell no, I'm too old for you; but back in the day I would have danced you right into oblivion."

I laughed. "Well I am sure there are lots of things you could be doing."

"Never you mind what I *could* be doin', I'm talking about what you *ought* to be doin,'"
He said pulling on his thrift store overcoat.

"Don't you worry about me; I'm doing what I love. I'm content."

"*Doing* what you love and *being* in love ain't the same thing. You need to get out more."
He was right and although I was successful in business, romance eluded me, not that I minded because I was too busy trying to expand my business into wholesale pastry catering and perhaps a small dessert café; especially because Dexter Ambrose continued to steer a lot of important business my way prompting me to think about expanding my current locale.

I was finally able to make an offer on a chic spot in the middle of the business district and
was working out the numbers one day in the back of the shop when Mose said I had a call from City hall. All kinds of thoughts

went through my head; thinking that perhaps someone had gotten sick and wanted to shut me down, or maybe someone important wanted my *new* space and went straight to the top get it. When I answered, it was the Mayor's Chief Assistant telling me that I'd been referred by three reliable sources and wondered if I would be able to prepare a dessert buffet to accommodate a gathering for three hundred people at the grand meeting hall in two weeks. It was an opportunity that could easily get me the seed money I needed for my new store.

I went to work immediately and only took me a couple of days to assemble three culinary students together and the additional equipment needed to fill the extensive order for the upcoming gala. They were quick learners and had a lot of talent of their own and was glad for the extra cash I paid them and the use of my name in their resumes.

On the day of the delivery, I got another call from Mayor's office asking if I could bring an extra person to help, since a last minute illness left them shorthanded in serving. Thankfully Max was available.

"Way cool Miz B." he said with a grin when I told him.

I had been able to afford a more reliable van and as we loaded it up I checked off items to make sure we had everything. I was just locking the door and getting in behind the wheel when my cell rang. I cranked the motor and began to drive and answered the cell. "Hello?"

"Miss Bronte, this is Mosely. I'm in the drunk tank. But I swear I ain't been drinkin'. I got a god-awful pain in my gut and got dizzy. I fell and hit my head. I need to get outta here or they gonna send me to *Ovfields.*"

I had heard of the place, it was for the disenfranchised who had no place to go or couldn't get decent care, even in this country with its socialized medicine.

"Mose, I can't come now. I have an important engagement."

I heard a strangled sigh. "That's okay Miss Bronte, you done enough for me already. Thanks anyway."
Guilt attached itself to me like a leech as I drove to the Mayor's hall. It ate at me like a piranha as I set up and I felt awful. The tuxedoed and gowned gentry filled the hall after nine for apéritifs and dessert. Everyone exclaimed over my presentation of the dazzling array of chocolate, fruit and sugary confections.

It was almost midnight and I was clearing up when I saw Max in the corner talking animatedly to a guest who as listening with rapt attention.
Oh no! I thought, the mayoral staff was going to hand me my head for letting the help interact with the guests. I went over to extract him.

"I apologize if he bothered you," I said to the man politely.

"Not at all, He has some pretty innovative ideas," He said handing Max a card.

"Come see me when you graduate. I might have something for you in our R&D department."
Max beamed and I knew I was about to lose the best help I ever had.

~*~

After driving Max home I went to my apartment but couldn't sleep. I tossed and turned fitfully, and as soon as the sun rose I was up, showered and dressed and raced downtown to the precinct. I was greeted with the ever stern-faced officer Montrose and told him I'd come to bail out Mosely.

"He's going to Ovfields." he said not bothering to look up at me.

"Why? He said he wasn't drunk."

"He's always drunk. You don't know him." He continued writing.

"And you do?"
He glanced up me. "Just what's your interest in him anyway? He's way too old for you."

"That's disgusting even for you. Look! He called me. I've come to bail him out."

"And what's he gonna do once he's out huh?" Officer Montrose said.

I was shocked at the loud octave his voice had taken. "He has no money, no real job, and no place to live. I'm not going to let him loose to roam the streets and be an embarrassment."

That was an odd choice of words. I straightened my back and strengthened my resolve.

"For your information, he has a job, *and* a place to stay. He's going home with me, and if you don't let me see him, I'll just have to go over your head." I glared right back into his angry eyes and he knew I meant business.

"You're as stupid as he is." He said going to the door behind him and punching in a code, then disappeared inside. I could hear muffled laughter before the door closed and supposed the old man was doing what he did best and that was make people laugh. A moment later Officer Montrose escorted, a tired looking rheumy eyed Mose in. I signed the necessary papers. Gave my address so they would have proof that Mose had a place to stay and we left, but not before he passed by an inebriated prostitute handcuffed to a chair and said, *"Damn girl, your eyes are so crossed I bet when you make love you think you're in a threesome."*
Several officers laughed out loud, but Officer Montrose' lips were tight as he put his head down.

I stopped at the store and picked some shaving essentials and a tooth brush for Mose, then took him home and let him bathe. I fixed a brunch of juice, coffee eggs, and bacon and cheese biscuits and then offered him the couch to rest. He fell asleep instantly and I went into my small office to finish up some paperwork.

When he awoke, Mose told me that he hadn't been drinking but that he'd fallen and hit his head. Officer Montrose just happened to be the one to find him and took him in.

"He took me to the hospital first, but hauled me in as soon as they said I was okay."

Anger went through me. *What's with him anyway?*

~*~

Two days later Mose was missing again. I couldn't find him anywhere and I was frantic. The old man had me in stitches whenever he was around and I was growing quite fond of him. It rained for the next three days and I worried for the old guy. At the end of the fourth day, I closed up and went to deposit the receipts in the night vault. I recognized the shadowy figure leaning against a garbage bin as Mose and he was bleeding from his nose and mouth. Officer Montrose was standing next to him.

"What the hell did you do to him?" I screamed running to the old man.

"Nothing. I…"

But I didn't want to hear. I dialed emergency on my cell and within moments I was with Mose in an ambulance rushing to the hospital.

Officer Montrose appeared a short time later in the waiting room but I didn't want to talk to him.

"You have to listen to me. I went looking for him. He…" he tried to explain.

"Look! I don't know what you have against a defenseless old man and just because you've never been in the position he's in doesn't give you the right to always be on his case; you've crossed the line this time and I am going to report you."

He was about to rebuke me when the Doctor appeared. He told us that Mose had stomach ulcers and his liver was in a bad way. He was stable and they would know more the next day when the tests came back and that we should go home and get some rest.

Outside, it was still raining and I couldn't get a cab.

"I'll take you home, the squad car is just over here, "he pointed

"I'd rather have a root canal with a steam shovel." I hissed.

"You're as mule headed as he is, " he said grabbing my arm and pulled me toward the car. "Get in or I'll arrest you for something."

"Like what?"

"For being so damned pig headed and so damned beautiful."

He pushed me gently into the car, got in the other side started to drive.

"My address is…"

"I know where you live, *he* had you down as a contact." We both knew who he meant.

We were both soaked and I told him he could at least come in and dry off. Within five minutes were at each other's throats. He told me I was a fool for taking in strays and I condemned him for being a bully.

"Why do you bother him so much? He can't hurt you." I yelled.

"He did hurt me."

"How? By making fun of you? He's a comic, he makes fun of everybody—it's what does. He probably does it to hide behind his inadequacies."

"He's hiding from his past—and from me."

"Oh stop it. He's just an old jokester."

"He's my father," he yelled.

I was stunned into momentary silence. "What?" I said just above a whisper.

"Well I guess I should say he's the seed I came from," he said sarcastically.

"But he's…"

"White, yeah I know. So you see it ain't always black men that abandon their families."

I didn't know what to say and went to him, but his glare stopped me from reaching out to him.

"Don't feel sorry for me. I don't need your pity and I'm not sorry he's out of my life. My mother died loving that old fool. She followed him from place to place until she just couldn't anymore."

It all made sense. The old man was too educated to have been a career drunk. There was sorrow in his inebriation, I sensed it but ignored it.

"I'm sorry Mr. Montrose."

"Daniel— originally Daniel Collins, and he's Melvin *"Mosely"* Collins. Montrose is my mother's maiden name. I had it changed legally afterwards."

The man was weighed down with pain. His huge shoulders slumped as he sank to the couch and held his head in his hands and cried. I was moved and wanted to hold him and tell him about forgiveness. I touched him and he turned to me. His tear stained face was handsome in the soft lighting of my living room.

"Look I am not going to profess to know everything you've been through, but I can tell you this, if you continue to allow your feelings to take all of your positive energy you'll end up with nothing but hopeless fatigue both mentally and physically."

"You don't know anything about him?"

"Did it ever occur to you that he's changed? I mean he's been working steadily for me for the last seven months."

"I know," he said softly.

"You know?"

"I kind of went by your shop a few times, I saw him in there. I was surprised you trusted him with your cash and your store."

"He's been quite a help to me."

"Yeah, probably just trying to make up."

"He doesn't owe me anything," I said.

"You kept him from getting locked up that first day, that's something."

"Maybe you should just try and talk to him," I said. He snorted sarcastically "Believe me lady we don't have anything to talk about."

"He's sick and in the hospital, what if he dies?"

"Then I hope hell is ready for him."

"You can't mean that," I said.

"Yes, I do."

I sighed, there was no use in trying to get through to him, it was late and we were both exhausted.

"Look you can sack out here on my couch if you want, your father did once. I'll go and see him in the morning. He shouldn't be alone." I got up and headed towards my bedroom when suddenly he stopped me.

"Thanks for the offer but I guess I'll just get on home. "

"Well good night then," I said walking him to the door. He leaned against the jamb and looked at me.

"So you want to tell me your story?"

"I don't have one.

"*Everybody* has a story."

"Have a good night Officer Collins- Montrose." And I closed the door.

It was late and I was vacillating between taking a shower and just going to bed. I opted for the second and went to the bedroom and got out of my clothes, donning my most comfortable *if* relatively unattractive nightwear. I couldn't get Daniel out of my mind and I kept trying to convince myself that is was because I wanted to somehow fix whatever was wrong between him and his father. But in reality it was his smoky dark eyes, impressive physique and the curve of his lips that offered little to no smile that made me warm all over.

I'd just removed the bedspread when I heard my doorbell. I went to the peephole and looked. It was Daniel. I opened the door and in a moment he had me in his arms.

 Was it because I hadn't been with anyone in a long time? Or was it because I wanted him, needed him? It didn't matter because like every romantic movie I'd ever seen I was kissing him back with passion that came from I don't know where. We never made it to bedroom— not right then anyway because he slow walked me back to my couch and laid me on it, without ever removing his lips from mine. His mouth was all over me as we struggled to get me out of my clothes. In moments I lay naked before him. I didn't care about anything except having this man inside me. He undressed quickly, stopping only to don protection and then lowered to me. He moved my legs apart splaying my cavity wide to accept him. Placing the head of his penis against me, he moved in, not hard but purposeful enough cause me to gasp. He kissed away any discomfort and then moved frantically inside me. I called out his name but he didn't seem to hear me as he plunged deeper and harder. I looked at him. His eyes were closed and his teeth gritted as though he was trying to rid himself of all the angst of his past into me. His groans of ardor gave way to a strangled sob as he made love to me and I let him for as long as he needed to, as long as he could until his angst was replaced with undeniable sexual hunger with a force that astonished us both. He kissed and sucked my lips and I bit into his shoulder to subdue the grunts of erotic passion that threatened to spew from my lips.

Finally spent he lay spent on top of me; I smoothed his tightly cropped curls and soothed him with light kisses.
He sat up, pulling his shirt previously discarded shirt across his waning erection.

"I'm sorry Sally."
I sprang up. "How did you know my…"
His eyes held a glint of mischief and I saw that they were indeed his father's eyes.

"I'm a cop. I can get whatever information I want. You call yourself, Saljon' which is sort of an acronym for *Sally Johnson*, the name you had when you lived in the United States, and Bronte is because?" He waited for my answer.
Embarrassed heat suffused through me. "I like the Bronte novels, so I sort of borrowed that last name." I said sheepishly.

"It fits you." He said with a disarming smile, the first I had ever seen from him.

There was a sudden and uncomfortable silence between us and I was abruptly embarrassed by my nakedness and what I'd just done. "Look, I really should explain about what we just did. I'm really not the kind of woman who...."

He placed his finger across my lips. "Hush, you don't have to explain anything to me. I was attracted to you the first day I saw you. I just let this thing between my father and me get in the way."

"Speaking of that…" I said getting up and putting on my clothes.

"I can't talk about it now Sally, I just can't."

It was a warning statement. Somehow I understood and didn't press him. He asked where my bathroom was and went to clean up, then with a sad smile, left my apartment.

I showered and climbed into bed naked, but it took a long while for me to fall asleep.

~*~

The next morning, I went to the hospital to see Mose.

"You didn't bring me no chocolates?" he asked when I arrived.

"You have stomach ulcers, you should never be eating chocolate and had I known…"

"Damn Doctors! They're so stupid they have to open their fly when the want to count to eleven."

I ignored the crude joke and went to him. "Mose, I know that Daniel is your son." I said calmly.

He was silent for a few moments. "He tell you about me?"

"A little."

"Did he tell you I'm so dumb I got hit by a *parked* car? Or that I thought I could get a *book* of matches at a library?" He was still making jokes, but he was trying hard to cover up his pain.

"Mose, I think he wants to talk to you, he just doesn't know how."

"Why would he want to talk to somebody so worthless and stupid that I could trip over a cordless phone?"

"Stop making jokes Mose, this is serious." I yelled and was instantly sorry.
Suddenly tears were in his eyes.

"I let him down Miss Bronte. I destroyed everything in his life. I loved him and his mother, but she died and it's all my fault."

"Then you have to tell him Mose, you have to."

"It's too late," he said sadly.

"No it isn't old man!" The voice from the doorway startled us both, "You tell me right now to my face that you love me, that you didn't really want to leave me with those people."

"I didn't know what else to do son. I had no money no, no prospects; I couldn't drag you down to where I was going."

"You were my father!" Daniel hissed and moved to the bed.
I got up and let him stand close.

"I was a failure!" Mose yelled back.

"Then you were *my* failure! The only thing I had left."

"Your mother... she..."

"Died loving you and never said a word against you. She told me to be strong and to look after you. But how could I do that when you left me. You left me with strangers."

"They were good to you,"

"I' didn't love them, I loved you. I didn't want them I wanted you."

"Do you think you'd be what you are today if I'd let you stay with me, traveling from place to place, ending up in slums and finally the street?"

"You could have discussed it with me?"

"You were a child!" Mose yelled.

"I was *your* child," Daniel yelled back.

"I thought about you every day, never stopped loving you and knew I had done the right thing by you even if you didn't and don't want to believe that."

They were both crying now and I felt like an intruder. I started to move away but felt my hand being taken. Daniel was gripping it.

"It's because of her that I'm even here. It took the kindness of this stranger from another country to let me open up, just a little."

"She's a gem alright and her spirit is richer than any of her finest chocolates." Mose said in agreement.

Daniel sat on the edge of the bed. "Pop, we need to clear the air. If we're going to get to know each other again, we have to talk."

I pulled my hand from Daniel's and wiped the tears from my face. "Well! I have a business to run and you two should get reacquainted." I walked to the door.

"You mean you don't want to hear about how I was so poor that my TV was an Etch-A-Sketch? How the time I was so poor I went trick or treating on thanksgiving." Mose joked.

I *was* laughing this time and waving good-bye.

"How about that winter we had a house warming party just to get body heat?" I could still hear him calling out as I left. I had almost reached the elevator when Daniel called me on my cell.

"How did you get this number?" I said softly.

"I told you, I'm a cop and I can get anything I want."

"And what *do* you want?"

"You… tonight."

"It's not going to be as easy as it was before."

"I can wait."

"I gotta go." I laughed.

"Me too. He's telling me about his nurse who has teeth so big she has to clean them a shoe-brush."

I was sure he could hear me laughing all the way down the hall.

Everything in my life was coming around in full circle. Business was booming, and I had fallen in love. It felt good to be wanted, held and loved. I knew this was the beginning of the rest of my life and once Daniel got over the pain of the lost years with his father I was confident that he would share his life with me. Together we would be a family with his dad. It would take time before he came but when he did; I will be ready for him.

Hard Lesson

I thought I knew it all and I wished I'd listened to the clichés and what I thought was just motherly rhetorical bullshit back then. When I think of my rebellion and flagrant disrespect of my parents, I want to wish it away like it never happened because I know now that I am one of the lucky ones.

For the longest time I blamed my bad attitude and boredom on living in a small and what I considered as a dull insignificant town in Nebraska. My mother and I argued constantly about everything, from the way I dressed, to the music I listened to. *It was too-loud-too vulgar* and of course the dance moves that went along with it was even worse according to her. My father loved me I'm sure of that, but he let my mother do all the parenting.

~*~

Day after day it seemed like the same thing, we'd have loud ear splitting fights about my room which she said was a horror and I considered *messy-chic*. She chastised me about picking over the food she prepared, telling me that I should be happy that I had someone to not only buy the food but fix it as well.

Yeah! Yeah... I'd heard it a million times and I was sick of it.

I often told my best friend Stephanie that I dreamed of going to Venice Beach California where the sun shined all the time, where every day was a party-fest and you could do whatever the hell you wanted. But that dream seemed a long way off if ever but I didn't want to think about having to spend the rest of my life in this hick ass town.

~*~

I was a few days short of my eighteenth birthday but could pass for twenty-one if I applied the right make-up and wore fashionable clothes. Thanks to my mother's classic runway model genes I had a terrific figure and Johnny Malone—the school science nerd said I had the best legs at Sprague High. Not that it mattered what he thought and while I liked it that he noticed me, I was really interested in his older brother Nicholas. I dreamed about that man night and day with his tall dark looks and that dreamy little scar just above his right lip. His jet black hair was thick with just a hint of a wave and his lean body was strong and straight. There'd been rumors that he'd been in and out of trouble a few years back and had even spent time at a state correctional facility. But that just made him all the more exciting to me. I'd often see him on the corner in town leaning against a wall with one leg propped up in back, smoking or chugging a beer housed in a brown paper bag and my heart would race a mile a minute.

He was almost always with a different girl, but most recently he was with Callie Bonner, a petite redhead from the wrong side of the tracks. Not that we *had* any tracks, but the division between the middle class and the poor was a mile wide and we just didn't mix. It wasn't so much *where* Callie had been born, but how. The town gossips whispered that her mother had slept around and when she had gotten pregnant and accused the owner of the department store where she worked, things took a bad turn. Of course the man vehemently denied her allegations and she was promptly fired and she soon found out that no one would hire her. Literally shunned, she moved across town and began to drink—a lot. By the time Callie was born it was said that she had alcohol fetal syndrome and it was a wonder that she had survived at all. By time she was into her teens it wasn't uncommon for men to be in and out of their house and everyone was equating Callie with her mother's actions and began to treat her like it.

It was no wonder Callie took up with Nick. He, in a sense became her boyfriend and her protector and I hated her for that because *I* wanted him.

~*~

I was a good student but I didn't apply myself and mostly went to school just because most of my friends were there. Mid-semester we were informed that our school had been selected to enter the National Science Project Championships and everybody was ecstatic about it. I couldn't care less because I was only interested in getting to California and being with Nick Malone of course. I only went to Science class because Johnny was there and I knew I would be able to get bits of information about his brother Nick.

When the teacher matched us off into groups and assigned us our projects I saw my opportunity to get closer to Nick through Johnny. As luck would have it, I was placed in another collection of science nerds and I pleaded with one of the girls in Johnny's group to switch places with me, imploring her with lies about how much *I really liked Johnny.* She couldn't stand him and jumped at the chance to switch.

Johnny was elated with the change and suggested that we meet at his house twice a week since he had all the equipment and everything set up in his basement to begin our assignment. He was such a hard core nerd but I was beside myself with joy because I was hoping to be able to see Nick up close at least two times a week—more if I played my cards right.

The first time I went to Johnny's house on the pretense of brainstorming about the science project, I dressed like I was going to a dance club with plenty of make-up and perfume and it was a good thing my mother was too busy in her sewing room to see me before I left or she would have flipped. Unfortunately, it was a complete waste of time and effort because Nick wasn't even at home that day.

~*~

One afternoon I was over my friend Stephanie's house who was trying everything she could to keep me occupied.

"Hey Marisa, you heard about those girls?"

"What girls?" I said absently as I filed my nails.

She began telling me about a news article on how several girls from neighboring towns were missing. The police had no leads on where they might be or if they had in fact been abducted in opposed to have run away. It had been a few months since the first one had gone missing and the trail had grown cold.

"They're probably in Venice California where I want to be," I said churlishly.

A few days later, I saw Johnny with his brother at the grocery store. Nick was cool and suave and this time, thankfully, he didn't have Callie Bonner hanging on his arm.

"Hey what's up Marisa, you coming over tonight?" it was Johnny trying to be every bit as cool as his brother and failing miserably.

"Oh? Do we have a meeting this evening?" I said trying to sound more grown up than sixteen.

"Well yeah, you were supposed to bring your research material."

I had totally forgotten, but I knew I could get Johnny to do all the work anyway with just a small amount of emotional suggestion.

"Well I've been having a bit of trouble with that and I was hoping you could help me," I said with pretended shyness.

"Sure, I have a lot of it anyway. We just talk it out with the others," Johnny said excitedly. By then I had caught Nick's attention.

"Well now…" he said in a voice that was all bass and full of innuendo. "Who do we have here?"

"I'm Marisa Bascomb." I said teasingly.

Nick's dark eyes were glued to me or I should say my breasts which had just the right amount of puff and cleavage against my blouse.

"So you're coming over tonight eh? Maybe I should stay home and see just what you two are doing in our basement." His tone was playful but his full attention was focused on me.

"Of course I'll be there tonight." I breathed up at them.

The rest of the afternoon dragged on and I could hardly wait until six. Johnny's folks were out for the evening and the other two people in our group had already arrived. The basement wasn't large but it was pleasant and well lit. There was a table in the corner with papers and a weird looking model made of wire and wood that I assumed was the beginnings of our project. The three of them were standing around another area talking at once. Johnny waved me over and I gave him a half smile and ambled to where they were. I listened as they squabbled and conferred over the science data notes and discussed over possibilities of the project. I pretended to be interested but nothing was further from the truth. They were so engrossed they didn't even notice when I moved back to the couch and was about to sit when I heard movement upstairs and then heard the muffled voice of Nick singing one of the latest rap tunes. I needed to get up there and had an idea.

"Hey Johnny I'm kind of thirsty. Do you have any soda?" I asked.

"Yeah, hold on a sec I'll go up and get some," he said tapping the keys of his laptop expertly.

"Hey you're busy, would you mind if I go up and get it?"

"Cool! Holler if you need any help," he said absently. I literally ran upstairs to the kitchen. It was empty but I could hear Nick humming and followed the sound to the family room. He was slouched in a large easy chair with one leg slung over the arm watching TV, as he swigged from the can of beer he was holding.
I strolled in front of him and stopped.

"Johnny said there was some beer in the fridge," I lied. His voice filled with lechery. "Johnny doesn't drink beer," he said, "But I bet you do."

"It's alright," I smiled and walked with seductive promise back to the kitchen. I heard him shift in his seat and knew he was watching me; I bent over allowing my short skirt to rise just short of my lacy thong panties.

I heard his footsteps as he came up behind me. Pressing himself against me he reached in and grabbed another beer from the bottom shelf.

"Soda is on the top shelf," he said against my ear.
I felt the rise of his erection and while it made me nervous I was thrilled that I could have this effect on him. He moved away and popped the can open and took a long slow gulp. I took out some sodas *and* a can of beer and turned.

"How old are you?" he asked.

"How old do I look?" I said smiling seductively.

"Not old enough to be drinking this beer," he said taking it from my hand.
I could tell he was enjoying this cat and mouse game and I was completely at ease with it but I did get a little jittery when he moved closer to me. His face was inches from mine and I was dead sure he was about to kiss me. His hand reached out and it looked as though he was going to touch my breast but he merely reached around me and placed the beer back on the shelf and grabbed another soda and put it in my hand with the others.

"I don't want to be accused of contributing to the delinquency of a minor."
I was about to deliver a clever retort of my own when at that precise moment his cell phone rang. He pulled it from his pocket and looked at the caller ID.

"Hey babe, how's my little sweet dumplin'?"
I figured he was talking to Callie, but his eyes were glued on me.

"Sure baby, I can pick you up, maybe we can continue our little…" he hesitated then whispered to me. "This is kind of private."

I went back downstairs, but my mind was not on any science project. I was busy with ideas on how I was going to be Nicky Malone's new girlfriend.

~*~

Three weeks later I was called into the School counselor's office. A tearful Mrs. Bonner—Callie's mother stood between two men who later identified themselves as detectives.

"You're in the science group with the Malone kid aren't you?" one of them asked after we were introduced. They went on to ask me if I had seen Callie in the past week or so. It appeared that she was missing no one knew where. I told them that she wasn't in our project group.

"Did you ask Nick? I think they were dating?" I offered. The counselor said that he'd been questioned at length, and was quite distraught over her disappearance. They continued to question me but all I could think of was, poor Nick and how devastated he must be about Callie. When they told me I could go I didn't return to class, I slipped out of the building and walked all the way to the Malone house hoping to find Nick there—alone.

When I arrived I heard loud music and Nick's laughter which seemed odd under the circumstances. I rang the bell and in a moment he snatched the door open, his face full of mirth.

"I just heard about Callie I'm so sorry." I said mournfully.

If he wondered why I wasn't in school he didn't let on.

"Come in" he said, his face taking on a more appropriate morose expression.

I stepped in and he lowered the music. I told him about the detectives and Callie's mom being at our school.

"What did they want?" he said on alert.

I told him they asked if I'd seen Callie at the house during my visits for the science project. He looked pensive but I mistook it for sadness and I went to him and put my arms around him. Immediately his body molded to mine. He needed comforting and I was going to give it to him.

"It's Okay Nick they'll find her I know they will."

We sat and talked for a while or at least I should say I rattled on like disc jockey on crack. I told him about wanting to leave this hick town and go to Venice Beach, and how I felt I never fit in. It never occurred to me that he wasn't offering much in return and I chalked it up to him just being a good listener. When I switched

the conversation to Callie, he looked sad and I hugged him again.
He held on tight this time and told me how difficult it was.
It felt so good in his arms. Although I knew it was wrong, I
wanted to kiss him; I wanted to be the one to bring him peace
during this difficult time. I initiated the first kiss and in moments
he was all over me. My only thought at that moment was that if
Callie never returned then *I* would be his girlfriend.
Suddenly he pushed me away.

"Look, you better go Marisa."

"But I don't want to go."

"I need to be alone right now, "he said not too
convincingly.

"Do you really want to be alone Nick?"

"No, that's not want I *want* at all."

It was like his words were a magnet and just pulled me into his
arms. This time I made no pretense of resistance. I let him
maneuver me back toward his bedroom and slam the door shut.

~*~

When I woke up, I had to admit his room was worse than
mine ever was. I was tangled in dingy, sweaty bed sheets, with a
lumpy smelly pillow and the place next to me was empty. I tried
to tell myself that although I was wrong for sleeping with Nick I
did it to comfort him.

I heard muffled laughter coming from the other room. I
got up and dressed and made my way to the door and opened it
quietly. I was about to step out when I heard him.

"Don't worry, it's all set and it looks like I just might
have another surprise for you—er, look I'll talk to you later,"he
said when he saw me and switched off his cell.

His smile was dazzling, but his *special* interest in me seemed
somehow lessened.

"Look Marisa, I don't know what came over me, I mean I
shouldn't have—*we* shouldn't have…"

He was looking down at the floor and I was so moved. I went to
him.

"I wanted it Nick, I wanted it to happen."

"It was wrong and I didn't know it was your first time, it's just that I was so upset about everything and you're so beautiful."

I was enthralled with the compliment. "I'm glad I could be here for you."

"You're pretty special you know that?" He said clipping my chin playfully. I blushed like the silly school girl I was. Suddenly he perked.

"Marisa, were you serious about going to Venice Beach in California?"

My heart began beating like crazy. *Did he want to go with me?* "Sure, I'm just trying to save a little more money."

"Look, I have to go out now, but maybe we can talk about it. Give me your cell number and I'll call you in a couple of days."

Nick's *couple of days* turned into two weeks. Oh I saw him alright, riding around in a brand new Ford Expedition and to my utter disappointment he was almost never alone and had a different girl in it all the time.

~*~

Our science project or I should say Johnny's and the groups' project was complete and I had no real reasons to go to the Malone house anymore. It depressed me and my irritation spilled over into day to day arguments with my mother. She was always on me about shit, like cleaning my room or staying out too much. I couldn't wait to get out of there.

I tried to call Nick a few times at his house since that was the only number I had, but he was either too busy to talk to me or he wasn't at home. I was so irritable and antsy I thought I would lose it and wondered if he had changed his mind about the Venice thing.

Then one night almost a month later, he did call.

"Hey sweetness I got some great news. It looks like we're going to California—that's if you were serious."

We? Had he said we? I was beside myself with joy. "Of course I'm serious. When can we go?"

"As soon as possible baby, when you do think you can get away? I mean I don't want your folks all over my ass before we're even off the block."

Nick and I were going to be together in the very place I'd always wanted to go. I told him that my parents were going out to dinner with friends next friday evening and we could go then. He agreed.

"Uh look baby, don't bring a lot of shit. I got some cash and I can buy you whatever you need when we get there. After all the climate there is a lot different than it is here."
I told him I was just going to bring a few things because I didn't want to raise suspicions either.

~*~

Friday evening I was on my bed with my headphones on and thumbing through a magazine when my mother popped her head in and informed me she and dad were leaving to go meet with their friend for dinner. I waved her off like she was a bothersome fly and never even looked up.

As soon as I heard the car door slam I went to the window and when they had driven off I hurried to my desk and scribbled a brief note to my friend Stephanie and placed it in a stamped envelope, knowing that Nick and I would be long gone before she even got it.

I hurried to get my large leather hobo sack filled with a few of my favorite clothes and CD's, some cash I had taken from my mother's *emergency* fund and went to rendezvous with Nick at the place he'd told me.

I ran all the way, stopping just long enough to drop the letter in the mailbox.
I wanted to leap right into his arms when I saw him but he stopped me.

"Hi ya babe, come on we gotta get going." He said looking around and hurrying me into his SUV then ran around and got in.

"Nick, I…" But he pulled me over and kissed me hard shutting off any protestation and I tingled all over.

"It's gonna be okay baby, we're on our way and it's gonna be just you and me."

He gunned the motor and we started out. As soon as I saw the sign that indicated that were leaving Nebraska, I bit my lip with reservations. I searched inside my bag, for my cell phone. I found it and began to dial.

"What the hell are you doing?" he said angrily and grabbed it from me.

"It's okay I'm just leaving a message for my mother. I'm not going to tell her where I am or anything just that I'm okay and I'll call her later."

A nervous smile settled over his face. "Don't do that baby; they'll track us down in no time. Let's get a little further out and then you can call okay?" He said taking my cell phone and putting it into his shirt jacket pocket.

I agreed and let my hand drift over to caress his thigh.

"It really will be nice won't it Nick, with just you and me?"

"You betcha doll. Say, reach back get that thermos. We'll have a little toast to our future."

I unbuckled my seatbelt and got the blue thermos, opened it and poured out the brown liquid in the cup.

"What is it?" I sniffed it and scrunched my nose.

"Brandy—the best. I want you to start enjoying the taste of it because it'll be just a small part of the good life you'll have if I have anything to do with it."

Liquor wasn't new to me, but expensive spirits were. I took a sip and it burned going down but after a while it was smoother and he urged me to drink some more. He turned on the radio and I was feeling pretty good and dancing in my seat. Nick laughed then admonished me to re-buckle my seatbelt.

"Don't wanna lose you now baby." He said pinching my cheek.

~*~

I don't remember falling asleep but when I awoke he was half carrying me as I leaned against him towards the door of a shabby motel.

"Where the hell is this?" My mouth felt like it was filled with sawdust

"Gotta save our money if we're gonna make it last, by the way, did you bring any?" He asked.

Groggily, I told him I'd brought everything I had which totaled $600.00 and few singles at the bottom of my bag. He took it all.

"It'll be safer with me," he said.

He switched on the old style T.V. and turned back the covers on the single saggy looking bed.

"Why don't you get some rest I'm going to find us some food and I'll be right back, okay baby?"

I smiled weakly and he made me promise not to call home from the room until he returned.

"Let me talk to them. I want to tell them that you'll be okay that I'll take good care of you. I'll tell them that we'll be getting married. Just wait for me honey and we'll talk to them together. Promise me."

"I promise," I said looking at him through my droopy lids.

He kissed me and left.

I didn't realize at the time that he hadn't taken any of *his* bags out of the car nor had he given me my cell phone back.

My head was aching something terrible from all the Brandy, but I waited for him and then I waited some more.

I must have finally fallen asleep and when I awoke it was close to three in the morning and Nick still hadn't returned. It dawned on me that I didn't even know his cell number nor did I know his license plate number. A cold chill washed over me as the realization that I'd done something really stupid, but evaporated like a mist when I heard the key in the lock.

I let out a sigh of relief, then horror gripped me as two strange men entered.

They were smiling lecherously as they looked me up and down. A scream welled in my throat but it was stilled when one of them who had been holding a white square cloth onto which he poured a clear liquid moved to me and covered my face as a cold blackness covered my world.

~*~

My hands tingled and my mouth was dry and pasty when I awakened. I tried to move but I realized I was bound tightly. My heart was beating so fast it hurt my chest and my head pounded. Something was covering my eyes and my mouth was gagged. I heard a shuffling sound and I scrambled away hitting a wall of some kind. I tried to scream but only a guttural moan escaped my lips.

"Shh! don't move?" the whispery voice said.
I felt hands untying the eye-band. My vision was blurred as I tried to focus on the person who was now loosening the gag and pulled it down. I blinked but could see nothing.

"Who…who are you?" I rasped.

"Callie Bonner and you're Marisa Bascomb right?"

"My God Callie, they've been looking for you, where are we?"

"We're in a truck I think. I can feel it moving sometimes."

"But how… Oh no! They must have hurt Nick." I struggled against my bonds when I heard her chortle.

"Nick is just fine." She said grittily, "He's the one who put us in here. He's selling us."

"What? But he said…"

"Yeah I know, I fell for his same lies. I thought he loved me too."
I was suddenly ashamed. Not only of things I had thought and said against her, but for the things I'd said and done to my mother.

"Callie, do you have any idea where they're taking us?

"Mexico, I think. I heard them talking."

My eyes adjusted to the darkness and I saw a little of her and gasped with horror. Her clothes were torn and dirty. Her lips were swollen and she had bruises on her arms and legs.

"Oh shit Callie, what happened?"

She began to sob softly. "They're gonna do things to you Marisa, bad—horrible things."

I couldn't believe this was happening.

"Have you seen Nick at all?" I asked.

"Not since he drugged me."

I remembered falling asleep and knew he had done the same thing to me.

We heard laugher outside. Callie hurried and replaced my gag and covered my eyes then I heard her move back to her place in the darkness. Keys and latches sounded and the creak of a rusted door opened.

"Well now, this one here with the pretty *yella* hair ought to suit our clients real nice." A gruff, phlegmy voice said.

"Yeah but we gotta test her out first," another man said. "We wanna make sure she's ripe and ready."

The laughter was frightening but not more than the sound of their footsteps coming toward me. I tried to move away but rough hands grabbed me. I couldn't see and I couldn't scream as I felt my jeans being pulled down then off. I tried to kick out but all I felt was dead air.

"Easy now little filly, this ain't gonna hurt— much."

I struggled against my bonds as I felt myself being slammed face down to the floor. I heard the unmistakable sound of belts being loosened and I tried to scream, but only the garbled sound of a moan escaped me.

The pain that shot through me almost made me lose consciousness as I felt my rear explode with pain. The man pushed himself into me without thought or care.

"Virgin ass; Just like I like it. " I heard him say and pumped until I thought I would die. The second man liked his sex a little more traditional, but in *all* orifices. It seemed to go on

forever as they took me in ways I'd never thought could happen to anyone.

When they were done, I could hardly move but I tried anyway until one of them grabbed hold of me and I felt the pinch of a needle in my arm, then oblivion once again.

~*~

Time had no meaning. I didn't know if it was day or night or how much time had passed. We were moved from one conveyance to another several different times and twice more we were assaulted. I was bruised and sore everywhere and I tasted coppery blood from my swollen lip.

"They like it when you fight." Callie whispered to me after the second ordeal was over and the men had left.

They hadn't given us much anything to eat and only the barest sips of water and a bucket in the corner of truck for bodily elimination. The two men came two more times, but this time they took turns between Callie and me. They even tried to get us to do things to each other, but I vomited and they left in disgust.

A day or more must have gone by and I knew my mother was frantic. I was suddenly sorry for every bad moment I'd ever given her and promised myself that if I ever got out of this I would change my ways and be the kind of daughter she wanted. I don't know how I thought I could do it but I vowed I'd find a way out of this hell.

~*~

The truck had been bumping along a rough road for more than an hour then suddenly it stopped. We heard the clank of the latch then coarse hands pulled us from the back. The gag was removed and the band was snatched from my eyes and I shielded them from the blinding sunlight. Callie was a blur as I saw her being pulled toward what looked like a cabin. A moment later I was taken inside also.

Callie was standing in the center of the room facing a rusty metal desk. Our hands were still tied although they'd been loosened from time to time to allow the blood to flow.

A door opened and Nick came into view. His eyes were cold and hard as he sat behind the desk.

"No matter what you might be thinking about me…" he said as though we were both strangers to him, "there is no escape from this situation. The more you fight the more harm will come to you."

"Nick…" I started, but he held up a hand.

"You're dirty, hungry and thirsty and I can remedy that, all I need is a little cooperation. Now Callie here has been with us a little longer than you so she knows the routine—you on the other hand…" He pointed to me. "Have to learn. So why don't you just start by getting on your knees and crawling on over here."

"What?" I rasped incredulously.

" Come to me ON YOUR KNEES!" he shouted. When I didn't move he nodded to one of the men standing behind us. I felt myself being shoved onto the floor.

"You can either crawl over here like I asked you to, or you can let my friend here enjoy his favorite pastime, you're in the right position for it."
Remembering the horrible pain of the past hours of degradation I moved slowly toward Nick. I hated him, but I couldn't let it show. When I moved around the desk and was at Nick's feet, he grabbed me by my hair so that I looked up at him.

"Now, just so you know, I get paid a pretty hefty sum of cash for young ladies like you and Callie there. I almost have enough saved to leave our sad little *piece-of-shit* town and start a new life. You've always been a bit of a problem to your mother as I hear it so the cops will probably think you just ran away."

"My Mom, oh Nick please let me just call and tell her I'm alive; at least just that."
He cupped my face in his hands. "But you're not alive little darlin'. Not anymore, not where you're goin' and your folks will never find you."
Sobs tore through the room long before I knew it was me who was crying.

"Now," he said rising. "I got a wash bowl and some clean clothes for both of you right in there so go and get yourselves clean up. We'll be passing you on to the next contingent in a little while so you might say…this is next to our last contact. Once I hand you over to your new friends and I collect my money, that's it."
His laughter was horrible as he left and the two men shoved us toward the bathroom.

As pitiful and grimy as it was I was never so happy to see a small bar of soap and hot running water in my life. The men took our soiled things and when we came out wrapped in towels there were clean but cheesy looking garments on the back of two chairs. They told us to get dressed and stood there smiling as we did, trying to hide as much of ourselves as we could.

"No need to hide *chica*, we know every inch of what you both got," One of the abductors laughed. Then they showed us their guns and told us if we tried anything they would go back and kill our families.

I couldn't believe the hell we were in and how my selfish needs and inconsiderate behavior got me into this mess. My mind was running through *any* idea I could come up with to let someone—anyone know what was happening to us.

As they herded us to a car, a thought hit me. *The letter!* I had mailed that letter to Stephanie. I told her not to tell anyone anything but I knew my mother would get it out of her.
A thin glimmer of hope coursed through me; somehow I was going to get Callie and me out of this.

~*~

They drove us around in that rickety rusted car for hours and in what seemed to be in circles as some of the landmarks kept repeating. They talked bawdily about how they'd abducted other girls from other towns and even joked about how one of them who hadn't cooperated was *never* going to be found. *Buzzard food*! They had laughed.

Callie had been with these men longer than me and I could see by the dead look in her eyes that she had given up all hope. I wanted to ease her fears by telling her that someone was looking for me, but her glazed stare made me know that nothing mattered to her anymore.

It was dusk when they stopped at a small roadside diner and pulled us out.

"You don't want to give anything away," Nick said as he put his arm around me possessively and I felt the gun pressing my side. One of the other men grabbed Callie and fondled her.

"Hey!" Nick said. "Cut it out, you've had your fun; they're being passed on now."
The man made a fake pouty face and gave her one more squeeze the urged her forward.
Inside, they slid us in a booth at the back of the diner and sat on the outside of us. The bored waitress came over and kept her eyes trained on her pad as she took their order. I was hoping she would look at me and maybe she could see how scared I was or I could signal her with my eyes. When she finally did look, Nick took my face in his and kissed me. He was smart, he knew all the tricks.

After she'd brought the coffee they'd ordered, we waited. A little while passed and two young men entered and came over laughing and shaking hands with Nick and his two ruffians like they were old friends. After a limited discussion, one of the men extracted a thick manila envelope and slid it over to Nick. He took it and glanced inside.

"Looks like it's all there, nice doing business with ya."

"Then we will take out merchandise and get going Senor," one of the newer men said
My heart was pounding. In minutes we would be on our way to Mexico where I was sure there was a good chance we'd never be heard from again.

Everyone got up; I clung to the table shaking with fear. Nick showed me his gun and yanked me up, gripping my arm possessively. They slow walked us toward the door. Just before we got there two laughing policemen entered and headed for the counter and sat down.

I could feel Nick tense as he focused his eyes ahead and kept walking. Suddenly Callie broke away from the man who was holding her and ran at me screaming and slapping me.

"You stay away from my man you whore!" she yelled, and then whispered, *"Play along Marisa."*

She kicked at me as Nick and his henchmen tried to pry us apart. The other men lowered their hatted heads and left the diner quickly. In a flash I saw that Callie had reached into Nick's waistband and got his gun. The cops jumped off their stools.

"Hold on lady, just hold on, you do not want to do anything foolish."

"They took us!" she screamed, "They're kidnappers and those two leaving are in on it," she pointed toward the two who had left the diner.

Both officers leapt from their stools and drew their revolvers as one called into his shoulder radio and the other one ran to the door.

"Halt!" he said.

After that everything happened at once, I saw Nick lunge toward Callie and the next thing I heard was the sound of a gunshot, then a burning in shoulder. I looked down to see a stream of blood stain the front of my dress as I sank to the floor. Screaming voices assaulted my brain as the light became dimmer. *Hold on! Just hold on Marissa!* I heard Callie say and then total blackness.

~*~

I awoke in a hospital bed in Tifton Arizona. My hand felt warm and when I moved, the grip became tighter,

"Marisa? Baby—oh my baby."

It was my mother. She was crying and squeezing my hand. My father looked like he hadn't slept in days came forward with tears in his eyes.

"Don't be mad Daddy, please."

"You're okay now sweetheart that's all that matters right now."

"I'm so sorry." I cried.

My mother explained that when they got home later that evening after their dinner, she hoped I was asleep but checked on me anyway. There had been many times I had left well after everyone had gone to bed and she was hoping this had not been one of those times.

"When you weren't in your room, I figured you'd sneaked out again," she sighed through her tears."

"Mom I'm sorry, so sorry."

"It was late but I called Stephanie and she said she hadn't seen you; when you hadn't gotten in by morning I called the school and you weren't there either. That's when I went to the police, but they told me that there was nothing they could do unless you were missing for at least twenty-four hours."
My father stepped close to the bed.

"We didn't know what to do or who to call. It wasn't until Stephanie came over with your letter that said you'd gone off with Nick Malone that we could give the police a place to even start looking," he said.

They went on to tell me that they went to the Malone house and questioned Johnny at length, but found that he was completely innocent of his brother's actions.

~*~

I'm safe now, but after I was discharged from the hospital, I didn't leave home for months. Nick and his cohorts were prosecuted after Callie and I testified and he is serving a seventy years in jail with a possibility of parole after serving no less than forthy for human trafficking.

The news media congregated on the Malone lawn for days and followed them relentlessly. They finally sold their home and moved away. I was sorry for Johnny because he had not been involved in any way.

Callie and I are friends and are almost inseparable. Her mother goes to regular AA meetings and has a new job. While I want to forget the horrible ordeal we had been subjected to, I felt it was important to share my story. I wanted other young women to know the dangers of female abduction also known as human slavery. I'm still in therapy a full year later, but I'm functioning normally and even established a guarded friendship with a boy from the neighborhood.

I'm a different person, but one thing didn't change, and that is the love my parents have for me and I will forever love them for it.

When the Music Fades

"Oh come on Sandra you're no fun. It's only a jazz club."
My friend Jaleena Thomas had been begging me half the day to
go out with her but I was too busy studying to be a Physician's
Attendant.

"You're the best head operating room nurse at that
hospital and you supervise over fifty nurses and assistants, isn't
that enough?" She asked.

"Not for me. I have dreams and aspirations." I said
patiently.

"Well couldn't you *aspire* on Monday and come out with
tonight?" she pouted childishly.

After another twenty minutes of begging she finally wore me
down. One sleek black dress and high heeled glittery pumps and
a fluffed short curly hairdo later, we were on our way.

~*~

We took a long cab downtown to *Razz,* a nice supper
club—a little high end but as I would later learn, well worth it.
Jaleena found seats at the bar and I was a little annoyed because I
never liked the way women looked perched on bar stools, but she
said it was the best place to see the band and of course—to be
seen.

Men drifted over and started conversations and offered to
buy us drinks but we weren't interested—*I,* for one reason and
Jaleena obviously for another. It was 10:00 when the band came
onto the small stage. The quartet played smooth jazz sets and a
few couples got up and melded closely on the small dimly lit

dance floor. Jazz wasn't really my thing and I was still nursing my second weak Vodka and cranberry juice cocktail when the base player stepped up to the mike. *"Ladies and Gentleman, for your listening pleasure, I give you Mr. JC Hadley!"*
The room exploded into applause, catcalls and whistles, and the women, I noticed moved closer to the stage.

The spotlight circled the room then rested on a bare spot on the stage. A moment later, a very tall, extremely handsome, muscular brother wearing a gray silk suit, open-necked shirt and brown kid leather shoes stepped into the light, a gleaming saxophone hanging from a strap at his side.

"I'd like to start with an original favorite of mine called *Moonlight Desire.*"
The smooth timbre of his voice and polished diction actually made some of the women in the club sigh out loud. I had to admit, he was one good looking man with his walnut brown skin, thick curvy lips that he kept wetting slowly with his tongue. I couldn't see the color of his eyes, but when he closed them his lashes feathered down like they had been brushed with wax. Licking his lips again, he placed the sax to his lips and began to play.

His music was intoxicating and I could tell he put his heart and soul into each melody. His last song, *Leavin' but still Lovin'* seemed to be a special hit with the ladies because they went wild. When he finished and left the stage, he was almost knocked off balance by the women that ran up for his autograph and hopes for a little of his attention.

"Well," I said turning my back to the scene. "It looks like there's a star in the room."

"Girl! Every woman in here wants to get with JC, he's hot as bacon on a griddle."

"I guess he's all right," I said nonchalantly.

"Forget you bitch…" she teased, "You know he's fine and you know if he came over here you'd be gettin' the wet panty syndrome just like the rest of us," she laughed.

"Sorry girlfriend, I'm not interested."

"Well you better *get* interested, because he's coming this way and I've been coming in here long enough to know he *ain't* coming for me."

My head bobbed up and I looked in the mirror behind the bar and sure enough JC did *appear* to be coming toward us.

"Good evening ladies, I'm JC Hadley did you enjoy the show?"

"Hi I'm Jaleena Thomas and I sure did." My friend said batting her eyes faster than the blades on a ceiling fan.

"...and who's your friend?" he said ignoring her obvious attempt to get all of his attention.

"This is Sandra Blake, she's my best friend."

"Well now Miss Blake, I don't recall seeing you here before."

"Jazz isn't really my cup of tea." I said trying desperately to ignore his bedroom eyes.

"Oooh that stung," He said feigning a hurtful smile and clutched his chest playfully.

"I love Jazz." Jaleena chimed in.

His smile faded just a bit as he looked at her as though she were a bothersome fly. "And do you like champagne?" he said to her.

"I sure do."

She was all fluttery as she adjusted her wide butt on the stool.

"Well, why don't you go find us table and I'll make sure to send over a glass when you get there."

I was puzzled by his remark, but Jaleena jumped up from the stool and ran to find a place to sit.

"Now that we're alone..." he said turning back to me.

"Look, Mr. Hadley..."

"JC—but I'd rather you call me Johnny—that's my real name John Claudel Hadley; and that little lady—is information that only a select few know."

"I guess I should be honored then," I said indifferently. Jaleena was hollering and waving from across the room.

"Looks like your friend found us table," he said.

JC snapped his fingers and the bartender came over. I saw him slip some money into his hand and whisper something to him, then I heard him say, *The house brand, not the expensive stuff and keep it comin' for her.*" He pointed at my friend, "You *know* what to bring us," he said looking at me then started walking toward the table. At first I wasn't going to go but I didn't relish sitting on a stool at the bar by myself so I picked up my purse and followed. When we got to the table, Jaleena was seated but, JC leaned over and whispered something in her ear, rubbing her bare arm seductively.

"For real?" she said looking at him shocked.

"That's what he said," he gestured over to the bartender who wore a smile as wide as the Grand Canyon.

She leaned down and whispered to me. "Looks like I might be able to get my freak on, I'll be back in a bit." She winked, got up and bustled her way through the tables back to the bar.

A few minutes later a waitress brought over a wrapped bottle in a tub of ice. Her icy stare didn't escape my notice nor did the look of pure adoration when she looked at JC.

"The *house brand* I suppose," I said through pursed lips. He extracted the bottle and poured."Piper Heidsieck, the very best."

"Thanks but I'm not much for champagne."

"Just a sip, I'm hoping you'll change your mind—perhaps about Jazz too."

I offered a thin smile and glanced over at the band.

"What about dancing?" he asked.

"What about it?"

"Do you like it? I mean you don't seem to care for Champagne and you've pretty much dissed my music so I was just wondering if you like dancing."

"I do."

"Well do you want to dance with me?"

"Are you asking?"

"I am," he said extending his hand.

I figured *oh what the hell*; it was only a dance not a marriage proposal. I got up and allowed him to lead me to the dance floor.

He was a lazy slow dancer, making me do all the work. Women bumped into us on purpose all in an effort to get his attention while ignoring me like I was yesterday's news. He'd smile and acknowledge with each one, but held me tight.

"JC!" the voice was loud and grating over the music. "I need to talk to you right now!"
I felt his arms slide away from me as he turned toward the sound. A young woman stood near us in a skintight short skirt and eyes that were shooting beams of fire.

"I'm busy right now." He said in a low voice.

"You didn't say that this morning when you was all up inside me."
The dance crowd mumbled and giggled. A *second* woman came up and stood next to the first girl.

"…and who the hell are you and why you out here yellin' at my man?"

"I'm *miss-gonna-jack-your-ass-up* if you don't get outta my face," the first woman said.
People were looking at us and embarrassment crept up my body like a wiggle worm so I excused myself quietly and went to find Jaleena.

"Sandra, wait!" I heard JC call out but I didn't want or need any part of his cat fight fiasco.

Jaleena was still at the bar and enthralled with the handsome bartender when I told her I was going home.

"Just a little longer, he's got to close up," she pointed to the bartender and pleaded.

"You stay, I'm going." And I left.
A misty rain had begun to fall and there wasn't a taxi in sight. I walked to end of the block with my handbag ineffectively covering my head when a black Lexus rolled slowly up alongside the curb next to me.

"Sandra, come on let me give you lift home."

It was JC. "Thanks but I'll get cab."

"Not this time of night and in this rain. Please, just get in."

He was right three occupied cabs had already passed me, the rain was chilling and I didn't feeling like walking to the bus-stop and probably have to wait at least thirty minutes for it to come so I relented.
He reached over and opened the passenger door and I got in and gave him my address.

"Look I'm sorry about all that back there."

"No skin off my nose." I said disinterestedly.

"Women… I guess they are just attracted to musicians."

"How lucky for you," I snorted.

"Why are you so confrontational?"

"I wasn't aware I was."

"Look! I like you. I could see you're a real lady and I'd like to get to know you better."
I thought about it a minute, but from the moment I'd gotten into the car and although he didn't answer, his cell phone never stopped ringing.

"I don't think so Mr. Hadley, but thanks."
When we arrived at my apartment he asked for my number but I declined, thanking him again and got out.

"I have cop friends, I can get your number you know." he teased.

"And I know people from the hood who will mess you up if you do." I said with a smile.

~*~

A day later I had just gotten home from work and my phone rang. It was JC.

"Look I'm a few blocks away and I thought you might like to get something to eat."

"How did you get this number?"

"I told you I have cop friends—nah I had *my* friend get it from *your* friend"

Something told me that although she hadn't said anything to me Jaleena had gotten lucky with the bartender and in turn she had a bout of loose lips in giving out my number. I told JC I was bone tired and thanked him for the offer.

~*~

I guess a man really goes after what he thinks he can't have and JC was after me big time. It's not that I wasn't attracted to him, I was, but I had no desire to get added to his list of brawling women admirers. He called almost every day and it was always the same thing, him trying to get close and me pushing him away. Jaleena told me I was being stupid.

"Shit girl, all he wants is a damn date, not your first born," she chided.
Maybe she was right, if I went out with him once, perhaps that would be the end of it, so I agreed to go to dinner and a show with him, and what a show it was.

The man took me to Atlantic City by helicopter where the headlining acts were *Rhianna and John Legend.* He told me that he had been tempted to take me to Radio City where the music of some of his favorites were having a once in lifetime performance. It included *Cyrus Chestnut*, famed guitarist *Martin Taylor* featuring the music of *Bucky Pizzarelli* and the famous *Clayton-Hamilton Jazz orchestra*. The only name he mentioned that I had ever heard of was *Chick Corea*, as I reiterated that Jazz was just a little too rhythmically confusing to me.

JC knew so many people; and even though a great many of them were women who kept coming up to him and acted like I wasn't there even as he held on to me, he didn't seem to object.

We took a limousine back home because he said he wanted to spend as much time as he could with me.

"I enjoyed the show very much JC, but the helicopter was a little pretentious don't you think?"

"You are one hard woman to impress," He said, "But I like that."

~*~

He continued to woo me and slowly chipped away at my resolve and soon I was inviting *him* over to dinner—which he was almost always late for.

We'd been seeing each other for a month and after dinner out one night he invited me up to his place for a nightcap. It was a typical *playa* pad; complete with a king sized bed and a played-out mirrored ceiling. We drank brandy, laughed and an hour later he was on his knees in front of me.

"Let me love you Sandra." His hands slipped up my dress.

The brandy had warmed me and made me giddy. I liked the rough feel of his hands gliding up my thigh, and his soft seductive voice. "Just let me show you how I feel."

Before I knew what was happening, he'd removed my panties and his face was plastered against me moving his tongue so expertly that I didn't have time to protest. The exquisite feeling of it raced through me and all I could do was arch to meet his face.

We spent hours making love. He was intense, powerful, and insatiable. The more he gave, the more I wanted. The only downer was that I couldn't stop watching the little red light on his answering machine as call after call registered.

J.C. loved to walk and talk and we often took strolls in the park or along the canal as he tried to explain the concept of Jazz to me. One night he brought out a stack of CD's.

"Okay now I know you think you don't like Jazz, but I think you may be able to relate to something more contemporary."

He placed the disc in the player and the melodic voice of Norah Jones filled the air.

"Wow I love her. I never would consider her jazzy though," I said.

"There are all kinds and believe me, there's a lot of artist that you know and probably like if you would just give them a chance," then pointed out music contributions by *Abby Lincoln, Nancy Wilson and Diana Krall*. I really like the smooth sounds of their music and told him that I probably was just focused on the voices and never gave the actual music rifts a chance.

"Now that's my girl, growing and glowing," he said as he kissed me.

It wasn't long after that that I knew I was falling— in spite of every effort I made not to do so, in love with J.C.

~*~

"You've been getting it good huh?" Jaleena said one day.

"I have no idea what you're talking about," I said sheepishly.

"*Cover-Girl* and *Mac* makeup can't give a woman that kind of a glow. It's a shine that only comes from a good deep lovin'."

She was right, I was on cloud nine. I felt satiated and cared for.

JC and I went out almost every weekend even when he *didn't* have a gig in town, and when he did I sat proudly in the front seat as he played and especially for me. After he each set he would come to the table and give me a kiss and I could feel the bitch-eyed glares of the multitude of women who I knew would have killed for a small amount of the attention I was getting. I wanted to tell JC about my growing affection for him and hoped that he would offer me the same, but every time I started to broach the subject his cell phone rang or he was being texted.

One evening when I knew he was *not* going to be playing, I wanted to surprise him by bringing a dinner basket I'd prepared and took it to his place. He met me at the door in his bathrobe and told me he'd had a fever all day and just needed to sleep.

" Oh you poor baby, If I'd known I would have made some chicken soup instead of fried chicken, potato salad and apple cobbler, not to mention your favorite beverage, Remy Martin,"

I said smiling, holding up the covered straw basket and trying to step inside.

"Aw baby that's sweet, but I don't want you to catch this awful thing," he said with a light cough, "The good thing is; I still have an appetite." he said taking the basket. "I'll call you the second this thing passes," he said putting two fingers to his lips in one of those *fake ass* pretend kiss things and closed the door. I was a little miffed but being in the medical profession I fully understood contagious viruses and it was nice of him not to want to infect me.

I didn't see him for more than two weeks, and when I called, my messages went to voicemail. He made two late night booty calls and I tried to tell myself that it was because I missed him that I let him even disrupt my sleep pattern that way. His visits were getting a little sporadic and when I asked him about it he always made excuses with sweet loving and small gifts.

Things hadn't worked out for Jaleena and her bartender friend so she pretty much stopped going to Club Razz so I *only* went when JC was playing, sometimes literally forcing her to go with me so I wouldn't have to sit by myself until he finished his set.

~*~

Three months into our relationship I was thinking about having a little get-together so that JC could meet some of my friends and co-workers. As we lay in bed one night, I told him about my plan and he became a little edgy.

"Baby, I kind of like it with just you and me. We don't need other people."

"I know we don't *need* them JC, but I *want* them to meet you, perhaps come and hear you play."

He sighed and looked at me with that lazy but intoxicating smile of his. "Sure baby; when do you want to do this?"

"Well I was thinking next Saturday."

"Damn, I have a week long out-of-state gig starting Friday. Maybe we can make plans when I get back."

Needless to say I was disappointed but I had a bright idea. "Say I have some vacation time coming, how about if I join you?"

I was so confident that he would want me with him that I was already thinking about what outfits I would take.

"You don't strike me as the roadie type. Besides, we're going to be playing at several places and I don't want my sweet baby traipsing all over like some kind of camp-follower."
He kissed me lightly on the nose, then my lips and the next thing I knew he was between my legs and I forgot everything except the delicious pleasure he was giving me.

I saw him once more before he left for his trip and when he was gone and even though it was only for a long weekend, I couldn't believe I was missing him so much, it wasn't like me to behave like a lovesick school girl.

Janelle called and asked me to go with her to a new club. I really wasn't in the mood but I knew she was still smarting from the break up with the bartender.

"Come on Sandy, I hear it's the newest hot spot. If we don't like it, we can leave. It'll help take your mind off JC," she cajoled.
She was my best friend, so I gave in so I got dressed and we went but my thoughts were only of my man.

~*~

It was a nice place, a little dark but plush and cozy. We'd been there about twenty minutes and had just ordered our second round of drinks when suddenly Janelle grabbed me.

"We gotta go—let's go"

"What?" I asked nearly spilling what was left of my first *Appletini*.

"Let's just get out of here Sandy," she hissed under her breath and was half pulling me out of my seat.
…And that's when I saw him. It was JC. He was with a young girl who looked as though she could be *Alicia Keys'* twin sister. She was smiling at him and he was grinning like the cat that ate the cream as he toyed with her shoulder length, wavy-*non-weaved* hair. They were at a table several feet away and she leaned over, he kissed her deeply.

78

Rage boiled in me like unleashed devils from hell and I
wanted to go over and throw my drink in his face. But I
remembered those other women at *Club Razz* the first time I met
him. I was *not* like them and I wouldn't debase myself that way
but I had to let him know I'd seen him. I got up and walked
nonchalantly by his table and intentionally knocked into it so that
their drinks sloshed over the tabletop.

"Oh I'm sorry… why Hello JC," I said sweetly and
noticed his adam's apple move nervously as he gulped.

"Do, er… I know you?" he said.
I couldn't believe my ears. Just a few days before the man was
moving inside my pussy like he was rotating an oil drill and *now
he didn't know me?* I was beyond anger but I checked it.

"We met at Club Razz… remember?"

"Oh so you're a fan of my music." He gave me a lopsided
grin then wrote his name on his drink napkin and held it out to
me.
I eyed him with carefully veiled contempt. "I already have your
autograph and your number—but you a nice evening."
I walked away with as much dignity as I could muster but
couldn't help overhearing the woman say, *who was that hag?"*
and his answer. *Damned if I know.*
My world had blown apart. JC was a dog plain and simple and I
had fallen into his trap.

~*~

I didn't hear from him that evening but the next day my
cell was blowing up like a land mine with messages and texts.

Two nights later he woke me up out of a dead sleep with
apologies saying that the girl was the daughter of a big promoter
and how he was looking to get signed to a record deal but I
didn't want to hear anything he had to say and hung up on him.
He called everyday all through the day for weeks until finally I
changed my home number and blocked him from my cell.
He sent flowers, wrote letters and sent gifts. I peed on the
flowers and returned them *and* the gifts unopened. He came to
my house but I threatened to call the police if he continued to

harass me. When all options failed he enlisted my friend
Jaleena. I loved my *bestie* but she was always a sucker for a sob
story no matter how lame it was.

"Sandy he said he was sorry. He doesn't know why he
did it. He just wants to talk and try and explain," she said trying
to convince me. But I wouldn't hear of it. I just wanted to forget
him.

~*~

Months passed and I had just about gotten over JC when
one day all hell broke loose at the hospital. There had been an
explosion at a building site and *everyone* was on extended call.
By 11:00 that night my head ached like a ten pound weight was
sitting on it. I was irritable, hungry *and* sleepy and the
combination of those three things didn't make for a happy
operating room nurse and I was glad my shift was finally over.

I was heading toward the nurse's station to sign out when
I heard a commotion in the waiting room area. Several other staff
members and a few orderlies were looking at something and I
pushed through them to find out what was going on. Five women
were arguing, pointing fingers at each other and using the foulest
language I'd ever heard to describe each other's bodies, hair and
faces.

*"Yeah well you better take your scraggly lookin' weave
and fake ass-dragon-lady nails and be on your way."* One of the
women said.

*"And you better roll your tootsie roll blubber lips out my
face before I knock you out."*
I looked at the two orderlies. "What's going on here?"

"I'm not sure—the one with the blond streaks came in
with a guy who'd been shot. They're taking him in now." He
nodded toward the O.R.

"Well you better get security in here before these babes-
in-stupid-land tear each other to pieces," I said, then went to the
nurse's station to sign out for the night.
I was slipping on my jacket just as Dr. Kelson sped by me like he
was on roller skates.

"Sandra, I need you in O.R. 3 stat!"
Had it been anyone but him I'd have told them to find someone else because my shift was over. But I liked Benjamin Kelson, he was smart, handsome and he adored his plump, dimpled-faced Alabama born wife Irene. It did my heart good to see a successful, good looking black man who was in a *committed* relationship and didn't take nonsense from anybody; and was a great physician to boot.

"Right away Doctor."
I signed back in then went, and scrubbed up and entered the operating theater.
The anesthetist on call was prepping the mask over the patient's face.

"What do we have?" I asked.

"Gunshot to the chest, a punctured lung—looks like he might lose it."
I adjusted my mask and went over and prepped the utensil tray. Another masked nurse went over to adjust his IV tube.

"Hey baby doll, you got nice eyes," a raspy voice said.

"You must be the Romeo I heard those women were fighting over out there," she said from under her face mask.

My hands were stock still as the slurry but familiar voice struck my brain. There was no doubt, it was JC. I went over to him with Dr. Kelson who leaned down to him. JC knew it was me instantly and was about to speak when Dr. Kelson began talking.

"Mr. Hadley you have a bullet that's dangerously close to your heart. We're going put you under now."

JC's shocked eyes never left mine until they glazed over and I saw a tear escape and slide down the side of his face. The operation lasted more than three hours and just as Dr. Kelson was about to close up, the heart monitor began an irregular pattern.

"Hold on, we have a pressure drop here." The anesthetist said as he looked at the gauge.

Everyone flew into action as we began working on JC. As much as I despised him for what he'd done to me, he didn't deserve to die like this.

Dr. Kelson was able to save his life but he did lose a lung and his heart would never be the same.

JC was in intensive care for a week and a half and not one of his women came to see him. I took pains to avoid him when he was awake and went in only when I knew he was under pain meds and asleep.

We were short staffed one day and I had to go in to check his vitals. His eyes were closed and I prayed he would stay asleep when I checked his pressure, tubes and bandages.

"Sandra," he rasped.

He was looking at me through half-opened lids.

"You're improving nicely Mr. Hadley, you should be able to go home in a few days" I said clinically.

"Sandra, talk to me please."

"I am talking to you. I'm sure you realize a lot of things will be different for you and you will have to take it easy from now on."

"You know what I'm talking about Sandra. I was a fool—a stupid fool. You're a good woman."

"Tell me something I don't know," I said adjusting the fluid knob.

"How can I make it up to you?"

"You'll have all you can do to try and get better Mr. Hadley and that's what you should be concerned about."

"Is there any forgiveness in you Sandra?"

"Yes JC there is and I forgive myself for not following my first head and leaving you alone. I forgive myself for falling in love with you and I can even forgive a dog even after it has bitten me but I will never trust it again."

"Let me try and make it better for us Sandra."

I couldn't believe what I was hearing.

"Us? There was no *us* when you denied even knowing me. I would have been there for you, not like those hoochies who were out there fighting over your worthless ass. You lost a good woman and you'll never again find happiness the way you did with me."

"Sandra please…"

But I was on a roll and wouldn't let him have word in edgewise.

"By now I'm sure you've been told that one of your lungs is gone, so you'll never again play the sax the way you used to—if at all. So you see, you may not have loved me, but you lost two things that loved you—so you just try and get some rest now. Another nurse will be attending you from now on until you leave."

The sound of his sobs and my name on his lips rang in my ears as I left his room.

For a scant moment I entertained going back to him, but men like him don't change and if they did it wouldn't be overnight. I had to forget the pain and move on with my life and he would have to live with his, no matter what it was.

~*~

A year later, I was still single but happy with someone new in my life—a doctor who cared about me and made JC Hadley a distant memory, but I must admit, he crossed my mind from time to time. I couldn't help wondering how he was and it wasn't until the following Christmas while reading the newspaper that I saw in the obituary section, *JC Hadley, renowned saxophonist, age 35,* had died.

Sometimes, late at night I still hear the ghostly soft cords of a saxophone but I move closer to my man and let the music fade.

Never too old, never too young

Not everything in a person's life is perfect. Sometimes no matter what you do, something will go wrong. I raised two daughters in the same house and loved them both equally and because their father left us early and moved to the Philippines with a woman he'd met at a club he frequented, and it was left to me to bring them up alone.

I did the best I could and often went without so they would have everything I could afford to give them since their father only provided me with divorce papers and nothing else. My girls were beautiful and smart and because I was raised strict, I didn't want to impose those same harsh constraints on them, but I made sure they knew right from wrong and were respectful.

It was no secret that drugs was taking a hold on our country. I used to read the papers and see all the horror stories about how drugs infiltrated communities and ruined every life it touched, including those who did *not* indulge. I knew the problem wasn't only with the local dealers. It went much higher than that and there was nothing we could do about it and nothing the politicians *wanted* to do about it as long as the secret big money kept rolling in. I made sure my two girls were well aware of those and other social dangers and I was confident that they were two well adjusted, intelligent, level-headed young ladies.

I'd always had a dream of my girls going to college and making me proud and allowing me to able to enjoy my golden years basking in the joy of their scholastic accomplishments. I never dreamed that I would end up raising my eldest girl's three illegitimate children and be subjected to a second lifetime of pain, embarrassment and dishonor. *Was it because we don't want*

*to believe our own children can have such despicable habits that
we miss them?*
It's like a wife who circumvents every sign in front of her that
tells her that her husband is cheating but she ignores it. *Did I not
want to see what was right in front of me?*
~*~

Norella, my oldest was sixteen and excelled in school,
her sister Andrea, fourteen was smart but struggled with testing.
Noree—as I like to call her, always helped her sister with her
schoolwork and I was so very proud of their closeness and her
willingness to help. They squabbled like typical siblings but for
the most part they loved each other and enjoyed being together.

Things began to change when Noree was in her junior
year in High school. She became morose, distant and eventually
combative. I began to notice that she stopped helping her sister
and became short with her at every turn. When she stayed home
she went to the room she shared with Andrea, often locking her
out and played her music so loud I had to threaten her if she
didn't to turn it down. I didn't even think anything when her
mode of dress changed. I figured she was wearing what all the
young girls were at that time. It wasn't until I noticed a shadow
in the back of her almost transparent blouse one day and pulled it
up.

"Norella Jean Cufton, I know that's not a tattoo I'm
looking at."

"Chill Mom, all the kids are getting them. It's no big
deal."
It was *huge* deal and I was on fire. I asked her for the name and
address of the tattoo artist because I was going to have him up on
charges. She looked at me like I was crazy.

"Do you really think I gave him my right name and ID?
He thought I was 18 and I proved I was."
I couldn't believe she was admitting this right to my face but she
was right, those people didn't give a damn about anything except
cash and the fake ID's they saw on a daily basis wasn't a concern
for them. Noree knew I was a hundred different kinds of pissed

but it didn't seem to faze her. A tattoo wasn't something that could be washed off and neither could any of the things that began to occur later.

~*~

There are things a mother does and will always do. One habit of mine was checking on my girls before I went to bed. I usually peeked in and would smile when I saw them asleep like baby bunnies. One night I had the urge to go inside and kiss them as they slept and to make sure the covers were securely tucked around them. I noticed Noree wasn't in her bed, but rigged it like she was. I woke Andrea.

"Where's your sister?"

"I don't know mommy?" her eyes were large and luminous in the dim light coming from the hallway.

"Has she done this before?"

My daughter never lied to me and I didn't want her to have to start now when none of this was her fault. "Look honey. I'm worried and I know you are too. She's gone out before hasn't she?"

"Yes mommy," she said looking at her hands, "But she always comes back in a little while... except for the other night and this time."

"Is it a boy?"

"I don't know. I think she just wants to hang out with her friends."

Some friends! I thought. I told Andrea to go back to sleep, shutoff the light and I settled myself on Noree's bed and waited. The clock on her bureau read 12:30.

I must have dozed because the next thing I heard was the safety gate at the window on the fire escape being pulled back. She must have greased it good because it hardly made a sound. She stepped in the room and I heard her begin to shed her clothes in the darkness. I snapped on the lamp beside her bed.

"Where've you been?"

Her eyes widened with surprise, then reduced to slits. She was weaving a little as she ignored me and finished undressing.

"Come on out to my room; I don't want to wake your sister," I hissed.

"Tomorrow, I'm tired," she said dismissing me.
What happened next could only be construed as a nightmare. I yanked that young *heffa* by her hair and snatched that narrow ass from the room. She began to push against my arm and we tussled until finally we were in my bedroom.

"Now you just settle down young lady!" But she just sucked her teeth and turned to leave. I did something I had never done before. I grabbed her and slapped her and she slapped me back—hard. My own flesh and blood had hit me. I stared at her like she was a monster and that's just what she looked like with her hair all over her head, her red bleary eyes droopy and anger filled.

"You're on something aren't you?" I said ignoring the stinging on my cheek and peering at her closer.
I half ran back to her room with her dead on my heels. I grabbed her jeans and began searching the pockets while she pulled at them and screamed at me to mind my own business. Andrea was awake and crying by then, but I was determined to find what I was looking for. Nothing was in her pockets or her handbag. I questioned her relentlessly and then my eye caught a small foil ball stuck in the corner of her discarded bra. I picked it up and she flew at me like a she-demon.

"Give me that you bitch. Give it to me!"
She clawed at me like a demented rabid animal. This was *not* the child I had given birth to. That's how I found out my daughter was on crack.

Our lives were a nightmare after that and everything was on lockdown. She stole everything and anything she could to get money for her habit and it was foolish of me to think that I could help her at home, but I was embarrassed. She disappointed us in every way imaginable and Andrea was losing weight and in tears all the time. I knew it was not fair to her having Noree at home and I tried to get her help and she was in rehab four different times. But each time, after promising to change her ways she left and slid back into her life of drugs and debauchery. It nearly killed me when Andrea came home crying hysterically one afternoon and told me that she had seen her sister being arrested near her school for trying to solicit sexual favors from the school crossing guard—a devout Christian man who immediately called the police. I tried everything even counseling to learn how to handle my situation, not only for my sake but Andrea's as well.

Things only got worse, she began to steal from our neighbors and once I came home to find her having sex in my bedroom with a man that was older than me. I picked up an umbrella and beat him out of my house like I was tenderizing a steak. I knew things couldn't stay the way they were. Either Noree had to straighten up or she had to leave. She chose to go and I had to let her.

~*~

She had been out of the house for a year and each holiday was a sad affair without *both* my daughters in attendance to celebrate. The rest of the family, aunts' uncles and cousins knew about her and was gracious enough not to talk about it, but did ask if she was okay from time to time.

"She's as okay as she can be in a situation like hers." I'd say but I knew she would never be my little girl again.

~*~

It was January and three major storms had hit Detroit one after the other. Snow was eight feet deep in some places and the plows couldn't get through for days. Thankfully, our building, while not the nicest in the neighborhood was at least warm and dry. The weather was beginning to let up and I was pulling a pie from the oven, noticing the time and that Andrea would be coming in at any moment. I smiled when I heard the elevator and knew it had to be her. I heard her keys, but it seemed she was fumbling. Puzzled, I went to the door and opened it and there she was, her school satchel slumped over one shoulder and holding up her bedraggled sister with the other.

"She's sick mom."

I pulled them both inside. A fit of coughing overtook Noree and she was shivering frightfully because she only wore a thin jacket, a pair summer slacks and sneakers with ripped soles, and... she was pregnant—very, from what I could see.

"Lord! Lord!" I cried and pulled her to the couch. "Get some blankets Andrea."
I began to pull off her soiled clothes. She as a mass of old and new bruises and of course needle marks. Tears cascaded down my face as she turned away and huddled into the warmth of the couch. *How could my child have come to this? Was it my fault?* As though she read my mind, her cold skeletal fingers gripped mine and she rasped out.

"You didn't have nuthin to do with this Mama, this was me —all me." And she coughed until I thought her chest would cave in.

I bathed that girl and dressed her in one of my cotton nightgowns. I hugged her close when she shivered and spoon fed her even though she could hardly keep the food down. Two days later when she was able to get up we talked. She said she had no idea where the father of her baby was and I surmised that she didn't know *who* he was either.

"I stopped using three months ago mama."
But that meant nothing because she was due to give birth within the month if not sooner. If she was using those first six months then there was a good chance the baby would be affected.

I prayed that things would be different and for a while they were. Color returned to her face and she was almost the same with Andrea. I took her to the doctor, bought baby clothes and *Pampers*. I sat up with her when she couldn't sleep and used the rest of my vacation time in order to be with her when she gave birth.

The following month on Valentine's Day, Jarel was born and as I suspected he was a crack baby. It broke my heart to see him shiver and scream—his little mouth stretched white from howling for hours on end. The doctor said he would have to withdraw on his own so I did what I had to do, I bought ear plugs for everyone and we brought Jarel home. I tried to get Noree to engage with her little son, but she couldn't stand his screaming and squirming and while she didn't *appear* to be back on drugs, she smoked cigarettes to excess.

"I don't want you smoking in the house. It's not good for us or the baby, especially in his condition."
She didn't answer me but leaned out the window or smoked in the hall.
Even though I knew it was unfair I moved Andrea into my room and let Noree stay with Jarel in their old room, hoping that they would bond.

"Will he ever stop that crying!" she screamed one night when Jarel seemed almost spasmodic.

"It's not his fault." I said picking him up.

"Oh yeah go on say it. It's my fault, I did this to him." She screamed.
I was silent and I guess that was all the excuse she needed. "You think I don't feel your accusing eyes on me every time he yells? You don't think I know that you blame me? Well I don't need this crap."

Before I could utter a word she grabbed her coat and purse and left. That was the last we saw of her for two years and I was left raising my youngest daughter *and* a grandchild.

~*~

Doctor visits for Jarel were many and expensive, but the physician looked at me with his big blue eyes and a smile. "Mrs. Cufton, this young man is a fighter and he's going to be okay because I think he knows he's loved."

I held Jarel all through those difficult days and nights and he held onto me as he fought against the raging fire of withdrawal inside his body. I'd rock him, walk with him and pray. There were days when I thought his little heart would burst or his clenched fists would break a bone. Still I sang to him and I prayed for him. Sometimes when it got to be too much for me I'd lay him in his crib and go to another room and cover my ears.

Then one night there was silence— which is the loudest sound in the world when you're not expecting it. Panicked I ran to the bedroom and to Jarel's crib expecting to his lifeless body because it was all too much for his little soul. But he was sleeping. His little chest rose and fell evenly and his mouth was poised perfectly with sleep. I couldn't believe it and didn't want to leave the room but I was dead tired and needed rest myself and forced myself not to kiss his little forehead for fear of awakening him from the first peaceful moment he'd ever had. I went to bed but awoke several times to check on him, and to my absolute prayerful joy he was still breathing normally. It seemed that the crisis of his birth had passed.

Jarel was two when I got a call from a police department in New York City who said twin female infants had been left in a tenement with a note that said to *Call Mrs. Ann Cufton at…* and my phone number. The officer told me that they were in the custody of child protective services and that I should come and clear things up. I knew right then that Noree had gotten herself into trouble again. With tears in my eyes I left the kids with my neighbor and got a flight to New York City. The authorities questioned me and I questioned them. There was no doubt the twin girls belonged to Noree because they looked just like her when she was born. There was a lot of paperwork and they were satisfied that related they agreed to let me take them home. I assume the courts were so full that they were glad to have them off their hands.

"Mom! They're beautiful." Andrea said when she saw the girls.

"Yes they surely are."
Fortunately and to my utter amazement, they were drug free. Perhaps Noree had learned a lesson with her first child. If that was the case I knew it had to have been a struggle for her because that's a monkey that never gets off one's back.

Tyra, Monique and the now two-year-old Jarel proved to be a handful, but they brought me so much joy that I'd almost forgotten what it was like. At first I was too proud to seek assistance from the state, but I was entitled to food stamps to get milk and other things the kids needed. The first case worker was a snotty new college graduate who looked down her nose at me as I filled out forms and told her my story. She sat there like in her limited work experience she had heard it all before. I wanted to slap an explanation into her, but I figured I didn't owe her a damn thing. Later, a more amiable social worker advised me that I could get *Permanent Guardianship* of the children, which is granted by the juvenile court after it is proven that it's in the best interest of the kids that the birth parent(s) are unfit and should never have physical custody of them. It would also mean that Noree would be prohibited from petitioning the court to terminate the preeminent arrangement once it was granted. Since she had abandoned her children, it was felt it was the best thing to do for their safety and wellbeing.

To my surprise I was also entitled to some small compensation to aid in their upbringing which took a little burden off our already strained finances. My job allowed me the luxury of working at home three days a week and for the other two I hired a reliable sitter because I did not want to put any further encumbrances on Andrea.

~*~

Enrolling Jarel in first grade was a day I will never forget. The girls were walking by then and a whirlwind of energy if you didn't watch them. I had just left Jarel in class hoping that he wouldn't cry or hide the first day; and he didn't. The second he saw the other kids in the classroom and all the colorful pictures on the walls he just ran in and began to play. I have to admit, he was a special little boy.

I took the twins for a snack and then to the park. They played in the busy box then ran me ragged as they headed towards the slide. A little boy about four years old was running by us carrying a small toy truck. I saw it before it even happened but couldn't stop it. He fell headlong over his untied sneaker laces and onto his stomach with a thud. He started screaming and I told the girls to stay put and went to him.

"Hey there little man." I said soothing him. Immediately his arms went around my neck as a mixture of snot and tears wet the collar of my blouse.

"What happened?" I heard a male voice say.

"He fell." I looked up at a young man with concern on his face and holding what looked like two large reference manuals.

"Hey Petey old man...you were running again weren't you?"
The little boy shook his head.

"I thought we talked about that. Well come on and let the nice lady go and we'll head on home," he said disengaging the boy's arms from my neck. But Pete was having none of it. The second he saw my girls on the slide he let go on his own and ran over to play with them, the pain of his fall forgotten.

"Well I guess we could stay a *little* longer," I heard the man mumble. "Hi! My name is Reese Maxford."

"Well Mr. Maxford, you really ought to be more responsible with your son. He could have gotten hurt badly and I'm Ann by the way." I hadn't meant to sound terse, but it was important to watch children every second.

"He's my nephew and you're right. It's just that I have to study for this an exam and I never can find the time. The park was pretty empty so I figured it be okay for an hour or so."

"Well kids can get into trouble in a short minute—Law huh?" I said looking at the manual then gave him a quizzical look.

He grinned. "I know what you're thinking; I'm a little long in the tooth to be going to college."

"I wasn't thinking that at all—well maybe. I guess I'm a little jealous, I never got to finish myself."

"It's hard when you have kids. How old are your daughters?" He said glancing over at the kids.

"They're my twin granddaughters and they're two. I also have a Grandson he started first grade today."

"Are you serious? You're a grandmother? Wow, you must have started when you were..." He stopped when he saw my smile fade and I looked away. "Oh hey look I'm sorry I didn't mean it like that."

"No problem, they're mine and I love them and just to add a little more fuel to your already shocked system, I also have two grown daughters, one is in her first year of college-she's nineteen."

"And the other?"

"Almost twenty-two." I could almost feel him aching to get up and run away from me as though he could impregnate me just by sitting there.

"Kids having kids." He clicked his tongue, "That little boy there, he's my baby brother's who *just* turned Seventeen."

"What are *you* doing out with him?"

"Cliff—that's my brother, is in trade school. I had some time so I told him I'd take him for the day. Little Pete usually stays with his mother, but that's not a very good situation either."

"I know what you mean."

Reese shook his head and chortled. "I just don't get these kids. They go out and have these babies and have no idea what it takes to raise them. Kids need things and my brother and his girl think they're still entitled to have fun and live out their teen years as though the kid doesn't exist."

"It's an age old dilemma and I guess they know they have us to fall back on."

"I know what you mean. I just can't say no, especially to that little crumb snatcher," He said looking over adoringly at his nephew.

~*~

The tinkle of the ice-cream truck brought the heads of all three kids to full attention. I dug in my purse because I knew my two would be hobbling over on chubby legs and pointing at the ice cream man.

94

"Allow me—a little thank you for coming to Pete's rescue; besides it's not every day one meets a fellow babysitter of sorts."
I smiled.
"You should always do that?" he said kindly.
"Do what?" I grimaced.
"Smile, yours is terrific."
Embarrassment crept up my legs but I threw it off as being a hot flash.

~*~

One Saturday Andrea, the kids and I were in the food store buying groceries when I heard Reese's familiar voice.
"Ann! Nice to see you again."
I noticed Andrea's eyes as she looked at the two of us.
"Hello good to see you too, um—this is my daughter Andrea. This is Mr. Maxford." I said introducing them.
"Nice to meet you Andrea. Your mom is a very special lady.
"She sure is."
 The minx said and gave me a *whoo!-he-is-fine* look.
"Hungry Man dinners?" I clicked my tongue as I looked in his cart. "You'll never get proper nourishment eating those."
"Not easy making a home cooked meal on my schedule."
"You should taste my mom's cooking Mr. Maxford. She makes the best scalloped potato soufflé in the whole world."
What was that little scamp doing? "I'm sure he isn't interested in my culinary attributes Andrea."
"Oh I'm interested… quite interested." His eyes were smiling at me.
Andrea innocently put some can goods in the cart and then looked at him smiling.
"Well it just so happens that we're having it Friday night with baked chicken and garlic veggies. If you call us at this number…" The little matchmaker was putting our number on a piece of paper and handing it to him. "And let us know if you can come and I'll set another place."

"Terrific, I mean if that's okay with your mom."
His eyes were doing some kind of pleading glances. I hesitated and felt Andrea nudge me.

"Well, I suppose it would be okay."

"Good! I'll bring something gooey and sweet for the kiddies."
He smiled, said goodbye then walked on to another aisle.

"And what did you think you were doing young lady?" I asked my daughter.

"Mom, couldn't you tell? He's totally into you. If his eyes were any brighter I'd have to wear a pair of those *Miami Vice* sunglasses."
I tried to pinch her but she dodged me.

"And it looks like we need to go shopping for a new outfit for you," she said pushing cart out toward the checkout.

At first I thought Reese might be interested in Andrea, after all they had college in common, even if their ages weren't. But as time went by he came by often and showed me nothing but interest and respect. He even took us all to see the latest animation film and the kids just loved it. When he finished school ten months later, he asked us— kids and all to come to his commencement and it was there I met his mother.

"So you're the one who put those extra pounds on my son. He said you were a good cook."

"Thank you, I—we, well he does like to eat and I like to cook." I stammered, nervous as a school girl.

"He's even told me you made some of his favorite dishes, but he didn't tell me..."
Oh no! Here it comes... you were so old and had so many kids; I thought and tried to think of a proper retort.

"You were so pretty," she said.
I blushed and signed with relief as I tried to keep Monique— whom I was holding from pulling off my earring.

"Here, hand her to me, you go on over and congratulate my son, he's been looking over here like an expectant bridegroom."

Monique went to Mrs. Maxford without a moment's hesitation and began playing with her beaded necklace.

"Your mother is nice." I said as I approached him.

"She's the best. I knew she'd like you."

"But…"

"Look Ann, it's going to be a while before I get on my feet as a lawyer, but I want you to know how I feel about you and the kids."

I had to stop him. "Look Reese this really isn't the time or place and these children are *my* responsibility. I would never expect you to…" But he cut me off in sentence.

"Will you hush a minute woman? I need to tell you something."

Married? Gay? Serial killer?—no, he'd never admit that. All kinds of thoughts invaded my brain.

"I was married once and my wife and child died during the birth. I never wanted to feel anything again, but I did—I do. I think I'm falling in love with you.

I looked at him and blew out a cleansing breath. "You do remember I have a slew of young kids don't you?" I said.

"I don't care if you have five kids or a dozen; I just want you to give *me* a chance."

"It won't work." I said glibly.

"It won't if we don't try and I'm willing to do that."

"Okay while we're both in confession mode I think there's something I need to tell you. Those kids mother…" I pointed to where the children were playing ring-a-round-the-rosie with Mrs. Maxford, "…my eldest daughter is a drug addict."

I waited for him to draw away from me like a leper, but he didn't so I continued. "There's probably little hope for her because I hear about her occasionally and she's still in clutches of that narcotic. It's why I've taken full and permanent custody of the kids. If anything happens to me, then they will be cared for by Andrea—it's all documented."

"Andrea is entitled to her own life, why can't I be part of yours?"

"Because I'm afraid it will be too much for you."

"I'll do whatever it takes. We can go slowly if you want, but I am anxious to be part of your life and your family."

"Look at the age difference, it will never work."
He reached over and touched my face, then leaned in and kissed me. "I don't care about our ages and let me be the judge of that."

"Hey you two," It was Mrs. Maxford, "If you're gonna act like a couple of teenagers then you need to go somewhere."

"Mom, we were just talking," Reese said.

"Well Andrea and I are taking the kids for some ice cream cones and then to the amusement park where we will be going on some serious rides. You can come and get them when you're through...*talking*?" Mrs. Maxford winked and Andrea smiled at us.

"Okay mom," Reese said too quickly, "we'll see you later."
Had this been the plan all along? Were they scheming for this?
~*~

Reese took me to an early dinner and then to The Wexler, the most premier hotel downtown.

"I want our first time together to be on neutral ground, because woman, I don't want anyone we know hearing you when I do what I am going to do to you," he grinned.

Inside the room I was apprehensive, after all I wasn't a teenager and it had been years since I was with anyone sexually but Reese put my mind at ease quickly when he noticed my agitation.

"I'm not looking for perfection Ann and I hope you aren't either because I got really skinny legs," he said.

If that was all that was wrong with him then I certainly didn't care. "I'm just going to go in the bathroom and take my clothes off," I said heading toward the washroom.

"If that's what you want, but sooner or later you're going to have to get comfortable with me because I'm going to want to see you naked—a lot," he grinned.

I thought about it for a second then decided *what-the-heck*, if he was going to run then this would be the place to start. I turned away and began to disrobe and then I went to him. He swiveled me around to face him then reached around and slapped me gently on the butt.

"Is that a tattoo on your thigh?" he asked incredulously.

"No…it's five little tattoos, four red hearts for each of my kids and one broken one for the one that is lost. It can be filled in if she returns."

"That's a lovely sentiment, but I have to admit I never thought you'd be so adventurous."
I explained that I couldn't believe I did it either, especially after I had chastised Noree about hers. "But she had been underage and these…" I stroked them gently, "is a reminder."

Reese kissed me gently, then leaned down and hovered over the patches of red and black ink, then licked each of the tiny red hearts.

"Okay sexy grandma, what's your pleasure?"

"Lower…" I said and then fell into the delight of his manly passion.

~*~

Reese and I were married two years later. I'm sad to say that my eldest daughter never returned home and spent many years in and out of rehabilitation facilities. Reese was exceptional in his efforts in trying to see that she got the best care; but the additive monkey on her back was bigger than anyone could handle and eventually she succumbed to eternal sleep.

A mother burying her child is no easy thing and her funeral was the saddest event of my life, but each time I look into the faces of her children; I see hers when times were good; and at night when I am in the loving embrace of my husband I am satisfied.

HIP-HOP TERROR

As a senior in college I never thought I would be crawling into the seedy underbelly of the hip-hop world trying to find my missing sister Tiffany. For as long as I could remember all she cared about was the music and rap artists on television that made the thug life seem easy and exciting. *MUSIC TV* and the similar stations flaunted rump shaking young women exhibiting as much of their sexual attributes as primetime censorship would let them get away with; and my sister was enthralled.

~*~

While I wasn't particularly in love with hip hop, I came up in the time of Grandmaster Flash and the Sugar Hill Gang where the only real bad word was *damn. But* ever since what I deemed the *new* Rap culture made its debut, everybody and his sorry-ass-singing-brother wanted to be a Rap artist. Little did they know or seem to care that the *real* money was in producing and promoting. In the eyes of the young if it wasn't sexually explicit right in your face with degrading lyrics than it wasn't worth it. All the young bloods in the neighborhood did anything and everything they could to perform in a club, with the hope it would get them to a stadium or in booty-shaking music video as soon as they possibly could. Only a few had *real* talent, the rest were mimicking the *all-readys* and the *has-beens or* being duped and used by shyster pretend music moguls.

I can remember chastising Tiffany for spending so much time in front of the television watching the sexy videos, mimicking the outrageous moves and singing the sordid lyrics.

"Girl, if you knew history or chemistry as well as you know that song you'd be passing your tests." I chided.

"And if you had any business, you'd be minding it," she snapped back.

She never used to talk to me or anyone that way, she used to have respect. She was heading for a bad end and my parents and I couldn't do a thing to stop her. If they grounded her, she found a way to sneak out. If they punished her, she would run away causing my mother to have an acute asthmatic attack from worry. Our father who was on heart medication cried for her because now she was missing and I lamented that if she were here now instead of out there with *JoVEY* I would let her watch as much HIP HOP as she wanted as long as she did it here safe at home.

JoVEY AKA Joey Mendoza was a small time hood rat with aspirations of being the next big thing in music. A local seedy club let him perform and they weren't particular about who they let in. If you *looked* eighteen, then you *were* eighteen, even when the fake ID was as obvious as a mole on a witch's chin and girls of all ages flocked to his shows like bees to honey and my sister Tiffany was no exception.

~*~

If my parents had any idea what I was about to do they would freak and lock me up until I was on Medicare. But my mother was distracted and grief stricken because Tiffany—her baby had been missing for more than two weeks. The police were of little help since they were over-burdened with gang shootings, murders and other crimes. Even the detectives who took the missing persons information were aloof and informal. Nobody seemed to care so I guess it was up to me. I ran myself ragged questioning everyone I could in the neighborhood to see if they had seen any information about my sister. But no one had seen her for quite a while. I hated seeing my mother so distraught and I knew that I had to find Tiffany and although becoming a hip-hop groupie wasn't something I'd thought I'd ever be doing, it was the only way.

Everybody thinks they know the Hip-Hop scene but there was a whole other seedy underworld in the music culture that the general public didn't know about and it my intention to enter it and find my sister.

~*~

Club Xenon was the most popular underground meeting place for established and wannabe artists in the city. Every Friday and Saturday nights there were no less than five or six high profile celebrity artists performing and producers scoping out the competition or just coming to see if there was any new and worthy talent.

It was almost twenty miles away from my home and things didn't start jumping until 10:00 and usually went on well into the wee hours of the morning and sometimes beyond depending on who was there.

I knew the acceptable dress code ranged from classy chic to sassy ho; so I donned a short, tight black leather skirt, a *Kimora Lee* fashion top and a *Baby Phat* studded purse. I wasn't *Niki Minaj* or anything maybe a little closer to a slimmer *Jill Scott*, but my outfit made me look like I belonged. I knew I would have no trouble getting in. All I needed was attitude and twenty-five dollars.

Once inside, I wasn't surprised to see several white men dressed in the urban styles of the culture they shunned by day but sneaked around in at night. In order to try and belong they talked like us, walked like us, but didn't *ever* want to wake up permanently in *our* skin.

The club was bustling with familiar people from the world of Hip Hop music and their cohorts. Every one of them had a big burly bodyguard who looked like he could take down an army of Sumo wrestlers single-handedly. The women were all colors, sizes and ethnicities, with each trying to out-do the other with their over-the-top skimpy outfits and ostentatious hair styles. It was like watching a game unfold with everybody vying for the win. I was appalled to see so many girls who I was sure were underage with stars in their eyes hoping to be chosen out by any of the visiting musical royalty to sit in the V.I.P area. The club itself was a huge refurbished warehouse, with corners, nooks and private rooms filled with people doing things I didn't want to think about my sister Tiffany ever being involved in.

As I moved toward one of the multiple bar areas I passed an alcove where a girl that couldn't have been more than sixteen, giving a lap dance to man who had clandestinely exposed himself to her undulating bottom. Another couple stood against the wall engaged in a long spit swapping tongue kiss which disgusted me. I moved a little quicker and bit my tongue as hands rubbed along the curve of my behind or brushed my breast. Men rubbed their hard members against me and when I looked at them with anger they merely licked their lips offering a suggestion of how they could pleasure me orally. Luckily, I found a seat at the far end of the long horse-shoe shaped bar, but it was impossible to get the attention of any of the busy bartenders.

"Can I buy you a drink?"
I looked up at the man who had made the offer. He was medium height and thin as a rail. His pants hung low on his waist exposing his stripped underwear. His brogan shoes were suede with gold colored laces and his bald head was covered with a baseball cap that was turned around backwards.

"Thanks, I can buy my own." I said dismissing him. Besides, I'd heard about how certain drugs were put into drinks and women could barely remember the degrading things that might have happened to them later.

"That's not very friendly." He smiled crookedly exposing a front tooth that had a quarter caret diamond looking stone pasted on it. But just looking at him told me that there was no way it was real unless he was drug dealer which was entirely possible. He did look however, like a man not used to being denied or ignored and I shivered a little when his eyes turned cold, but the smile was still there. "Suit yourself there's plenty of other ho's."

He turned walked into the hip twerking bodies on the dance floor.

~*~

Someone squeezed by me tapping the mahogany bar and waving a fifty dollar bill. The gold lion's head pinky ring had two brilliant rubies for eyes and glinted magnificently even in the dim light of the bar area.

"Yo BayZee! Lemmie have a Dewers; neat."
The bartender nodded and proceeded to fill the order.

"You must have some clout in here. I've been waiting fifteen minutes; they've been ignoring me like I was yesterday's news," I said to him.
He barely glanced at me, but took his drink—which arrived in record time and sipped it and left the money on the bar. "Thanks BayZee and hey; give the lady what she wants and keep the change."
I was about to explain that I didn't want him to buy me a drink but all I could see was his back as he walked away in the slickest, neatly tailored and obviously most expensive black suit I'd ever seen.

"What'll you have?" The waiter said.

"Merlot." I answered, "but I'd rather pay for my own drink."

"Suit yourself" the bartender shrugged, picked up the fifty and went off to prepare my drink.

I surveyed the room, hoping to catch a glimpse of JoVEY, but it was impossible in the sea of bodies that moved like a dark wave on the ocean. I took a small sip of wine. I wasn't much of a drinker but even I knew this was a watered down version of an actual glass of wine. But I sipped it to at least *appear* to be part of the scene. All the while I kept darting my eyes around to see if I could see my sister, but it was difficult. I needed to circulate and search for her.

I took my drink and weaved my way through the throng of dancers. The music was loud and people were really spellbound with it, the liquor and I'm sure—drugs. Girls were doing the most decadent dance moves, twerking and grinding their pelvises against the distended crotches of men just standing there accepting their favors. One young woman was sandwiched between two men; her skirt pulled high and I almost gasped when I saw that she wore no underwear. One of the men slipped his hand between her legs then brought it back out and forced it between her lips, which she suckled erotically. Another woman sat on the lap of a man whom I thought I recognized as a singer from *UV1-Soulvision* and she was obviously performing a sex act right out in the open. Disgusted, I turned away.

A young woman slammed into me, causing the wine to splatter on her and me.

"What the hell is yo problem bee-otch?" she slurred, looking me up and down.

"I'm sorry, I didn't mean..."

"You're sorry all right—a sorry ass. Look at my top. I just got it off lay-a-way and you done ruined it."

"I'm sure a little seltzer water will get that right out." I tried to explain.

"Stupid heffa... get the hell outta my face."
I moved around the girl quickly and headed for the ladies room hoping to dab at the stain on my own top. It was a unisex bathroom with men *and* women standing around, talking, smoking weed or groping one another. To my shock a man stood near the stalls with a woman who was on her knees with a dog's choker collar around her neck.

"One dollar and she'll clean you good when you're done in there." He said yanking at the collar and nodding to the stall. I wanted to throw up. My sister could never be part of this lifestyle, even she had to see that. I knew I had to start asking questions if I was ever going to find out where she was.

As I entered the stall, I was suddenly pushed in from behind. My heart raced as I felt myself being shoved over the dirty toilet.

"You make one sound and you'll be drinking toilet water."

I fought to keep from passing out as my body shook with fright.

"When a man offers you a drink you should be more polite."

I recognized the voice; it was from *Mr. stud tooth.* I felt him yank my skirt up and press himself up against my panties as I struggled to get free of him.

"This is what all you ho's come here for, a little fun and a lot of release." His hand moved over my butt and then under to my mound and I squeezed my legs together tightly.

"Ooh girl, yeah that's it, work them muscles. Is that what you're like on the inside?"

His hand moved to the waistband of my panties and I knew I was in serious trouble.

"Maybe I'll call some of my boys and we can run a train on you. A snooty booty like you can stand to be taken down a peg."

I was scared to death. I began to kick backwards but he held me fast. His hand was on the waistband of my panties, ready to pull them down.

Then suddenly I felt blessed air as someone snatched him off me.

"You gettin' ready to push up on my woman Lover Man?"

The voice was unmistakable. It was the *Dewers* man from the bar.

"Whoa, chill out Salik, I didn't know she was your ho. You need to put some signs on your ladies' man. How a brotha gonna know?"

"All a *brotha* needs to do is ask."

I turned in time to see the one called *Lover man* make a hasty retreat.

Sighing with relief I was about to thank my savior, when he grabbed my arm and pulled me from the stall. Draping his arm possessively around me he walked me out of the bathroom.

"Just keep walkin'" he whispered in my ear.

Now what had I gotten myself into? Was he going to finish what *Lover Man* started? I tensed, my eyes searching for an avenue of escape. As if he knew what I was thinking he held me tighter, moving me toward the exit.

Cool air caressed my face as he walked by the bouncer at the door."Enjoy your evenin' Salik." The man said lasciviously. He ignored the bouncer as he urged me toward a gleaming black jaguar parked nearby.

"Get in!" he growled.

"Look…"

He opened the door and pressed against me. "*G E T I N*," his voice was an ominous whisper.

I slid into the seat, my mind desperately trying to devise a way to get out of this new situation. He got in, started the engine and took off down the street. It was late and there wasn't much traffic. He came to an abrupt halt in the darkness of the entrance of Lockland Park. I knew this was it; this was where he would rape me or worse leave my lifeless body by the side of the road. He turned to me, and even in the half-light I could see the hard handsomeness of his face.

"Just what the hell did you think you were doing? Slumming for the night?"

"Excuse me?" I said perplexed.

"You've never been in that kind of club in your life. Don't you know what goes on in there?"

"What makes you so sure?"

"Are you kidding, you stuck out like a cotton-ball on a pile of coal. Why do you think *Lover man* went after you?"

"Because he's a slime-ball."

"He's a sexual predator. Although I must admit you're a little older than his usual prey."

I was incensed at the insult. "And who do you think you are? *ICE-T* from *Criminal Intent*? And what kind of name is *Salik* anyway? It sounds like a dollar-store joke."

"Where do you live, I'm taking you home, and I'd better not ever see you at Xenon again." he said ignoring my insult of his name.

"I have to go back."

"Why? To get yourself raped or killed?" He yelled.

"I've got to find my baby sister, she's only fifteen. I think she might be with some creep named JoVey."

"Joey Mendoza?" He whistled lightly. "He's a bad dude. How the hell did she get mixed up with him?"

"I found a card in her room. He was looking for girls to be in his video. His number was on the back."

"I haven't seen Joey for more than two weeks." He mused rubbing his chin.

"I'm so scared something bad has happened to her. Look, you're in that world, maybe you can help me. I can give you money," I said excitedly.

He smirked. "You couldn't afford me even if I was so inclined,"

"It's not much, but you can have all I have saved and maybe I can get some more from my parents; please." but all he did was snort out a laugh.

"This is dangerous what you're doing. You don't know me, how do you know I won't take your money *and* you?"

"If that was going to happen you wouldn't be sitting here telling me about it," I answered sardonically. My sister's life was at stake, I knew it and I had to do something and it didn't matter what as long as I got her out.

"Maybe…maybe you're interested in a little *something else?"* I tried to sound seductive but somehow it didn't come out that way.

He just looked over at me and smirked. "Where do you live?" He said quietly.

I wasn't about to give him my address so that he could come back and harass me or worse. I was frantically trying to think of a fake address when I heard a muffled cell phone ring. I was surprised to see him reach under his seat to retrieve it.

"Detective Young."

I was stunned. *He was a cop*?

After a short conversation, he snapped the phone shut and turned to me. "Now will you let me take you home?"

~*~

On the way, he told me how he'd seen *Lover Man* follow me when I entered the ladies room. He said he had heard what he'd done to young women in the past and couldn't stand by while another woman was brutally taken advantage of. He apologized about my sister and said he was on a big undercover investigation and very close to making an arrest. "Look I'm sorry about your sister but I can't compromise the entire operation by getting sidetracked."
I knew I had to convince him to help so I took tact. "How do you know you can trust me? I just might go back and squeal my head off about who you are."

"And risk your own safety or that of your sister—I don't think so. Besides you're probably already on somebody's radar, if ever there was a woman who didn't belong there it's you." He said.
I let the slight pass, but I needed his help.

"Please, I've been to the local police, no one will help. I have to find her before it's too late."

"I said I can't—not now. Maybe when this is over I'll be able to help you."

"It might be too late then." I was in tears.

"Look just give me your address so I can get you home and I'd better not see you at Xenon again," he said gruffly.
I pleaded with him again but it was no good. He left me at my door, tearful and hopeless.

~*~

I ignored his warning and returned to Club Xenon the following weekend. This time I was dressed in an ostentatious glittery extra short dress and I let my hair fall to my shoulders in soft waves. My strut let everyone know I belonged there as I strode through the crowd and glaring right back at anyone who gave me the eye. I spotted Salik at the bar, a slim willowy blond leaning against him. I walked right to him and pressed my body close to him then turning him to me and kissed him, taking his tongue into my mouth like I was suck starting a Humvee.

"Been missing you lover," and I kissed him again to hide the shock on his face. I felt his arm snake around my slim waist. Releasing his lips, I turned to the girl.

"Beat it bitch!" the tone in my voice and the color of my skin let her know I meant business in a place where she was outnumbered and surely unwanted by the regular female populace.

I saw Salik's eyes dart around for a moment as he pulled me into him, and hissed into to my ear.

"I thought I told you not to come back here."

I ground myself against him as I'd seen the other women do to men. Pressing my lips close to his ear I nibbled and whispered back. "And I told you I have to find my sister. If you don't help me, I'm sure the thugs here would love to know that Five-O is in the house."

He breathed in hard and I felt a stirring below his belt. "It's nothing personal. It happens when any sexy woman throws herself at me," he said.

"I'm nothing like them and I'm not throwing myself…" I tried to move away, but he held me close.

"You started this so we'd better keep up appearances," he said and kissed me again. "So, what's your name?"

"Mikia." I said, "And yours?"

"It's Earl but you better call me Salik or better yet, how about—baby."

He spun me around so that I faced the crowd but still leaning against him as his hands moved lazily over my hips. I was about to tell him that he was enjoying himself a little too much when I saw them.

It was Tiffany and a slick looking Hispanic who could only be Joey Mendoza. He was medium height and as stocky as a bull. His shaved head had tribal tattoos all over it that coiled down and around his neck. He glittered with more bling than *Mr. T* ever had and he moved with the self-assurance of a jungle cat. Tiffany didn't look happy and I could see a small bruise below her left eye.

"That's her! That's Tiffany." I said and started towards them but Earl pulled me back.

"Be cool." He turned me to him once again. "Just be cool."

Two burly men approached us. "Evenin' Salik, enjoying yourself?"

"Hey, my man Dusty, what's goin' on?" he bumped the man's fist with the *brother* handshake.

"Not much, except I heard a rumor that we may have mole up in here. This new lady?"

The man's eyes scathed over me and I fought not to shudder.

"Yeah this is Cookie because she's got a pussy that snaps like a cracker."

I clenched his hand; and to anyone looking I hoped it appeared like I was just giving him a love squeeze.

"Yeah always been lucky like that," the man said his eyes still roving over me.

"You got to be kiddin me Dusty—A cop? In here?" Salik said with mock astonishment.

"Yeah that's what I heard." Dusty said. "Say, I have that stuff you wanted. How about we go and have a taste."

The man's feral eyes never left mine.

"Sure Dusty, whatever you say."

He leaned down and kissed me and smacked me smartly on the butt. "Stay here baby and have whatever you want, I'll be right back."

"Bring your lady," Dusty said.

It was more of an order than a request and somehow I knew Earl dared not refuse.

I followed them to the back and up a flight of stairs, Earl made sure I was between the men so that I couldn't be seen by Tiffany.

~*~

Inside the plush office there was an ornate bar with long rack of crystal glasses, a cherry wood desk and a long brown leather couch.

"Make yourself a drink if you want; and one for the lady," Dusty said.

"Naw I'm good, and she drinks what I give her when I give it to her," he said cupping his private area.

Dusty laughed out loud. "I got you man," He went to a wall and moved a picture aside exposing a safe. He stood in front of the tumbler so we couldn't see as he opened it and extracted a square package. With a small sharp knife he slit it and extracted a line of fine white powder.

"Have a snort. It's the best nose candy you'll find anywhere," he said.

"Man I was about to take my lady and get my freak on." Earl said rubbing at his crotch.

"It' will make the experience that much better. Maybe she'd like some too."
It was clearly a challenge.

"I don't need any stimulation to please my man." I said trying to control the fear building inside me.
Dusty took the knife and held to his own nose, snorting up the fine powder. He closed his eyes as the euphoric pleasure cloud hit his brain.

"Go on then little lady. Let me see what you can do to your man, unless of course you're FIVE-O and in that case *can't* do it."
He thought *I* was the undercover cop? He'd never really seen me there before and Earl had been in deep cover for quite a while so I understood his caution.

"Why don't I show you what I can do without any help from the white line." I said remembering the words from a Law and Order episode.
Never in my life had I performed a sex act in front of an audience. I looked at Earl, he smiled, but there was something behind his gaze—a pleading, but for what I didn't know. I did know that if we had any chance of getting *us* out of this and Tiffany to safety we'd both have to comply. I knelt in front of Earl and unzipped his fly, but he held onto my hands.

"My woman follows *my* orders Dusty. You know how it is, I don't want your boys here…" he looked at the other bodyguards that had followed us up into the office, "to get all fired up."
I saw Dusty tense as two of the men took a step forward. I had to act. I ran my hands up Earl's strong thighs and then reached inside his crotch opening. I felt the warm steel strapped to his inner leg and I hesitated a mere second.

"What's the matter Miss Pussy cracker? He ain't up enough? cause if he ain't I sure am?" Dusty challenged. Everyone laughed except Earl.

"He will be," I said and pulled him free and pasted my mouth against him. He gripped my shoulders but it was more of a gesture of pushing me slightly away. I heard Dusty move to get a better view and I went full speed ahead and took Earl into my mouth. With long noisy slurps I pleasured him and I knew it was too much for him. I said nasty things in between and told him I wanted to feel his heavy balls.

"That's right, roll them bitches like marbles," Dusty said huskily.
All of them were focused on what I was doing and I was scared to death as I reached in and unstrapped the gun. I knew Earl was close to climax. His breathing increased as a moan crawled up and out of his throat. Just as I felt he was about to burst, I yanked the gun free and spun around waving it haphazardly. Through a drug haze, Dusty reached for his own gun but I shut my eyes and fired. I felt myself being pushed down and the gun snatched from my hand. I covered my ears as the report of gunshots filled the air. Then the sweetest words I ever heard, *"POLICE! EVERY BODY FREEZE!"*
I looked up, hardly noticing Dusty's body guard leaning against the wall holding his hand against his bloody shoulder. Dusty himself was trying to catch his breath as blood poured from a wound in his chest. I pushed myself to my feet and ran from the room screaming for Tiffany.

Moments later I heard her calling my name and then she was in my arms.

"I'm Sorry Mikki, I'm so sorry."

"It's okay now. You're safe. We're going home."

After what seemed an eternity Detective Earl Young cleared us through and had an officer drive us home.

~*~

It was two weeks before he came to see me. "I'm sorry about the delay, but there was a crap-load of paperwork and pre-trial hearings. How's your sister?"

I told him that Tiffany refused to talk about what had happened during her time with Joey Mendoza and we had to put her in a counseling program. "But we're hoping she'll be okay in time. We're just glad to have her home."

There was an awkward silence between us and I was embarrassed but I needed to tell him why I did what I did that night. He held up his hand to stop me.

"Look it's me who needs to apologize for putting you in that position. There's nothing I can say to make up for it."

I told him it was water under the bridge and neither of us could do anything about it.

"But if you're free maybe dinner might be a start." He offered.

"I'd like that," I said smiling. "But after what I did for you, it had better be some dinner," I teased.

His laughter filled the air and I knew it was the start of a new and very special relationship.

What a man

"What you need is a date!"

If she'd heard that statement one more time Brooke was going to kill Jeraleese Wilfort—the office ditz-busy-body-turned-match-maker. Ever since Jeraleese found what *she* deemed as *her* Mr. Right and who had given her a gaudy *muddy-looking-maybe-not real* two caret *diamond ring,* she felt it was her right to try and find a suitable mate for every separated, divorced, widowed and single person in the entire office building. After multiple and the annoying habit of getting all up in hers and everyone's business, Brooke was forced to take her aside and tell her in the nicest way possible that she really should *"let people try and find their own solutions to their dating difficulties. "*

Probably embarrassed about being called out Jeraleese's retort was loud, insulting and in the middle of the clerically occupied office break-room.

"Well maybe if you would just take my advice Brooke you wouldn't have to resort to being with *BOB* every night." Every female head turned and looked at them. They all knew that *BOB* was the acronym for *Battery operated Boyfriend*, because secretly each and every one of them had one.

It was true and no secret that Brooke hadn't dated in over a year and a half, not since she'd found out her low-life lover Miguel Montez had three women from three different races and two them pregnant at the same time. *How could she have been so stupid?* The signs were all there. Miguel almost never wanted to go out and constantly made excuses. He told her she was a great cook and they didn't need to eat nasty restaurant food. When she insisted he take her to a movie, he always chose the last show and usually a flick that everyone had already seen.

But when it came to his lovemaking he was like a machine gun, hot ready and full juicy ammo.

It all came to an end however one weekend when he'd told her he was going to see his mother in Bound Brook New Jersey.

"She's my mom and she don't get to see me that much. It's just for the day I'll be back on Monday. You know how it is right baby?"

Brooke never really liked New Jersey and it was a good enough reason *not* to accompany him—*not* that he had even asked—ever.

She decided to take the weekend opportunity to treat herself to a nice quiet Sunday brunch at the South Street Seaport pier. It was a great spring day and the train being practically empty was another veritable pleasure to the usual crowded weekday grind.

She stopped at a local café for a vanilla latte and a honey almond Muffin, bought a newspaper and strolled to the pier. The area was busy with visitors but nowhere near the chaotic crowd of people that frequented the area during the regular work week. She spotted a table close to the railing by the water and sat. The slight breeze blew her through her hair and she pushed it back, took in a deep cleansing breath and was satisfied with how nice it felt to be able to relax and appreciate the day. She didn't even want to think about the conversation she'd been putting off having with Miguel about their relationship but she knew it was inevitable. She'd wanted it to work, she really did, but while their love-making was off the chain, he didn't seem to want to put in the effort it took to keep them in couple mode. They'd had previous skimpy discussions about it but he always placated her with smooth words followed by spectacular sex. The man was a veritable insatiable animal when it came to lovemaking and she couldn't count how many times they'd made the sheets wet or how they'd ended up on the floor with him still pumping wildly inside of her. He was a deliciously dirty sexual being and excited her with whispered decadent words as he moved inside her. Sometimes it was slow and methodical, other times hard fast,

forceful and almost *always* in a combination of English and Spanish. *"Aye mami, your chocha is good—muy Bueno, so juicy; you make me want to fuck you forever."*
She would get wet panties every time she remembered the evening he came home and she was sitting on the couch reading, and he just came over pulled off her jeans and panties and spread her wide then pasted his face between her legs. He ate her deep and from crack to crack, pushing his tongue so deep in her she thought she would die from the pleasure. Every so often he would stop and look up at her, his face shiny from her frequent releases, *"You like it Brooke? You like my tongue in your pussy?"*
She didn't have to answer; but he knew by the way she pushed herself down hard on his face and devoured his tongue.

He was a man who seemed to never get tired of going down on her and he never cared where. If the urge hit him and they were out in public he would find a spot where he could indulge his hard-on, or satiate his appetite to taste her. Having never done anything quite like it before, the thrill of being in danger of being seen by someone was titillating. While all that was good, she still wanted to be a couple with him. She wanted to get to know his family and friends and go out more. She wanted him to get to know *her* friends and maybe enjoy some local trips and vacations together. She just wanted to be more like other couples, like the ones she was now watching walking hand in hand and just seemed to be enjoying being together.

~*~

She was just about to settle her teeth into the muffin when she heard a familiar voice. Brooke turned quickly knocking over her Latte and looked over where she saw Miguel talking in rapid Spanish to three kids—all under the age of five and they were calling him... *Popi?* The woman sitting opposite him, obviously in her last month of pregnancy was smiling at him adoringly. With her Muffin forgotten, the spilled Latte dripping off the table and onto the ground Brooke leapt up from the chair and went over to him.

"Going to see your mother huh?" She said trying to hold her anger in check.

His face grew pale as he began to stutter out an excuse.

"Miguelito, who ees thees?" The pregnant woman said. Brooke was about to say non-ya—short for *none of your business* when suddenly she heard another voice call out his name. This time in hardcore *hood* English,

"Michael!"

They all turned and stared wide-eyed at the two hundred and fifty-five pound mountain of a girl about twenty or so lumbering toward them wearing shoes with the heels running over the side of her swollen ankles and her cheap V-neck blouse barely containing her mega-breasts. Her scowl could have scared the face off a clock but Brooke had to admit *and* appreciate that her nails and hair were done up in high fashion and perfection.

"Where's my money mutha fucka?"

"What are you doing here?" Miguel hissed.

"I called your brother, he told me where you was at," the girl said.

Miguel had a brother? Brooke hadn't even known that. The girl continued her tirade as Miguel swallowed and blanched.

"You know I got to get to the clinic on Monday and you out here with two hoochies and some weasely lookin' rug rats." Brooke resented being referred to as a *hoochie* but there was no way she intended doing anything about it given the girl's ginormous proportions and uncontained anger.

"And now who ees thees Miguel?" Little Miss Chiquita asked now getting her broody feathers in fluff.

"I'm Lafeena—his girlfriend..." she pointed at Miguel before continuing, "And who the hell are you?" the girl said looking the woman up and down.

"I am hees wife," she said proudly then clarified, "Well a*lmost* hees wife." She waved a tiny cloudy diamond in her face that looked like it came from *Family Dollar*.

"Yeah well *almost* only counts when you miss the rail I'm about to throw your ass off of," Lafeena said advancing toward her.

The two women started yelling at each other and the kids all began crying at once.
Brooke had had enough. She wasn't about to stay in the midst of this fiasco and was about to walk away when the middle child latched onto her leg and held on tight, tears and snot smearing her brand-new Kelly-green Capri pants. She looked down at the little boy. Always a sucker for a child, Brooke picked him up and his arms instantly locked around her neck like he was afraid someone was going to steal him.

"Aye Dios Mios, Ladies! Ladies! Can we talk about this rationally?" Miguel said in his smooth Latin voice.
They all stopped and glared at him with enough venom to poison a slew of gang-banging malcontents. *Now he wanted to talk?* It was all too much for Brook and she handed the child over to his mother and was about to walk away again when she saw what looked like an entire Asian family hurrying toward them. The short bandy legged red faced man whom Brooke assumed was the patriarch was pulling a lovely young woman by the hand toward them, her face frightened and wet with tears.

"You there!" the man called in clipped English, "Your name Miguel? My daughter say you her love. She cannot love you she marry Jimmy Lau."
That was the last straw. This scenario had every intention of becoming the international smack-down of epic proportions and Brooked wanted no part of it and walked away.
The minute she got home she packed up all of Miguel's belongings and set them outside the door with a note: *Take your shit and keep going.*

She wanted to put the whole episode behind her and tried to lose herself in her work. She loved her job except for that busybody Jeraleese the self-proclaimed guru of perfect matches and didn't want to hear anything else she had to say.

~*~

It was a hard struggle at times but Brooke excelled and finally attained a position that placed her next in line for the senior management position. She worked even harder doing what she did best and that was to make sure everything ran smoothly.

Her boss, Linda Murtin had started the company with little more than a dream and whatever she could beg borrow or steal from her maxed out credit cards and help from relatives. Now she was on the *A*-list of who's who of Event Planning firms that commanded the highest profiled clients, society had to offer.

Brooke wasn't a bit surprised when she called her into her office late one afternoon just before she was leaving to go home which was something her boss had taken to doing more often of late. She really didn't mind because she usually had nothing going on except a *Lean Cuisine*, diet soda and a re-run of *How Stella Got Her Groove Back* waiting for her at home anyway.

"What's up boss lady?" They'd become friendly enough for her to be able to call her that.

"Well," Linda said swiveling around to face her, "We have a gig—an important one."

"I'm all ears." Brooke said.

"What you might be when this is all over… is all nerves."

"It can't be that bad." Brooke chortled.
Linda got up and paced the room, her sleek Donna Versace suit hugging the lines of her lean athletic figure.

"It's for someone I know—a man."
Brooke looked pensive, there was something else here.

"You and he were…" She waited to see if Linda would finish.

"We were high school sweethearts in Florida; we even went to the same College. Girl, I did things with that man I wouldn't admit to under oath. I loved him." Her tone grew quiet and pensive.

"What happened? Why'd you break up?" Brooke knew she was riding up the *none-of-your-damn-business-highway*, but she had to give it a try anyway.

"Lots of reasons; it was all so stupid but the fact of the matter is, we parted and it wasn't pretty."

"If you're that uncomfortable, why take the job? Why not refer him to a competitor?" Brooke asked.

"I suggested that, but he insisted. I got the distinct impression he was challenging me somehow. He had no qualms about reminding me that he was the best at what he did and I should know that and which is why he wanted the best."

"Sure sounds like a challenge to me," Brooke said.

"I reiterated several times that I thought it would be in both our best interests that he go with another company."

"I gather he didn't agree."

"He had the nerve to almost insult me by saying that I sounded like I didn't have faith in my own company."

Brooke had never known Linda to back down from a challenge of any kind and this was beginning to sound personal.

"Maybe he's just looking to get back in your life. You know how men are; they're little boys dressed up in church clothes trying to act all big and bad," Brooke said.

"I don't think it's that."

"So then you want to go ahead with the job but *you* don't want to be all that *involved* is that it?"

"It's probably just better all-around."

"When was the last time you saw him?"

"More years than I want to admit to," Linda said with a laugh.

"Well, "Brooke said with a little snort. "It's been my experience that men don't look all that good after a while anyway. I'll bet you a four course dinner that he looks like two bags of highway dog mess,"

Linda gave her a sardonic smirk. "Did you happen to see the Music Awards last week?" she asked.

"You know I did. I had to see my boy Bijon Clique." Bijon was a new sexy singing import from England—the black part, who had taken America by storm.

"Well did you happen to see Monique Questor after her win was announced?"

"Yeah I saw her; she was wearing the hell out of that Versace sheath. It looked like liquid silver."

"And the guy she hugged later when they were interviewed in the green room?"

"Goodness yes. Even the Hershey factory doesn't have that much sweet looking chocolate and those eyes and lips. He must have been *eleventy-seven* feet tall..." Brooke stopped prattling; when she noticed Linda wasn't saying anything.

"Oh hay-ell no! *He's* the Client? The guy you..." Linda nodded.

Brooke had to compose herself. Now she understood why her boss was so nervous, the man was ten different kinds of fine with a healthy amount of gorgeous chaser and a voice so deep that came all the way from the earth's core.

Linda looked at her earnestly. "It's a big job—not black tie but it should be a well-designed event."

Brooke could see her boss was stressing over this and she had to let her know she was in her corner one hundred percent. She calmed herself and put her work-game-face back on.

"Don't worry, by the time we're finished with him his tongue will be hanging out like a thirsty lap dog," she said. Linda threw Brooke a knowing glance. "You don't want to go anywhere near his tongue, trust me."

"Ooh girl..." Brooke said then collected herself for a brain storming session.

~*~

The event was scheduled for a month away and while that sounded like a lot of time, in reality it wasn't when every detail had to be better than perfect for three hundred of the most influential people living in and flying into Chicago. Brooke knew she had her work cut out for her and she didn't intend to disappoint. "Leave it to me." She said with a confident smile.

When she got home that night Brooke went on the Internet to find out all she could about the mysterious man who had her boss's usually well reigned in emotions all tied up in a knot. Harrison Gaitlin of *Gaitlin Public Relationsl Inc.* rose to prominence when his company landed a lucrative soft drink deal to advertise at the Super Bowl, followed by deals with three of the largest annual parades in the country. After that there was no stopping him and everything he touched seemed to turn to green—as in money and lots of it. It was also rumored that he was currently in communication with a Parisian company seeking to do business with him and an Asian conglomerate had been wooing him to start negotiations for business there as well. He was single, thirty-eight and he liked to snorkel, mountain climb and sail on his own forty-eight foot Catamaran named *Sea wind.* There were many pictures of him at various events and engagements and almost all of them showed him with some of the most influential and astonishingly beautiful women in the world.

The next day Linda contacted his office, introduced herself to a supercilious administrative assistant and asked her to send over the event proposal. It arrived by messenger an hour later. After reading over it several times, Brooke chose *Le Chic*, a pricey dinner and dancing spot in the Barrelhead section of the city for the event. It was the equivalent of Tribeca in New York right down to the cobblestone streets and vintage street lamps. She got samples of invitations from the engraver they often used and a book of floral designs for the table center pieces. After collecting menus from several notable caterers and bartenders, she went to work on her presentation.

~*~

A couple of days later she contacted Harrison Gaitlin's office set to up a meeting to go over and coordinate the specifics but was told by the snooty administrative assistant that someone would be over to finalize everything before the end of the workday.

Brooke went over her presentation three times and was pleased with the content. By three o'clock when there was still no word from the Gaitlin office she called again and was subjected once more to the annoyed tone of the Admin.

"I believe I said *before* the end of the workday and…" there was a pause, "3:02" does not normally constitute the end of a workday here. We will be in touch."

And she hung up.

Bitch! Brooke thought with irritation.

At 4:00 she was drumming her fingers on her desk with impatience and at 6:30 she was packing up to go home when there was a light tap on her office door as it was pushed open. A head popped in—a very good looking movie star quality head.

"Miss Finely?"

"Yes I'm Brooke Finley."

"Jamal Mendoza—Harrison Gaitlin's confidential aide." *Okay*, she thought to herself, why had she been expecting a *female* associate from Gaitlin's? Mentally chastising herself for being just as discriminatory as men were in similar situations. His name inferred he probably had a black mother and a Hispanic father which made her heckles rise as she immediately thought of Miguel.

He held out his hand and she shook it, taking in his impeccable *John Vervatos* suit. She was quite familiar with expensive menswear, most likely because Miguel *never* wore any.

"Please have a seat." she pointed to the chair opposite her desk. Her ire at his tardiness was not abated even as fine as he was, but she knew that she had to make this presentation work for Linda's sake if nothing else and tried to put her irritation aside. With her lips pinched she retrieved her portfolio and gave him a copy of the proposal. He thumbed through it slowly, giving no indication if he liked anything or not. She fumed inwardly; her eyes squinting into slits wondering what the hell he was thinking. She was damn good at her work and knew the proposal was flawless. There might be something they would probably want to change here and there, but *shit on a stick, what the hell was taking him so long*?

Wrapped in her own thoughts she hadn't even heard him when he finally spoke.

"Miss Finely?"

"Oh, Yes?" she snapped to attention.

"Is this it?" He said.

Was that it? She thought angrily. She worked her ass off on that proposal it was exceptional even *if* she thought so herself.

"Yes it is—but if there's something you'd like to change…"

He didn't even let her finish as he closed the binder with a sharp snap. "Did you read the profile that was sent over?"

"Yes I…"

"Well then it should have been obvious that the new office and condo complex that is being built is catering to the idea of a simpler lifestyle. It won't be all angles and fluff." He said tapping the folder.

Brooke wanted to climb across the desk and jab her finger into the middle of his forehead. She'd show him angles when her finger dug straight into his brain and pulled it out—*would that eliminate enough angles for his ass?* But her business sense prevailed.

"Something with a little more pizzazz perhaps?" She offered trying not to sound condescending and fought not to grit her teeth.

"Well not really, just something a little more free and easy," he said. "After all, these clients are looking to invest in a project that will not only make them a profit but helps the community as well."

His annoyed patience didn't escape her.

"Mr. Mendoza, I assure you our services are the best you'll find anywhere and if our fee seems a little high I'm sure Ms. Murtin would be happy to negotiate…" She surmised it *had* to be about the money—after all it was *always* about that. People with it always wanted the best but didn't want to pay for it.

"Trust me Miss Finely it's not the money, if it was I wouldn't be here. Look! Why don't I give you a couple of days

to come up with something else, if I don't like what you have…
well we'll just have to seek other options."
Brooke's mouth dropped open like a fish out of water fighting
for air, but before she could utter a word, he was up and out of
the office.

"What the hell just happened?" she thought to herself. No
one had ever questioned her work before. People had made
suggestions here and there of course but never had anyone told
her it wasn't good enough. The rage factor kicked in and she was
so hot she had to loosen her collar and use a discarded folder to
fan herself. She had a good mind to go in and tell Linda that she
ought to tell Harrison Gaitlin that *his* company wasn't good
enough for *them* and maybe he should just take his business
elsewhere. But that would reflect badly on her and make her look
almost as though she was incapable of doing what needed to be
done and she couldn't have that.
On the way home, her mind was thrashing around thoughts about
what *Mr. Afro-Latin-macho-hunk* felt *free and easy* was.
~*~

All that weekend she wracked her brain trying to drum up
with a concept and by Sunday afternoon she came up empty. It
was unusually warm and she was tired but she decided exercise
might help to ease the mounting tension of impending failure.
She got into her sweats and slipped a headband onto her head.
Tucking her keys and ID into her pocket, she fast walked to the
park, stretched, and did her deep breathing routine before starting
her run.

She ran for thirty minutes at a high paced gait then
slowed to a fifteen minute trot. Finally tired and sweaty she
slowed to a fast walk, then brought it down to a slow step until
she got to one of the hard green park benches and sat, took her
pulse and allowed her heartbeat to settle to its normal rate.

Looked around she noticed a couple sitting across from
her. The young man was rubbing the girl's swollen belly gently
as she looked at him tenderly. Several feet away a family of four
sat on a blanket as the mother handed out paper plates and the

father uncovered plastic containers filled with sandwiches and other finger foods like chips and pretzels. An elderly couple passed by her walking slowly, the woman's arm hooked into his, while he patted hers lovingly. *Family, Commitment, Love,* that's it!

Brooke got up and raced home and went to the spare room which served as her office and began putting her thoughts down on paper. Monday morning she was well pleased with her final work and dialed Gaitlin Associates and asked for Jamal Mendoza. After she was connected, she told him that she was positive she had exactly what he wanted. He told her he had meetings all that day and when she *gently* reminded him that time was of the essence he agreed to make some time for her.

"Alright Miss Finely, I'll be finishing up with a potential client at *Lashers,* why don't you meet me there say around 6:30?"

What does he think? I have no life? She thought, but said; "Of course, I'll see you then."

~*~

When she arrived at the trendy restaurant with its round tables and Corinthian leather lined booths, Jamal was sitting at the bar with his back to her. She knew it was him instantly by the neat cut of his slightly curling hair lying against the collar of his suit jacket, not to mention that his broad shoulders would catch the attention of *any* female as it did hers.

"Good evening Mr. Mendoza." She said walking over to him.
He glanced at his watch and gave her a small smile.

"Right on time," and stood up and offered her the empty stool next to him. His killer smile made her stomach gurgle like an oil rig gas pocket.

"On second thought why don't we take a booth," he said and ushered her toward one where there weren't too many people.

She declined his offer of a glass of wine, opting for spring water as she handed him her new proposal. Again he perused it coolly as her crossed legs shook nervously under the table.

"Not bad," he said finally.

That was it! Who needed his know-it-all attitude?

"Mr. Mendoza, this is a good proposal. I personally investigated each and every one of these vendors. Granted, two of them are start-ups, but everybody deserves a chance and isn't that what you wanted to portray? A concept that was free, easy and new*?"* she accentuated the word *new*. She thought he was about to give another one of his curt remarks and headed him off.

"Look! I never turned away a client in my life but if…"

"Whoa," he said holding up two hands to ward off her machine gun mouth. "I like it. It's crisp, its innovative it's good—really good."

"Well why didn't you say that in the first place?" she said trying not to pout.

"Maybe I just wanted to see that pretty little temper, I knew it was in there."

"Do we have a deal Mr. Mendoza?" she said ignoring his flattery.

"Of course we do."

"Good! Then I'll send over the finals by courier tomorrow." She gathered up her papers and pushed her chair back.

"Have a dinner with me," he said.

She smirked at him. "Oh and if I don't then I guess it's a deal breaker?"

"No, we have a deal. I'm just hungry and want some company."

His smile was infectious but she refused to give one of her own. She *was* hungry and had been even *before* she'd walked in the place. "You know what?" she said sitting back down and placing her portfolio and purse on the chair next to her, "I think I *will* have dinner and you know what else?"

He raised a brow and listened.

"I'm going to eat like a field hand—like Aunt Hesta's pet pig. I am *not* going to eat a small salad with low fat dressing and a glass of Perrier with lemon. I want a mega-size bowl of French onion soup, then I'm going to have a steak—a great big one with fingerling potatoes and all the trimmings like sour cream real bacon bits and a nice glass of Sauvignon Blanc to wash it all down with. Think you handle that? You *still* want me to have dinner with you now?" she said looking him right in the eye.

His eyes were smoky. "Oh yes... He said as a seductive smile curled his lip, "I can handle *all* that."

After she had received the signed copies of the finals along with the first installment check, she spent the next few days fine-tuning the preparations for the Gaitlin fest. Jamal called every day to check on her progress and every day she gave him the same terse answer, *its going fine!* The one day he *didn't* call—and she hated to admit it, she missed him.

~*~

The day of the gala Brooke was running around like a chicken with its head cut off. Her last stop was *Table Top Choice*—the best but newest caterer she'd ever taken a chance on and spoke to Romilda the owner, who was getting things together in the small but efficient kitchen.

"It's got to be right *and* on time Romilda please."

"Don't worry Ms. Finely you're giving us this wonderful opportunity, you think I'm going to blow it?"

Later that evening as she was simultaneously putting on her lipstick, shoving her foot into her new almost too-tight *Kate Spade* pumps while listening for the taxi she'd called to take her to the venue, she went over various details in her mind. Driving herself was not an option because she didn't want to get wrinkled and sweaty before she even got to the venue.

Limousines were lined up and down the street as high-powered couples and mega-moneyed singles exited them. Inside, the building—she had to admit was gorgeous. Low hanging tulle twists in soft greens, blues and purples cascaded over soft lights complimenting the sophisticated but under-stated décor. The crowd milled around sampling fancy appetizers assorted wines and champagne. Much to her chagrin Brooke found herself clandestinely searching the crowd for Jamal but he was nowhere to be found. She was sure he was there somewhere and positive he would most likely *not* be alone and it irritated her that she hadn't thought of asking someone to accompany *her*, but who?

At first Brooke thought that Linda would punk out and not show up—that seeing her old love might be too much for her. But she smiled when she saw her enter a few minutes later wearing a short, deep purple sheath with only a strand of pearls to accessorize.

"You look wonderful boss," Brooke said.

"So do you," she said looking around.

"I haven't seen him," Brooke leaned over and whispered.

"Who?" Linda asked.

"*Him* who you are pretending you're *not* looking for." Linda ignored her and took a glass of champagne offered to her by an impeccably dressed and impressively tall waiter, as they both stood off to the side and out of the way watching the efficient personnel do its work.

"You did well Brooke, everything is gorgeous. I love the tulle and the lights."

"I'm glad you like it, the food is great too I hope you get a chance to taste it."

"I'm afraid the butterflies in my stomach probably won't allow that."

Brooke was about to tease back a response when suddenly there was the sound of thunderous applause and whistles as the crowd nearest the side door parted.

A suave smiling Harrison Gaitlin went up to the podium and waved down the applause. The crowd quieted, looking at him with fascinated anticipation. He reached into his inner side pocket and withdrew a pair of glass and placed them on his nose.

"A true sign that I'm not as young as I pretend to be," he said in a low sonorous voice.

The crowd laughed then quieted once again as he positioned the
mic to speak and there was momentary silence. Just then Linda's
cell went off with Whitney Houston's *I'M YOUR BABY
TONIGHT* ring-tone blaring loud and clear.
The audience laughed and Harrison's eyes went right to where
they were standing then went right on with his talk.

Linda struggled to find the *vibrate* set button in the dim
lighting when the ring-tone went off again. Even Brooke could
feel the heat emanating from her when Harrison stopped
speaking and every head turned to look at her.

"I think I got the message the first time," Harrison
jokingly.

"Sorry," she stammered offering a weak embarrassed
smile.
Linda set the phone to vibrate and took a deep breath and
listened as Harrison resumed. A second later Brooke heard the
vibrate buzz when Linda's phone went off yet again. Linda
stepped back a few feet to answer and whisper into it. Brooke
saw her head jerk up like it was on a marionette string. She saw
her boss's face grimace and she went over to her.

"What's wrong?" she asked her.

"Uncle Hez!" she said turning off her phone.

"Your Uncle Hezekiah from Florida?

"Yes! What the heck is he doing here?"

"A better question is how did he get *here*?" Brooke said
waving her arms.

"I have no idea."
Brooke had heard about Linda's good but hearted-loud talking,
fun-loving uncle who liked nothing more than eating, dancing
and sneaking a feel on any woman's butt whenever he could.

"Okay don't panic. I'll just go out front and look for an
old geezer and head him off, um what does he look like?"
Brooke said; but before could get an answer…

"Harry Gaitlin! Boy is that you?" a laughing voice
sounded from the back of the room.

"Too late!" Linda murmured as they watched her Uncle Hezekiah lumber forward with his white pants, black shirt and lord-forgive-him, blue suede cordovan shoes with red laces.

Brooke glanced over at Linda and saw her close her eyes as probably surmising that all this hard work was about to blow up in a cloud of embarrassing smoke.

"Ladies and gentlemen," Harrison Gaitlin said into the mic. "I'd like you to meet the coolest, hippest old role model in the world. Mr. Hezekiah Murtin."

"Who you calling old?" Hez said as he walked up to the podium where he pulled Harrison into a bear hug.
Everyone applauded politely, but after Harrison spoke at length about how Uncle Hez was behind unifying the people in the most drug infested parts of Florida and help drive out gang lords and drug dealers making the neighborhood safe and single handedly lobbied for reevaluation and re-zoning to obtain a healthier portion of tax relief benefits, they clapped thunderously as Harrison continued.

"I had a great father but this man was a father to everybody and I am thrilled and proud that he is here tonight."

Harrison finished his speech and invited everyone to enjoy the food and festivities, while he and Hez sat at the front table and from what Linda and Brooke could see were having a good old time reminiscing. When the dance music started Uncle Hez had everyone, including a man with a bunion boot on up and doing the electric slide and the Cupid shuffle and several other dances no one had ever heard of.

~*~

Brooke and Linda were standing near the ice fountain sculpture when they saw Harrison walking toward them.

"Um, I think I'm gonna go powder my nose," Brooke said.

"You won't have one if you take a single step away from me," Linda whispered.
Harrison stopped in front of them and Brooke felt Linda stiffen. His eyes were bright and his smile full and genuine.

"Hey there girl, he said softly.

"Hey yourself," Linda said.

There was an awkward silence and Linda finally introduced Brooke. "Have you met my event manager?"

"Not personally, but I've gotten nothing but glowing reports from my second in command—Jamal Mendoza, and I must say you did an excellent job," he said looking around admiringly.

Brooke lost her smile at the mention of Jamal's name as she shook Harrison's hand. Linda chimed in when she noticed the awkwardness.

"Listen Harrison I want to apologize. I completely forgot Uncle Hez I didn't know he was coming in; my service told him where I was and well I just want to thank you for doing what you did. I know it made him happy."

"Are you kidding? A lot of what I am today is because of what he taught me which is why I invited him."

"You invited him?"

"We've kept in touch over the years. I'm surprised he never mentioned it to you."

"Well I guess there are some things he can keep to himself."

"He's quite man."

"Linda smiled. "He'll be talking about this night forever," she said looking over at her dancing uncle.

"He's not the only one I wanted to see." Harrison gazed down at her.

"About my nose…" Brooke broke in, "It's probably as shiny as new quarter I'm just going to go and…" But Linda grabbed her hand, staying her.

"So…" Linda said clearing her throat and changing the subject. "Did the arrangements meet your clients' expectations?"

"Exceeded them," he said taking her hand. "But I think I should tell you I didn't all need this to get their money. I needed this to swallow my pride and get to you."

The band began a slow lilting rift of a jazzy *Chris Botti* song. "Dance with me," he said.

When she hadn't moved Brooke freed her hand and gave her a little *go-on* pinch, then grinned with dreamy delight as he gently led her boss out onto the dance floor.

"What about you fine lady, you think you can keep up with these fancy feet?"
Brooke jumped, turned, then frowned. It was Jamal.

"You think I can't? Just bring it and show me see what you got." She sashayed out onto the dance floor, beckoning him to follow.
As he folded her into his arms he leaned down to whisper in her ear.

"I think you ought to know that I'm going to be inside you as soon as I get the chance."
She didn't move away and wasn't the slightest bit put off by his sexual self-assuredness.

"Think a great deal of yourself don't you?"

"No, I just know what I want and I go after it."

"You think it's going to be that easy?" she said.

"If I wanted easy, I'd settle for anyone, what I want is you."

"You don't even know me." She leaned back and looked in his eyes.

"We can remedy that anytime you like—say starting with dinner tomorrow night,"

"And then what?" She said.

"Well we'll just see what happens," he winked, "but I think I should warn you, I am insatiable."
She moved her mouth close to his ear. "And I think I should warn *you* that you better bring your best game because this pussy ain't no joke."

He threw his head back and laughed as he held her closer, the weight of anticipatory passion filling his mind as he thought of the nights and days of passion to come.

Crash Course

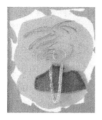

Meetings, deadlines and magazine setups—that was my life and it was a busy one. The turmoil of working for a popular educational periodical was beginning to take its toll. I had stumbled into my editorial position at *The Learning Curve* quite by accident. It was more daunting than I'd expected with scheduling changes, artistic egos and of course the late articles that always seemed to plague my portion of the magazine more than the others. We were always a minute away from deadline and the 11th hour was constantly looming over my head.

On top of everything else, my boss decided to volunteer me to teach a creative writing course at a Community Center across town. It was one of those *give–back* programs that I wasn't really interested in and even less so when I found out that the group I'd be teaching were troubled students, non-violent parolees and a few bored housewives. Of course he made it sound like it would be worth my while, but the last time I saw any real raise was when I *raised* my venetian blinds to look outside my living-room window.

"Saaja" he said, "You're the right person for the job and I know I can count on you.

Yeah right! What he could count on was the Ad's and subscriptions that this endeavor would generate for his business. But he committed me and I had to do it and I was two kinds of mad about it. It wasn't like I didn't have enough to do all day, now I had to dedicate two nights a week for the next three months to a bunch of people who wanted nothing more than to be home watching *Two Broke girls* or *Law and Order criminal Intent re-runs.*

On the first evening of my *unwanted* assignment, I figured there was no way that most of these people were going to come out after having worked all day just to take a course in writing. So without any real attempt at preparation I devised a lukewarm initial presentation and an even less substantial lesson plan because I was positive I would be facing a bunch of bored malcontents who would probably rather be anywhere other than where they were.

~*~

Tuesday night I went to the Lake Zion Community Center in what was in a pretty unsavory part of town. All sorts of characters loitered around the area but because of the bored and severely overweight but mean looking security guard, thankfully none were in front of the building which put my mind at ease. I was immediately surprised at the sheer size and neatness of the place considering its locale. It was freshly painted with some rather respectable and interesting artwork displayed on the walls—all done by local artists. I was particularly drawn to one scene of a young woman standing in the middle of the sun with her face and arms raised. It said so many things to me as I enjoyed the non-traditional color choices and shadowing of the piece.

"Thought provoking isn't it."
I turned to the deep voice that had spoken to me.
"It's pretty good." I said turning back to the picture.
"So are you here for the writing class?"
"Saaja Adams, I'm here to *teach* the writing class."
"Oh Yes, Sid Grafton said he would be sending someone over I'm Gordon Martin the evening director, welcome."
"It wasn't my idea. I kind of got roped into it. I have a ton of things I *could* be doing." I said irritably. I could almost see his heckles rise.

"Well Miss Adams it appears that you're not up to the task, so why don't I just go to and call Sid and get someone else."

He turned on his heel, showing me a right fine tight butt and walked back down the hall.

Oh no he didn't just turn that big brawny, 6ft foot fine frame away from me! Anger raced up my spine as I hurried to catch up to him.

"There *isn't* anyone else. I guess you could say I pulled the proverbial short straw so I'm all you got."

He turned to face me, his eyes burning as much as mine.

"In that case I certainly hope you take a better posture with the students Miss Adams. These people have been through enough shit—if you'll pardon my insensitivity. They don't need anyone coming in here with a *holier-than-thou* or *can't-be-so-bothered attitude.*"

His voice had risen then lowered as a couple of young men passed by and stared at us.

"Look, just show me where I need to be," I said trying to reign in my annoyance.

"Down the hall, last door!" he said sternly and stalked away.

I glared at his back. No matter how fine he was, with those dreamy brown eyes, shiny bald head and a chin-cleft so deep a sofa could rest nicely in it, his pomposity was way over the line for someone in his position.

I stalked toward the direction of the class, with angry thoughts crashing around in my brain. W*ho did he think he was? The Dean of Temple University? He was just a Pencil-pushing-part-time-director of youth center for goodness sake!* I thought irritably.

I found my class and walked in and my eyes almost popped when I saw that every seat was filled. Young men, old men, teenage girls and middle-aged women.

Humility wended its way around me as I went to the small desk in front of the room. A low cat-whistle sounded.

"Now that's what I'm talkin bout!" an appreciating male voice said from somewhere in the back.

"You got that right, and how come none of my teachers didn't look like her?" another man said, and almost everyone laughed.

I knew had to grasp the situation quickly. I had to make them respect me.

"Well..." I began as I walked around the desk and leaned against it. "... probably because sometimes women like men who can express themselves with the written word and not just calling them out like hood rats," I said.

"You mean like that Shakespeare stuff?" someone asked.

"Not exactly: Shakespeare was a playwright and a poet, but he wasn't the only one. I was thinking of something more attuned to us."

"Oh you mean like *Def Poetry Jam*." The same guy called out.

"Something along those lines, but also story telling. For instance..."
I began running off Urban book titles and authors, *PAYBACK IS A MUTHA, FLY ON THE WALL, SHOULDA, WOULDA, COULDA*, and *WORDS OF WISDOM* by Reverend RUN formally of RUN-DMC.
You could have heard a flea squeak from the moon it was so quiet and when I was done every eye was on me. I had their attention and for the *right* reason.

When the two hour session was over, I heard them exclaim that they wished it was longer and bombarded me with questions about black authors and writers. As they filed out, my mind was already working on a new and *improved* lesson plan and projects. I couldn't' keep all the thoughts in my head about the things I wanted to teach them. I was gathering my things and readying to leave the classroom.

"So you're a writer?" The voice was soft, low and with a tinge of hardness to it.

"I dabble. I'm an editor at The Learning curve." I said to man about 5'11 with dull flat eyes that watched me so intently it made me nervous.

"I'm Clyde Wells and before you hear it from someone else. I'm on a parole. I killed a man."
My blood seemed to slow in my veins and I must have taken an involuntary step back.

"Nice to meet you Mr. Wells," I didn't extend my hand and I knew that was impolite but I was being cautious.

"I think I'm going to like your class. Maybe I can put down some of *my*... incarceration experiences on paper."
His tone was threatening and his smile was oily and confident.

"I'll bring some study materials that might help you at the next class." I was gathering up my books and purse, anxious to be away from him.

"Can I walk you out? It's late and anything can happen to fine young thang like you," he said.
I couldn't think as fast as he was talking but I knew I didn't want to alone with him.

"Well I have to see the Director first." I said hurrying to the door and out to the dimly lit hall.

Just like in every horror movie ever made, the corridor was completely empty and the space looming ahead of me seemed too long, shadowy and menacing. I turned to go the other way to the outside, but Clyde had taken hold of my elbow.

"The Director's office is this way."
He began to urge me toward the dimness of the hall.

"Well I...um guess it can wait." I turned to the exit.

"You don't have to be afraid of me you know. I'd never hurt you."
It was the way he spoke, slow, deliberate; almost tasting each word before he said them and it almost made me want to drop everything and run. He inched closer and I was glued to the spot.

"You're pretty, real pretty. I wonder what your head would look like nailed to a wall."
I was almost faint with fright.

"Practicing again Clyde?"
I breathed a sigh of relief when I heard the familiar voice of Gordon.

"Yo! Mr. Martin." He said with jocularity, "You should have seen me, I was excellent. I had her goin'. I know I'm gonna get that part at the city playhouse next month."
He turned back to me; his face lost its hostility and was almost comical. My relief must have been as apparent as a cupcake at bake sale as I looked at Gordon.

"Miss Adams; I see you've met Clyde; our resident acting student and future academy award nominee. He's had two bit parts in a local cable production, a walk-on in a popular soap opera and is presently auditioning for a role in an upcoming locally produced indie film and he likes to channel Tony Montana from *Scarface* or Denzel in *Training Day*."

"Yeah but I had you going didn't I Miss Adams? I'm buff, I'm bad. I'm gooood." The young man sang.

"Okay Clyde that's enough acting for one night. I'll see you on Thursday."

"Right-O Mr. M. and hey sorry if I scared Miz Adams," and away he went down the hall rapping out a popular song, acapella.

"He's right, he *is* good. He had scared me half to death. I thought he actually *did* kill a man. I thought he was going to kill me or worse…"

"Clyde couldn't kill a blind roach on a broken crutch and as for the *worse* is concerned he's also gay so you have no worries there."

"I didn't mean…"

"It's okay, Clyde likes to stay in character as much as possible but he's harmless."
I decided the best thing to do was begin slicing up and eating my humble pie as soon as I could.

"Look Mr. Martin, I'm sorry about before. I was in a snit. It had nothing to do with you."

"It's Gordon, and I should hope not given the fact that we'd just met."

"Well you weren't exactly the epitome of grace either." I said trying to make it sound light.

"Yeah well I have to apologize about that; I have a lot of things on my mind. They're thinking of closing the center."

"Don't tell me—budget cuts right?"

"Yep!" he sighed, "Good programs like these are always the first to go."
We walked to the exit and he locked up. "Well good night Miss Adams."
And he turned and walked down the street. I was miffed. He hadn't even asked to walk me to my car. As a matter of fact he didn't seem the least bit interested in me and while I didn't know why, it made me testy all over again and I told my best friend Fatemah the next day.

"That's just your ego girl. You're used to men responding to you and this one isn't. Maybe he's gay."

"I hope not, it would be a loss to some lucky woman."
I wasn't thinking along those lines for myself because I was in no way attracted to *Mr. Attitude.*

~*~

At my next meeting with the students I brought each of them—at my own expense, a small writing journal.

"Sometimes there are things you want to say that you just can't say to anyone else. Other times there may just be random thoughts you want to remember for future reference and use. Write it here, it will help you keep track." I was filled with humility as I watched each of their faces when I handed them the notebooks.

By the fourth class, everyone was embroiled with the prospect of becoming an author of some kind. I was quick to tell them how hard it was to become published, but how rewarding it was if and when it happened as well.

~*~

One evening I arrived at the center early and wrote four movie titles on the board. *WAITING TO EXHALE, TWISTER, A STREECAR NAMED DESIRE and CLOSE ENCOUNTERS OF THE THIRD KIND.* I figured many of the younger students had never seen read or even heard of *Streetcar* so I'd used my almost defunct library credentials and got a copy of the movie from the library near my home and we spent a class looking at and discussing it. Then I told them to pick a movie and completely re-write it using any characterization and situations they wanted, but keeping close to the story concept.

A week later they handed me their papers. Some were typed others were written in long scribbled script and still others written in childish capitalized penmanship. I spent the weekend reading them and quite frankly, I was blown away by some of the talent. The creativity and imagination was mind blowing. I was in awe of the minds that were stuck in the mire of an existence from which they would probably never leave and all this innovative potential would be lost if they closed the Center. I knew had to do something. My mind ran a mile a minute when I got to work the next day as I made phone calls to find out who I could see about the center closing. First it was the County, then on to City Hall.

The meeting with the mayor was productive and because I had been lucky enough to call in a few favors, a few city and legislative leaders we were able to garner some additional funding—with some modified stipulations of course. I couldn't wait to tell Gordon and excitedly asked my boss for his home number and address. He was reluctant at first but after I explained everything he gave it to me and I called, but there was no answer. I started to leave a message on his machine, but was too excited to sit still and wait. I had to tell him the good news. I drove over to his house so I could leave a message in his mailbox in case he wasn't home because I was that excited about letting him know what we needed to do to keep the center open.

I arrived at his small but neat house on Hesper Street and was about walk up the steps to leave a note in his mail slot when I heard a voice from the yard.

Maybe he'd come home and was relaxing in his yard and was on his cellphone. This was even better because now I was going to be able to give him the good news in person.

I went to the side gate, opened it and stepped in and walked a short distance toward the back. I was mentally preparing an apology for intruding and found out that's just what I had done—intruded. He was in his hot tub with his back to me and— he wasn't alone. A honey hewed women was sitting astride him with her eyes closed in euphoria and from what I could see she was rocking back and forth in a motion that could be construed only as sexual. His large hands were rubbing up her sides and I saw his long, thick tongue begin to lick down her breasts then twirl around her nipple. The scene was erotic and I felt heat creep up my legs to my middle. I had to get away before they saw me. I turned to leave and bumped into a pliable, but strong body. I looked up and there stood Gordon Martin. Confused, I looked over at the pool to make sure I wasn't going crazy. I felt him take my arm and maneuver me back through the gate.

"Miss Adams? What are you doing here?"

"I... I..." stammering I looked back to the gate.

"That's Cedric, my identical twin brother—well identical in looks anyway. We don't share the same tastes in temperament, women or obviously decorum," he said looking over at the gate. I let out a breath. *His twin!* My goodness they were totally the same.

"You wanted something?" he asked.

"I um... *Why couldn't I focus?* Maybe because I was wondering how Gordon would look and feel in a hot-tub with me surrounding him like that woman was doing his brother.

"I think I found a way to save the center."

"Let's go to the Café down the block. My brother could be entertaining for some time, and the women he plays with can be pretty vocal if you catch my drift."

I did, and the last thing I needed was to hear some woman in the throes of passion while I had been as celibate as a nun for the last year and a half.

Later as I excitedly made my proposal about the center, he seemed less than impressed.

"I already went to the Town Council and the County they don't seem interested in keeping the center open, he said taking a sip of his beverage.

"Then we'll have to *make* it worth their notice," I said leaning forward with excitement.

I told him about some pretty famous people we'd edited books and articles for over the years and that I was sure I could get one or two to help us in our endeavors.

"What's the use?" he said despondently. "When they have their mind set on something that is not going to benefit them, they take particular pains in making sure they get what they want and never mind what we need."

"You know…" I said as I sat back, "you don't strike me as the type to give up. I know you love this job and I can tell you enjoy helping people."

"You don't know how I've tried. I've been through this before in other towns. They don't care, nobody does so why should I? I'll just be placed in another position somewhere else and it will all begin again."

I sat back, annoyed at his attitude. "Well if you're not going to try then I will. These people want a chance to do something creative for themselves. If you can just see the talent, it's amazing."

He pursed his lip and looked away, but I could see that he was lying, he did care. He was probably just frustrated at the amount of red tape he'd always had to face. I reached out and touched his hand, and he let it stay before he drew away like I had burned him.

"We can do this. It might take a little time and a lot of effort but we can do it." I said, but failed to convince him and I left him sitting forlornly at the café, but not before telling him that I'd do everything I could to see that the center had a fighting chance. Then, I went to work.

I obtained permission from three of the students with the best short stories and poems to submit them to a few contests. I sent out some poetry to several paper and small publishers, and also the first draft of a novel called *Desperate Love* from Mrs. Sylvia Roberts a bashful housewife who almost never spoke in class, but had a whole lot to say on paper. I didn't tell her I was sending it because after getting to know her a little better, I knew she'd had enough disappointments. It was a long-shot, but I wanted to try anything.

Normally I used the weekends to relax and unwind, but now it was filled with writing to county clerks and the Ombudsman about saving the center and my usually perfectly set dining table was now littered with pamphlets, manuscripts, and papers. When I received no answer, I petitioned relentlessly to see an official at the State level. It took a multitude of phone calls and long waits, but I finally got a hearing one month shy of when the center was due to close.

~*~

It was late Saturday night, my hair was all over my head and I looked like last's weeks clothing sale at Hubba-Bubba's when suddenly my doorbell rang. Opening the door, thinking it was my friend Fatemah—no one else would dare come to me at that hour, but it was Gordon Martin.

"I know it's late and I have no business asking you for anything, but I want to apologize and ask you to let me help."

"How did you know where I lived?"

"Your resume, your boss sent it when he first recruited you for the assignment."

"Oh so now you want to help after I've done all the work— work *you* should have been doing, now here you come."

"I deserve that and you're right but there must be something I can do."
I looked at him for a long moment, and then stepped aside to let him in.

"Well you can get in here and get your tongue ready to lick…"
His eyes widened as he looked down at my less-than-sexy-outfit. "Envelopes, I need you to lick envelopes for mailing some of these manuscripts and poems I'm sending to local newspapers and publishing houses."

"I hope you have a wet napkin," he winked, "licking envelopes can be dry work,"
I gave him a smirk.

"Say, isn't everything done by email now" he said taking off his jacket.

"Yep, but I am following up with hard copies just in case."

~*~

After we finished with that task we sat and discussed strategies about the center. It was 2am when we were done and I fixed him an early breakfast of chicken and waffles—he didn't drink coffee but he adored tea.

"I take it with honey if you have it."
I did because that's how I took my tea as well.

We talked until dawn and when I couldn't stop yawning, I told him I had to get some sleep.

"Me too," he said rising stiffly. "Guess there'll be no hearing a *fire and brimstone* sermon this morning," he said with a stretch, "I'm going to go home and sleep in."
So he was a church man. But it didn't look like he was going to make it as tired as he was.

"Look, it's a ways across town, why don't you just lay out here on the couch. Its comfortable and when you wake up I just might let you take me to lunch," I offered with a smile.

I could see he was about to decline, but his droopy lids made up his mind for him.

I bought out sheets, a pillow and a blanket and handed them to him. "Have a good night—um I should say morning," and giggled my way to my bedroom.

I was literally crawling into my bed when I heard a light snoring come the living room. I had to smile, he was dog tired and so was I.

~*~

Gordon started calling me almost every day after that. He was now relentless in his pursuit to help in keeping the center open.
He even had flowers sent to my job, with a card that said.
"Thanks for lighting a fire under me."
Little did he know he had lit a fire inside me that was past due to be an all-out-blaze. I don't exactly know when it started but every time he was near me I wanted to touch him. I wanted more from him than I'd wanted from any man for a long time.

As I entered class the next week, two students and an older gentleman nearly rushed me. They had received word on their Poetry. One was to be in a very popular magazine and the other two was in a small press chapbook and they were giddy with delight.

"You did this Miss Adams and I am stoked," said the younger of the two. The older man could only hold his notification letter with reverence. "This is real fine Miss Adams and I thank you."

There had been no word from anyone about the closing of the Center and the day of the hearing was looming over us.

The day before the meeting I received white flat envelope. I'd seen it a dozen times before when I had sent my own manuscripts out to publishers—back when they had been accepting them that way. It was thin and I knew it was the typical one page rejection type letter, the first of the few students' works I had sent in. I glanced at my watch, I had a meeting at a senator's office that I had written and called no less than a dozen times, and finally got a meeting and I didn't dare be late. I stuffed the envelope in my bag, vowing to read the bad news later, vowing to never even let any know that I'd sent their manuscript using my return address of course lest they be put off by a first rejection.

~*~

I was waiting in the outer office of the State Department along with Gordon and three students who had taken time off from their badly needed jobs to be with us.

"Stop fidgeting," Gordon whispered.

He was right, I couldn't keep still. I scrounged around in my bag looking for a tissue and pulled out the crumpled envelope instead. I figured I would read the rejection now while I waited and absorb any guilt of having sent it at all later. I tore it open and began to read.

Dear Mrs. Roberts. We have read your synopsis and first three chapters and wish to make an offer to publish... My eyes nearly bulged from my head. I leaped up and Gordon did too. He thought I was going crazy. I couldn't help myself and threw my arms around him and just squeezed, then I handed him the letter.

"It's Mrs. Roberts's book! They want to publish it."

He beamed at me. "That's great, she'll be so happy and this could actually help us, show them in there that we have made a difference."

I couldn't wait to tell her but I wanted it to be special and I wanted to tell her by herself so that the others wouldn't be put off. Now if we could get past this one last hurdle we'd be home free.

But it wasn't in the plans of fate. We were turned down flat, even after I'd proved my case with the accomplishments of the students. The center was closing.

Later that evening as I sat at my dining table and drank two *appletinis*, I finally understood Gordon's frustration. It was no use. How would we be able to make a difference if all our worthwhile programs were going to be cut off? I decided that I didn't want to drink alone and called a taxi and went to Gordon's house—taking a thermos of the brew I'd been indulging in. If he had a woman with him when I got there, *then she would just*

have to get the hell out, because this is my pity party, I thought
sourly. I rang the bell and got no answer; I remembered the hot
tub and went to the back. It too was empty, but inviting. I wasn't
drunk but I did have a bit of a buzz and I stripped down to my
undies, turned it on grabbed the thermos and stepped in.
The hot bubbling water soothed and relaxed me, with the help of
my mixed drink concoction of course. The only thing that was
missing was the crooning voice of Luther Vandross singing *Here
and Now*, Teddy singing *Turn off the lights* or Freddy Jackson
singing *Rock me tonight.*
I don't remember much after the first fifteen minutes; then the
feeling of being carried.

"Damn fool woman! You want to drown? You're as
pickled as three week old cucumber."

"Let's make love Gordon," I said sleepily as I wound my
arms around his neck.

"You're in no shape to make love."

"What do you mean? I have a great shape, men adore my
shape," but my head was too heavy to hold up and I let it flop
onto his chest.

When I finally did wake up it was about 1 a.m. and I was
groggy and had a banging hangover. I knew I was in Gordon's
house but I don't remember anything else. I got up and waited a
moment until the room stopped spinning and saw that I was
completely naked. *Shit*! I wandered down the hall and passed a
closed door and went further until I found the bathroom and
showered, then rinsed my mouth and smoothed back my wild
hair that had me looking like Macy Gray in that *HBO* special.
The shower helped a lot and my headache was subsiding a bit but
I needed something to take my mind off it altogether. *Coffee? Oh
that's right; he didn't drink the dark brew.* I wrapped myself in
the too-large cotton robe that I found hanging on the back of the
door and went to find Gordon. I went back to the closed door and
quietly pushed it open. He was lying on the bed with a sheet
covering half of him and the TV on. At first I thought he was
asleep.

"That's my robe you're wearing." His voice was low.
I waited a full two seconds then undid the sash and took it off.

"Then I guess you'll be wanting it back," I said and threw it on the foot of the bed.
His eyes drank me in as I stood before him unashamed. He folded the sheet back and moved over. I slid in beside him and immediately his hands worked over my body like a concert pianist. I melted against him as he delighted my body in ways I'd forgotten existed.

"Remember when you tried to get me to lick all those envelopes?"
I grinned.

"Well now I get to show you what this tongue can really do."

"Bragging or fact?" I challenged.
A sly smile curled one side of his lip as he tore the sheet off us and moved me into position.

"Open up and see," he said.
I don't know what came over me, but my legs slid apart like they were greased with Crisco on a hot griddle. Immediately his face was pasted between my thighs as he made me forget my headache and everything else in my mind. The sounds that came out of me were almost unrecognizable as I allowed him to supply me with as much passion as his lathering tongue could give.
Later it was my turn to show him what I had and to get what I wanted. "You have condoms?" I asked.
He reached over and opened the drawer in the night table. It was full of shiny squares.

"I guess you're used to having a good time."

"Nothing like being prepared just in case and then is my twin brother remember?" he said and pulled out a packet and waved it at me. *Magnum for Maximum pleasure.*

"Full of yourself I see," as I read the packet out loud.

"Nope, just preparing you," he said tearing it open and slipping it over his erect penis.

"Well then I think we just better get to it," I said and pushed him back and took my time in bringing him to the brink of erotic desire time and time again.

Gordon made love to me for hours and in every way that I liked. Finally when we were both exhausted I fell into an easy sleep in his arms.

~*~

His phone woke us and I figured it was some woman calling him and I didn't need to hear him make halting explanations and I got up to leave. But he held me tight in his arms and spoke into the receiver.

"Yes! Of course. I'll be…we'll be right there."
As he got up and headed to the bathroom to shower he explained that the stenographer who took down the proceedings at the hearing had gotten in touch with a group that aided neighborhoods with *at risk* programs such as ours. Sandy—that was her name, met us an hour later along with two gentleman who said they would see to it that the Center would not be closed with the help of some last minute private donations, but we'd have to help as much as we could with bake sales and anything else we could to show good faith seed money. It was like a dream come true and Gordon was bursting with idea.

I got my boss to run a story in our local magazine and donations trickled then began pouring in, most from some of the minor celebrities and entertainers that we had interviewed favorably. Not wanting to be outdone and always in line for a photo op, the Senator who had *initially* refused our request came out to endorse the good works of the center and with it a nice check to seal the deal.

~*~

We had a grand re-opening and everyone was there. I even managed to get the associate editor of the publishing company that accepted Mrs. Roberts's book to come down and make the announcement. Sylvia Roberts was in shock as she ambled forward with tears in her eyes and hugged me tightly. "I couldn't have done this without you." I was so happy for her and the others.

By the time word got out, we had to try and find room for all the people who had expressed an interest in creative writing. I was able to get two of my work associates and even Fatemah to come down and help. To my surprise local authors came to the center and shared their struggles to show these people that they had worth and that nothing should stop them from continuing to share their written words. All we could hope for now was that Clyde got the part he'd auditioned for.

As for me, I now share a household with Gordon and we're getting married at the end of the year. I look back on where I was and know that this was where I was meant to be, not only with a man who adores me, but being able to make a difference in the lives of people who just needed a chance.

Mirror Images and Broken Vows

Alisa and Brenda, identical twins, that's what we were. So much so that it was almost uncanny. Brenda was younger than me by eight seconds and was a mere 1/8 of inch taller than I—which was our only distinguishing feature and hardly noticeable. Other than that we were like one person right down to the dimple in our left cheek and the mole just above our top lip. Our father said that during my mother's cesarean the doctor had to disengage my sister's arm from mine before I could be delivered. *"She was hooked onto you as if holding on for dear life,"* he'd said, and we've been super close ever since.

Because of our ability to fool even our parents on occasion, we were able to get away with almost anything. For that reason we grew up pampered, spoiled and did pretty much anything we wanted. Brenda and I perpetrated many deceptions over the years including at school *and* employment. At my insistence we did however attend different colleges and while I excelled in most subjects Brenda had trouble with quite a few. Twice I stepped in to take tests for her and no one was the wiser. She reciprocated when once during a summer job at a downtown retail store I was invited to go on a week-long trip to the St. Lucia with some college friends and Brenda took my place and no one even had a clue. We even had the gall to switch boyfriends once just to see if they could tell us apart—they couldn't, but what I didn't know was the Brenda had let *her* man take liberties with her that I had not even thought about doing with mine. I was able to fend him off and when we finally told them about the switch and her boyfriend swore he knew it all along, but we all laughed about it for days. However we found out later, that our pranks would not *always* going to be a laughing matter.

~*~

We told each other everything and did everything together, but when one of her work buddies—Courtney Bettis introduced Brenda to the new Acquisitions Officer Lewis Palmer he went wild over her. Lewis was good looking, smart and ambitious. He had a great smile and my heart was bursting with joy with how much he seemed to adore my sister. He never commented on how much we were alike and was completely taken with Brenda from the first day he met her. It wasn't long before he was showering her with gifts, trips and almost anything that would make her happy. When he asked her to marry him and presented her with a four caret canary yellow diamond ring the following year she was over the moon and our entire family was overjoyed for her. I couldn't have been happier for my sister but I had to draw the line at her insistence to me trying to find a husband just so we could have a double wedding.

"Brenda, I will be happy to be your maid of honor but I am *not* going to go on some stupid man hunt just so that we can have a double and completely ridiculous ceremony and honeymoon together. We're not kids anymore and we have to put those childish antics to rest."

She pouted for a while, spoiled little witch that she was, but soon she was caught up in her wedding preparations and let it. I was happy for her and I secretly had high hopes that I would be lucky enough to find a man who adored me the way Lewis did my sister.

~*~

Lewis insisted on paying for the entire matrimonial event and allowed Brenda to do whatever she wanted. All he wanted to do was get fitted for his Tux and stand beside her as she became his wife. I must admit that it was a lot of fun trying on dresses and watching Brenda primp and preen like a fairy princess. Time flew by and before we knew it the big day had arrived. Our father struggled to hold back tears of pride as he escorted her down the aisle in her eight thousand dollar *Lazaro* wedding dress. When the minister asked… *who giveth this woman*… our father handed her over to Lewis who looked like the happiest man on earth as he took her hand and kissed it. Each had written vows and while I thought it was pretty corny because almost everybody never adhered to that bullshit, I was happy for them.

My sister—imp that she was couldn't help pulling one last trick on Lewis at the wedding. Between the ceremony and the reception and after the pictures were taken, Brenda convinced me to switch into her wedding dress and go into the ante room where Lewis and the groomsman were and see if anyone would know it was me. I flatly refused, but she begged me and said that it was something that they could laugh about with their children someday. I reluctantly agreed and quickly changed into her dress and she into dusty rose colored maid-of-honor gown.

We walked in the room where Lewis was talking and laughing with his groomsman and his eyes lit up as he walked over and took my hand. He was about to kiss me but I turned my head telling him I had just repaired my makeup for the reception.

"Alright darling, but let me see you for just a minute," he said against the backdrop of whistles and catcalls from his groomsmen. My eyes turned to Brenda pleading with her to intercede. As he began to escort me to the Bride's holding room, Brenda moved forward to protest, but he held up a hand.

"It's okay Alisha, we'll only be a minute, I promise." The best man—a tall lanky white guy with a Kirk Douglas cleft and two other groomsmen came over and surrounded me. "No worries; your sister is in the best of hands," they said with smiles.

Inside the small room, Lewis took my hand and spun me around. "Never has any woman been more beautiful Mrs. Palmer."

I smiled shyly but didn't say anything lest my trembling voice give me away.

"In a few hours we will be on our way to Cancun where I can love you until you can't take it anymore and I can give you all of this..."

To my shock he took my hand and cupped it right over his rock hard erection. I snatched it away quickly giving him a look of admonishment as I whispered, "no, not now."

But he wouldn't be deterred. "Let me just take it out and you can do that thing you do on the tip," He said in a soft raspy voice.

This was getting out of hand. I had to get out of there. When his hand went to his zipper and I panicked even more and I was ready to run when there was a knock on the door. It opened and Brenda's head popped in. She gestured wildly and then came over to us and began playfully pushing Lewis toward the door and back to his laughing groomsmen. He stopped momentarily and pulled me to him and whispered something so decadent in my ear that I blushed clear down to my toes.

After he left I sank onto the tufted bench.

"That was close," I breathed a sigh of relief "And what the hell do you do to the tip of his..." I couldn't even say it. But she just laughed as we quickly began to disrobe and change clothes again.

At the reception she was all innocent smiles as she and Lewis danced and looked so much in love that I almost forgot about the trick we'd played. I was truly happy for my sister and hoped that she'd finally grown up and that we would always have the memory of this and other antics we'd perpetrated over the years.

~*~

Bad news hits quick and unexpected and just before their first anniversary our parents were killed in a head-on collision by a driver who was under the influence of alcohol and drugs. The driver survived with a cracked rib and two broken finger. I often wondered why *they* never died but managed to kill good people.

He hadn't even been wearing his seat belt but it appears the demons that controlled his existence took good care of him while our parents died horrifically. Brenda was inconsolable and Lewis who tried desperately to ease her pain but could do nothing; and at the funeral she clung to me for dear life, just as she'd done when we were born.

"How could this happen? There's so much I never told them. She cried.
I reassured her that they knew how much we loved them and they us, but Brenda didn't seem to want to hear any of it.

~*~

Things became a little quirky after that and I knew something wasn't quite right with my sister. She'd become even more withdrawn and distant even with me. I invited her out for lunch to try and find out what else was going on.

"Lewis is pressuring me to have a baby," she said.

"I thought you wanted a family." I said.

"I do, just not right now."

"Are you afraid?"

"No—well maybe a little, but mostly because I'm not sure I'm cut out for motherhood."

"Well I would have thought that was something you should have talked to Lewis about *before* you got married."

"We were too busy having a good time; I guess he just thought it would be a natural progression."

I knew she loved him but quite frankly I thought she was within her rights to tell him that she just didn't want to start a family just now or the fact that she didn't feel she might ever be ready.

"I do think you should talk about with him Brenda,"
She said that she would approach the subject when she was ready. I shook my head in acquiescence but I still had a nagging feeling that there was more going on.

Three days later there was a fire at my apartment complex. I didn't sustain any fire damage but the water and smoke damage was extensive and the insurance wouldn't be able to assess the destruction for days.

"Come right over and stay with us, goodness knows we have plenty of room," Brenda offered.

Lewis was nice about it but I knew he was used to having my sister all to himself. Maybe it had something to do with that *thing she could do to the tip of his....* Well anyway it was what it was and I hoped to be out as soon as possible. But it was not to be. The insurance company was dragging its feet and the building manager—after my fifth call, said that they had not released an all-clear occupancy certificate as yet.

~*~

One night when I got a raging case of the munchies, I padded in sock-feet down to the kitchen for a snack. It was close to two a.m. and as I got to the corner of the kitchen I saw Brenda seated on the counter, her head thrown back and her legs over the shoulders of her husband as he pleasured her orally. I backed up and tip-toed back to my room and let my stomach rumble until morning breakfast.

They were both seated at the table; Lewis impeccably dressed taking a sip of his coffee and reading the Wall street Journal. When I sat down he got up and gave Brenda a kiss and nodded at me politely and left.

"Bren, I think I'm going to stay at the Claremont until my apartment is ready." I said to her thinking about the sight last night on the counter.

"No! You can't. You have to stay here. I need my sister here with me."

"I really should go Bren, I should have done it in the first place—besides the insurance company pays for it."

"Why? Don't you love me? I like having you here with me; it's almost like it was when we were kids."

"But we aren't kids anymore. You have Lewis; he's the one you should be focusing on."

"Oh sure just leave me here with him when all he wants to talk about is babies and where I go on my days off."

That part was true, even I had noticed it; she was always going on extended runs after work, lengthy shopping sprees or the gym on the weekends. She pleaded with me to stay and I did. After all she was my baby sister even if it was only moments.

Unfortunately she insisted on bringing me in on some of their marital issues which I tried hard not to get involved in. I started eating a good many of my meals out and came home either while they were watching a television program or asleep. Brenda insisted however, that we always have Sunday dinner together—which of course I had to practically cook because she was practically useless in the kitchen.

One Sunday evening as we sat at the table, they were continuing a discussion that had started in the living room that I had caught bits and pieces of from the family kitchen. When I heard her raise her voice, I went to the door and announced that dinner was ready. Hoping that my culinary offerings would quell some of the discord they were having, but I was dead wrong.

"You just don't want to hear anything I have to say Lewis, it's always all about you," she said after swallowing a fork full of potato salad.

"Of course I listen; all I'm saying is that because of our work schedules we have so little time together. The weekend is all we have right now."

"I like to run after a stressful day you know that, and sometimes I need to be with friends or my sister."

"Your sister is right here," he said eyeing me, "all the time."
I was positive he hadn't meant it the way it came out but the meaning was clear.

"I offered to go to a hotel but…" I started to say.

"Yeah I know, but *she* needed you," he said to me with a surly grin.

~*~

The next Saturday I told them I would be at the library all afternoon and then most of the evening with friends. I was halfway across town when I remembered that I had left a book and two videos I'd borrowed from the library and since they were on hold for someone else the fines would be triple so I turned the car around and went back to Brenda and Lewis'. I let myself in and was on my way upstairs when I heard Lewis.

"What do you mean you don't want to?"

"I'm not in the mood," I heard my sister say.

"What's gotten into you? All of a sudden you're having a problem with this?"

"It's not all of a sudden. Didn't I do it two nights ago?"

"So we're keeping count now? And besides your sister was here so I had to keep quiet."

"It's no wonder you're louder than a train horn," she said. His voice had grown softer. "That's because you suck me so good girl. Ooh that thing you do with your teeth and then your tongue right on the tip drives me wild. Here baby, just touch it, it's all ready for you,"

I was stock still; I didn't want to even look in the direction their voices were coming from. The only thing I could do was to ease right back out. I turned and slowly took a step and landed right on a squeaky floor board. I turned and looked at them just as they looked at me. Words wouldn't come and I stood looking like a *peeping tom.*

"Great, just fucking great," Lewis said turning away and adjusting himself back into his slacks and left the room.

I stayed away that night and in fact I didn't come back for two days. When I finally did return, it was late but they were sitting at the dining room table eating. I went in and sat down.

"Look, I'm sorry I walked in on you the other day. I don't know what to say. You know I love you both but my being here is a problem. I'm going to stay at hotel until my apartment is ready."

Lewis didn't say anything, but Brenda nearly leapt out of her chair.

"No! What are families for if they can't help each other," she cried.

Every Day Stories

I went to her. "Brenda, I love you and this is your home, yours and Lewis's. Whatever is going on between you two does not need the added complication of a family member."

"I need you Alisa. I need you here. There are things on my mind and …,"

"Baby…" Lewis soothed, "That's why I'm here."

"Please Lewis, I can't do this right now." And she stalked away and ran up to their bedroom and slammed the door.
Lewis's shoulder's drooped. "I don't know what's wrong. Everything was so good in the beginning."
I knew I was taking a chance on butting in but he sort of kind of opened that door.

"Lewis, did it ever occur to you there maybe things in a Brenda's life that she might not be ready for, or even want."

"Alisa, you're my sister-in-law and I love you, but I think it's time you let Brenda live her life and figure things out for herself," he said softly but with firm conviction.

"I'm here because my sister said she needed me," I retorted.

"What she needs is to stand on her own and not have you interfere—and I mean that in the nicest way possible."
By then Brenda had come back downstairs.

"He's right Alisha, I need to stand on my own. There are things on my mind and I just have to deal with it."
But I knew my sister; she wouldn't deal with it and whatever was on her mind she was probably never going to address it."

"Bren we are family and I don't want to *interfere but…*"
I threw Lewis an indulgent look.
Lewis stepped between us.

"I'm her family too Alisa and I love her more than you can ever know."

"Then why are you forcing her to have a baby when she is clearly not ready?" I shouted but confused when he looked from me to her then back at me again.

"I haven't even mentioned children," he said.
I glanced at my sister.

"Of course I'm hoping just like any man would, but I figured it would happen when the time was right."
Now I was staring at her completely puzzled. The look she returned was almost like a *Star Trek Vulcan-mind-meld* that was as close to begging as she could get without saying anything.
I looked at Lewis again and gave him a half smile.

"Well perhaps I misunderstood. I thought she might be hinting at something like that. I guess I got it all wrong."

"Well maybe it's something she and I need to talk about—privately," he said.

"You don't have to beat me outta here with a *get-lost* hammer," I said with humor trying to ease the mood. "I'll just get my stuff and I'll call ya later."

I stayed at the hotel for a week and finally I received notice that I was allowed back into my apartment. It wasn't a total disaster, but I had to replace carpeting, wall paper and two appliances, but a least that would keep me busy.

~*~

I had some men friends I *played* with but I wasn't serious about any of them which is probably the reason none of them lasted very long. Somehow there seemed to be something missing with them but I couldn't figure out what. There were some who delivered the sex goods okay and one of them even did me so good I thought my hollering would bring two police dogs and a S.W.A.T team. Then there were those mediocre lovers—the ones who always *thought* they were rocking my world but weren't doing shit except annoying the hell out of my anxious libido. Of course there were two that took me to the best restaurants in town and bought me all kinds of nice trinkets but couldn't just one of them have all the goods—looks, money and could grind me like a Columbian coffee bean?

Things must have gotten better with Brenda and Lewis because she started calling me all the time again and we'd talk and giggle for hours just like we used to. There was no more mention of babies and I figured she and Lewis had resolved that particular issue and seemed to be spending much more quality time together.

Then one night about six months later she called me and she kept hemming and hawing—not getting to the point so I knew something was wrong.

"Come on Sis tell me, just spit it out." Brenda didn't speak right away which wasn't like her.

"I need a favor," she finally blurted out.

"*How much* of a favor?" I laughed into the phone.

"It's not money."

I knew it couldn't be that because Lewis gave her a monthly allowance that could feed a family of four for weeks. But there was something in her voice that made the hairs at the back of my neck prickle.

"What is it? Lewis hasn't done anything stupid, because if he has…"

"Of course not Alisa, stop being so dramatic," she said.

"Well what then?" I said impatiently.

"I need…"

The suspense was killing me. "Yeah, you need…"

Another long pause, then… "I need you to be me."

"Oh is that all." I said with relief. For a moment I thought it was real trouble.

"What is it? You need to bow out of work for a few hours?"

We hadn't done anything like that for years but it wouldn't be hard.

"No, it's more than that. I have to go out of town and I need you to be here…with Lewis."

I didn't think I heard her right. "What?" I couldn't believe it. "You want me to impersonate you with your husband?"

"Yes." She said quietly.

"Oh hay-ell no girl." Then went on to tell her on how many levels that was insane I was *not* going to do it.

"You know I wouldn't ask you if it wasn't really important."

Her tone was charged with pleading and I knew the only thing that bred that kind of desperation was another man and I had to call her on it.

"Who is he?" I asked trying to control my anger.

"I can't talk about it right now, but if you love me and as your identical twin sister you will do this one thing for me and I swear I will never ask you to do anything like it again, I promise."

"Brenda, I know we've done some crazy shit back in the day. But this is a matrimonial line I just can't cross—I won't cross."

"Please sis, I need to go—it's only for a few days. I'll never ask you do another thing, I swear."

"Brenda, what the fuck is going on? Who is this man?"

"It's no one." Her answer was quick and final.

"You've never lied to me."

"And I'm not lying now. Come on Alisha please. It's just for a few days."

"How few?" I asked suddenly cautiously.

"Seven."

Her voice was a whisper and I could almost see her cringe expecting the tirade she knew I was about to lay on her.

"Seven days?" I shouted into the phone. "Girl the whole world was created in six where the hell are you going without your man for seven days?"

"It's just something I gotta do... and there's something else too."

I rolled my eyes. "Isn't there always? What?"

"I need you to work at my office as well."

"Brenda just because I freelance doesn't mean I'm not on call."

"I know but that's why it will be so easy for you. Please Alisha I really need you to do this for me," she pleaded.

She was a receptionist so her job wasn't all that hard. "What about Lewis, he's your husband, don't you think he'll know the difference."

"How? Remember at my wedding when I made you put on my dress? He never knew you weren't me."
I remembered all right. There was no way I could un-hear the whisper in my ear of his intentions to put me in *deep-dick hold* on our honeymoon—or *their* honeymoon, I should say. But this was different there would be no way I would be able to fool Lewis for seven full days. I had to refuse this ridiculous idea.

"No sis... I'm sorry I can't."

"Yes you can. Please. I need you to do this. I promise I'll explain everything later."
After much arguing, pleading and even a threat of bodily harm— to herself not me, I finally relented with conditions. The primary one being that she cut the trip down to five days.

We agreed and I met her at her job that next Friday while Lewis was at a late business meeting, drove her to the airport in *her* car then proceed on to *her* house. My mind was in a panic as I wondered how I could ever have agreed to this. We hugged at the airport and she promised she would explain everything when she got back.

I took my time driving back to her house as a million scenarios went through my mind.
Finally I pulled into the garage and took a deep breath before entering through the side door to the kitchen. Thankfully Lewis wasn't home yet and it gave me an opportunity to go up to their bedroom and find something familiar of Brenda's to wear. The phone rang and I stared at it like it was tentacle monster. Finally I picked it up; it was Lewis asking about dinner.

"Um... baked chicken with peppercorn, basil potatoes and salad."

"Really? What'd you do hit Alisha up for her recipe?" he laughed.
Stupid! Stupid! I had made that for them when I was staying there. "Um yes." I was offering as limited responses as possible and hoped like hell my sister had at least one chicken in her refrigerator. He made small talk then asked me more than once if

I was okay. I told him I had cramps, grateful for thinking up the excuse so fast.

"Well I'll you later hon. Love you."

"Um… me too," I said and hung up quickly.

~*~

I did my level best to stay out of Lewis' way when he got home. I prepared the dinner—used too much basil in the potatoes, and over cooked the chicken, after all if Brenda was supposed to be cooking it, it couldn't be perfect. Then I went to the bathroom and locked myself in and got into a nice hot bath.

"You okay in there?" Lewis said rattling the door knob

"Be out in a minute," I said.

I waited until I didn't hear him and got out of the tub, dried off and dressed in Brenda's baggiest sweat pants and largest top I could find. I went downstairs to the kitchen and heard Lewis turning on some music in the den. I noticed that while I had been in the tub he had set the table in the dining room and brought out the salad and tongs. I bent down to the oven to take out the potatoes and jumped when I suddenly felt his arms around me as he whispered something exceptionally naughty in my ear and felt his erection hard against my backside.

I wiggled gently away from him. "Lewis what about dinner?"

"It'll keep. I want my dessert first."

"I…I've got cramps." I moved around him and went to check the table.

"Yeah, it's like the second time this month." He said with irritation before plopping down in his chair.

"It happens sometimes."

"Maybe you should see a doctor," he said.

"I'm just crampy that's all."

"Perhaps a suck on a *little Lewis Midol* can help that."

I glanced up and corralled my horror to see him rubbing his exposed heavy headed erection.

"Lewis!" I said and went to the kitchen to get the rest of the food.

I made sure I stayed up as long as I could; waiting for Lewis to go to sleep. I thought about sleeping in the spare room but knew it would only raise more questions. No matter how far to the edge of the bed I went, Lewis always found a way to snuggle up against me in his sleep. What had I expected, after all he thought I was his wife.

The next morning I awoke to find his hand on my bare breast so I very gently dislodged it from my very erect nipple and laid it back down and got up.

~*~

The next two days passed pretty uneventfully. I stayed out of his way as much as possible, but there are some things that married couples can't avoid, like the small touches when he passed by me, or coming into the bathroom when I was taking a shower and his eyes all but devouring me. I prayed for the week to pass quickly.

Brenda called me every day at work but she never gave away much of what was going on with her. Two days before she was due back, Lewis phoned and said he'd be working late and he and his business associate would have dinner out.

Great! I thought. For the first time since this whole thing started I would be able to relax. I poured myself a glass of wine and thought with any luck I would probably be asleep when Lewis got home. I poured myself a nice hefty glass of Merlot, put on a CD and curled up on the sofa with my *kindle*. The strains of *CAUGHT UP* by *Usher* filled the air and I stopped reading to sing along. Two glasses of wine and three songs by *Alicia Keys'* later, I was feeling warm, cozy and buzzed. It wasn't until I found myself dancing to *LET'S GET IT STARTED* by the *Black Eyed Peas* that I noticed the bottle was empty.

I didn't even hear Lewis when he came in and when I saw him standing in the doorway with his brow knitted in consternation. I shimmied over to him.

"Come on let's dance." I pulled him to the center of the living room.

"You been drinking Brenda?" his eyes revealed his puzzlement.

I tugged at him until he started to move jerkily. I was sweating from the wine and exertion and the silk t-shirt clung to me. I saw his eyes trained on my taut nipples, but I didn't care because I was feeling too good. The music ended and almost immediately a seductive reggae tune started.

There's something about island music that just speaks to the hips. Mine began to roll and turn like they were oiled. I felt like a python as I slithered around Lewis, rubbing against him. The peasant skirt I was wearing flared when I turned revealing legs that were soft and curvy. I moved closer and caught the scent of his cologne. Something like a small beacon at the back of my brain kept trying to tell me something, but I refused to listen as the music took hold of me.

Suddenly Lewis's arms were around me, and his body pushed against mine, his lips parted and his tongue feathered over mine. It was so sexy and I began grinding my middle against him. His erection was so hard it hurt my leg. Again the warning and again I ignored it.

"No cramps?" he said.

"I'm finished with them," I murmured against his neck.

"That's real good news baby." He crumpled my skirt up in his hand and then roved over my bare buttock.

"Where's your panties woman?" his eyes were glittering with excitement.

"Why? What you want ain't in them right now."

"Damn right," he said and moved his finger over my pussy.

I gasped as he parted my labia and teased me until my body began to release the juices it stored up for moments such as this. He pulled my legs up and over his strong ones, holding me against him; the barrier of his clothes didn't even matter because his fingers were caressing my backside quite nicely.

"Oh Lewis, I want… I want…"

"Go on baby, tell me what you want."

The words popped from my mouth like water on a hot griddle. "I want it hard, long and deep." I breathed at him, my nostrils flaring with yearning.

"Then lay yourself out for me, because tonight you'll get all that."

I went to the couch and leaned over it with my back to him. I perched one bare foot on the cushion then pulled my skirt up exposing my solid, runner's behind. Over the music I heard the rustle of his clothes as he shed them. The cool air teased between my legs as I waited with anticipation. Without preamble I felt myself being splayed apart and then his tongue as it began its pleasure dance. I moaned with delight as Lewis brought me to heights I'd never experienced. From crack to crack from *taint* to crevice he consumed me. Each time I released and thought it was over, he was at it again licking and lapping me until I thought I would die from ecstasy. My stomach was aching by the time he pushed himself inside me and colored lights exploded before my eyes as he began to pump.

"Condom," I said breathily. But he only answered with words of carnal love bordering on obscene and I had never been more excited in my life and made me want to give back every bit of what I was getting. He couldn't get enough of me. We made love in every position and I gave no thought to anything except the pleasure.

It wasn't until I awoke the next morning with an earth trembling headache tucked securely under Lewis's muscular arm that the veil of betrayal and dread cascaded over me. *What had I done?* I tried to slip out of the bed but Lewis stirred and pulled me close again.

"No baby, stay with me. I can't believe how deep I was in you last night." He said sleepily.

I hushed him and rubbed his hard flat back until he fell asleep once again, and then I slipped quietly out of bed and from the room.

~*~

I avoided Lewis most of that and all of the next day and told him that I was meeting some friends and would be home late. I had to get hold of my sister but she wasn't answering her cell even after I'd left several frantic messages. When I got back to the house it was late and Lewis had fallen asleep on the couch, he looked so peaceful. I didn't want to wake him and tiptoed upstairs, undressed and fell into a deep sleep.

Early the next morning; I got up and went to a local coffee shop so that I could get my thoughts together and to try and reach Brenda again. I was frantic with worry and left her a message that if she didn't call me back, I was going to tell Lewis everything.

I used my pent up nervous energy to take a long walk around town before driving back to Brenda and Lewis' house.

I hadn't expected him to be home in the middle of the day and almost shrieked when I saw him in the kitchen filling a picnic basket.

"Lewis, you didn't go to work today?"

"Nope and we're going to the Cove." He said winking at me.

I told him I had a headache and that I just wanted to lie down.

"No worries sweetheart, the clean crisp air will take it right away—not to mention the goodies I packed for lunch."

He was insistent and figured it was go with him on the picnic or risk a day-time bedroom romp.

It was an hour's drive and although I had been there before it was still one of the most beautiful and peaceful places in the state. We found a secluded spot, although there was no one around the middle of the week and Lewis wanted to make love almost immediately but I persuaded him to *wait until later*, hoping like hell there would *be* no later.

Ordinarily I wasn't as concerned with creeping with another woman's man especially if *he* started it, but this was my sister's man and you just don't do that. As ashamed as I was of my behavior I couldn't help remembering that Lewis had done

170

things to my body that I only dreamed about and if Brenda was getting it like that, there was no reason on earth why she should be anywhere but in *his* bed. I was damned mad. I was mad with myself for doing something unspeakable and mad at my sister for asking me to impersonate her and *super mad* that she *was* getting and currently missing out on the kind of loving that I desired all the time.

It began to drizzle so we packed up and headed home. By the time we got there it was a full-fledged thunderstorm and had knocked out the electricity in the entire neighborhood. Lewis lit candles and I groaned because his lascivious grin told me he had more on his mind. I told him my head still ached and he suggested *we* lay down in the bedroom and he would stroke my temple.

"I'll nap in the spare room for a bit. If I feel better I'll come in later," I said with the sweetest smile I could muster. Less than an hour later, with the storm still raging outside, he stood in the guestroom doorway stark naked and ready. His smoky voice filtered over to me and before I could say a word, his mouth was devouring every inch of my body.

"I love you baby, I love the way you smell, the way you taste. I love the way you feel in my arms and I love the way you love me back," he said nuzzling my neck.

I was in heaven and I was in hell.
We spent the rest of the night romping, eating fruit, drinking chardonnay and making love. Nothing mattered. I pushed every thought of what I was going to tell my sister or even *if* I was going to tell her out of my mind. I was locked in a tumultuous sea of guilt and regret and what about Lewis? He didn't deserve this treachery. I wasn't in love with him, but I was caught up and craved the sexual attention he gave me.

Brenda was due back and it couldn't come soon enough for me. It was to be the same scenario. I'd go to her job as usual, leave her office—pick her up at the airport and then she'd drive *me* home then continue on to hers and no one should ever be the wiser.

Instead, all hell broke loose.

There was a meeting at her job that lasted most of the morning and there was a brief I had to prepare—which I had no idea how to do. I made an acceptable excuse and was given a time reprieve. Obviously they valued Brenda and her work ethic and I didn't want to ruin that when the CEO asked me to attend a lunch meeting with him and a new client.

It was almost two when I got back to Brenda's office and the answering machine was blinking. I turned it on to speaker, while I thumbed through her files looking for one of her presentations. *Alisa! Where the hell are you? Call me at the San Diego Police Department as soon as you get this. Please! And hurry.*

I stared at the phone as confusion and fear gripped me.

"Alisa? Why did she call you Alisa?"

My blood chilled as I turned and looked right into the stunned face of my twin sister's husband, the man I'd been making love to for the past few days.

"Lewis...I... what are you doing here?" the words died on my lips as recognition registered on his face. He slammed the office door shut and advanced toward me.

"I came to take my wife to lunch, what the fuck is going on?"

I tried to lie but he was having none of it.

"Cut the bull? You're not Brenda. I should have known. She never rode my face the way you did. What is she doing in San Diego?"

"I don't know Lewis, I swear I don't know."

"Horse shit! She tells you everything. Now why is she calling you from an out of town Police Department?"

I was shaking so hard I thought my teeth would rattle out of my mouth. "I have no idea, but I'll find out." I looked up the number for the San Diego Police department and dialed. I told the desk sergeant who I was and that my sister had called me. He

informed me that Brenda Palmer had been charged with assault and battery and she was currently lodged in their jail.
I couldn't believe it, there had to be a mistake. He went on to tell me that bail had been set but there was to be a hearing the next afternoon.

~*~

Lewis and I took the red-eye to California and he didn't say one word to me all the way, but the tension in his body told me he was on the very edge of exploding with anger.

More shock greeted us when we arrived at the hearing. Sitting in the same room with Brenda was Courtney Bettis, her boss and the *same* woman who had introduced Lewis to her. The poor woman who had been reasonably attractive now had two black eyes, a broken arm and her nose was packed and bandaged. *What was she doing here? Had there been an accident?*

As the story unfolded, both Lewis and I dropped our mouths in shock. The court reporter read the transcript aloud before Brenda was asked to sign it. *Brenda Palmer found her lover, Courtney Bettis in bed with another woman and attacked..."* it read.

What? It couldn't be. My twin sister—the one I'd known everything about all our lives was a lesbian? It would be laughable had it not been so tragic.

Brenda evaded looking us and was forced to pay damages that included all of Courtney's medical bills, a little for pain and suffering and agreed to an order of protection. Lewis seemed to age before my eyes as he came to grips with two things; his wife had been dishonest about her sexual preference and we'd both played him.

Outside the courthouse, Brenda tried to explain that she was Bi-sexual and not a lesbian and that she really *did* love him.

"You love me?" he shouted. "You love me so damn much that you lied and what's worse you allowed your sister to impersonate you? He snorted out a laugh.

"It's all my fault Alisa didn't even want to do it. We never meant for it to get this far."

"But she did agree to it now didn't she?" He smirked. "I should have known. You never showed the kind of creativity in bed that she did."

"What?"

My sister's eyes glared at me so coldly I could only look at the ground. "You slept with Lewis?"

"I didn't mean to. It just happened."

"You bitch!" she screamed at me.

"You forced me into it," I screamed back."

"We talked about the ways to avoid that, but obviously you both had other ideas," she glared at Lewis.

"You can't blame him. It was us—you and me, we did this." I said.

"You screwed my husband?"

"It was wrong, I was wrong and I'm sorry." I was being genuine.

"Lewis how could you not know she wasn't me?" Brenda said to him with tear filled eyes.

"I guess the same way I couldn't know that you liked going down on women."

She looked down with shame. "I wanted to tell you I just didn't know how."

"You and Courtney…" he grunted. "I guess she had an agenda all along when she introduced us. It was to keep you close and cover yourselves as well."

"It was foolish I know, but…"

Lewis threw up his hands to stop her from going on. "I was the one who was a stupid fool, but I won't be ever again. Both of you can go to hell and take Courtney with you because I'm sure that devil-bitch knows the way."

And with that he hailed a cab and left.

~*~

That was six months ago. Brenda and I haven't seen each other in all that time. I moved to Philadelphia and worked as temp at an Advertising agency. They really like me and want me to consider working full time. But of course I can't think about that until after the baby is born—mine and Lewis's. I called Brenda to tell her about the baby, I felt it was the right thing to do, but she hung up on me.

The last I heard Lewis had taken a job overseas and no one has heard from him since.

My child will be a constant reminder of my foolishness, but also a gift that lets me know that the world goes on no matter what and I live with the hope that someday I be able to mend the broken fences between my twin sister and me.

The most unlikely man

Jasper Smoot was a big pain in my neck. He'd been after me to go out with him for more than a year and just couldn't seem to take no for an answer. He was a slim meek mild-mannered man of about 5'9, a mere inch taller than me, with sallow skin and round dark eyes. He wasn't horrible, but he was definitely no *Shemar Moore* either. His hands were a little too soft and I don't think I could ever be serious with a man who had feet smaller than mine. He wore the same outdated blue pin stripped suit and black thick soled cordovan lace-up shoes every day.

His hair was cropped short and he didn't appear to have much of a butt, or anything else of worth in the sex department as far as I could see and knew I could never be seen with someone like him.

Okay I admit I may be a little conceited but it's not my fault. I was graced with my grandmother's earthy hips, small waist and dancer's legs that went on forever. I can't help it because I'm light skinned with Mariah Carey hair and green eyes. It's how I was born. People have old me all my life I was gorgeous and I guess I thought I was privileged to do what I like to anyone I liked when I felt like it. I didn't have to chase men they chased me, and I enjoyed the company of every type that came running when I crooked my little finger. I was used to being with the cream of the crop—tall, handsome men with skin tones ranging from onyx to milk. Only those with money and a lot of it dared approach me and I was used to having the best there was to offer. I went to the best clubs, ate at the finest restaurants and enjoyed premium seats at any sold-out performance of any show or ringside event. And while I could certainly understand Jasper's fascination for me, my annoyed confusion couldn't comprehend why he thought he even *remotely* had a chance. I doubted very seriously if he'd even been to an elite restaurant or enjoyed the finer things I was used to. But still he tried, and each and every time I turned him down.

I was growing bored of working and was on a mission to find the tallest, handsomest, richest man I could and make him my husband. I didn't care what color he was or where he came from or who he belonged to. I just wanted him to be able to tell me that I didn't have to work ever again if I didn't want to, someone who would give me a platinum American Express card with *his* name on it, along with a big house where I could bring all my purchases to. It was hard work weeding through all the high-profile men to find just the right one and even *I* had to take a break. But I was also beginning to experience a dry spell in the male/companion/lover department and as much as I tried to ignore it, I couldn't. Some men with whom I'd had made previous arrangements began canceling or made excuses; and none of my usual booty-call friends were returning my messages or text. I did find ways to occupy my time but it involved me spending my own money and I didn't take to that very well.

~*~

My office cohorts were big pranksters; and I had even been the butt of one or two of their best *gotchas*! But even with all my smug arrogance I didn't really want to participate in the jokes and pranks they had played on poor Jasper. But this time when they told me what they wanted to do, it was just too funny to pass up. We set it up with me pretending that I didn't have a partner for a dinner dance that is held annually at a place called *Club Affirm.* I was by coffee machine in our office break room pretending to be upset over the fact that I had bought an outrageous outfit, but the man who was supposed to take me had to go out of town on business. My buddy Gwen, who was in on the joke waited until Jasper came by to get his morning cup of Java before she began her sympathetic tirade.

"Oh Charmaine, that's so sad. Girl what are you going to do?" She said to me with a wink.

"I don't know, I am supposed be a judge at the dance and its important. I guess I just won't go." I sniffled, struggling not to laugh. I heard Jasper clear his throat and pour his coffee. I saw Gwen swivel her curvy hips over to him.

"Say Jasper, you have any plans next Saturday?"
He hemmed and hawed before answering. "Well I... uh I..." he stammered.

"Charmaine has a dilemma and I think you might be just the one who can help her out."
He looked over at me and I gazed back with blinking sad eyes.

"I know its short notice and you probably have a hundred things you'd rather do than go with me to some stupid dance." I said.

"Please Jaspee..." Gwen puckered her lips and played with his collar allowing her finger to graze his neck.

"Well um sure. I'll be happy to take you."
Like I knew he wouldn't. We couldn't help but pour it on.

"You'll have to get a Tux and some new shoes."

"Um sure, I can do that." he said eagerly.

"Good," I said straightening and started back to my cubicle.

"Um what's your address? " I heard him call out.

"I'll call you in a couple of days with the details." There was no way I was going to have him show up at my place before time—oh hell no. On the way home, Gwen and I couldn't stop laughing.

"Girl you ain't right, I couldn't believe those crocodile tears you were shedding," she said.

"You weren't any better you lying snake, but this is going to be too funny. I wish I could be there to see his face."

"Me too, but there ain't no way I'm going anywhere near *Club Affirm.*"

Only a few people knew about our joke, and it was hard to keep them from spilling the beans because they were laughing so much.

~*~

The atmosphere at work began to change. There was talk of a merger and everybody was in an uproar. The slackers suddenly became productive and the overachievers nearly killed themselves with long hours and extra work. *I,* on the other hand decided to use my womanly wiles that had never failed me, to achieve my purpose in retaining my position.

Herbert Salton, the President of the company was making trips down to our floor frequently to meet with various managers and the upper supervisory staff. I tried my level best to acquire information about the secret meetings from the few men that were included, but their mouths were shut tighter than a miser's bank account. I made it a point to dress sensibly everyday just in case Mr. Salton came down but when you have a figure like mine it's hard to hide what I have to offer. I made sure I was within eyesight of him and his staff every chance I got and I knew it was just a matter of time before he noticed me. The wedding band on his finger meant nothing to me, it only advertised that he was not available but if he didn't bite then he could probably put me in touch with some of his important business partners who could.

~*~

The evening of the joke on Jasper, I called him and said that I had to make a stop at a sick relative's house and that I would meet him inside *Club Affirm* within the hour. He offered to come and take me wherever I wanted to go and had in fact arranged a Limo to ride in. That was certainly an unexpected surprise, but I had to forgo the elegant transportation in order to go along with the joke.

By eleven o'clock Gwen was on the phone laughing her head off. "Girl I would give a month's salary to see Jasper's face right about now."

"There's no way he would know that *Club affirm* is a gay, bondage club and he's the new meat." I giggled back.

"He's gonna be mad as hell on Monday girl."

"So what, did he really expect someone like me to be seen with him? Not on your life."

"Speaking of being seen, what happened to that investment banker you were planning on going out with this weekend?" Gwen asked.

I winced, hoping she'd forgotten that I'd mentioned him. "He had to go to Amsterdam or Paris—I forget which, on business." I said making an excuse.

"Well maybe he'll bring you back something expensive and sparkly."

I didn't know what to say, the truth was I hadn't heard from Melvin Kirkwood in over three weeks. We'd had some wild sex but he failed to pass my erotic standards—like most men actually, but their money more than made up for it.

Monday morning, we were all waiting for Jasper to come in in. The office was taking bets that he wouldn't show, but he did. Gwen and I were standing off to the side and watched as Jasper braved the gamut of giggles, sniggling remarks and guffaws with his head held high. For an instant I felt really bad about the trick we'd played on him.

Later during a meeting, he looked over at me with sad eyes and I'm not sure if they were sad for him or for me. There had been no apologies or talk about the joke and I figured that he thought this was just another crude joke we'd played on him.

~*~

The merger looked like it was a go. The next few weeks were a flurry of super confidential meetings and classified memorandums. Mr. Salton still smiled at me whenever he came down and I wondered what was taking him so long to make his move.

A few weeks later, I was working late one evening when Jasper poked his head into my cubicle. Ordinarily I would have been gone but I'd taken an extra-long lunch hour to get my nails done and to do a little shopping and I figured my staying a little later might look good in case any of Mr. Salton's cohorts came down after hours as they sometimes did these days.

"Charmaine, I was wondering if I may have a word with you."

He was so damned polite. I knew what was coming and decided to make my apologies and leave.

"Look Jasper, if this is about *Club Affirm,* I need to apologize for that. I really did get hung up with a sick relative and it took longer than I expected; I guess I should have called." I lied.

"Things happen and I'm willing to let bygones be bygones…" he said ignoring my half-hearted attempt at an apology. "If you'll allow me take you to dinner and you agree to…"

He hesitated and I raised a brow wondering if he had to gall to ask me what I thought he was going to ask me.

"…If you will agree to spend the night with me."

The laughter that exploded from me reverberated throughout my office. "Spend the night? Me— with you? Jasper, are you crazy?

His gaze never left mine, giving me time to cease my jocularity.

"Things are changing here Charmaine; there might be a chance that I may be in a position to see that you go where the company goes."

He sounded so self-assured that my instinct told me there might be something to what he said.

Hell! What was one night? I'd done one *nighters* before. Besides, by the time I finished rocking his world there would be no telling what he'd do for me *in* and *out* of work.

I still intended to keep Mr. Salton on the backburner so I had to make sure this little episode would be just between us.

"All right Jasper, I'll have dinner with you."

"And spend the night?" he added.

"I'll stay all night." I said it like I was giving him a gift.

He smiled and said he would call me with the details. It was the same thing I'd said to him about Club Affirm. When the smile left my face, he assured me nothing was going to be amiss.

"Don't worry Charmaine; I don't intend to leave you hanging in a gay bondage nightspot the way you did me. I promise you will enjoy our evening."

~*~

The date was set for Friday night. I left work early and went to great lengths to make sure I was going to be a knockout. There was no telling who might see me, even though I figured Jasper would be taking to me a Diner or another mundane, local eatery.

At 7:00 sharp he rang my bell and when I opened the door I couldn't believe my eyes. He looked like Jasper, and he was the same height, but without his glasses and with the new expensive suit and polished shoes he looked like a totally different person. He held out a single long-stemmed American beauty rose.

"You look lovely Charmaine. Shall we go?"
Normally I invite my male guests in for a drink but I didn't bother with those niceties with Jasper.

Outside, a sleek stretch limousine purred at the curb. The chauffer opened the door and Jasper held my arm gently to guide me in.

"This is nice, I guess you been saving your pennies eh Jasper?"
He just smiled and pressed the bottom on the intercom.

"Yes Mr. Smoot?" the soft spoken chauffeur said.

"Did you get the air report Joseph?" he asked.

"Yes sir, its all clear and we'll be at the heliport in about fifteen minutes."
Heliport! I was stunned. "Jasper, where are we going?"

"You'll see."
I almost fainted as we arrived to a large corporate building near Beverly Hills. We entered and took the elevator to the roof. A

pilot waited as we made our way toward the helicopter. I was scared out of my wits but my excitement overrode it.

Fifty six minutes later we landed in San Francisco and then whisked off in a tricked out hummer to *Chateau Andre*. I was impressed that Jasper even knew about a place like this, but when the Maître' addressed him by name I almost fell of my black silk Vaneli pumps.

After we were seated at a lovely table he proceeded—in fluent French, to order three different wines for the three course meal we would enjoy.

"Jasper, you are just full of surprises aren't you?" I said looking around at the sophisticated crowd.

"There's a lot you don't know about a person until you really get to know them."
I must admit that although I was all set to be bored to tears, I found Jasper to be quite entertaining and never guessed that he had such a broad range of interests, including sky diving, deep sea exploration and of all things, ballroom dancing.

It was close to eleven when we finished dinner. He took me to a small exclusive piano bar for an aperitif and dancing. I was feeling giddy and found myself laughing at his lame jokes, and suddenly Jasper didn't seem so bad and I was really beginning to enjoy his company. He told me that he owned a house on Martha's Vineyard. *"It's only three bedrooms but its waterfront and the sunsets are gorgeous....*He also had a small boat but if things went the way he hoped they would, he was striving to get something better.

He asked me to dance and to tell you the truth when the music slowed and he had me in his arms and held me close I felt calm and safe. His cologne teased my nostrils and the even though he was thin, his legs were strong and tight against my thighs. He began to sing softly and I was amazed at his deep melodic voice.

It was one AM when he escorted me from the club. "Did you have a good time Charmaine?"

"I really did Jasper, I can't tell you how much."

"I wanted it to be a beautiful time for a beautiful lady."
He looked down, then back up at me, his eyes woeful. "Look Charmaine, this was a wonderful evening. You don't have to go through with the rest of it."

I felt sorry for him just then. The poor man probably never had or would have anything near as good as me.

"A deal's a deal." I said.

"Really?" he eyes lit up like a child with a new toy.
I hated weak men, but I guess I owed him and I was positive it would be over quickly. "Just lead the way." I said.

Again, I was floored by the elegance of the hotel he took me to. Everything was top of the line, from the fluffy bathrobes to the champagne and strawberries by the king sized bed. A small gold plate was on the nightstand and held a slew of different types of condoms. There were two bathrooms and when I went in to undress, I would have killed to have a relaxing soak in the large Jacuzzi tub. When I came out wearing only lacy panties, thigh high stockings and my pumps, he was in the bed covered with sheet, his eyes devouring me. I shook my curls until they waved around my face, then I looked at him sultrily. Judging from the way he was covered up I figured I would have to walk him through everything.

I went to him, and he pulled the opposite side covers back. I slipped in and moved up against his body. In a moment his hands were on me, teasing me.

"I'd like to show you how I feel Charmaine, will you let me?"

How pathetic! I thought—but glibly said, "Sure, knock yourself out."

He kissed me and it was nice in a soft sort of way. It was when he raised my hands above my head and began a rain of sucking and kissing down my chest that I felt myself getting warm and excited. I had never noticed or had reason to notice how long and thick his tongue was and as he licked up and down my thighs I thought I would go mad. I kept moving, hoping he would get to the point of my excitement, but he didn't, he stopped and looked up at me.

"I know what you want Charmaine and I am going to give it to you, but a lot of the pleasure is in the getting there." His voice was low and sexy. He murmured against my inner thighs and vibrating so close to my pleasure spot that I thought I'd die from the want.

"Do you want my tongue?"
I was beside myself with yearning, "Yessss, I do." I moved my hand over his head hoping to guide him, but he grabbed them and pinned to my sides.

"Then say it."

"I want your tongue Jasper; I want it so much, please." I said wiggling myself to him.
He teased me even more, his tongue making feathery motions until finally he gazed up at me.

"Then hold yourself open for me, so I can eat it deep,"
I was pulsating with the thrill of his words and my legs fell apart like they were on oiled hinges and I reached down and pulled my lips apart. Instantly his tongue began exceptionally rapid strokes. I rose up to meet him, but he moved away, causing me to moan out my anguished disappointment and need.

"You want more?"

"Yesss more," I moaned.

"Then give me your clit."
Without any rational thought I exposed my secret nub for him and writhed like a demented banshee when he tickled and sucked it and wouldn't let go. I was amazed at his wiry strength in keeping me pinioned with just the motion of his mouth and I was surprised to find that I liked it—I liked his control. He didn't let up for close to an hour and by then I was hoarse from moaning and my stomach hurt from so many pleasure releases.

"I know how you like it Charmaine, turn over."
I begged him to wait, but he touched me in every place that held bliss and I complied and turned, raising myself onto all fours. Wetting me once again with his tongue, I felt him slide in me—

and he *kept on* sliding in me. No one would ever know that Jasper Smoot could fill a woman like he was doing me. I thought he'd finally reached bottom when…

"Just a little more; you can take a little more can't you?" *How could that be*? I had never been with a man who had such length and I wanted it all.

"Yes Jasper, give it to me give me all of that long cock of yours." I pushed back and painfully took the rest of him.
He moved in me so expertly and so wonderfully that I found myself calling out his name over and over.

It was 4 a.m. and I was exhausted.

"Shall we go again?" he smiled rubbing himself.
I begged off, telling him I needed to sleep a bit and he smiled and covered me with the sheet. He was kind and sweet and I knew I had misjudged him. He held me and I fell into a deep satisfied sleep.

~*~

When I awoke hours later, the bed was empty beside me. I figured Jasper was in the other room with a whole banquet of goodies; after all, everyone was always hungry after great sex. I pulled the sheet around me and padded to the other room. It was empty. I called out, but there was no response. Panic struck me as I searched for his clothes. They were gone too. I rang the front desk and asked if there were any messages from Mr. Smoot. The stuffy concierge told me there was no one registered by that name, but a message had been left for me.
I refused to believe what was in my mind. I looked for my clothes but they were gone, then searched for my purse but it too was missing. I had nothing, no clothes, no money, no credit card not even my driver's license. I dialed the front desk for the clerk to have the message brought up to me but he told me there was no one available and that the room I was in needed to be vacated as soon as possible. I told him I had a little problem and pleaded with him to send a maid to my room.

When she arrived, a short fat Hispanic woman with an attitude when she saw that there was no way I could leave a tip, she asked me what I wanted. I told her that someone had robbed me and had even taken my clothes and if she could please find me something to wear I would make sure to send her a generous tip when I got home.

"Where ees home Senora?" she asked rocking back and forth on her worn out clogs.

"L.A. but I promise…"

She waved her hand dismissively speaking rapid Spanish as she walked out of the door. A few minutes later she returned with a maid's uniform that had seen better days. It was too tight, too shirt and faded from too many washings. It was horrible but it was better than nothing.
I went downstairs and asked the clerk for the message. I tore open the white envelope and instantly recognized Jasper's neat handwriting.

Charmaine, by the time you read this I will be on my way home. You can find your own way. You will learn that you can't treat people with such flagrant disrespect without repercussions. Last night was just a taste of what you will never know again.
I also doubt that your intended involvement with Mr. Salton will do you any good because he and his family relocated to another city the day before we left for our little tryst. I am also sorry to say that your wallet and credit cards seemed to have fallen out of your purse somewhere in the ghetto of L.A. There will be no need to return to work as you have been terminated. I will give your empty purse to your friend Gwen when I fire her upon my return. You see, I have been named the new CEO and the first of my duties is to get rid of all the dead wood.

Good bye.
JS

He signed his initials with a flourish. I couldn't believe it. He had this planned all along.

I was angry beyond belief, but the fact that I had no way to get home and no job when I got there concerned me even more. I was about to leave when the clerk called me back and told me that there was a little matter of the outstanding hotel bill.

Life has been a challenge for me ever since that day. Every bill for that night came to my house, from the Stretch Limo right down to the single long stemmed rose he'd brought me. As if that wasn't bad enough, I had gotten word that everything we had done had been taped and everyone in the office heard every word I said. I started getting calls from so many men asking me for dates and women teasing me about my date with Jasper that I had to change my number—twice. I am unable to find work because no one would give me a reference. All my old friends seemed to have fallen off the radar and last I heard, Jasper Smoot married Beatrice the sallow face administrative assistant and they were living large in Beverly Hills.

I learned a valuable lesson that day and the days since. You have to pay for what you do and someday you will have to *pay the baker whether you like his pie or not.*

Campus Stripper

Both my parents had been killed in an auto accident and I was living in a hellish situation with a distant relative on my father's side. *Aunt Marlene*—as she asked me to call her, was interested in one thing and one thing only and that was men and having a good time. The small house we lived in was constantly filled with the dregs of the town who barely worked and were almost always drunk.

I liked school and I loved books and spent long hours at the library or in the park reading. I hated being at home listening to bawdy jokes and drunken raucous laughter well into the wee hours of morning. I couldn't escape the muffled giggles and loud moans when Aunt Marlene decided to let one of her *friends* stay over.

The only time I ever got a real compliment from her was when we put on a school play rendition of *A star is born*. Afterwards my favorite teacher approached her.

"Allie is my star pupil you should be so very proud of her. She's made the dean's list three times in a row and I am positive she will continue to excel when she gets to college."

I won't lie, going to college had been on my mind for some time but I knew there was little to no chance of me ever being able to go.

~*~

It was getting close to high school finals and I found it hard to study with so much noise so I spent more and more time at the library. I a hardworking student but was still surprised beyond my wildest dreams when the Guidance Counselor informed me that I'd received a partial scholarship from Shawnee State University in Ohio.

"Ms. Croom your English teacher, contacted then on your behalf. It isn't much Allie, but it'll help. Of course you'll have to find a way to get the rest of the first year's money before you can enter."

"I will, I promise."

I went to see Ms. Croom to thank her for what she did for me.

"You deserve a chance Allie, and they certainly need to attract more students. They are a small school but provide an excellent academic curriculum. Your room is included the first year and I know you will do well Allie."

I hugged her and thanked her once more. I was literally over the moon and raced home to tell Marlene. As usual, the house was filled with her low-life friends who used it as an encampment to do whatever they wanted. Marlene was in the cramped, smoky den playing poker with four of her friends.

"Get me a beer will ya hon?" she called out.

I stopped at the refrigerator, which held little else and extracted a can and handed it to her.

"Pop it open for me. I just had my nails done." She waved her long, outrageously manicured fingernails at me.

"I need to talk to you a minute, it's important," I said to her.

Charlie Hinch, who was sitting at the table with her, reared back in his chair, his ferret-like eyes roving over me.

"Hey there Allie darlin', you lookin' real good these days."

I ignored him and waited for Marlene to answer me.

"I ain't got time right now Allie honey. Go on and fix yourself something to eat, we'll talk later."

I knew it was no use, and just as I turned to walk out, I saw Charlie reach over and give her a kiss but his eyes were focused on me.

I was disgusted by their behavior and I couldn't wait to be out of there.

I fixed myself a cheese sandwich and went into my small stuffy room at the back of the house. I waited well into the night, when Marlene's *guests* finally began to drift out to their cars to leave. Hoping to catch her before she went to bed, I left my room. As usual the house was in total disarray with beer cans, bottles and leftover fast food cartons strewn everywhere. I knew she expected me to clean it up and I would—but not until I'd spoken to her about money for college. I walked into the living room and quickly turned away as I saw her and Charlie in an almost naked embrace.

"Allie you ought not to walk in on a person like that," she said pulling her blouse together. Charlie on the other hand lay there with his legs splayed and pants undone.

"I told you I needed to talk to you, it's about school," I turned my head and stammered.

I heard the rustle of movement and then footsteps walking toward me. I turned, it was Charlie. He slowly zipped up his pants in a suggestive manner and grinned.
I hated him and had from the beginning. He reminded me of a slimy, slithery snake with his black oily hair and long veiny nose. I'd always heard that he was a dangerous man, and just the sort Marlene would take up with.

"Can I talk to you now?" I asked annoyed. "Alone!" Charlie went back and draped his arm over Marlene's shoulder, allowing his hand to brush suggestively over her breast.

"Charlie's a good friend; you can talk in front of him."

"I'd rather not." I sneered.

"Look Allie, I ain't got time for this, are you going to tell me or what?"

I knew there was no way Charlie was going to leave, so I had to go on and say what I wanted to say.

"I'll be graduating from high school in June. That's three months away. The counselor told me I had a small scholarship, but the rest has to be paid before I can go to Shawnee University in the fall."

"So?" she said tritely.

"I don't have the money; I was hoping you'd be able to help."

"And I don't have any money to give you. Perhaps it would be better if you just got yourself a job."

"I *have* a job at the diner, but it doesn't pay enough and I won't be able to work fulltime once I start school."

"Well you better get another one because I sure can't help you. I mean it's enough that I keep a roof over your head and food in your stomach." she said with a giggle as Charlie nuzzled her ear.

It made me sick and I wanted to shout at her about how I did all the housework and took care of her when she was too drunk to do it herself. I wanted to cry but I didn't dare in front of Charlie. She must have noticed my look, because she nudged Charlie away.

"Look Allie, you're a good girl and I wish I could help out, I really do. But things are pretty hard right now. I didn't tell you, but it looks like I might lose the house."

She was lying and I knew it, the small house was already paid for, so it meant she couldn't come up with the yearly taxes. They didn't amount to much so I was sure they had to have gone unpaid for some time in order to be in a foreclosure status.

"Well then," I said. "I guess I'll just have to find another way." I turned to walk out of the room and heard Charlie yell out to me.

"Hey Allie, maybe I can work something out for you."
I ignored him. I'd rather die than accept a dime of his money.

~*~

I dreaded the next two months, knowing that college was drawing closer and the chances of me getting in was slim to none.
One night just as my shift at the diner ended, one of the night waitresses came over to me.

"Here!" she said handing me an envelope.
"What's this?" I asked puzzled.
"Just a little something from the day-crew and me."
I was so touched and wanted to cry. I hugged her tightly. "Thank you so much." I said with heartfelt emotion.

"It ain't much, but we thought it might help."

I hugged her again and left with tears of gratitude in my eyes.

As I walked home I wracked my brain trying to figure out how I was going to get the rest of the money for school.
As I approached the house, my heart sank. Marlene was having one of her *get-togethers*. Cars lined the street in front of the house and rowdy laughter and cursing emanated from the open windows. She might not have money for the yearly taxes, but it seemed there was no end to it for buying cigarettes, beer and marijuana.

I steeled myself to fend off a barrage of groping's and lewd comments and entered the house.

"Surprise!"
I almost jumped out of my skin when I saw the slightly weaving crowd of Marlene's friends standing under a banner decorated with diplomas, caps and gowns that read, *Good Luck Allie!*

Marlene moved forward wearing and outrageously scanty outfit and hugged me tightly. I could smell the liquor on her breath.

"Allie Honey, I have a surprise for you."
I could see Charlie smiling like the devil he was in the background. She pulled me over to the lumpy couch and sat down with me. Reaching into her bodice, she pulled out a folded white envelope. "Here!" she said proudly.
I took it and turned it over in my hand. "What is it?"

"It's your future."
I looked at her with puzzlement.

"Go on open it," she urged.
Slowly I ran my finger under the flap and tore the envelope open. Inside were two money orders. It was for the full amount I needed the start of my first college year. I gasped aloud. "How?" I asked looking at her.

"Funny thing…" she started and I hardly noticed her nervousness. "I had this little ole insurance policy tucked away. Plum forgot all about it."

"You cashed in your life insurance policy? I can't let you..."

But she pushed my hand back. "Now don't you worry your pretty little head about that. It wasn't doing me no good laying in the drawer so I cashed it in.

I was still excited, but then remembered the house taxes. I put the money orders back into the envelope and handed it to her. "I can't take this." Her face paled as she glanced back at Charlie quickly. She shoved it back. "Sure you can honey."

"You'll need it for the house. I won't let you lose it."

"Oh that! Don't worry; there was enough to take care of everything. The taxes will be paid this week. This is for you."

"Really?" I could barely contain my happiness. I hugged her tightly. "Oh thank you. You won't regret it. I'm going to be the best student. I promise I'll get all A's."

"You'd better," Charlie chimed in. "Marlene is really counting on you doing just that."

I was so happy about being able to start college that I didn't even care about him.

"Thank you, so much Aunt Marlene." I hadn't called her that in years and I saw her flinch a little when I said it.   The others crowded around me, patting me on the back and wished me well. The next thing I knew Charlie had spun me around and was hugging me close—too close.

"You make us proud Allie, ya hear?"

I felt stifled in his grip and glanced over at Marlene who had a queer, embarrassed look on her face. I extracted myself from his sweaty embrace and offered a small insincere smile.

"I will Mr. Hinch, I surely will."

~*~

I graduated from high school with honors and Marlene didn't even bother to come. It was just as well because I knew she'd never come without Charlie and I didn't want him there.

No one offered to drive me to Ohio which wasn't that far since we were on the border of Michigan, so I packed a suitcase and a duffle bag and bought a bus ticket. Marlene and Charlie were still asleep when I left, so I write a quick note of goodbye and promised I would write or call when I could.

~*~

I had arrived. I was standing in front of the Shawnee University Administration Hall, beaming with pride and anticipation. It was a bustle of activity with students from all over the surrounding counties and other cities. Parents were dropping off their kids who were carrying trunks or bags of everything they would need for the next few years away from home. I felt a little sorry that I had no one, or that everything I needed was all I had with me. Still, it all seemed too good to be true and I expected to wake up and find that it was all just a dream.

But it wasn't and I wanted to leap for joy when the clerk handed me my class roster and room assignment. I was in! I was in college.

~*~

My roommate Carol Brisco was a pretty African American girl who had lived right in the same county as I did, but we didn't know each other since she lived completely on the *other* side of town—even poorer than ours but as much as anyone didn't want to admit, it was better kept by the residents there and didn't look half as shoddy as ours did.

She was shy and didn't share too much about herself except that she had obtained a full four year scholarship. We had some of the same scholastic interests and we had two classes together. She seemed apprehensive at being friendly and for the first few weeks and kept to herself even though I made every effort to engage her. It didn't take long for me to find out that she was a far better student than I was and seem to have a natural ability concerning logic and I enlisted her help in some of my studies. It's also how I learned that she wanted to be an educator and I knew it was the right choice for her because she was good at it. The one thing however, that I knew interested her more than anything else… was clothes. She loved the latest and the greatest. She was always impeccable and matched to a *T* even in ultra-casual mode. She watched the local infomercials and sales programs on the little television she'd brought with her and exclaim over some sweater, blouse or slack set. I grew concerned when she started ordering more expensive things and I had to finally chime in when I saw her searching the online sites and purchasing high-end apparel.

"Carol…" I said one evening as I watched her peck away an order for a *Tory Birch* handbag starting at four hundred seventy-five dollars. "Are you really going to buy that?"

"Sure, with the money my folks saved with my tuition they can send me what I need. It's one of the perks of being an only child," she giggled.

It wasn't only the handbag, it was clothes, shoes, and fashion jewelry and absolutely *nothing* that contributed to her education.

~*~

The first semester sped by with lightning speed. I was amazed at all I'd accomplished in such short period of time but still horrified by all there was left to do.

Carol didn't hang out with me except in our dorm room, but she started going out with a popular group of sophomores and seniors. "You should come with us sometime Allie; these girls really know how to party."

But I declined because partying was something I didn't have time for. My mind was strictly on my studies which gave me little time for anything else—until I met Frank Durant, all 6'5 of him with sparkling eyes and hair the color of a raven's wing. I had been hurrying to my social science class one morning when I collided right into him. Books and papers flew everywhere.

"I'm so sorry," I apologized and made an effort to retrieve everything as fast as I could

"It's not your fault. No one expects to run into a human wall this early," he joked and helped pick up my books.

"Thanks!" I said as I took them haphazardly and ran on toward the building where I was already late for class.

"Hey! What's your name?"

I heard him call out. But I was in too much of a hurry.

Later that day, I went to the commissary for dinner and was engrossed in a Criminal behavioral Studies text manual.
"Well that's not very nutritious."
I looked up and there was the giant I'd crashed into earlier.
"Well actually I already ate *real* food. This…" I pointed to the chocolate cake on my tray, "is just a little reward to myself."
He smiled and my heart started doing the stupid pitter patter dance of infatuation.
"I'm Frank Durant by the way. Mind if I join you?"
A blush crept up my face. "Not at all; I'm Allie Morrison." I condensed some of my books that literally took up half the table and a chair to make room. He sat down and even then his height was still amazing. He made small talk and before I knew it we fell into a comfortable, easy conversational pattern about the school, the area and his family.
He was very good looking with his angular jaw line and deep-set green eyes. But it was his bone straight, jet black hair that caused me to stare.
"Choctaw!" he said when he'd caught me gazing at it.
"Excuse me?" I said turning my gaze back to his face.
"I'm one quarter Choctaw Native American, hence the dark hair. My eyes are compliments of my Irish mother."
"I didn't mean to stare." I said apologetically.
"It's okay. I'm from Oklahoma; a lot of us have this look."
He was quite a jokester and I surmised it was just his way of getting people's attention off his height.   Afterwards Frank walked me back to my dorm where we stood outside and talked another few minutes.
When I finally went to my room I noticed that Carol wasn't there. As a matter of fact, she'd taken to coming in quite late the past few evenings and had missed several classes. There

was no way she'd pass her exams if she kept up her current extra-curricular activities, whatever they were.

A couple of hours later just as I was coming out of our small bathroom, she came in. She looked tired and I could see that she was wearing the remnants of some garish makeup and her hair was styled as I'd never seen it before.

"Carol, are you okay?"

"I'm fine," she said and hurried passed me and into the bathroom. When she emerged a few minutes later, her face was clean as she padded to her bed wearing just her under-things and fell across it. In a moment she was fast asleep. She was still asleep the next morning when I tried to rouse her but she brushed me off and told me she had a late class. I left the room and told myself I would check on her during my lunch break.

I hurried downstairs and out the front and stopped fast when I saw Frank sitting on the top step.

"Good morning, I thought I'd walk you to class. Do you mind?"

"Not at all," I said like it was nothing, but inside my heart was jumping with joy and fell into step with him.
That was beginning for Frank and me. He was a senior and getting a degree in Business Economics and Agriculture.

"Going for my Master's and Ph.D. as soon as I finish, don't want to waste time," he said with a lady–killer smile.
He loved to talk about his family, his career choice and all the things he wanted to do in life.

"I want a family someday Allie, a great big one. I want to share the love in my heart with a good woman and kids to go with it."
He was always starry-eyed when talking about his future and it filled my heart.

As time went by, our friendship grew into more and it didn't take a genius to see that I was falling in love with Frank. I never said anything to him, but it was almost impossible to hide how I felt and I was hoping he had some real feelings for me. I really couldn't tell because although we kissed a few times, he never tried to go any further. Then one evening as we walked back to the dorm, he just said it like it was the simplest thing in the world.

"I guess I ought to come right out and tell you that I'm in love with Allie."

"Are you sure it's not just my divine personality?" I joked.

"*Including* that but I can make a list if you want, but I think you get the picture."
I did and as he entwined his fingers with mine I walked with him in blissful happiness.

~*~

Midterms had me so busy I didn't notice the passage of time or the mail that was building up on the small battered cheap wooden desk the school had provided for me. It wasn't until I received a call from the campus finance office that I knew something was wrong.

"Miss Morrison, I'm sure it's just an oversight but we haven't received your tuition for next term," the finance Officer said with a knowing smile.

I didn't know what to say. I'd completely forgotten. I had no money of my own and no idea what to do. I was enjoying college and I was excelling quite well. I knew I had to call Aunt Marlene. I punched in her number and much to my annoyance Charlie Hinch answered who was making inane and barely disguised inappropriate conversation. After repeatedly asking to speak to my aunt he finally put her on. I raced through my dialog about the money, pleading with her to try and help me. She listened then told me to wait a minute. I heard muffled voices on the other end and the next voice I heard was Charlie's.

"Don't you worry your pretty little head about a thing Allie; a check will be sent express mail tomorrow."

I sighed with relief. "Tell Aunt Marlene I said thank you and I'll pay her back every cent."

"Oh you surely will honey and I'll tell her."

I was still on pins and needles for the next twenty-four hours. *What if she changed her mind and didn't send the money? What if the envelope got lost?* It hadn't gotten lost but she certainly made me sweat for it because I checked right up until 3 o'clock—well after mail delivery the next day and the money *still* hadn't arrived. I must have paced a dent in my dorm room floor from worry. Two hours later I was seriously thinking about calling my Aunt again when the finance officer rang my cell and said that money order for my tuition had come in. I *yipped* with joy and wish I could have shared my good new with Carol but again she was in our room.

~*~

I spent the next weeks after class in the study hall and the library preparing for upcoming exams. I was so happy when Frank understood when I told him I couldn't see him because of my studies and often fell asleep with an open book on my chest. I was awakened one evening by the sound of Carol throwing up in our small bathroom. I sat up and waited for her to come out.

"Are you Ok?" I asked.

"I'm good," she said.

"Carol I'm worried about you. You've missed quite a few classes and you look like hell. What's going on?"

"Nothing, I'm tired is all, I just want to sleep."
She didn't even bother to change into her night-clothes; she just plopped onto her bedspread and was almost instantly asleep.

I lay awake for a few minutes and wondered if I should speak to the counselor about her, but I didn't want to get chastised for meddling.

~*~

One Friday after my last class, Frank was waiting for me outside.

"You, milady are about to be kidnapped," he said and made a corny sweeping bow.

"What?" I laughed.
He took me in his arms and kissed me tenderly.

"I've rented a room at a nice little Bed and Breakfast in Spring Harbor. I figured we both could use a weekend break."

He had so much love and affection in his eyes that I knew there was no way I could go another minute without having him make love to me. He'd been patient and kind, but I knew it was time and mostly because I wanted it too. At precisely 6:00 that evening we were watching a most beautiful sunset out of our bedroom window at *The Spring Harbor Manor.*

"It's all right isn't it Allie? You do want this as much as I do don't you?"

I knew what he meant and I knew he was a lot more experienced than I was and although I was nervous, I did want him—I wanted him more than anything. I leaned into him and pressed my lips against his. It was all the invitation he needed. Gently and sweetly he brought me to the precipice of need. I wanted him so much that I didn't much care how it happened. Thankfully his cool head prevailed and he extracted a small square from his pocket.

"I want you to know that I love you and I want everything to be right with no worries," he said huskily.

I knew it was hard for him because we'd talked about it and it had been quite a while since he was last with anyone and now he was about to bring me to womanhood. He began kissing me everywhere and as soon as I was naked he kissed me *everywhere* still. I moaned under him as he allowed his mouth and tongue to bring me to an agonizingly sweet passion. He whispered sweet things and I wanted him so much that I tried to get him to make love to me right then and there.

"Please" I begged in emotional agony.

"Soon love, the idea is to distract you from as much discomfort as I can sweetheart."

I was touched by his thoughtfulness. It was too bad that Aunt Marlene would never know the kind gentleness of a man like Frank instead of the insensitive jerks she was used to.

When we returned to Campus early Sunday morning, I kissed him and sent him off to his own dorm. Happiness filled me as I went to my room but my joy turned to worry when I noticed Carol's bed appeared not to have been slept in. As a matter of fact everything was exactly as it had been before I'd left. A queer feeling washed over me. *Something was wrong*, I could feel it, especially since Carol been acting so funny and every time I tried to question her she became even more uncommunicative or defensive. When she hadn't returned the next morning, I was really troubled and I spoke to Frank about it.

"Don't worry honey; she's probably out with her boyfriend or something."
She never talked about anyone like that, but then why should she, we weren't as close as some of the other roommates, but I was still concerned.

~*~

A week later I received a call from the Dean's office asking me to come over. When I got there, two worried faces glanced up at me. I they were Carol's parents and they said they hadn't heard from her in days. I was questioned at length, but I couldn't offer them any comforting information. The Dean tried to dispel their fears by intimating that sometimes, young girls wound up with the wrong type of boy or got caught up with an unsavory crowd.

"Our daughter isn't like that and besides she was calling us every week, now there's nothing," Carol's mother said trying to hold back her tears. The dean was sympathetic and promised to look into it further.

The campus became a bedlam of activity when the police arrived on the scene. Detectives questioned everyone including and *especially* me about Carol's habits and friends. I wasn't much help and asked them if they would let me know if there was any news. When another week passed and there was still no word, Carol's parents asked to have her things shipped home, so I packed them neatly and waited for the courier to pick them up.

I could only imagine their angst about their daughter and knew that they would never give up on waiting for a word from her. The vacated space was given to another girl who wanted to switch rooms with her current noisy roommate, but she spent most of her time with her boyfriend and didn't engage me much.

Frank graduated with top honors in June and I sat proudly watching him make the valedictorian speech. Later when he introduced me to his parents, I nervously smiled as his mother grabbed me in a tight hug. They were good solid people and later during dinner they talked incessantly about how proud of their son they were. I was proud too and very comfortable in their familial company.

~*~

End-terms were approaching and I was ashamed that I didn't think much more about Carol as my studies and *other* activities occupied my time. There had been no more monetary scares and I was on cloud nine. My choice of Criminal Justice as a major and Journalism as a minor was grueling but I worked hard and I was getting outstanding grades. I went home during some holiday breaks but it wasn't a good situation for me as the household climate hadn't changed so I usually ended back on campus early.

~*~

The passage of time had little meaning for me because I was young, busy with my studies, being elected president of the student body, the leader of the debate squad, tutoring coach and of course in the throes of first love. It was a great time for me and I enjoyed every minute of it. Frank began his Master's program while interning part-time at a local Advertising agency two towns away so I didn't get to see him much, but we talked and e-mailed as much as we could.

Before I even realized it I was a senior with graduation hot on my heels. It was only two months away it dangled before me like a deliciously sweet confection. As if things couldn't get any better, I found out that I'd been given the honor of Salutatorian *and* introducing our keynote speaker who just happened to be a well-known mega movie star and philanthropist. I was giddy with happiness. I told frank and he was over joyed for me and said he hoped he would be able to attend the graduation but is conflict with a career opportunity that had been offered.

"I'm so happy for you honey, and I hope I can make but if not, I feel we are going to be great together for a long time." *What did that mean? A long relationship? Engagement? Marriage?* I didn't want to think of anything that would have me living my life without him. And even though I had told him about my home life he said that none of that mattered because I was sweet, strong and the kind of woman he always wanted.

A month before commencement and after being fitted for my cap and gown, I returned to my dorm room and saw a large, official manila envelope on my bed. I picked it up and saw that it was from the financial department. *Oh no! Not when I'm so close.* I tore it open.

Dear Miss Morrison, we regret to inform you...
It went on to advise me that I wouldn't be able to graduate with my class because the last installment of my tuition had not been paid. I hurriedly phoned Aunt Marlene.

"Well honey, we wanted to talk to you about that. We're coming down to see you tomorrow."
We? I hoped she wasn't referring to Charlie. He was the last person I wanted to see.
As bad luck would have it, he was the *first* person I saw when I'd agreed to meet Aunt Marlene at the Cafe in town when they came.

"My! You're really looking good Allie. You've filled out in all the right places." Charlie said when he saw me, his thick tongue rolling over his lips like a garden slug. Aunt Marlene remained seated and seemed nervous and jittery.
I didn't want to be there any longer than I had to, so I made my plea to her about the tuition as quickly as possible.

"Well honey..." she began, "It's not as easy as all that. There's been some problems." She was fidgeting with her hair and her eyes kept darting back to Charlie who sat next to her with a snake-oil salesman type grin.

"I promise I'll start paying you back every cent as soon as I get a job. Please, this is very important." I pleaded.

"Well that's what Charlie—what *we* wanted to talk to you about."

I noticed beads of sweat break out across her lip.

"Charlie is a partner in a little a business. He was thinkin' well…."

She was having trouble so Charlie decided to help her out.

"Yeah Allie, I got this little business over in Buford. You can make some real nice cash."

I slid my eyes over to him. "Doing what?"

"Well, you can start out being a hostess, you know— selling cigars and cigarettes to the patrons."

"And then?" I knew there was more.

"It's a gentleman's club Allie, you can get top dollar for dancing," Marlene chimed in.

"Stripping, isn't that what you mean?"

"It's exotic dancing and there's a hell of a lot of money to be made," Charlie said defensively.

I looked at Marlene. "You can sit there and let him suggest this to me?"

She rubbed her hands together nervously. I could see I was not going to get much support from her and looked at her with sorrow.

"It's okay Aunt Marlene I'll find a way to get the money and thanks for what you've done so far. I promise I'll pay you back every penny."

I got up to leave, but Charlie was quicker and barred my way.

"Don't you mean pay *me* back?"

Then it hit me. The money hadn't come from any insurance policy; it had come from Charlie. My mouth dropped open in horrified disgust as he urged me back into the seat.

"I'd say you and me got some business to transact Allie."

I dragged my eyes over at him, repulsed by his slimy grin.

"I'll make sure you get your money as soon as I get a job." I nearly spat.

"Well it's not just that. Your ole Aunt Marlene here agreed it would be a good idea for you to earn your keep for all the years she took care of you. It's time to pay the piper."

"It's not my fault that my parents died and I'm grateful for all you've done for me Aunt Marlene…" I said to her but with my eyes right on Charlie, "but I won't be taking my clothes off for anybody." I slid out of the booth and headed for the door. In a few steps Charlie caught up with me and gripped me tightly, his nose pressed close to my ear.

"Watch it Missy, you don't want to end up like your little roommate."
Horrified I turned to face him. "What do you know about Carol?" I glared at him.
He backed away and grinned.

"All I'm saying is that you might want to rethink your decision."
He let me go and went back to Marlene.

~*~

Dazed, I walked along the street, not knowing or caring where I was going. How could Marlene have allowed this to happen? I was her flesh and blood. *Why had Charlie mentioned my roommate? Did he know something about her? How?*

I was still in deep thought when I approached my dorm.
"Miss Morrison?"
I jumped as my eyes focused on the stocky man in an ill-fitting suit standing before me.

"I'm detective Paul Novane."
He flashed a gold badge at me and my heart turned to ice. "Is it Carol?
He looked blandly over at his partner who was standing a few feet away.   "I'm afraid so. She's dead."
I fought to keep a wave of dizziness from consuming me.
"How?" I murmured.

"We believe she was strangled, we can tell more after the autopsy."

"Oh no, no…" tears welled in my eyes. "Has anyone told her parents?"

"We called them before we came over here. They're coming to claim her body tomorrow," he said dejectedly.

I hadn't been close to Carol but I was still filled with grief and wished Frank was with me for support.

"Do you have any leads on perpetrator?"
He looked back at his partner and gave him a knowing look.

"Criminal justice major I gather?" He asked.

"Yes, how did you know?"

"Terminology; and actually we do have the name of a person of interest." He said.

"Is it someone from the here?" I said wondering, because no one had ever come to the dorm to be with her

"We have a name and wondered if she might have mentioned him to you—a Charles Hinch?"

I felt the color drain from my face. *So that's what Charlie meant when he said I didn't want to end up like my roommate.*

"Miss Morrison?" He said.

"No she never mentioned him. I didn't think she even knew him." I half whispered.

"Do you know him?"

"Did he kill Carol? " I asked with burgeoning anger.

"We're not sure, but perhaps you need to come to station to answer some questions."

"Why? You don't think I had anything to do with it do you?"

"No we'd just like to talk to that's all."

Later as I sat in the detective's cramped office numb to the core after having heard the evidence he presented, he showed me photos of Carol's poor dead body, I told them how and everything I knew about Charlie, including the remark he'd made to me earlier.

"We've had our eyes some illicit operations he's been involved in for a while now. We have reason to believe that he has been blackmailing and extorting favors from young college girls in turn for paying their tuition or some other family crisis. We also think he's dealing drugs out of a dance club he manages as well."

I wasn't at all surprised by Charlie's dirty dealings, but I was stunned to the core when the detective proposed a sting operation that would involve me.

"No! I can't. I've never done anything like that."

"We'll have undercover personnel throughout the club. You'll be perfectly safe. I promise."
But I just couldn't do it. I was too upset and yes I was afraid. Detective Novane drove me back to school, advising me not to discuss the situation with anyone until they could sort out what they were going to do.

~*~

Frank accompanied me to Carol's funeral and never had I seen such sadness. Her parents were devastated and seeing her mother's agonized grief made up my mind. I knew then that I had to do what I could to help bring her daughter's killer to justice.

The next morning I contacted detective Novane. Then I called Marlene and told her to put Charlie on the phone.

"All right I'll do it." I said trying to hide the revulsion in my voice, "but only until I get the money for graduation then I'm out."

"Sure, sure; I knew you'd come around. When you see the kind of money you can make, I probably won't be able to get rid of ya," He laughed into the receiver.

He told me that I would have to come in for the next three nights for training, after that I'd be ready and he expected me to work at least three or four nights a week.

"What about school? I don't have my last tuition and I'm due to graduate soon."

"You be there and the money will be there," he said

I despised him. I hated that he'd probably killed an innocent young girl and I hated him because he was in my life.

As luck would have it, Frank had some extra time between classes and work and wanted to spend it all with me. It wasn't easy convincing him that I was too busy studying to see him and by the third brush off, he wasn't happy.

"Fine!" he said irritably, "I'll be with my friends. I'm sure we can find a diversion or two."

He stormed off, with me fighting back the explanation I wanted so desperately give him and that he deserved.

~*~

The club was in the next town only a few miles away. I noticed on my first night that there were many girls my age and a few women well into their late twenties and early thirties. They took me to a dressing room where there were racks of costumes and dresses that I wouldn't be caught dead wearing under other circumstances, then told me how to approach gentleman with a tray of cigars and cigarettes. The first night wasn't too bad except that I had to fight off the groping hands and indecent proposals of drunken men. I skipped the next night, but Charlie called my dorm while I was on my way to class the following day to tell me that one of the girls had called in and that he needed me at the club. I tried to make up an excuse but he wasn't having it.

"Maybe your Aunt and me ought to make a trip over there and have a talk with your Dean"
I was too close to graduation and I couldn't have him making trouble for me so I agreed.
I was about to put on one of the lesser sleazy dresses when Jaycee a girl closest to my age but had hard lines in her face that said she was a lot more worldly.

"Mr. Hinch said you should wear this tonight." She held out an outrageously skimpy outfit.

"I can't wear that, I won't"

"Yes you will!" It was Charlie standing in the doorway. As soon as Jaycee saw him she dropped the outfit on the chair and left hastily.

"You see how things are done. You're on the pole tonight," he said.

"I can't—I...I...don't know how."

"No worries the men out there will tell you what they want, you just dance. You can do that can't you?"
I didn't say anything and he sauntered over to me and leaned down.

"I can make it real easy or real hard for you. I can dope you up and use you anyway I want or let anyone else use you if I want. Your Aunt owes me and I intend to collect so you get that sweet little ass out there and rub on that pole, or..."
I couldn't believe it as he unzipped his pants and took out his penis. "...rub on this one."
He stroked himself suggestively. I hurriedly picked up the indecent garment and held it close to my chest, staring at him.

"Good, I'll give you some privacy—for now." And he turned and walked out, readjusting himself zipping up his pants as he went.
I undressed and donned the embarrassingly lewd costume. Sweat broke out on my forehead and for a moment I was dizzy as I heard he music start up and heard Charlie addressing the raucous crowd and applause then whistles and cat calls as I assumed once of the girls began her routine. I was looking for something—anything to cover my almost exposed breasts when Charlie re-entered.

"It looks good on ya Allie, but you'll look a lot better when it's off."
He disgusted me.

"What do you say you and me have a little drink after the show?"

"No thank you. I just want to do this and get out of here," I said.

"Darlin' when you see the money that's gonna be thrown at ya you'll be beggin' me to stay on. Now you go on out there and make us both some dough."
He slapped me on the backside, making my skin feel like a thousand spiders were all over me as I walked passed him.

I stood in the wings off the stage waiting to go on. As I peeked out, I could see that the club was crowded with seedy looking men and to my surprise a few women and I almost lost my nerve.
Relief covered me when I saw detective Novane and three others—whom I assume were undercover cops, weaving drunkenly into the room. They were stumbling and boisterous, but managed to keep their faces shadowed out of the immediate view of the bouncers who stood around the club. One of them was laughing and yelling out loud. "Girls! You got em, I want em," he slurred waving a wad of cash.

"This way gentleman, have a seat right down here in front!" I heard Charlie say.
I sank back into the curtain and prayed that everything would go as planned and that this ordeal would soon be over. A few minutes later he came back to me.

"Allie baby, we got a full house and some big spenders out there. Now you get out there and strut your stuff and make some real dough tonight."
One of the bouncers came over and whispered something to Charlie.

"Well now it looks like it's going to be a very lucrative night for everybody," he grinned.
The introduction music began and I broke out into a sweat.

"That's your cue Allie, go out there and wow em!" he said lasciviously and reached out to touch me. Afraid as I was, I didn't relish his hands anywhere near me and I circumvented his contact and slid out onto the stage.

Rude comments and cat calls began immediately and drunken men began lunging at the stage. I began to move amateurishly slow and the cat calls soon became hisses and boos.

I glanced at Charlie in the wings and his face was dark with anger and threat. I began to move more suggestively, twerking and gyrating the way I'd seen others do and how most women did on explicit music videos. Drunken men leered and waved ten and twenty dollar bills up at me then throw them up onto the stage. I saw a satisfied look on Charlie's face as he slithered to a dim corner and sit down with a dangerous looking scarred faced man.

A series of *boos* resounded and loud yells of *take it off and get on the pole!* Filled the room.

I caught Charlie's angry gaze, but he continued talking to the man.

The catcalls were getting louder so I slowly reached around and undid the sequined bra and removed it but kept my breasts covered my hands as best I could, and threw it out into the crowd hoping that would suffice.

Out of the dimness a hand reached up and caught it. A wave of dizziness overcame me so severe I thought I was going to die on the spot when the figure holding it stood up. It was my boyfriend Frank.

Words froze on my lip except for his name that barely had a sound. He just stared at me and if it had been a look of disgust I might have been able to handle it, but it was his expressionless face that told me he was sorely disappointed. I wanted to go to him, but suddenly all hell broke loose as two drunks were trying to climb up on the stage and grab at me. Two bouncers were hurrying to the stage shoving Frank aside when suddenly...

"Freeze! Police!"

Relief washed over me as uniformed officers stormed in. Everyone began running and I was being knocked around every which way by people climbing onto the stage and running in every direction searching for a way out of the club. In a blur of activity just as I saw Detective Novane and his men handcuff Charlie; I felt strong arms around me. "Come on let's get out of here."

It was Frank. I was relieved but afraid too. How was I going to explain all this to him?

He took me to the back and we waited until put on some decent apparel.

"Frank, I need to explain about this." I said pulling on my blouse.

Just then detective Novane entered. "Miss Morrison, are you alright?"

I shook my head.

"We got him. I'm sure Hinch's cohorts are going to want to cut all kinds of deals. I can't begin to thank you for your assistance. It's all over; we got everything we came for."

I smiled shakily and looked at Frank. He reached up and pushed a wayward curl away from my face.

"I knew something was wrong, so I followed you that day and saw you talking with that creep in the diner and then to the good Detective. I had to know what was going on. He let me in on everything. You were always safe honey, because I was always right here."

I began to cry. "Even when I first came down here?" I sniffled. He laughed and hugged me, "Yes, I was right here in the shadows."

"Why don't you two get going, we'll finish up here," Detective Novane said.

As I was about to leave that seedy den of horror wrapped it the arms of the man I loved, the detective stopped us.

"Oh by the way, there's a twenty-five thousand dollar reward for Charlie Hinch's capture. It looks like it's all yours Miss Morrison. I'll call you in a week and you can sign for it." Frank and I left and never looked back.

"Say," he said as I got into his car, "You think you can show me that little dance number you were doing up there?"

"Not on your life buster. I want to forget this whole thing." I laughed and pulled the door shut.

~*~

Later that week, we found out that Charlie was in serious trouble in more than one state. Aside from blackmail allegations and drug running, he'd also been implicated in the murder of Carol. He was going to jail for a long time. With the reward money I paid my last of my college tuition and sent the rest to Carol's parents.

As I proudly left the podium after accepting my diploma, I couldn't wait to get started on what I wanted to do which was study criminal law and eventually marry Frank.

"No worries honey, we'll make sure all your dreams come true," he'd said.

Those words stayed with right up to the day I said *I do* to the only man who I will ever love.

The Fairest Gentleman

I was too through with northern corporate America. After ten years of loyal service and staying late and going above and beyond the call of anybody's duty, the new blond, twenty-four year old senior manager, who'd been working for Langstone Technologies for about five minutes brought me into the conference room and told me my position was being eliminated because,

"You don't possess the skillsets for the direction that the company is going in."

Resolving myself not to get as ugly as I could have, I did have one question for this new brain-dead office showpiece. "Would you mind telling me what the skill-sets are that you say I *don't* possess?" I politely asked.

She looked at me with bright canary egg blue eyes and said: "They haven't been officially defined yet."

"Then how do you know I don't have the skills?"

Her face reddened. She knew she was caught in a dead-in-water-corporate-sponsored-stock excuse for firing people. With a glare that could cut stone, but a smile that let her know I knew more than she ever would I politely gave her a little advice.

"I realize why you're here and how you got here. However I'm not sure what you'll be doing—if anything, but if you intend to be the hatchet-person, don't use that bullshit excuse on anyone else that you just gave me. It makes you sound uninformed and stupid." Then with the dignity I possessed from the moment I walked into that company, I gathered my belongings and left the *Langstone* Corporation.

~*~

They'd given me a decent severance package and while I was determined that I would make no major decisions so soon after the trauma of my downsizing, I did just that. I sold my condo and my car, packed my things and moved myself to Alabama—my grandmother's birthplace.

Things had certainly changed in the town of Summerdale. Blacks were living quite well in upscale neighborhoods and I was happy to find a small house in a gated community that had all the amenities I had become accustomed to.

Armed with a Master's degree, superb references and determination I went job hunting and was elated to find that I was received with genuine interest in my ability to do the jobs being offered. It took one week, hardly enough time for me to get situated in my new home before Human Resources Reps from the three different companies called telling me I had the job. Now my dilemma was which one I was going to take. Finally I settled on the one that offered a little less money but a lot more position and prestige, hoping it would eventually open the door for me to even more lofty exposure and it was closer to home.

By the end of the fourth weekend however I was socially bored to tears. Thumbing through my phone book I searched for people who hadn't moved away or died and finally found the name I was looking for. I hadn't seen or spoken to Carline Daniels in years and wondered if she'd even remember me. I dialed her number, expecting a cool reception but hoping she could at least direct me toward something more sociable than staring at the paint on my living room wall.

"Hello Carline? This is Paulette Mason." I had to move the receiver away from my ear when the high-pitched shriek ripped through the phone.

"Paulette? Gurlllll, where you been?"

I winced at her southern country drawl. I told her that I'd just moved back and was hoping to hook up with old friends. If she was surprised by my call, she didn't let on and asked when we could get together. I was immediately ashamed of the fact that I hadn't kept in contact and that she exhibited the country charm and friendliness as though no time had passed and seemed so happy to hear from me.

"Let me give you my number and address. You need to come over and say hey to Big Mama." She said.

I wrote down the information noticing that it wasn't in the best of areas and I thought I'd left all that behind me. I wasn't excited about taking any steps backward.

I did hook up with Carline and her maternal grandmother who was just as big and loving as I remember not to mention her still able to make the best macaroni and cheese in the world.

~*~

Carline insisted I come with her to a club the following weekend. I told her I didn't have a car yet and she quickly offered to pick me up and I gave her my address. "Oh by the way, what's the dress code for where we're going?" I asked.

"Dress Code? Honey the code is that you should wear something as nasty-stank as you wanna."
Her laugh was loud, bawdy and crass. Unsavory visions circled my mind when I thought of the club she was going to take me to but figured I'd suffer through it this one time only. Besides, if I didn't get out soon I was going to burst into tears.

Saturday arrived and when I peeked out of my window and saw Carline pull up in front of my house in her ten-year-old dodge with *Ja-Rule* blaring from over-sized speakers, I was almost sure I'd made the wrong decision in reconnecting with her. I was positive when I saw her step out of the car wearing a blood red tubular dress that was so tight I could see the cellulite dimpling her expansive derriere. I'd always thought the object of wearing a thong was *not* to be seen but that certainly wasn't true in Carline's case since it creased her middle and made her ass cheeks move like two rambunctious kittens playing under a blanket. I opened my front door and with a forced smile then waited as she teetered up the four concrete steps on heels that were way too high and grabbed me in a bear hug.

"Girl... You're still skinny as a pole bean—but you look good. Is that your real hair? This is a weave but it's a good one, I go to Miz Pinkies down on Sutter St. and...,"
She was talking so fast I hardly had time to listen or answer. She had on too much of an unfamiliar perfume and her makeup although flawless was unneeded because in spite of her weight, her face was even prettier than I'd remembered. Her teeth were white and straight and her eyes were as clear as summer day.

I was ready to go, but manners dictated I invite her in. To my relief she said we'd better get going because it was almost an hour's drive to the club and parking was terrible if you didn't get there early. As we drove, she chatted on and on giving me updates on people she thought I ought to remember. All the while I was running an academy award winning makeover for Carline in my head. I was almost bursting with ideas on how I was going to change everything about her.

To my surprise the club, *Chez Gerard,* was in Clayton County nestled on the corner of a series of high-end boutiques, exclusive Jewelry stores and small neat office buildings. There was a line of people standing outside a velvet rope where a large, well-muscled bouncer in a dark suit stood sternly picking and choosing who would be allowed in and who had to wait.

Carline rolled her plump hips right up to him, pulling me along. His expression didn't change but I was impressed to see that he reached down and unlatched the velvet rope to let us pass.

Inside, I watched Carline as she greeted almost everybody. Several handsome men came over and planted a quick kiss on her chubby dimpled cheek or gave her a hug.

"Hey Carline, when you gonna stop messing around and marry me?" one said.

"When you die and come back single, with no kids and lots of money," she said to him with a laugh.

We entered the main room of the club. The music was jamming and the bar was full of good-looking people. Mostly women since that seemed to be the way of the world these days. People were dancing, talking, laughing and having a good time.

The bar was jumping and the bartenders were working like a turbo machines. The music was good and I couldn't help moving to the beat as Carline pulled me toward the end of the bar.

"What you drinkin' she asked."

"White wine and I got it," I said reaching into my purse.

"The hell you do. This is your first time home in ages girl this night is on me."

Everyone seemed to know Carline, and our order was filled in moments. I leaned against the bar and perused the area and that's when I him; and my eyes nearly popped out of my head.

"If that ain't a hunk o man, I don't know what is." I said half under my breath.

"Who?" Carline asked looking right over the object of my admiration.

His pecan skin was smooth as a baby's and his smile was wrapped around teeth that were *just-left-the-dentist's-office* white. His hair was cropped short with waves that were brushed back away from his face. He was a big man, thick and meaty like a lumberjack, and when I saw him walk toward the bar I knew there was grace in his soul.

"Right there walking toward the other end of the bar," I gestured.

"Aww girl that ain't nobody but my cousin Junior, he moved here from Clater County right after you grandma passed."

"A junior what? Refrigerator?" I said racing my eyes up and down his frame.

"Girl please, come on, I'll introduce you."

His name was Randall but they called him junior because he was the smallest of his three brothers. Whew! I hated to see the size *they* were. He was polite but I scowled inwardly at his singsong country drawl and his clothes were so mismatched I couldn't believe he even knew what a suit was.

"You want some more to *drank?*"

I winced at the misuse of the word and declined politely.

"Okay, it was nice meetin' ya. I'll see y'all later." He left and walked over to a small crowd of women who shrieked and exclaimed over him like he was Will Smith or something. *What did they knew about male sophistication*, I thought meanly.

~*~

I'd accepted the position offered at SB Communications as the senior head of Marketing. Donald Trayton, the Vice president of Production was tall, handsome and smart, just the sort of man who was in my league. The thing was I felt no spark which was unusual for me. But it was just as well, because office romances never worked and almost always jeopardized the woman's employment status but hardly ever the man's.

For the first few weeks I stayed late getting the lay of the land and building strategies. One night after I'd finished going over the SOP manuals to make sure I was familiar with all of the company's policies and procedures I decided to stop at a sandwich shop on my way home and pick up what was to be my dinner. I was looking up at the menu items trying to decide, when I felt the air shift beside me.

"The pulled pork will have your mouth watering like a bull after a cow." I turned and let my eyes travel up the barrel-like chest to the familiar face of Randall.

"Oh, good evening Randall."

"Call me Junior, everybody does."
That name didn't suit him at all and I refused to address him by it.

"I don't eat much pork." I stated with my nose turned up like I smelled something disagreeable. His laugh was loud.

"Then you need to get on up outta the south. Pork is a main staple here. Carlie said you were raised here so I'm sure you've been introduced to bacon at one time or another."

I let the offhanded insult slide and ordered a chef's salad paid for it then gave Randall a barely polite smile as I left.

Two days later Carline called me on the phone. "Paulette, whatcha do to that man?"

"What man?"

"Junior. He's been calling here four times a day for the last two days asking questions about you."

"I don't know why he should."

"Come on girl, you ain't been in the big city so long that you don't recognize when a man is interested in you do ya?"
I laughed. "I hardly think Randall has designs on me, and if he does it's just because I'm new," I said.

"Well if you don't want him, then stop looking so good because there's a line of woman just waitin' to get at him. Mayleece Cummings wants to marry him in the worst way," she laughed into the receiver and I closed my eyes at the thought of what a *Mayleece* looked like.

"You don't remember my baby sister Eunice do ya? Well she's a lawyer now and she's gettin' hitched. It's gonna be at real nice hotel in town called the *Ritzy Glitzy* or something, it's supposed have a five star diamond rating so it must be the bomb."

"I think you mean the Ritz Sheraton. Yes, it is one of the finest hotels in Alabama."

"We're all going, why don't you come along?"

"Oh I couldn't."

"Sure you can. Look, Junior's been holding off going because ain't got no date, you can go with him."

"What about Mayleece?" I asked with no intention of going.

"If he'd wanted to go with her he'd have asked her by now."

"I don't think so Carline, but thanks for the invitation."

"Well you think about it, you might change your mind."

~*~

Carline told me that Randall owned a contracting company and had five employees working for him and even though he was crazy busy, he was always looking for new clients.

I called and asked if he'd come over and look at my deck which needed some repair work. Three days later he came over and gave me an estimate. I watched him through the kitchen window while he measured and took notes. His muscles jumped and bunched under his tee shirt and his thick neck looked strong and appealing. He didn't make much small talk this time, but was still friendly as he handed me the estimate and advised me that it was always good to get three estimates and I would find that he was competitive and is work spoke for itself.

~*~

I went to church with Carline on Sunday and it seemed the whole Collins and Daniels clans were there. At the end of the service I had shaken more hands than a newly elected president. Carline's grandmother insisted I come over to for dinner and when I tried to refuse, she called Randall over. "Junior, you bring Paulette on over to the house, she's having supper with us. I'll ride with Essie."
I started to protest but she was already walking way.

"It's best not to argue, just go along; it's much easier that way," he said with humor in his voice. He escorted me to his truck opened the door and I got in and sunk down low in the seat hoping no one would see me in a contractor's truck on a Sunday afternoon.

Dinner was the typical southern fare, too much of the very best of everything. My mouth watered over the platter of fried chicken, mashed potatoes with dark rich gravy, collards and turnip greens, macaroni and cheese and of course the best potato salad I ever tasted. I thought I had no room for dessert but made some for the piping hot deep-dish apple cobbler.

I insisted on doing the dishes and Randall came in to help. Carline whispered to me on her way out of the kitchen.

"He near bout gave Big Mama a stroke. He ain't never offered to help with the dishes before."

Later, I thanked them for a great meal and the laughs and asked Carline if she would mind driving me home.

"I'll take you, it's on the way," Randall interjected.

Protesting was out of the question as Carline gave me her best *"uh huh"* look and winked.

We rode in silence for a while and just before he got to my house he turned on the radio, the soft melodious voice of Boyz II me singing, *I'll make love to you* drifting into the air.
"I was wonderin' if you'd like to go with me to Eunice's wedding next month."
I hesitated trying to find a believable excuse.
"I'd really like it if you'd go with me," he continued quickly.
I thought about it for another minute. *How could I refuse? When else would he get a chance to show off someone as sophisticated and dress-savvy as me?* She thought.
"Of course Randall, I'd love to go."
~*~
Two days before the wedding I treated Carline to a beauty treatment session at the *Serenity Garden Day spa,* then took her over to the *Bronze Beauty* make-up counter for a lesson on applying barely-there cosmetics. Our last stop was the BIG PEACH EMPORIUM, specialists in stylish plus size eveningwear.
"I ain't got the money for all this, "she complained.
"I don't *HAVE* the money for all this;" I corrected "It's my treat to you for being such a good friend."
In reality I didn't want to be anywhere near her if she wore one of her tacky ill-fitting outfits.
The only other thing that bothered me was what Randall would wear to the nuptials. My outfit was going to be stunning and there was no way I wanted him beside me wearing any Bo-hunk country ass clothes. I called him.
"Hi Randall, I was wondering if you were going to wear a tuxedo for the wedding."
"I hadn't intended on it, I have suit. I wore it to Eunice's Graduation."
I grimaced. Eunice had been out of school for years.

"Since this is such a special occasion—and I know you want to look your best on her special day, perhaps you should think about renting a tuxedo," I said too sweetly.

"Do you think it's necessary?"

"Yes!" The word came out of my mouth like a frog leaping off a hot rock.

"Well if it's that important than I think you should come help pick it out."

"Of course." I leaped at the chance, relieved that I didn't have to drag him kicking and screaming into my *Fashion makeover arena*. I was a genius.

He didn't bat an eye when I coerced him into an expensive tux, shirt, shoes—the works but I was shocked when he bought everything instead of renting them. "You never know when I might need it again," he said with a mind blowing smile.

~*~

When Randall came to pick me up at my hotel room on the day of the wedding, I was aghast at how utterly handsome he was all dressed up, even though he was clearly uncomfortable in the finery and almost bashful as he offered me his arm. I couldn't hide my surprise when he escorted to black Lexus sedan.

"What no truck?" I teased.

"It's a special day, with a beautiful lady.."

The ceremony was lovely. The bride and groom recited loving vows and to the delight of everyone, the guest soloist was a member from the renowned singing group, *Boyz to Men*, and an old friend of the groom. Everyone looked nice, but I was especially proud of Carline who looked like an angel in her soft green sheath evening dress with white crystal beads and seed pearls. It was a marvel that had taken inches off her copious frame.

I had a wonderful time and actually enjoyed being in Randall's arms when we danced. A couple of times when he left me to dance with other female guest I found myself oddly irritated.

After the wedding as we prepared to go back to home I fully expected to ride with Randall. I was disappointed when he told me Carline would take me then sauntered off to a lovely woman who awaited him in the foyer.

I was silent most of the way and fuming inwardly. Men just didn't leave me by the wayside that this big country ass Bohunk had done just that. By the time we reached the town border I had to know.

"Carline, who was that woman waiting for Randall?"

"I don't know and I don't expect he knows either. Women are always chasin' after him," she said as she waited at a red light.

"I didn't figure him much for one night stands."

"Aww it ain't nuthin, he might just be takin' her for drink."

I didn't figure that, not with the way the woman was smiling at him when they left.

~*~

I didn't hear from Randall until two weeks after the wedding when he called to find out if the following Saturday would be a good time to begin repairing my deck.

"That would fine, if in fact you don't have anything else to do— like taking someone you don't know out on a date."

I don't even know where the comment came from, and I was utterly embarrassed, especially when he didn't even respond to it.

He arrived so early Saturday morning I was still bleary eyed from sleep and in my worst looking PJ's when I opened the door.

"Thought you might like one of Big Mama's cinnamon rolls," he said handing me a plate wrapped in foil and then went back to his truck to get his tools and began his work.

I showered, dressed and made myself a cup of coffee— asking him if he wanted a cup. He said maybe later, so I just sat down and enjoyed the cinnamon roll. I knew if I kept eating like that I would be as big as Carline and I was not about to let that happened and ate only half.

I kept going out and asking Randall questions about what he was doing and I'm sure I was being annoying—which usually wasn't me. It didn't appear like he was going to mention the wedding, so I did.

"Did you enjoy yourself at the wedding Randall?"

"Did you?" his answer was immediate but I detected no malice.

"Yes, it was an elegant affair, and you were quite dapper." I said smiling.

He stopped working and stared at me for what seemed like a full minute.

"That's important to you isn't it?"

"What?" I asked curiously.

"Making sure that you look good and the person you're with looks good too."

I hesitated and he took it as a confirmation to his statement. The jangle of my phone interrupted the thick silence between us.

"Excuse me." I said entering the house and picking up the cordless phone. It was Helen Jackson, from my old office up North.

"Hey girl how's things?" I said. We spent a few minutes catching up and I was happy to hear the new person they'd hired in my stead wasn't working out. There was even talk of trying to woo me back.

"Well that will happen only if the price is right." I said to her.

She asked me about what was going on in the romance department and I told her nothing was even remotely on horizon.

"Believe me; it would take an army of clothiers and make-up specialists to get these country-fied people into the 21st century."

I told her about taking Carline for a complete spa treatment and makeover and her laughter urged me on to keep her entertained.

"Girl! I had this date for a recent wedding and I'm telling you if I hadn't taken the *big-hefty country-ham-hock-of-a-man* to get the right clothes they'd still be laughing at his multi-colored zoot suit he might have worn." We giggled then laughed uproariously as I went on and on. I twirled around on my stool and saw Randall standing at the deck doorway. The blood drained from my body down to my feet. His eyes were glazed and the brief fury etched on his tight lips was replaced with a teeth-grinding statement.

"I just came in to tell you I have to replace two rotted railings."
I told Helen I'd call her back and went to him.

"Randall...I...I..." how could I explain away the insulting conversation I was sure he'd overheard?

"I'll send one of my workers over next week, he'll finish up."
I didn't know what to say and all I could do was watch him pack his tools and leave.

~*~

If Randall said anything to Carline about my behavior she didn't show it. I was sure he hadn't because she was the kind who'd be all over me in defense of a family member. On Sunday when she called and asked if I was going to church, I told her I had a headache.

"Come on girl, praising the lord will cure any ache or pain you have. At least for a little while anyway, I'll pick you up in a half hour."

The last thing I wanted was to see any of them and I certainly didn't want to go to any dinner. I wasn't dressed when Carline arrive but she pushed me into the shower and had a suit on the bed waiting for me when I got out.

Seated in a back pew, I saw Randall walk in with big mama. He looked toward us, inclined his head and I knew the acknowledgement was for Carline and not me. Afterwards I begged her to take me home before the Sunday dinner invites started and seeing the pleading in my eyes, she did.

Three days later, I left my office and saw Randall walking with a gorgeous curvy female with red hair and wearing what was easily recognizable as a *Donna Karen* pantsuit, *Jimmy Choo* pumps and her makeup was flawless. I walked faster to catch up with them.

"Hey Randall," I said smiling at him and his lady friend.

"Hey yourself," He said with a smile but didn't bother to introduce us so I did.

"Hi I'm Paulette," she shook my outstretched hand and smiled sweetly.

"I'm Mayleece."

My smile held. She wasn't at all what I'd expected.

"Is the deck work okay? Is there something you needed?" Randall asked and I stumbled over my words trying to find something to say.

"Oh nothing and yes the work is fine, I was just going to say that I hadn't received the invoice for the Deck work yet." I lied.

"There's still a couple of things that need to be done, you'll be billed at the completion of the job and after the inspection is okayed. I want to make sure it's up to *your* specifications."

The sarcasm in his last words was barely hidden and I knew I deserved it but certainly not in front of the gorgeous creature he was with.

"Thank-you I'm sure everything will be fine."

"Then if you'll excuse us…" He took Mayleece gently by the arm and led her away.

My face was burning but what's more a tiny squirm of what I instantly recognized as jealousy crept up my spine. *NO! I thought. That can't be*, Randall Collins was the last man on earth I'd ever be attracted to. Oh no! This would never do.

I began to curb my time with Carline even though she called me almost every day. I put her off most of the time, and other times I just didn't answer the phone at all. I figured that if I didn't return her calls she'd eventually stop calling me.

A month later I was at my wits end. I was lonely and bored and tried stretching out my work projects for something to do. Donald Trayton knocked on the door of my office one day a week later.

In the short time I'd been working for the company, Donald and I had settled into an easy professional relationship. Quite frankly I was so sure he'd be hitting on me that I practiced a few gentle insults to keep him in check just in case. But he never did and that worried me because I thought perhaps I'd lost my touch. Not that I wanted to touch him anyway.
 He came in to my office and shut the door.

"Are you All right Paulette? You seem a little distracted."

"I'm fine Donald; it's just that—well." I couldn't say it.

"Come on tell Uncle Donald." He joked.

"I'm bored—not with work mind you, but socially."

"You need to change that."

"I know but where does one go around here? It's not like when I was up North. There are eating joints and night spots every two blocks."

"What about that club you went to; didn't you have a good time?"

"Chez Gerard? It was okay."

"Sounds like a man to me."

"Puh-leese!" I said holding up a hand. "I wish you could have seen the men in there."

"Well" he said turning and heading back to the door. If there's anything I can do, just let me know."
He had his hand on the knob when I spoke up.

"Actually, there is. What about going out with me—purely as friends of course." I added quickly.

He sucked in his cheeks, pursing his lips as if in deep thought. "Sure, just tell me when." He opened the door and stepped out.

"Saturday?" I called out before he shut it. He stopped and looked back and smiled.

"Saturday it is, just text me the preliminaries."

~*~

If Donald was surprised by my choice of Clubs he didn't let on. I chose Chez Gerard again. It was ladies night and the nightspot was teeming with women on the prowl. I was relieved to be with Donald so that it didn't look as though I was as desperate as some of them appeared. I scanned the room, sure I was going to see Randall and probably Mayleece with him, but I didn't see him or her at all.

Donald was dressed like he'd stepped out of bandbox and more than one of the ladies made their appraisal of him more than obvious. We sat at a small bistro table and ordered drinks. I was all set to pay the tab, since I was the one who had asked him out but he held up a hand to stop me.

"No way, if the lady wants to have a good time, this gentleman will show her one." He said.

Donald was every bit the gentleman he portrayed, he didn't try to paw me or make suggestive conversation that had double meanings. Very soon I found myself relaxing and actually having a good time. But for the life of me I still couldn't help searching for Randall.

It was close to ten-thirty when I saw Carline. She came in wearing a dress that for once fit her and the color was stunning. She saw me, waved and hurried over.

"Hey Paulette, you feelin' better girlfriend? I figured you were under the weather because you didn't answer any of my calls."

I was immediately shamed by her graciousness in ignoring my bad manners.

"And who might this vision of loveliness be?" Donald asked standing up reaching for her hand.

I looked at his face and to my amazement he appeared to be positively enthralled with Carline. "Donald, this is a very good friend, Carline."

"I'm enchanted," he said kissing her hand sending her into schoolgirl giggles.

"Carline, this is Donald Trayton, a co-worker, and also a terrific friend," I said meaning it because after all he did come out with me tonight, even though his attentions were certainly not on me. Just then the air was filled with the strong seductive voice of Mary J. Blige.

"Oooohh" Carline cooed, "That's my jam."
She started circling her butt slowly. I closed my eyes; sure that Donald would sense my disapproval and excuse *us* to the dance floor. Instead, he got up and took her and led her out onto the floor.

Thirty minutes and four dances later, including two very slow ones, they came back to the table.

"Donny, you're some dancer I don't know how a girl can keep up with you," Carline laughed.

"You keep up just fine lady. How about another spin?" And off they went.
I was happy she was having a good time I had been sitting alone with nothing but a watery drink an impending headache and not one person had asked me to dance.

It was almost twelve when I saw Randall enter the club. He was so decked out I thought he'd just stepped out of GQ. A second later a woman—not Mayleece, entered and entwined her arm in his. He looked down at her and she puckered prettily up at him.
I didn't want him to see me sitting alone and searched frantically for Donald. *Where the hell was he?* I got up to go look for him on the crowded dance floor trying to beat Randall before he came my way, but the crowd made it impossible and before I knew it I was looking right up at him.

"Lose something Paulette?" He said.

"My date," I said trying to laugh as though it were a joke. "Oh here he comes."

Donald sauntered over with Carline in tow. I was about to cozy up to him but he was holding Carline's hand like he was linked to it by a chain.

"You know Paulette," Donald said. "I should chastise you severely for not introducing me to this charming creature sooner."

"I just love the way he talks—hey boo." Carline said when she saw Randall. She introduced her cousin to Donald and his date whose name was *Urtha*.

"Er Donald," I interjected, "I have an awful headache I was wondering if you'd take me home now."

"Of course," he said but I could see the disappointment on his face as he turned to Carline. "I'd love to call you if that's okay," he said to her.

Carline went to the table to write down her number. I didn't look up, mainly because the searing heat from what I knew was Randall's mocking gaze prevented me from doing so. Tucking the number in his breast pocket, then patting it to show her that he intended to keep it safe and close to his heart, Donald told me he'd go get the car. When he'd gone Carline leaped at me and hugged me tight.

"He's the absolute best Paulette. Did you know he's been to Japan? He speaks Japanese, Italian, and Spanish?" she said gleefully.

No I hadn't known any of those things about him. "He's a charmer all right," I said to her.

She bussed me once more on the cheek and told me she'd call me then trotted off into the dance crowd.

"Well, I guess I'd better be off, Donald's probably got the car by now," I said to Randall.

When I passed by him, he leaned down to me. "Enjoy your... date," he said sarcastically. With my back stiff and with as much dignity as I could muster I walked to the exit.

~*~

For the next few weeks, I was tortured with calls from Carline telling me about the wonderful and wild things she and

Donald were doing together. Picnics in the park, a movie day at his house where he actually rented an old-fashioned popcorn maker—but it was the hot-air balloon ride that really set my teeth on edge. Here I was with nobody and country-ass Carline was having the time of her life. How was that fair?

Our company picnic was fast approaching. I considered not going at all but everyone at management level was required and had a job to do. Mine was monitoring children ages seven through eleven on the game field. Each employee was allowed to invite four people other than immediate family members and I was surprised to see Randall there.

"He was kind enough to agree to coach the little league game at two." Donald said before trotting off to find Carline. Other than a terse obligatory greeting I didn't see much of Randall during the day but to my surprise and relief, it appeared that he had come alone.

~*~

Carline was constantly in contact with me, but I ducked her whenever I could. She was way too *country* for me and I didn't feel like being bothered and was glad if a bit perplexed by all the attention she was getting from Donald. I mean he could have anybody yet his fine ass was running behind Carline like he was on fire and she was the last fire hose in the world.

Helen from up North called again and told me she would love to come visit me during her vacation. We were friends but we were never tight, mostly because I think we knew each other too well. I felt she was a user and a gold-digger and she thought I was too ambitious. She was far prettier than I'd ever hoped to be with a figure that was movie-star perfect. She was the typical light-skinned-good-hair type of woman that all men seemed to covet and when she walked in a room full of men, she knew there wasn't a one in it she couldn't get. But I agreed fro to come and visit.

She arrived that next week wearing a pale peach suit that was so tight it had the gardener almost cutting off his pinky toe with his lawnmower as he watched her come up the steps.
We hugged and air-kissed and when I showed her to the spare bedroom she hardly had let me say a word before she said…

"Girl, when I got off the plane I was wondering what in the world you were doing in a *country-Bama* place like this." Her laugh was shrill and made my eardrums ache. I smiled but the *Bama* term she used suddenly irritated me.

"So." she said sitting on the edge of the bed. "Tell me about this man you re-designed for the wedding you went to."

"There's not much to tell, but girl these people are a trip you just wait until you see some of them," I said trying to detract any conversation about Randall.

"Well I'm ready to go. You pick the time and place."

I decided not to go to *Chez Gerard* over the weekend and instead took Helen to fine-dining eatery on the outskirts of town. She was bored instantly and found it stiff and pretentious. I asked the concierge if there was a place where two ladies of distinction might go for an after dinner drink. He said there was a place near *Woodcomb* where they'd welcome two fine ladies such ourselves.
I got the directions and twenty minutes later I was parked in front of what was little more than a storefront with my mouth wide open.

"We are not going in there," I said adamantly.

"Oh yes we are." Helen said exiting the car when she noticed three of the largest, darkest men walking into the place and walking toward the entrance.
I had no choice but to turn off the engine and to run and try to catch up.

Entering together, we looked around and as usual saw a bevy of women but this time and for the first time the man ratio was staggering and I wondered if we'd in fact entered a gay joint, especially when I saw that they were pretty much all dressed in jeans or extremely causal cloths.

"So many men and so few who can afford me," Helen said with a lopsided grin then perked up when she saw several men gaze at her with their mouths half opened.

"You ready to hunt?" she whispered to me.

Hunt? I didn't even want to be in this jungle.

There was no place to sit at any of the side tables so she headed to the bar. I almost fainted at the thought of sitting on a barstool looking like an advertisement for a lap-dance. Several men offered to buy us drinks, but I declined while Helen accepted, along with invitations to some very close and seductive dances. A diminutive, bald headed man came over and totally ignored me as he smiled up at Helen.

"Hmmm hmm, girl you look so good I could drank a tub full of your bathwater," he drawled.

Helen's brow arched into a severe arc. "I showered before I came so I guess you missed your chance," she said dismissing him.

A group of people nearby commented on the slight and one woman leaned over. "Girl, you sure got attitude and know how to use it."

They all laughed, but I was clearly uncomfortable. I sipped my drink slowly and hoped that not one of this country ass lumberjacks would want to sweat out my hair by asking me to dance. I avoided their looks and stares and glanced over the room. Then I saw him—Randall. *What the fuck? Was he following me or something? We hadn't even known we were coming here.*

He was dressed in a pair of loose tan pants, sneakers and his baseball cap was on backwards, but it was that plaid shirt that made me want to gag even if it did have a time containing his broad chest and shoulders. He looked over and saw me then turned away. I felt Helen's gaze go from him to me.

"And who is that *A number one side of beef?*"

I turned and faced the bar hoping that Randall noticed my back and disinterest.

"He's the one I told you about—the wedding?"

"Ohhh" her mouth pursed into pretty pout. "He's not so bad as a matter of fact; he's really kind of nice looking. I mean he's not Jason Momoa or anything, but that body… ooh girl now that's the kind of steel you want in your Cadillac." She shifted around. "He's coming this way."

I don't know why but the beat of my heart elevated.

"Good evening." He said.

"Oh hi" I turned and smiled, but it faded when I saw he was addressing Helen and not me. After the longest moment in the history of mankind I made the introduction.

"Randall, I'd like you to meet my friend Helen, she's visiting me from out of town."

"Nice to meet you Helen," he said with an earth moving smile.

"When Paulette told me about the men here, I know she wasn't talking about you." Helen cooed.

"Well it appears she doesn't share the same taste for *country ham* as you appear to."

"It all depends on how well it's been cured," she said looking him up and down.

Randall spent the next fifteen minutes basking in the sugary compliments Helen spouted like an open fire hydrant.

"I see some people I know, order what you like and tell the bartender to put it on my tab. I hope we'll get the chance to meet again," He smiled and barely giving me a curt nod before he excused himself. Helen turned to me.

"Okay, give me the 411."

"There isn't any. He's the cousin of a friend—are you ready to go yet?" I asked irritably.

"We just got here," She whined, "I'm going to have myself some fun and you should to."

Helen's idea of fun was leaving me alone for the next hour while she danced, drank and laughed with various men and couples she'd met.

~*~

On the way home I was moody and silent.

"Paulette, you look like somebody just shot your dog. What's the matter?" Helen asked me.

"Nothing, I feel a little headache coming on that's all."

"That *little* headache wouldn't have anything to do with *big* Randall would it?

"Hell no!" I turned to look at her, the wheel inadvertently veering to the left.

"Well then you won't mind if I sort of engage in a little friendly conversation with him," she said.

"Why would I care? If I want something that country, I'll go to the Rib Shack."

"Then it's settled—but would you mind keeping your eyes on the road?"
I swerved just in time to avoid another car.

After our night at the club Helen's cell phone rang incessantly and while she exchanged teasing pleasantries, she didn't accept any offers to take her out. It was like she was waiting for a special call and I had an idea just which one that was. When she finally began to get calls from Randall I knew immediately because she stayed in her room or lounged out on the deck for hours talking to him.

An emergency work proposal tied me up for the next few days I told Helen I wouldn't able to entertain her and I'd be late so she should go on and eat without me.

"No problem Paulette, Randall called, we're going to…"
It seemed that she and Randall were going somewhere or doing something every night. It made me so irritable I yelled at my assistant for no reason, I made stupid mistakes and I was frustrated to distraction.

Saturday morning as I sat on my newly renovated deck sipping my second cup of coffee, I heard Helen come downstairs, yawning loudly. She filled a mug and came out and sat down by me.

"So what time did you come in last night?" I asked her.

"You mean this morning—somewhere around three," she said taking a sip from her mug.

"You know..." I began, "I never figured you for the country boy type."

"Believe me, Randall is anything but a boy," she said with a laugh.

"You know what I mean Helen. You usually like your men like that coffee you're drinking—smooth and rich."

"Well that was true once but I believe he's a diamond in the rough. He's not like other men and he doesn't have to be. He's confident and comfortable inside his skin. Oh he may not have the GQ modal good looks, but he's sturdy and honest and he knows how to keep a woman—entertained."

That was the one thing *I didn't* need to hear about and the coil of jealousy that unwound itself in my body shook my spirit to the bone.

"You can get that from any man...in fact I'm sure you have." I tried to make it sound like I was teasing but I know it came out like a dig. I felt her shift and stiffen.

"People change—needs change.
I couldn't let this go. "Just what are you doing Helen? With all the men you can play, why are you playing with Randall?"
She stopped sipping her coffee, her hazel eyes boring through me—searching.

"You want him don't you Paulette?" she said in a low voice. "You're jealous as a neutered tomcat in a feline whore house."

"That's insane." I said with my chin held up indignantly.

"No! It's not. If you didn't think he was more country than a backwoodsman with four dogs living under his porch, you'd be with him right now. But he isn't good enough for you is he Paulette?"

"I never said that."

"Not in so many words, but the way you talked about him you acted like he's so backward that he uses toilet seats as picture frames or something. But now that you see someone else *might* be interested he's looking a little better to ya huh."

"I have no idea what you're talking about."

"You can't fool me we're two of kind with slight differences, but there are some things that are exactly the same; only I know how to be more honest than you."

"He's not even your type, why are you pursuing him?"

"Because, I want to and what's in a type anyway?"

"People get hurt when you play games Helen."

"Well since you don't care about him then you shouldn't give a shit."

I was quiet and pensive. *Why was I acting like I cared?* I heard her get up and come over to me and give me a hug.

"Stop worrying girlfriend, if I decide I don't want him, you can have him okay?"

"I'm not worried at all and in case you think you're the only one Helen you're not. Randall seems to be quite popular with the ladies."

"Yeah well tonight he'll be popular with one lady and that's me," she said and got up and went back upstairs.

~*~

I went to my office and worked all day and well into the night. I don't know if I was trying to keep busy to stop from thinking about Helen and Randall together or if I just needed to make myself tired enough to sleep without dreaming. When I finally decided to go home I was bleary eyed as a drunk on a three-day vodka binge. My bones ached and even though I was hungry I headed straight upstairs to my bedroom. I looked up and was face to face with Randall exiting Helen's room—and zipping up his pants. His eyes locked on mine but he said nothing. A second later Helen came out patting her hair and buttoning her blouse.

"Oh Paulette I didn't realize you were home. We're um… going out for a little snack; can we bring you back anything?"
It looked to me like she'd already been a snack.

My blood boiled, but I held my voice in check. "No thanks, I'm going to bed." I didn't say goodnight and hadn't meant to slam my bedroom door.

I was too tired to take a much-needed relaxing bath so I showered quickly and climbed into bed naked. As fatigued as I was, I waited and listened for Helen's return. *Why should I care if she stayed out for the rest of the night?* But still I waited and later when I looked at the clock and saw it was 2 a. m. and I still hadn't heard her come on, I finally turned over and went to sleep.

I had no idea when she'd come in but the next morning when Helen came down for coffee, I hinted that for the rest of her stay I would much rather she see her *friends* other than at my home.

"What friends? It's only been Randall and…"
"Well that's what I mean." I said cutting her off. "I just think it would be better if you did your *special* entertaining someplace else."
I saw her eyes narrow to slits, as though she were trying to read me. "Uh huh," was all she said.

~*~

Much to my heavily masked irritation Helen extended her visit another week but I saw very little of her as she and Randall seemed to spend most of her time together.
Carline invited me to Big Mama's after church for Sunday supper and while I was reluctant the thought of homemade food with a healthy slice of *whatever* pie was being served made my mouth water.

"You can ride with us…" she looked adoringly at Donald, "Randall is coming later with your friend Helen."
I declined the invitation and went home to sulk.

At the end of the week when Helen was finally getting herself ready to leave, she decided she had time for an early shopping trip. Randall called my cellphone, telling me he couldn't reach her cell and could I tell her he'd be a little late picking her up to take her to the airport, but they would be there in plenty of time.

"No problem, I'll tell her!" I said sarcastically and clicked the phone off.

About a half hour later she came in with both hands filled with shopping bags from *Beskers* and *Sumner a local* high end clothier.

"Randall called; he couldn't reach you on your cell he said he was going to be a little late picking you up."

"I always forget to charge that damned thing," she said.

"You know Helen, I would have driven you to the airport," I said.

"What? And miss the biggest, juiciest super-soaker kiss a girl can get from a man? Girl! Hell no. Here—I got this for you," and she tossed one of the bags over to me.

"I hope I can get all this shit in my suitcase, they're probably going to charge me extra." She laughed and went upstairs.

I opened the bag and inside was a gorgeous slinky maroon blouse. The tension between us was all me and now that she was going home I was suddenly ashamed of being such a bad hostess and friend.

I couldn't leave things the way they were and went up to her room. She had finished packing and was standing before the dresser mirror applying a tangerine colored lipstick over first her top then bottom lip. I could see her eyeing me through the glass. She put the tube in her purse and turned to me.

"You know Paulette; the sweetest wine doesn't always come from the prettiest bottle. Just like the most gorgeously decorated cake in a bakery window doesn't always taste good. You can't just assume that something is or isn't just by looking at it. Sometimes you have to have taste and then taste it again to get the full flavor."

"I don't know what you're talking about." I said as the doorbell rang.

"Of course you do and if I'm any judge of good character albeit jaded at times, I think you'll do what you have to do in order to get what you think you *don't* want." she said and to my

surprise leaned down and kissed me on the cheek and winked. "That's probably my ride,"
She said grabbing her garment bag and overnight case while I pulled her monstrously large and heavy suitcase downstairs.

Randall didn't come in when I answered the door but took the bags and went to put them in the truck as Helen and I hugged and said our goodbyes. I was closing the door when I heard her squeal with delight and call out Randall's name, then after a few minutes I heard the roar of his truck as they drove away.

I mulled Helen's statement over and over in my mind. I knew what she meant but the devil kept twisting it around and around in my mind until all I could see was her writhing in wanton abandon in Randall's arms. I wasn't sure why I was procrastinating; it had become increasingly clear to me what I wanted. *Why the hell was I fighting it?*

~*~

After Helen's departure Randall continued to treat me with cool indifference at church at the clubs or whenever we crossed paths. It was annoying and childish. I was distracted at work, I was eating way too much fatty fast food and my sleep was being affected.

One day when I'd been trying my level best to work on a project but couldn't concentrate, I finally had enough. There was one way to be done with this once and for all. *If the mountain wasn't going to come to Mohammad...* I told my assistant I'd be out for the rest of the day then called a cab and gave him Randall's work address.

The closer I got the madder I became. By the time the cab pulled up to the small building that housed his company I was a volcanic mass of anger. I threw the fare at the cabby, got out and stormed my way into the office. It was one big room really, with a couple of PC's, phones, some desks and chairs. Randall's eyes popped up and stared at me in surprise.

"I need to talk to you!" I said in a no-nonsense tone.
A man who had been speaking with him rose to leave. "I'll see you about this later boss," he said.

After the man left and shut the door. I leaned over the desk, planted my palms down and looked Randall straight in the eye.

"Okay, I was stupid and crass. I made a mistake, maybe even made a complete ass of myself. But it's been weeks and I would have thought you would have forgiven me by now."
He stood up so quickly I had to step back and look up at him.

"Forgive you? I don't give a rat's left hind leg about me, but it's how you been treating Carline that makes me so mad. She adores you and doesn't deserve your disinterest or your views about us *county-folk*. Looks are not as important to her as they are to you.
I wanted to interject but he wouldn't let me.

"In your eyes people have to fit your standards or they're just not even worth your time, but worthy of your ridicule. Well you just come with me you shallow witch and let me show you something," he said through clenched teeth.

Stunned and rooted to the spot, I watched him come around the desk, then grab me none- too-gently by the arm and pulled me out of the office. He called out to the same man he had been talking to who was standing outside smoking. "Hey Maxell, lock up for me will ya?"

"Right-o boss" the man called back.
I almost tripped trying to keep up with Randall's long angry strides. He literally tossed me into his truck then got in and started the engine.

"Where are we going?"

"Just sit there and be quiet," he said.
While I was incensed, something told me I had better do just that.

Fifteen minutes later we pulled into the visitor's parking lot of the *Howelton Hospital.* I was perplexed as Randall got out then pulled me out and hurried me to the entrance. He punched the elevator button then hauled me through the open doors. We got off on the fifth floor where he ignored the happy greeting of the young white nurse as he sped by her.

"You know Paulette; there are people in this world who don't care how you look. They don't care if you're fat, skinny, ugly or have a dragon's tail. All they care about is the love."
He pulled me to a large window where six or seven kids, black, white, Hispanic and East Indian huddled around Carline who sat in a comfortable looking easy chair reading from a large colorful book. One of the kids was on her lap, while another had his shorn head on her shoulder, another painfully thin child leaned against her leg. Each of them was touching her in some way.

"Every one of these kids has cancer of some kind and this is what *Fat-uncouth-country-can't-dress-to-suit-you* Carline Daniels does on her days off."
I was awestruck.

"If you like that, you're gonna love this."
He pulled me away from the window and back onto the elevator. Up to the fourteenth floor and down two long aisles we went until we came to a room with the door ajar. He opened it and a thin white woman lay on a bed with so many tubes in her it scared me. She turned her head and a smile appeared on her cracked lips.

"Hello Mrs. Givall, I was wondering if you've seen Carline today?"

"Oh yes," the woman rasped. "She came by early this morning and brought me some flowers then she read my favorite bible passages to me. She's such a sweet girl."

"You get some rest now; I'll come by and see you again real soon."
It went that way for three more rooms, then a lounge full of patients who sang Carline's praises.

By the time we went back to the elevator I was in tears. "Please Randall I'm so sorry... let's go. Please."

I was hysterical in the truck but he did nothing to console me. I didn't even pay any attention to where we were going, but the next thing I knew he had pulled into a short tree lined driveway and turned the truck off.

"Where are we?" I asked but I think I already knew.

"My house." And he got out and then got me out and took me up three stone steps. He opened the front door and pulled me inside.

"Randall…" I began.

"No, I've got something to say and I'm going to say it. You needed that reality check Missy and it ain't all you need, not by a long shot."

"Randall I don't feel well." I said wanting to go home and hide.

"You don't like the way I talk? Then I won't talk. You don't like the way I dress then I'll get undressed, but lady you're about to get what you need."
I took a step back, my eyes wide and glued to his.

"Don't even look at me like that girl I'm not about to rape you. But when I'm through, you'll be begging me for it."

"Like Helen?" I said regaining a bit of bravado," Did you have her begging for it?"

"This ain't about Helen and me."

"Why not, she said you certainly know how to please a woman."

"There are all kinds of ways of pleasuring a woman and Helen gets a great deal of delight out of seeing what *her* particular talents do to a man."

"Then I suppose you're saying nothing happened?"

"I didn't say that."

"So you're saying you didn't sleep with her."

"That's exactly what I'm saying. But my question to you is why you care what me and Helen did or didn't do."

"I don't," I said looking away from him.

"The hell you don't," he said and the next thing I knew I was in his strong beefy arms. He wasn't holding me with strength enough to crush my chest, but it was a strong firm embrace. His mouth bruised mine as he pushed his tongue pass my resistant lips and enslaved my spirit. I felt his manhood leap hard and urgent against my thigh and he moved around until it was situated right in the middle of my vee. It was hard and strong. There was a grinding movement and suddenly he stopped kissing me long enough to give me a sardonic smile. He was perfectly still; it was *me* that was grinding my hips against him. I tried to move away.

"It's not gonna be that easy Paulette, not this time anyway," he rasped.

He picked me up like I was a rag-doll and took the steps two at time to his bedroom then set me on my feet. He stepped back and began to remove his cloths. When he was in his shorts he backed up and sat in a large chair a few feet away.

"Now, it's your turn. Shed those high priced clothes, and that haughty ass attitude. Do the first part slow."

It occurred to me to resist but he was seeing passed all my facades, he had me and he knew it. I undid the tiny buttons that held my Versace dress together. Pulling it off my shoulders, I let it slide down my body into a puddle on the thick carpet and then I waited.

"Everything Paulette."

His voice was thick, his eyes steely on my body. I unsnapped my bra and let it fall. A slight slant of his lip told me he liked what he saw. He gestured downward and I slid my panties down and stood before him proudly. He shook his head from side to side.

"You still think it's about appearances don't you? Of course you're beautiful, but in that..." he pointed to my neatly trimmed vagina, "You're like every other woman in the world unless you can prove otherwise. Now come here and see if that stiff haughty attitude can take what I got for you,"

I watched nervous fascination as he slid his underwear off exposing his erection which was thick and ram rod straight. For a moment I didn't move and watched mesmerized as he began to stroke it up and down slowly.

"I'm not coming to you Paulette, if you want it then come and get it." He slid further down into the chair and ran a forefinger over the wet tip. I had no idea what was controlling but I went to him. He grabbed me by my buttocks pulling me forward so that his face was level with my stomach. He kissed me there and I gasped as his lips began to suck at my skin. His hands slid down and under me, I felt a finger slide over my damp mons, then slid into the wet crevice.

"Pussy juice is the one thing no woman can control when she's ready," he rasped.

I knew he was talking about how moist I was and I was turned on by his course phrasing of it. He pushed me back and got up from the chair and sat me into it, opening my thighs he knelt before me and pushed his face right between them. I opened like a cracked pecan and he shoved his tongue so deep inside I thought I would die with delight. The heat from his mouth devoured me and my legs parted even more. I was powerless to resist the pleasure that was consuming me. Cupping my ass cheeks, he pulled me forward and raised me higher, he tonged me deeper and I had to force a scream back down into my throat. He licked me ever so slowly then fast twirling his tongue like a whirly gig in the wind. I couldn't stop the ebb of pleasure and I gasped for him to stop. But he didn't, he sucked and licked until cum poured out of me in short bursts of creamy liquid. Still he didn't remove his face even when my breath began to slow. He turned me over so that my knees were on the chair and I was in a doggie position.

"Bring it back Paulette, bring it back to my tongue,"
He said. And I did it, I moved my ass back and before I knew what was happening he began licking me from crack to crack. He spread me open with his thick lumber jack fingers and flicked his tongue in me like a mini whip. Cum slid out of me so many times my stomach ached. No one had ever taken me like this and I couldn't believe the feeling.

He stopped long enough to run his fingers over my swollen lips.

"Hmmm, so puffy and sweet now," he said lapping at them again. I couldn't help myself it was like my swollen lips pushed out and begged for his mouth.

"You're so wet Paulette, so tasty," He said with his lips reverberating against my lips causing a new and wonderful sensation. *A man who could talk and eat you at the same time, now this was brand new.*

One of the things that my women friends often joked about was how a man ate you for a few scant minutes before he wanted to enter you or have you suck him. But Randall didn't rush like that. He tasted me so many times and in so many ways I felt like a raw piece of meat.

Finally he stopped and pulled me from the chair and over to the bed. He pushed me down and spread me once again. I was writhing wanting to get away from his short fast licks and deep delving sucks yet wanted him deeper at the same time.

"You like designer things Paulette? Well I designed this lovin' especially for you." And he slapped at my swollen lips gently. I closed my eyes and bit my fist to keep from screaming out with the pleasure pain of it. I felt him reach out to the end table then heard the unmistakable tear of cellophane. I opened my eyes and watched as he tore the packet and place the contents on himself. Spreading my legs even wider he leaned down and sucked at the pink maw once again then repositioned himself and plunged inside.

The feeling was explosive but I was well lubricated from his earlier licking as he filled every inch of me. He began to move with sensual agonizing slowness. The rhythm of his movements was so precise and deliberate I could hardly stand it.

"Stop trying to make people over Paulette. Stop trying to create people into what you think they should be." He rasped. *Was he really having this conversation while he was pumping inside me?* I thought.

"I don't give a damn what you think of me. I knew I could make you mine whether I was wearing an *Armani* suit or a pair of Wal-Mart jeans."

"Randall I..."

"I fell in love with you almost from the moment I laid eyes on you? He said and increased his rhythm.

My arms were around his neck as I listened and accepted the pleasure he was giving me.

"And girl if I have my way you won't be giving a damn about your clothes because I just may not let you wear any once you're truly mine."

My legs were taut as another bout of pleasure threatened to race through me. Still he moved in me and talked with words that became more and more sensual until finally I could hold no longer.

"You say it right now, say you love me," he hissed.
I didn't hesitate, not for a second.

"Yes! Oh Yes Randall, I love you. I do love you."
And at that moment we came in an explosion that threatened to toss us from the bed.

It took many moments for us to regain our breath and even longer to recoup our strength. Finally he leaned up on one elbow and looked down into my sweat-drenched face as he toyed with my taut nipples.

"Now, tell it to me one more time, who is it you love?"
I smiled. "You *Junior*, I love you."

Substitute Mom

Some women are just not destined to be mothers and every mother who bears a child is not necessarily motherly. Much to my sorrow I was in the first bunch. I knew early on there'd be no children for me since I had to have a hysterectomy in my mid-twenties and it had destroyed almost every relationship I had where a future was concerned. It didn't matter and I found other things to occupy my time. Mostly I spent a great deal of time and efforts doing what I could at my church.

It might be all about the new clothes on Easter Sunday but on Mother's day at the Mount Carmel Bible church it was all about the hats. It seemed that the bigger and more colorful the better. I hate to admit that it was my favorite time of year and my guilty pleasure was seeing the contest between the old female icons of the church and the new age upwardly mobile businesswomen on who had the best head gear.

I liked my church because it was lively and full of spice and had more secrets than a suspense novel. It was a place where people came to absolve and rid themselves of their concealed burdens. It was a place where although no one ever *asked* you your business because everybody somehow *already knew* your business. The ringleader of the nosey rumor brigade was that needle-nosed Lestina Rungo—a perfect name for her because whenever she found out something about *anybody* she'd *run* and *go* tell *everybody* about it.

My favorite person was Calhoun Tall-Crow-Rodriguez who professed to be being one quarter everything including Puerto Rican and Comanche.

"Mr. Rodriguez," I chided one day after Sunday service, "It's impossible to be one quarter of everything you claim you are."
He looked at me with mischievous eyes and dug into his high-water pants pocket and extracted a coin.

"Girlie, you see this here twenty-five cent piece?"
I nodded.

"Well for every one of these I got heritage that goes back before the civil war so that makes me one quarter of what I say I am."
There was no use in trying to argue with logic like that?

Another character I was fond of was *Ernestine Two-ways* Jackson. She always had two ways of doing everything and going anywhere, not to mention that she intimated she also liked her loving two ways—in and out and a reverse 96.

But it was still the Sunday hats that had me laughing. You never saw so many floral, netting and tulle laden hats in your life. The organist, Mrs. Cooper wore the same black hat but with a different adornment each and every Sunday. We called it the *puzzle hat* because you could see the zigzag stitches that were left *after* she tore off the old embellishment and replaced it with a new one. They were quite a bunch of characters.

Saturday nights were the loneliest for me and I tried to sleep it away so that I could hurry to the church on Sunday and busy myself with helping to prepare supper for the impoverished elderly members and the sick and shut-ins. After the service, everyone met in the large creaky basement where long tables were setup with bright plastic table cloths and pitchers of sweet tea and ice water. Off to the side, the kitchen staff were busy arranging their donated dishes—each pushing his or hers a little more toward the front. It was a contest about who could make the best sweet potato pie, coconut cake or crispiest fried chicken. Thank goodness for these competitive cooks, because without them we wouldn't have enough food to go around.

Sister Idajean was two hundred and ten pounds with arthritic ankles and a milky cataract in one eye but she made a roast beef that would put any famous TV chef to shame. Her mashed potatoes and gravy were legendary and you could make a meal on just that alone. Brother Clayton Jefferson said he prayed over his bread pudding before putting it on the oven and that's what made it extra tasty.

One Sunday, reverend Critchlow preached a hellfire and brimstone sermon so loud that it woke up four sleeping babies, and filled Coralee Strunk with so much Holy Ghost that she jumped up and knocked off another parishioner's hat. Unfortunately it had been bobby-pinned to a lady's wig which left her sitting there with tufts of gray and black hair sticking out all over her head.

I was preparing the dinners I would take to my assigned shut-ins and made sure I made an extra healthy sized plate for myself for later on.

I had five stops to make, the last being the 44th street tenement where the widow Purcell lived with her two cats and a one legged parakeet. She told me that one of the cats had gotten hold of the little bird and she grabbed the feline and pinched his tail until it let go. She then nursed the little bird until it was well and learned purely by instinct how to balance itself on one thin leg. It was quite sight.

I arrived at the dingy building and climbed the stairs to her apartment. I was in shape, but even these steps were a little too much for me and I was winded and tired when I reached the top. I rapped on the widow's door.

"It's me Mrs. Purcell, Gail Millen from the church." I had to yell because she was a little hard of hearing. I heard her shuffle to the door and begin to unlock at least four locks, two dead-bolts and an iron door stop before opening the door.

"Cain't be too careful," she said as she peeked at me before undoing the thick slide chain.

"I've brought your supper."

"I hope you brought me some macaroni and cheese this time. I didn't like them salad greens you brought the last time, damn things messed up my constitution."

We always had a conversation like this when I thought she could use a little more roughage and less artery clogging fat. But she reminded me she was eighty-seven years old and that she never smoked nor drank and had *cavorted* with only one man her whole life and with the time she had left she was going to enjoy eating all the foods she loved best.

"Yes Mrs. Purcell I brought the macaroni and cheese, and big slice of that coconut cake you like so well." I smiled at the small pale skinned woman.

"Bless you child and I hope it's Corrine's because Anna-Mae Cully can't bake for shit."
I stayed with her a while as she ate and I listened to stories I'd heard a dozen times before but it made her happy and gave me something to do.

I left her with assurance I'd return the following week with something special. I waited until I heard her bolt the door like it was Fort Knox before walking down the hall toward the steps. I noticed at the far end of the hall, a door was ajar and a child no more than eight months was old sitting on the floor with a tear stained face. I hurried over, knocked on the door and peeked inside. "Hello?"

There was no answer and the odor that emanated from the place almost made me gag.
I pushed the door open then leaned down to pick up the baby. It was so thin and sad. The child was whimpering and chewing and was about to put something in its mouth again when I saw that it was a huge cockroach. I slapped the wiggling thing out of the child's hand which instantly made it bawl loudly. I hugged the

child to me, ignoring the bad odor and obviously soiled pamper. Walking inside and calling out I was shocked to find the floor littered with and empty cans, bottles, fast-food cartons and half-filled containers of spoiled milk and juice. I called out again but there was no answer. I searched for a phone in order to call 911, but there was none and if there had been I would never have found it under all the debris. I put the child down and reached in my purse for my cell.

"Who the hell are you?" a small voice said.
I looked toward the sound and there was a little boy about nine years old standing in the doorway.

"Do you live here?" I asked.

"What the hell do you want?"
His mouth was firm and his tone angry, but I could see the fatigue and fear behind his dark eyes.

"My name is Gail, what's your name?"

"Nonya" He said.

"*Nonya*?" I repeated like a parrot.

"Yeah! None ya damn business."
I looked at him with irritation."Where are your parents?" It was a stupid question.

"Ain't got none."

"Of course you have." I said impatiently.

"We ain't got none right now."

"Why are you here alone?" I asked.

"Because I enjoy the solitude after hard day foraging for food at the local garbage dumps."
He said it with the intonation of a much older educated person and what kid his age used a word like *foraging*? I wondered ignoring his sarcastic tone.

"When's the last time you ate?" I asked.

"When's the last time you had some business of your own to mind," he said rudely.
I was done. I went over to him. The little brat stared me down like he was Evander Holyfield and we were about to go two rounds.

"Look! I am the adult, you are a child and you will not talk to me that way. And before you go off on a tangent..." I figured if he knew what *foraging* was, *tangent* would be a no-brainer for him... "I'm telling you right now I am not leaving you here alone with this baby. I going to call the police and you, *Mr. Smart mouth* will sit down and wait until they come."
His eyes widened. "Come on lady, don't call no police."
"The police," I corrected.
"Okay look, how about we make a deal. I'll clean up the place and make sure Crystal..." he said pointing to the baby. "Is changed and fed. You come back in ohhh say an hour and..." The little con-man was actually trying to get me to leave. "No way!" I said pushing the numbers on the dial pad.
Before I knew what was happening the kid ran to what I assumed was the kitchen and came back holding a bent steak knife with the tip broken off.
"Put the phone down." He said in a tone that was almost laughable.
I went over to him and snatched the dull rusty knife out of his hand.
"Dang," he pouted, "It was only a suggestion."
"Yeah well I *suggest* you sit your little tail down and behave."

I called 911 and while I waited for them to arrive I wanted badly to go get the food out of my car for them but I knew if I left the little mannish-man would most likely bolt and take the baby with him. I searched the place for some clean pampers, but of course there weren't any. I found a dingy pillow case and took Crystal to the sink and began to wash her as best I could then made her a makeshift diaper.
When the police arrived it took only a minute for them to assess the situation and get child protective services involved. One of the officers came over to interview me, I took notice of his name tag—*Anderson,* in black on gold letters. He took down

my information and told me that as soon the authorities arrived I could go.

"I have some food in the car it looks like he could use it." I said looking over at *Mr. Smart Alek.*
He said okay and I hurried down to get the package of church food I had intended to enjoy later on. Before going back up I saw a small bodega on the corner and went in to get some pampers. I also picked up a bottle, milk, a couple jars of baby food, soap and tooth brush and paste for the little smart mouth. When I returned, Officer Anderson was trying his level best to calm a now screaming Crystal.

"She's probably starving," I said putting the packages down.

When church folk cook the delicious smell can come through a brick wall and I could see the little boy eyeing the wrapped plates with longing.

"Go on" I said, but eat the food before you eat the pie." I said and he literally ran for the paper sack, then stopped and eyed me warily.

"What kind of pie?"

"What kind do you like?" I asked knowing that anything in that bag was going to be devoured.
He gave me a broad smile and it melted my heart to see a boyish innocence return to his face.

I changed the baby into a proper Pamper then began to feed her. The poor thing gulped the food and milk down so fast I thought she was going to choke.

"It's a shame isn't it?" the smooth husky voice said above me.

"Yes it is. What kind of person leaves children alone like this?"

"Desperate ones!" It was the kid talking through a mouthful of chicken and mashed potatoes.

"You!" I pointed to him, "Keep your nose out of grown folk's conversation and don't talk with your mouth full."

I turned my gaze back to the officer. "Sounds like a little old man doesn't he?" I smiled.

"Yeah. I guess some kids are just forced to grow up faster than others," he said looking around with disgust.

"Did you find anything out about him?"

"Just his name. Nathan Tiberius Hudson."

"That's quite a mouthful."

"You should have heard the explanation behind it," He chuckled.

He called the Child Services office twice more and was told that there had been a rash of child incidents and abandonments and they didn't have the room or the personnel to help us right then. They asked if he could find a family member willing to take the kids until a foster home could be found. After questioning little Nathan and got a firm, *"there ain't nobody,"* The officer was at his wits end.

"The only place is the 45th street Shelter, but that place is hell." His voice sounded almost like he knew from personal experience.

I thought for a minute. I was on vacation starting the next day for a week. They idea was preposterous; I didn't know anything about kids. But as I looked at the little boy who was using his finger to sop up every bit of gravy from the plastic ware I knew what I had to do.

"Maybe I can take them for a couple of days." I said.

Officer Anderson's head shot around and he stared me. "You?"

"Yes me."

"What about your... umm, husband?"

"Do I need one to care for two little kids?"

"I meant what if he objects."

"He can't because I don't have one."

His smile was immediate and brilliant.

"Well I sure ain't surprised she ain't got no man, she's bossy as prison guard," the little agitator chimed in.

We both looked at him.

"Maybe you can help these kids out for a day or two, maybe teach this little whipper-snapper some manners."
I smiled.

"But I have to warn you, If I can make this happen I intend to personally follow up to see how they're doing."

"Is that within your jurisdiction?" I asked.

"It is now." His eyes flashed a kind and just a little naughty lilt.
Crystal had finished the bottle and began crying loudly. Nathan walked over and took out of my arms.

"She gets gas a lot, she can fart like an old steam engine." He cradled the baby and patted her on the back until a loud burp exploded from her. Sitting on the couch he laid her across his little knees and moved them side-to-side and began to sing. Instantly the baby stopped crying, gurgled twice then fell asleep.

"He's good with her, he should be a lot of help to you." The officer said.

"He needs to be a little boy." I said softly.

By the time the Child protective investigator arrived, it was close to nine and Nathan was trying hard not to fall asleep. I had taken Crystal from him and was rocking her gently as she slept. It was agreed that I take the kids for the week-end at which time hopefully space could be found for them. I signed a release order and Officer Anderson carried a now sleeping Nathan down to my car. I buckled him in and Melvin had put the baby in a large soiled blanket next to me and wedged her in.

"You know I could give you a ticket for not having this child in a baby seat," he joked.

"Well officer we could just put her in *your* squad car and you can give yourself a ticket for not having one," I quipped back.
His laugh was raucous and almost woke the baby.

"I have all your information; here's my card in case you need to contact me day or night."

I looked at the card, *Officer Melvin Anderson.*

"I'll give you a call when I hear from the Child Services Bureau."

But somehow, I knew it would be a lot sooner than that.

I pulled into the garage of my small house on the west side of town and roused Nathan who groggily complained that he didn't feel like *"doin' no walkin!"*
I figured I'd take him in first because he was more apt to awaken and be afraid in unfamiliar surroundings. I put him in the spare bedroom and then went to get Crystal. Bless her heart she was wide awake but not crying a bit. I took her in and laid her on the couch and put the cushions around her. My curious cat *FuzzBall* nosed over to her and after seeing that she was no threat began to rub and purr against the little girl. I ran a warm bath for her in the sink and bathed her. It was pitiful to see the bug bites on her arms and legs which I soothed with Aloe and calamine lotion then swaddled her in an old white tee shirt. I made her a bottle and rocked her until she fell asleep once again.

I was bone tired, and after checking on Nathan once again I went to my room and looked up, *"Lord! What am I going to do with two little kids?"* Answers to your prayers don't always come immediately and maybe not the way you want but they do come.

That next morning I was awakened by the smell of bacon and for a moment I didn't know where I was. The voice of Brian McKnight blasted from somewhere in the front of the house and I got up and ran barefoot toward the sound. Nathan was standing on his tiptoes looking into a sizzling frying pan.

"What do you think you're doing?" I asked moving to him, but first turning down the radio.

"Waiting for a bus! I'm cooking breakfast what does it look like?"

"Give me that," I said grabbing the spatula. "Don't you know you could get hurt?"

"Lady, I've cooked more eggs and bacon then *IHOP* during an eating convention, but if you want to take over be my guest."

I wanted to laugh as he took his little narrow butt and sat at the kitchen table, but I didn't dare encourage him. I looked in the pan. The eggs were scrambled nicely with just a couple of shells that I could see, but the bacon was dangerously close to incineration so I made some more. I didn't want to hurt his feelings, so I picked out the shells then spooned and divided up the eggs onto two plates. I took out the ketchup and poured him a glass of milk.

"You like ketchup on your eggs too?" he asked.

"I sure do." I said grinning, then remembered his sister and got up to go check on her.

"Crystal woke up at six, I gave her a bottle. She'll sleep until the next ice age." He said matter-of-factly.

"How did you get so smart?" I said sitting back down.

"Books."

"Yes but you couldn't learn all those big words just from books."

His face lost its glow as it saddened. "Well, I was in this class for gifted children for a while, but I had to stop when..."

"When what?"

"When my mother left; I came home from school one day and Crystal was all alone. I waited but she never came back."

"How long ago was that?"

He shrugged. "Since Christmas."

I was stunned. "You mean you've been taking care of your sister alone all that time?"

I shuddered to think of what he had to do to in order get food.

"No biggie." He shrugged again.

"Wait just a minute." I said suspiciously, "Didn't the school check on you?"

"Yeah but I paid a whore to call and pretend to be my mother and tell them we had to go to out of town to my sick grandfather's and there was no one to leave me with. They didn't check, I guess there's just too many kids with crap going on.

No child should ever have to experience the hard life this boy had been subjected to and only with the help of some kind of guardian angel did he manage to survive as long as he did.

"Oh by the way, that cop called." He said chewing the last of his bacon.

"What Cop?" I hadn't even heard the phone.

"The one from yesterday that was giving you the googly eyes."

"Oh Officer Anderson."

"Whatever, he said he'd be by this morning."

Almost as if on cue the bell rang. Nathan got up but I gestured him back. "I'll get it."
It was Melvin and he had a box in his arms. I stood there staring like a school girl.

"Good Morning, you're early," I said suddenly self-conscious in my sorry looking faded pajamas.

"Good morning Ms. Millen. I brought a little something for the kids."
I moved aside and let him in.

"Mornin lil Dude," he said to Nathan. "I got some stuff here that you might like."
Nathan came over warily and looked in box. Melvin extracted some new underwear, jeans, shirts and socks. "I didn't want to take a chance on the sneakers; I figured we might go out later and see about those."
I could see that Nathan was excited, but taking pains not to show it.

"Cool," he said nonchalantly.
There were some little things for Crystal too. "Most of it is from my sister, she has twins about
Crystal's age and she's got tons of stuff."

I thought that was so sweet of him and offered the Officer some coffee—which I hadn't made yet.

"Just let me get dressed and I'll make it. I just want to check on the baby first."

"You go ahead, I'll check on her…" he said removing his hat then asked, "Where?"
I was about to answer when Nathan strolled over to us.

"In *her* bedroom" he said nodding over at me. "It's this way; I'll show you—so you'll remember where it is after we're outta here," Nathan said with an *all too knowing glance*.
I glared at him, then went to start the coffee machine.

After Officer Anderson left, I dressed the baby and told Nathan to get ready. I took them to the park which Nathan didn't seem to be so fond of.

"What are we doing here?" he asked.

"Having fun?" I figured kids knew what to do in a park, but he didn't seem to. I thought for a minute and then grabbed him by the hand.

"Come on I got it." His eyes lit up like a holiday candle when I took him into the library. He didn't even wait and half ran over to the children's section and began to peruse the shelves. Crystal was getting fidgety and I went over to Nathan.

"I'm just going to be in the toddler area right over there. Stay where I can see you all the time, you got me?" I made sure I had a no-nonsense tone in my voice.

"Yeah sure," he said never even looking at me put pulled several books from the shelf.

"I mean it Nathan."

"Okay, Okay, I'll be sittin' right there," he pointed to one of several bean bag chairs laden about the small children-only reading area.

In the toddler room I retrieved two *Child Proof* books and sat crystal on my knee and began to read to her. She wasn't taking it too well, but was enthralled with the interactive books with its animal sounds and car horns.

Later I took them to McDonald's for lunch—Nathan's reward for being a good boy and then home. Crystal went to sleep immediately, and Nathan settled on the couch with a book we borrowed from the library, but was soon asleep himself. He looked so sweet and peaceful and I planted a light kiss on his forehead. I was beginning to like him; I was beginning to take to both of them.

There was no word from the Child Protective Agency by Monday or Tuesday but by then two things were happening. I was worried about getting back to work the following week and I was getting really attached to the kids.

Melvin came over almost every day, which made me wonder how *his* family was taking him being out all the time. He took a lot of time with Nathan and informed him that he would see about him getting back into the school as soon as he was placed.

For the first time I saw fright in his eyes. "Why can't we just stay here. Miss Mill…" *that's what he called me.* "don't mind, I mean she kind of likes us right Miss Mill?" he said casting his glance over at me.

Melvin chimed in before I could answer. "It's not a matter of that Nathan. There's a lot involved, more than you know."

"Well I ain't going to no home where I don't know nobody. So you just find my moms and we'll go with her." He said then stubbornly opened a book and began to read, or pretended to.

On Friday, Melvin came over and his face was solemn and I knew it wasn't good news.

"A woman was found dead in the kid's apartment this morning. She had a photo of her and the children among her belongings so we can assume she was the mother."

"How?" I asked.

"Overdose."

We hadn't noticed the boy standing in the doorway of the living room.

"Nathan…" I said going to him but he brushed me off.

"No biggie, She was always shootin' up, it had to happened sooner or later.

I'll get our stuff together, guess me and Crystal will be staying at the shelter." And he went into the bedroom but not before I saw tears in his eyes.

I knew I couldn't let those kids go into a city run shelter. They would only separate them and who knew if they'd ever find each other again.

I partitioned for custody and while my being single wasn't a particular problem, my work schedule proposed a huge problem. I told them I would take a leave of absence until I could secure a good baby sitter for Crystal and I'd make sure Nathan got back in school. They weren't even considering it until a blessing came once again in the form of Officer Melvin Anderson and his sister.

"Your honor, this is my sister Lorna, she's married and a stay at home mom. I've talked to her and she said she will be happy to watch the kids until Miss Millen gets home from work," he said.

There was a lot of back and forth with the overworked state worker who made a compelling if routine speech about rules, regulation, interviews and home visits. In the end and with the help of my two new friends The judge allowed the kids to stay with me until the preliminaries with Lorna and her home was satisfactory and with the State work load took exactly two days.

Someone else had to take over my duties running food to the shut-ins on Sundays but I helped prepare the packages. Nathan was playing with some of the other kids and several girls

from the Sunday school class managed the babies and toddlers.
Melvin came by when he could and fell right into the swing of
helping out and soon it was like he'd always been there.
As we left later that afternoon he smiled at us.

"So, how do you feel about ice cream?" he was talking to
Nathan but looking at me.

"I might be lactose intolerant," the little scamp said.

"Fine, then you can have a yogurt."

"Then again I might not be if it's chocolate with wet
walnuts and a cherry," he giggled like the kid he was supposed to
be.

"That kid has got to stop watching the Food Channel,"
Melvin whispered as he ushered us to his car.

With the kid eating ice cream nosily, Melvin and I each
drank ice-cream sodas and watched families enjoying other
confections which I shared a little with the baby.

"Soooo!" he said drawing out the word. "How about my
sister watching the kids Saturday night and you and me go out?"

"Like on a date?"

"Well yeah, you know dinner, maybe a movie."

"I don't know,"

He looked at me. "Gail, there's a chance you might not get
Nathan and Crystal permanently but also a change you might—
adopt them even, but no matter what happened you also have to
live your own life too."

"I didn't know it before but I didn't have a life until they
came into it," I whispered.

"So does that mean there's no room for anyone else?"
I knew what he meant and I was flattered and interested, but
afraid too.

"I've been meaning to ask you about that. How come
there is no *anyone else* in your life?"

"There was a couple of times but one of them had an
issue with me being in Law Enforcement, and the other was a
little too into it, so much so he married my partner."

"Ouch!…" I winced. "That must be awkward."

"It was at first, but I soon found out that they were more suited for each other. I was their best man actually."

"You sound like a good man."

"I Like to think so—which brings me back to you and me."

I was edgy and shifted in my seat.

"Look I might as well be frank with you. I don't know what you're looking for, but I do know that eventually men will want children of their own."

"Whoa! All I'm asking for is a date not a marriage commitment."

I felt a blush.

"I'm sorry, I'm jumping the gun, but I like to get things out in the open quickly."

"Like?"

"Men want children of their own and I can't give them any." I said with finality.

"I don't think you're not qualified to speak for all men."

"I know what I know," I said evenly.

"Well let me tell you what something you don't know. Five years ago I was diagnosed with testicular cancer. They caught it early and radiation took care of the problem but it also took care of me being able to have kids, so you see you don't know everything," he said.

I was surprised and saddened for him. "Nathan and Crystal depend on me; they're beginning to care about me." I said.

"An abused child goes where the love is," he said. That was insulting and I got up to leave, but he stopped me. "It's the same with a man. Sometimes he can see the love that's missing from his life and he won't take the chance on letting it get away."

I sat down again looking at him. "What are you saying Melvin?"

"Those kids may need you, but I might need you too."

"How do you know, it's only been..."

But he shushed me.

"It's only been my whole life looking for someone who can give me what I want, someone to love and a family when it comes to that. I think you just might fit the bill."

"Can you give me some time to think about it?" I asked.

"Take all the time you need, as long as it isn't past August because that's when I take vacation and I'd like to take you and the kids to Disney world."

We did go to Disney world on his vacation along with his sister, her husband Conrad and the twins. I thought it a bit odd, but not after the third night when they insisted we have a night out alone and Melvin proposed, I suspect they knew it all along. I was so happy and of course I said yes. We were married in my church which was filled with familiar parishioners and even some of the shut-in's I had brought service for over the years. Two week after our honeymoon in Bermuda we were notified that that we had been granted custody of kids; pending adoption.

The following Sunday as we walked into church with the kids all decked out in new clothes, I was beaming. My makeshift family might have started out a little backwards but we are a real family and I'm a wife and a mother and able to give all the love I have to the new people in my life.

Drop Out to Graduate

I once overheard a young woman telling her young son to *sound it out* when he had trouble with a word in a book he was reading aloud. That's what I'd tried to do every day of my young life; it was what I was doing now. I sounded out the long word carefully *Ad-van-ta-geous,* then fingered down the page of the *NEW WORLD* dictionary, which not only used the word in a sentence, but in colloquialisms as well. I guess it was designed for people like me-the functioning illiterates of the world.

It was no surprise that I didn't know much. My mother left me with her widowed sister when I was six months old and I never saw her again after that.

Aunt Tilda lived in an old house on land that had been in her family for more than four decades in the Shenandoah Mountains of Virginia. It was a small ill kept parcel of land and the house was almost falling down. Her only source of income was from her deceased husband's social security and the remnants of a small insurance policy that he'd made sure was doled out in small allotments to make it last a little longer. Of course it wasn't nearly enough after I came along. A baby costs more than most people think. She supplemented her income by tatting doilies and leaving them at the general store to be purchased locals and the few camping visitors. We'd spend countless hours sitting in front of the big stone fireplace as she showed me how she used a small, metal shuttle to form the webbed cloth with designs so intricate you would have thought they were woven by angels.

Aunt Tilda taught me to make braided rag rugs from remnants of discarded clothes and old yarn. From a very young age I picked berries which she set up in jars for selling and some for us for the winter months and after a time I knew all about mountain herbs for various illnesses and complaints.

Every evening she would read to me from an old tattered bible but I suspected that she didn't actually *read* it, but had memorized the passages down through the years as they had been told to her. She died when I was seven and I became a ward of the State. I was moved down to Roanoke and cried for days because I had never seen so many people at one time in my life and it was too loud and bustling. I missed the cool mountain air and the peacefulness of our valley.

~*~

I was passed around from one foster home to another and no one seemed to care if I went to school or not—let alone learn anything. Social workers came around from time to time to check, but their caseloads were so heavy that I soon fell between the cracks.

By the time the state released me at age eighteen, I was living on the streets. No one has any idea what kind of life that is for anyone—let alone a young girl. I had to fight off men, women, even stray dogs that challenged me over discarded food. I learned quickly how to hide in alcoves and find places to sleep in the abandoned buildings or behind closed restaurants. Keeping warm in the winter was the most challenging and only on the coldest and snowy nights did I seek refuge at the shelters, all of which were overcrowded and teeming with vermin. Thankfully the YMCA allowed me to shower for Fifty cents a day and sometimes I even got a stale donut and coffee.

~*~

One day I was walking along nibbling around the brown spots of a banana I had found when suddenly I was wrenched rudely back.

"Hey! What's the matter with you can't you read?"

The man in the maintenance uniform glared at me as he pointed to a sign. The only thing I could understand was the big red circle with a line through it. I knew that symbol meant danger or go no further, but I couldn't read the words. When I looked down, I found that I was standing in wet cement with two footsteps behind me.

"Go on! Get outta here," he yelled, then went to smooth out the damaged area.
Tears flooded my eyes. I wasn't stupid; I just didn't have to proper training but I still felt like an idiot.

A short time later I got a job sweeping out and cleaning up at a local fast food place and within six months I was trained and promoted to the register when they found themselves suddenly shorthanded. I thanked my lucky stars for my good memory that there were pictures of food on the register or I would have had a much harder time doing the job.

I was finally able to find a room in a cheap motel not far from the job and for the first time I was making a little money and had a place to live—even if it wasn't the safest or cleanest place in the world. I got most of the things I needed from *Good Will* and secondhand stores and soon I felt like I finally had a semblance of a life. But I still couldn't read, and my math skills were poor. This really bothered me and then one day I had a brainstorm. I knew that local high schools held classes at night for foreigners who wanted to learn to speak English. I figured all I had to do was slip in and melt in with the crowd and listen and learn.

The school was across town, so I went one day before work and looked for the night schedule for the class I thought would do me the most good, but there was nothing posted. I expected that at any moment someone would ask me what I was doing there.
Finally a woman came out of an office carrying a bunch of books and I figured I had nothing to lose in asking her.

"Excuse me, can you tell me about some night courses in English and how much they cost?" I asked. She told me in a

surprisingly friendly tone that the class was free and held every
Tuesday and Thursday night from seven to nine. Free was good,
I could handle free but I would have to check my work schedule
because a lot of time I was asked to stay and do clean up. I knew
they were taking advantage of me, but I would make sure
everything was done in time for me to make the class.

After work that first Tuesday, I waited outside the school
until I saw a small group of Hispanics entering the building and I
followed behind and entered the class, taking a seat as far back
as I could.

"Buenos noches," The instructor said, then followed with
a full-fledged dissertation in fluent Spanish. If I thought I was
lost before, now I was really in the dark.
I slipped out of the classroom after about ten minutes and was
almost at the exit when I heard footsteps behind me.

"Senorita?"
There was no one else in the hall so I assumed he meant me. I
turned; it was the instructor from the class. He began to speak to
me in Spanish but with such a soft tone that I thought he was
apologizing for something.

"I...I'm sorry but I don't speak Spanish." I said.

"Ahh!" he said, "Than that answers the question as to
why you left so quickly. Do you wish to learn Spanish?"

I grinned sadly, "No, I can't hardly speak English good."

"You cannot speak English well," he corrected me,
"...and you cannot say *can't* and *hardly* in the same sentence,
because one means that you are totally *unable* to do something,
while the other means you can do it a little. Which is it?"
Was I getting lesson right there in the hall? I wondered.

"I...um, well I was looking to learn some stuff."

"Well then young lady what you need to do is to come
back tomorrow night and again on Monday. That is when the
English classes are taught."

"Do they got math and maybe some history stories?"
I could see him wince as I spoke.

"What is your name little one?"

"Sharelle Farley." I thought about lying, but I figured there was no point now.

"You be here at seven sharp tomorrow Ms. Farley and I will take you to see Mr. Hudson, he will be able to help you."

"Really?"

"Si, tomorrow at seven and do not be late, because I promised Concetta—that's my wife, I would watch that movie with Will Smith. Aye aye aye! I think she adores him more than me and I gave her a nice home and three children. What did he ever do but show her how to kill bugs with a big gun and fly an alien spaceship." he chuckled.

"Don't worry I won't be late," I smiled, because I'd seen and liked both of those movies.

He took out a pen and wrote something on a slip of paper that he'd extracted from his pocket and handed it to me. I looked at it stupidly.

"Say it, I wrote it the way it sounds, not how it is really spelled" he said when he saw my confused look.

I pursed my lips to sound out the name—*Kar-los Moon-yose.*"

"Si! That is correct, Carlos Munoz, that is my name."

"Cool! I'll see you tomorrow night then."

He smiled and walked back down the hall, calling out over his shoulder. "On time or…"

"I know, Concetta will *keel* you."

I could hear his laughter as I exited the building.

~*~

The next evening I put on a clean pair of jeans and a wrinkled but halfway decent sweater and went to the high school. I was afraid that Mr. Munoz might have forgotten and wouldn't be there, but as soon as I entered there he was, sweating and pacing like an expectant father.

"Ahh, Miss Farley, there you are—come, let's go." He hurried me along the corridor until we came to an empty classroom. Inside a tall balding black man of about fifty or so rose as soon as we entered.

"Mr. Hudson, this is the young woman I spoke to you about."

I was apprehensive because I was wary of men, even the so-called fatherly types.

"I'm Lawrence Hudson, and you are?" He said extending his hand.

"Sharelle Farley," I said quietly.

He spoke to Mr. Munoz for a moment then told me to choose a seat. A few minutes later, chatter in the hall told me that students were coming to class. I was shocked to see that most were older than I was, but there were a few younger ones too.

"Now, let's get started..." Mr. Hudson said.

I was happy that he didn't single me out with introductions and I didn't know much about teachers, but I soon found out that Mr. Hudson made learning to read fun. It was amazing how he incorporated pictures and things from everyday life to make us understand things easier. Don't get me wrong, he was quite a taskmaster and if you didn't do your homework, he punished you with extra.

 By autumn I was already reading simple books and had written three short essays.

"These are pretty good Sharelle, do you think you might want to consider a career as a writer?" he asked handing me back the paper with several errors in punctuation circled in red.

"A career in *anything* is all I want," I said blushing at his compliment of my work.

"You can do anything in the world you want, all you have to do is want it."

I read as many books as I could and I got better at it. Soon I was reading the newspapers right through and finally enjoyed the totally insane and unbelievable stories in the local tabloids that cracked me up. I wondered how people could read such nonsense, but I was glad just to be able to read it at all. Mr. Hudson told me that at the rate I was going I would earn my G.E.D in no time and he would see about help to get me into a community college. I couldn't believe it, *me*—in college. I wanted to cry with joy.

One Saturday as I was walking across the park reading *THE PROPHET* by *Kahlil Gibran*, I looked up just in time to see a jogger heading right for me. He had just taken a swig from his water bottle and didn't see me. Before I was able to move out of the way, we were a tangle of arms and legs on the ground.

"Damn it! This path is for joggers or didn't you read the signs?" The man said, his sandy hair tousled like a toddler's who'd just awakened from a fitful sleep.

"I didn't see no... *any* sign, and yes, I can read." I said defensively holding the book up to his face.

"Obviously *Gibran* doesn't describe walking and reading in any of his dissertations," He said rising then helping me to my feet.

"Well he should because he sure has a lot of opinions about other stuff."

"Opinions? The man was one of the greatest philosophical poets who ever lived."

"A Poet can't have an opinion?" I countered back.
By then he was smiling. "Ya know, you could be right. Maybe all this is just his opinion."

"Take this passage on *REASON AND PASSION*..."
Before I knew it we were in a full-fledged out-and out-down and dirty debate about the book.
Fifteen minutes later, I finally stopped talking.

"You hungry?" he asked. "Because if you're not, then you have got to be thirsty, you talk more than any woman I've ever met and you ask more questions too."

"There's a lot to know and I got a slow start." I murmured.

"Well let me buy you lunch and we can talk about it some more."

~*~

His name was Paul Brandt, he was twenty-six years old and had just returned from a two year stint in the Middle East a year before. It was the only thing I *couldn't* get him to talk about. Before we parted company, he asked for my phone number, but I didn't have one so I asked for his. "Unless you're married, which would mean you cheat on your wife and in that case we can forget phone calls or anything else." I said and eyed him carefully.

"I'm divorced, and here…" he handed me a card he'd extracted from his fanny pack.

"You always carry these in your pack?"

"That and my medical ID, in case someone comes along who shouldn't be *walking* on a *jogging* path and nearly knocks me unconscious."

"I apologized."

"Actually, you didn't, but you can over dinner."
A date, now here was something new. I must have hesitated a bit too long.

"Come on it's the least to can do after trying to kill me."

"You love to exaggerate don't you?"

"Only when there is a degree of difficulty," he said with a smile that was hard to say no to. I agreed to the next weekend. He said that was too long to wait.

"How about Monday night?"

"I can't!" I said it so fast he actually took a step back.

"Whoa! Maybe *you* have a husband or boyfriend *I* should be worried about."

"Do I look like I have a husband or boyfriend?" I half snarled.

"Why not, you're really cute especially when you get all fired up like that."
His grin was infectious and I smiled back. I'd bet he wouldn't think I was so cute if he knew that up until a few months before I couldn't read a whole book or even write very well.

"Tuesday would be better." I said.

"Cool, where can I pick you up?"

"How about if I meet you?" There was no way I was going to have him come to the *Buford Street weekly motel*. I could tell he knew something was mysterious but he let it go.

"Do you know *Huff's* over on Aldan Street?"

"Yeah I know it." It was a popular eatery.

"See you there Tuesday at eight. Deal?"

"Yeah it's a deal. If something comes up, I'll give you a call." I said waving goodbye.

~*~

A lot of things were beginning to look up for me and I felt really happy about it. Things only seemed to get better when a co-worker at the fast food place where I still worked told me about a gig she had coming up. "It's at some *La-de-da* house up in the hills and we'll get two hundred dollars each for three hours work," she said.

Her brother Rick was a groundskeeper there and he'd heard they were a having a huge gala and the catering company they'd hired needing help because of some other function that they had over-booked.

"I don't know Kerri…" I was suspicious because she didn't have the best reputation. I'd managed to stay away from trouble this long and I didn't want to ruin everything now.

"It's legit I swear. All we have to do is wear a stupid ass uniform and serve drinks and appetizers to some fancy pants pool partiers."

"Are you sure?"

"Scout's honor," she held up her fingers in the time-honored salute.

~*~

It was almost thirty miles up to the house and I thought I'd never seen anything so gorgeous. Rick identified himself over the intercom and a big wrought iron gate slowly opened to let us in. As we drove up, it looked like every light in the house was on and the driveway was filled with expensive, shiny cars complete with valet service. Rick drove us around back and told us which door to go in. The kitchen was as large as three rooms on my floor and people dressed in white chef's outfits were running around with tureens, trays, cups and glasses like mad. A woman wearing a polka-dot pantsuit and the biggest eyeglasses I'd ever seen came over.

"Are you the extra help?"
We nodded. I couldn't get over the hustle bustle in the kitchen nor the amount of food that was everywhere.

"Okay, you can change in there…" she pointed to door to the left, "Then we'll tell you what to do."
When I came out, the woman handed me a huge tray filled with small sandwiches, stuffed olives and some funny looking fish things I'd never seen before. Kerri had a tray with stuffed mushrooms, tiny meat patties, fried ravioli and pigs-in-a blanket.

I walked out onto the veranda and stopped every so often to offer a napkin and a selection from my try. These were the beautiful people, women with too much makeup and gaudy jewelry, and men with fake tans and bad hairpieces. They were people way out of my league and I knew I'd never be one of them. Kerri ambled up alongside me.

"See that woman in the gold pants? That's Mrs. Keene, don't get in her way she's meaner than a caged tiger on crack." Of course as luck would have it, avoiding her wasn't in the cards because she was coming right for me with her finger pointed.

"You there—yes you with the pony tail." She hurried over to me, struggling to keep her skinny feet from sliding off her way-too-high-backless pumps.

"Yes Ma'am" I answered politely.

"You march right back in the house and pin that hair up. The last thing I need is having my guests spit out hairballs the size of cotton wads."
I hurried back inside to do as she asked.

I must say it was the hardest money I ever had to work for since we were also responsible for cleaning up afterward which we didn't expect and when Rick dropped me off at 4 a.m. I was dead on my feet.

I slept like the dead but managed awaken in time to make it through work that day. But I had to fight to convince myself into going my evening class because I was so tired. But Mr. Hudson had told me so often how proud of my progress he was and that I was the best student in the class. I couldn't let him down by not showing up.

As soon as I finished my shift and on legs of lead, I grabbed my backpack and headed out. I was so tired and walked so slow to school I arrived literally seconds before the class was to start. Mr. Hudson was nowhere to be seen and that gave me a few extra minutes to sit and read over the assignment.

"Good evening all! Mr. Hudson had an emergency so I'll be substituting for him until he's able to return."

That voice! I looked up, *those eyes*. It was Paul. He saw me at the exact same moment I saw him and only the slight rise of his questioning brow registered his surprise.

"Okay then, let's turn to page 117," he said too loudly. My hands were shaking and I couldn't focus on the words.

"Would anyone like to share their thoughts on the passage—how about you?"

It took a minute before I realized that people were looking right at me and so was Paul.

My mouth was dry as a sand desert and as I looked down at the page, the words seemed to meld together in one big jumble. It was like before when I couldn't understand the words. I couldn't do it. Tears flooded my eyes and I gathered up my things and ran from the room.

I couldn't go back—I'd never go back as long as Paul was there. What must he think? I'd bet a sack-full of hill beans he'd never want to take a girl out who was so stupid that there was a time in the not so distant past she couldn't even *read Tom Sawyer.*

~*~

I'd begun to hate my life again but I couldn't stop thinking about Paul. But more importantly I couldn't stop thinking about what I was missing in class. I had been so close to getting that certificate and now I was nowhere. I'd decided it wasn't worth going back.

A week later I was sweeping up after the last customer had left and Kerri was in the back putting the day's receipts in the bank pouch.

"You didn't keep our dinner date last Tuesday," Paul's voice was low.

I stared at him, the broom poised in mid-sweep.

"I'm sorry sir, but we're closed."

"Sharelle..." be began, but I didn't want to hear anything.

"I said we're closed!" the words came out loud and harsh. His brow knitted with confusion and his eyes were sad as he shook his head and turned and walked out. Kerri exited from the back when she'd heard my voice.

"Everything okay Shar?"

I could only nod with my back to her so she couldn't see my tears and kept on sweeping.

I walked home slowly. I liked Paul there was no doubt about that and I felt as though my world was falling apart. In my room I didn't even bother to undress; I just lay across the sagging bed and cried. After a while I dried my tears and sat on the edge of bed facing the smudgy mirror on the wall in front of me. *Get it together girl he was way out of your league anyway.*
I turned on the small TV but I muted the sound, I wasn't really interested in anything anyway.

A soft knock sounded on my door. I was stunned and suspicious. Most people in this establishment were itinerants and welfare recipients and usually stayed to themselves. No one bothered to make any familiar connections.

"Who is it?" I purposely lowered my voice and sounded gruff.

"It's me Sharelle, I need to talk to you."
It was Paul. *How had found me?*

"Please, just for a minute Sharelle."
I snatched the door open.

"Well come on in Mr. Brandt, come see how the other half lives. Not only am I stupid, but I'm poverty stricken as well," I said glaring at him as he moved passed me.
He stood in the middle of the small dingy room, his handsome face a mixture of confusion and resolve.

"You need to come back to class."

"I don't think so, besides I'm bored with it anyway."

"No you're not." He said.

"And how do you know?"

"I spoke to Mr. Hudson."

"A lot he knows," I said trying to sound sarcastic.

"Look, if it's me you're trying to avoid that won't be necessary, I'm leaving," he said.

"Don't flatter yourself. It has nothing to do with you. I just don't want to do it that's all. I mean what's the damn point anyway?"

"The point is, you were trying to better yourself and now you're giving up."

"What's it to you?"

"I've been there."

"Yeah right!" I sneered.

"Okay, maybe I already knew how to read, but I was a hellion back then. I was lazy, missed a lot of school and ran with a really bad crowd. By the time I was seventeen, I had been in juvenile detention six times. I spent my eighteenth birthday in court and the judge said it was the army or jail, those were my choices. I chose the army and it was the best thing I ever did. They paid for my education and I found that I liked learning. It took a while but I got a degree then my Master's. Soon after I was certified to become a teacher...then..."

His whole face changed. It became hard and his mouth twisted almost like he was chewing on a stone.   "...then I got deployed to the Middle East. You think you've had it bad? You have no idea. The heat, the war, the poverty is its own kind of hell. And then there's the children... that's the worst because they're in the midst of it all in the most deplorable and uncertain of conditions. You have no idea what it's like to be under the constant fear that a bomb can drop on your village at any moment. Can you imagine living under that threat every single day? No child should have to go through that. I've seen so much death in all forms of its horror. I held fellow soldiers in my arms with their legs or arms blown off. For some I was the last face they saw before they breathed their last. It's something you can't get out your mind. It haunts your day and keeps you from sleeping at night."

Why was he telling me all this, to make me feel sorry for him?

"You have no idea how it can change a man. When I got back I was a shell and I began to drink, but even that couldn't make the images go away."

I was about to interject but he continued on.

"I knew I had to get myself together, and I did. It took some time, but I did it. I got re-certified and took some more classes to bring me up to speed and started teaching again. I was still drinking and I knew I had to do something about that, so I joined AA, it helped a lot but it was the nights that were really bad. When you're alone and your only thought is to try and forget everything that horrified you and the only thing that can do that is a bottle of anything, you can't imagine how bad it gets.

"Didn't you have a sponsor or something? Aren't they supposed to help you?"

"Yes I had one and they did help, but post traumatic syndrome is a hard nut to crack. One night I brought a bottle of rum, I intended to drink every last drop and the rest of the world be damned. I must have stared at it for an hour. I even opened it, inhaled the smell that made me want to drink right from the bottle. But I didn't, I ran."

"You ran?" I said stupidly.

"Right out the front door and down the street. I ran until my lungs stung in my chest. I kept running until my legs were rubber. I ran until I didn't know where the hell I was."

I looked at him curiously wondering…

"So what did you do?"

"I turned around and ran back."

"Back home?"

He snorted out a laugh.

"Well I *eventually* found my way back home but it was hours later. When I got there I was so damned tired I couldn't think about anything except hitting the sack. The last thing I saw before I closed my eyes was that bottle and the first thing I did when I awoke the next day was pour the whole thing down the drain. "

"Why didn't you tell me any of this before?"

"You never gave me a chance, like I said; you talk more than any woman I ever knew." He snickered, but then the silence was overwhelming, his soft voice, "Aren't you going to say anything?"

I stared at him. "Like what?"

"I just poured out my life's story to you in five minutes. You can at least say you'll go back to class and you'll get your diploma and go to college and how you'll go out to dinner with tomorrow night."

"College? Who are you kidding? I'll be happy with the GED."

"Not a woman like you. You like learning too much, I can tell.

"I'm don't think so."

"Look, I know seeing me in class that night upset you a little but you can get back on track. College is not out of your reach, we can research grants and student aid."

I sat on the edge of the bed. "So you don't think I'm stupid?" I asked softly.

"Of course not, besides; anyone who thinks that *Gibran* is just a conceited loudmouth is far from being stupid."

"I don't have much—this is how I've been living, it's all I can afford. But maybe if I get a better job and…" I was speaking rapidly and he put a finger to my lips.

"It's not where you live; it's *how* you live your life. I see so much goodness in you Sherelle. You're going to be okay, and if it's all right with you, I'd like to be beside you as you do it."

"Paul, there's a lot about me you don't know, a lot that's not pretty."

"When you're ready you can tell me your nightmares and if you think you can stand it I'll tell you the rest of mine. Maybe together we can find a place that will belong only to us and we can put those horrors behind us forever."

Paul was right about everything. I did go back to school and I got my GED Certificate. I enrolled in the community college at night but Paul insisted I move in with him and go during the day. "I'll support us, even if we have to eat Pizza or franks and spaghetti, and you'll finish quicker."

~*~

Four years later I got my degree and then went on to complete a Master's program in education and economics. I knew I wanted to be able to do what was done for me, so I became a teacher. Not only that, I made sure that I taught at least one class at night to give others an opportunity to fulfill a life-long dream of getting an education.

My life is changed because an education opened doors, but more importantly it opened up my mind to the possibilities of endless adventures. Paul and I plan to marry in the spring and we're moving up to Shenandoah and open a little school so that other kids won't have to grow up the way I did. He's a loving soul and I even when he tells me I don't owe him anything, not even gratitude I know that it was because I met him that I can be the person I always wanted to be.

High on the down low

"He's cheating on me." My friend Della cried.
I couldn't believe it. Gregory and Della Howes were the happiest couple I knew—or so I thought. I handed her yet another tissue and she blew her nose then wadded it up into a tight ball and cried some more.

"I'm so sorry Della I really am." I wanted to kill that no-good Gregory, how dare he cheat on my friend.

"My wedding is three weeks away. How could he do this?" she sobbed.
Shauna, her roommate walked in, swiveling her hips and cutting her eyes over to where we sat.

"I told you not to trust his trifling ass." She said taking a Heineken from the refrigerator.

"Hush Shauna, this is serious," I said to her.

"Girl please, I told her a long time ago she needs to be checking his whereabouts especially because his ass was always MIA. But she was so sure he was true blue as a summer sky."

"Not all men cheat," I said.

"Yeah well that may be true for some, but they *all* have the capability and *all* they need is opportunity."

I was well aware of Shauna's views on men and their dating habits. She'd had so many bad relationships that I was positive she wouldn't recognize a good one if it came along. Della jumped up and pulled her robe together, she hadn't been out in three days, not since she found out that not only did Gregory have another woman, but she was also pregnant with twins.

"It's not his fault; some hoochie seduced and tricked him by getting pregnant. They know he has a good steady job. She's probably looking for security," she yelled at Shauna.

"Shauna said taking a swig from the beer bottle. "If that skank knew half of what *this* hoochie knows she would be running the other way fast and you should to. Once a cheater always a cheater."

"That's not fair," I broke in. "If Della feels she wants to forgive Gregory that is her business, you have no right to try and dissuade her."

"Oh really and what do you think he's going to do? Never cheat again?"

"Personally I don't think he will, if he's sincere," I said.

"Then you're just as dumb as she is." Shauna said waving her hand then disappeared into her bedroom.

I was suddenly glad I was married and enjoying my fifth year as Mrs. Alyn Harvey. I didn't have to wonder where my man was because he was with me every night, and called me no less than five times a day.

I'd met Alyn at an Aids-walk six Years ago. If ever there was love at first sight this was it, but it wasn't him I loved at first sight it was the cute little brown and white Pekinese he was walking with. When I stooped down to pet him, the little dog began lapping my fingers and dancing around like a show animal.

"Wow this is really something. *Monster* doesn't like everybody." His voice was deep and throaty. *Too deep for an ordinary man of ordinary height.* I looked up and the sun kept me from seeing his face so I stood up and found that I barely reached his shoulder.

"You named this cute little puppy Monster?" I grinned.

"Hey, this is New York, you have to have protection." He didn't look like he needed anything except a Mack truck to haul his 6 foot 5 frame from place to place.

By the time we finished the walk, we were talking like we'd known each other for years. He was funny and didn't do or say anything that put me off. When he asked me to join him and a few friends later that evening for a drink I didn't hesitate. Never had I been in the company of so many high powered, uber-intelligent handsome men and beautiful women in my life. These people were confident and they didn't make me feel inadequate even before they knew I was completing my Master's Program in biology. Later as we left the restaurant Alyn told me that he knew someone at Columbia that might be able to help me credit wise or at least be a good resume addition. It resulted in me securing a position as the assistant to the head Science Professor.

~*~

Alyn and I were inseparable after that. The law firm he worked for kept him busy, but every chance he got he was with me. We went hiking; kayaking, sailing and rafting in Pennsylvania and I even joined his gym. I was not only making a little more money, but I was also in the best shape of my life. I was more than happy to keep *Monster*, when he had to go out of town for a few days and the little impish puppy loved it too. I remember the first time Della and Shauna came over and saw him.

"Where the hell did you get that fluffy little rat?" Shauna said looking at the dog and pursing her burnt orange colored lips.

"He belongs to Alyn." I said picking up the little fur ball and cradling him close.

"What kind of man has a frou-frou little dog like that?"

"A very sensitive one," I said putting the dog down on his little silk pillow.

~*~

Six months after we met, on my birthday, Alyn told me that he had something special planned. He told me to wear the most comfortable causal clothes I owned and sneakers.
I was curious about what he was up to and I soon found out. He had a little basket filled with twenty-five fortune cookies. Each one had a number and he said I had to open each one in sequence. It was a scavenger hunt. Each clue led me to a place where a small nifty gift was hidden. While they were hidden within three blocks of my apartment, it was exhausting but so much fun I could not stop laughing.

The first clue led me to *Ashanti's Lingerie Emporium* where the sales girl presented me with a gift wrapped box when I handed her the numbered clue. The second clue led me to my favorite spa where I enjoyed a full body massage, a relaxing foot bath and a *mani* and *pedi*.
It went on like that all day and I was sure that I couldn't go another step. The last of the clues had me in my apartment un-wrapping a gorgeous box from SAKS which held the sexiest blood red wrap dress I ever saw.

After I bathed and slipped on silky red thong panties and bra from *Ashanti's* and slid on the sheerest silkiest lace-topped thigh-HI's I owned, I put on the gorgeous dress then slipped my feet into black satin backless mules with rhinestones on the heel. My make-up was understated but flawless and dewy. I grabbed my purse and headed out the door by eight.

Downstairs there was a long black stretch limo with a fully uniformed driver waiting for me with the door open. I handed him the paper from the Fortune Cookie and he got in and off we went. When I arrived at *Hefesta's Tavern*, the concierge handed me a long stem white rose.

"Your party is waiting please follow me," he said with a smile and practiced bow.
I followed him to an elegantly set table, where Alyn stood beaming. He was resplendent in his Armani tuxedo and I knew I was even more in love with him than I had thought. He kissed me softly and we sat. His eyes were shining and he couldn't take his eyes off me.

"So, how was your day?" he teased.

"You know how it was. I'm exhausted—and grateful. You're so generous and so wonderful Alyn."

"It's your birthday and it was my pleasure. It makes me happy to see you happy."
I looked around at the elegant chandeliers, expensive furniture and crystal. I had never been in such a sophisticated and expensive place in my life and it made me feel like a queen.

"This is just beautiful Alyn, what made you pick this particular place?"

"It suits you and you deserve it."
The waiter came with the menus with no prices but I knew it didn't' make a difference to Alyn. I couldn't decide on what I wanted and left it up to Alyn to choose for me. We enjoyed a six course meal specially prepared by and brought out by the chef himself. After the dessert of fresh berries and cream, I couldn't help but smile until I thought my face would crack.

"I love my new dress." I said running my hands over the soft material.

"And I love you." His statement stunned me.

"You do?" I blinked at him.

"How could I not? You're everything a man could want Radina."
I felt a blushing heat race through me.

"I never thought…" I was too overwhelmed to continue.

"What? Tell me Radina."
It was all I could do to keep from crying. "I just never thought I could be so happy. You're like a dream come true." I reached over and touched his large thick hand. He clasped mine and grinned.

We shared an after-dinner aperitif, and when the table was cleared, the Matre D, set the rectangular bill folder in the middle of the table. Alyn reached into his pocket and I noticed a puzzled look on his face. He frantically began to search but was coming up empty. He looked at me sheepishly.

"Um, Radina, it looks like I left my wallet at home. Could you see about this? I'll pay you back."
I thought this a little odd because Alyn was so meticulous about everything. "Of course." I said without hesitation, but I was wondering if my already burdened Visa Credit card could handle the expensive dinner. I took it out and opened the leather check case and my eyes bulged. Attached to the bill was a two caret sparking diamond and platinum engagement ring. The bill read **WILL YOU MARRY ME,** in Alyn's familiar handwriting.

I began to cry. Alyn had come over and was on his knee, and placed the ring on my finger. "I love you Radina. You're the women I've been searching for all my life and I want to take care of you in every way."
I was too overwhelmed with happiness to speak. He handed me his handkerchief.

"Come on baby; don't cry people are going to think I mistreat you." He laughed.
I hugged him—clung to him in fact like he was my lifeline, and in a way he was. At that moment I decided I would be the perfect wife. I was going to love and honor him and never let him forget for a moment that he was the only man for me.

"Woman, people are beginning to stare. You better let me go so that I can get you home where I can give you what you want."

I separated myself from him and gazed at the huge sparking gem on my finger. "Can I call the girls first?"
His laugh was loud and sexy. "Sure honey you go ahead. I'll take care of the check and meet you in the foyer."

I could hardly wait to get to my apartment. I nearly ripped off his tux as I began to appreciate his body in the way I knew he liked.

"Girl, you sure know what to do with that mouth."

"Only for you baby."
By the time I'd brought him to the edge of several unrealized orgasms he was so tense I thought he was going to take me right there on my living room floor. We made it to the bedroom, but none too soon. His mouth made a trail of kisses down my chest, over my breasts and belly until he finally came to my trimmed patch. As always he began his teasing. He knew it drove me crazy but he kept it up for almost a half hour until I was wild and frenzied. "I like it when you want me that way Radina." He said.

"Please," I begged. But he wanted more. He liked to hear me tell him what I wanted.

"Go on baby, say the words. Tell me what you want and how you want it."

In the most decadent words I could find, I uttered my demands. His mouth went to work and my body was a quivering mass of jelly by the time he entered me. He was huge, so large in fact that I bit back a cry each and every time he took me, but I loved it and I took every inch of him inside me.

~*~

We were married three months later. Alyn insisted on it being a fabulous affair and it was. I always dreamed of a fairytale wedding and he provided that and more.
We purchased a brownstone at an exorbitant price on Strivers row and I couldn't have been happier. I guess I seemed smug to my friends, because Shauna finally told me she was tired of hearing about my new this my new that, and how my man satisfied me like no other could.

"Well now ain't you just the lucky one." She said snidely one afternoon when we were having a girl's luncheon.

"Shauna you don't have to be so mean about everything just because things aren't going very good for you right now." I said gently.

"Yeah well all I can say is, if things look too good to be true, they usually are."
I ignored her mean statements and concentrated on my big hunk of a man.

Alyn's job was demanding and he suddenly was asked to go San Francisco for a few days. Those days turned into weeks, but he called and sent flowers, and my life was never so complete. Oddly, I started getting hang-ups during various times at home. It didn't bother me at first, but then they started coming late at night and only when Alyn was home. I mentioned it to him and he checked Caller ID, but the information was unavailable.

' "I had some issues with a divorce client's husband. I hope it isn't him calling to make trouble."
I worried about Alyn, I knew how insensitive people could be and I didn't want him to get hurt.

~*~

One evening while we were out having dinner, we'd just left the restaurant when a pale faced white youth approached us. Immediately apprehensive I clung to my husband's arm.

"Can I speak to you a minute?" the young man's eyes didn't even look at me, but at my husband.

"Casey, this is not the time. I'm with my wife. Come to the office tomorrow." And before I could take a breath Alyn pulled me along toward our car.

"Who was that?"

"Just a case I worked on. Things aren't going his way, and he's been calling and trying to get a conviction overturned." I relaxed a bit. He'd handled it so smoothly I knew there was nothing to fear. However, the strangest thing happened when we got home. We were barely in the door before he grabbed me and kissed me so hard my lips felt bruised. He literally shoved my clothes up, tore my panties off and then undid his own clothes. He pushed me up against the door and entered me roughly and began to pound in me so hard I struggled to hold onto him. His face was an anguished mask and his teeth gritted in a snarling grimace. When he finished he moved away, breathing heavily, his head lowered.

"Alyn, is everything okay?" I asked smoothing my tousled hair.

"Yeah-look baby I'm sorry if I was a little rough. You just looked so good and when I saw Casey looking at you, I guess I got a little jealous."
Nothing could be further from the truth. That man never even noticed me.

~*~

Alyn was spending longer hours at the office. Twice I went by to bring him a surprise dinner for which he was immensely grateful. The third and fourth time, he wasn't there. I asked him about it and he told me he was with clients. I didn't want to sound like a jealous wife, I really had no basis for any suspicion but I couldn't help it I loved him so much.

I was disappointed that I didn't get pregnant and I was about to set up an appointment with my GYN to discuss the matter when I received a call from my elderly Aunt Bea, who lived alone in Iowa and was due to have a hip operation.

"You go sweetie." Alyn said, "I'll take care of everything here."

By then I had no problem getting a leave from work and since I took my lap top I wasn't totally unavailable.

The time dragged as I took care of my maidenly aunt. I loved her, but I ached to be back with my husband. I was away a month and when things looked like they were going okay; she suffered a mild panic attack.

"I'm sorry honey I have to stay a little longer. But I miss you and I will be back soon."

"You stay as long as you need to. Your aunt has no one but you."

"So you miss me?" I asked fishing for compliments.

"You know I do." He then lapsed into the raunchiest phone sex diatribe that had me pleasuring myself over the phone so he could hear it.

Aunt Bea recovered and a week later called me into her Bedroom.

"You go on home to that handsome husband of yours; Maize Conklin is coming to stay with me for a while until I'm on my feet again."

I refused but one thing you don't do is get on Aunt Bea's bad side, she was adamant that I go home and I went to the phone to make reservations. I was excited and wanted to get back to Alyn. They had two flights- one was the red eye at 6AM, but they had a flight with a few seats that night due to arrive at 2AM. I decided on that one. What a surprise it would be for Alyn when I slid naked into our bed beside him. I knew the rest of the night was going to be a non-stop love fest.

I had trouble finding a cab that hour of the morning, but finally I got one and when I arrived home I let myself in quietly. I removed all my clothes and went to the bedroom door and opened it. The illumination nearly blinded me from the multitude of candles burning in the room. The heavy scent of incense and Marijuana filled my nostrils, but the greatest shock was seeing that recently familiar white face jump apart from my husband's. It was the same young man from the street that day. He was in my bed, and what was worse, it looked like he *had been in* my husband. The bitter taste of vomit rose in my throat as I stumbled from the room. I was blind dizzy and could hardly stand.

"Radina, wait... please let me explain."
Had I heard correctly? What was there to explain? I hurried to don my clothes, throwing on everything haphazardly and backwards but I didn't care. Alyn stood before me his face unrecognizable in its anguish, but all I could see was the youth standing in the doorway, a half smile playing across his painted mouth.

"You remove your sorry ass from my house." I shouted at him.
He rolled his blue eyes over to my husband. "Do you want me to go honey?" he drawled in a sing-song voice.
I couldn't believe his gall. I went to him, pointing my finger in his face. "I said I want you out of here right now."

"Don't be all mad because you can't give your man what I can," he said looking me up and down with scorn.

"Casey please! " Alyn pleaded with the man.

"Alyn, how could you?" Tears ran down my face.

"Yes Alyn, tell her how you could." The young man said. "Tell her how I was the one who broke it off when you got married; I was the one who stayed away. Tell her how you keep calling *me* back."
I was stunned. "You mean this has been going on since we got married?" The years fell away in my mind.

"Girlfriend, it's been going on since I was eighteen years old and I'm twenty-four now."
I couldn't believe it.

"But you love me. You make love to me like no one ever has, you made love to me like a man makes love to a woman." I said to my husband who wasn't saying anything back.

"Of course he did sweetie. When men lives on the down-low like Alyn here he has to know how to keep *all* of his paramours happy—and we both know he has what it takes to do that now don't we?"

This piece of crap was in my house talking to me about my husband like I was supposed to understand and condone what had been going on behind my back. I glared at him with uncontrolled fury. My husband finally looked away from me to the young man. "Casey maybe you better go."
Maybe? How could he say maybe as if there was a choice?
Casey got up and took his time dressing, unashamed that I saw everything he had. I turned away and waited until he left our home.

I sank to the couch, my legs were weak and I was completely drained. The place beside me depressed as Alyn sat next to me and went to put his arm around me. I didn't want him to touch me—not ever again and I moved away.

"Don't touch me."

"Please honey let me explain…"

"Explain what? That you been creeping—and with another man no less? That there's a chance you have given me a death sentence?"

"I just didn't know how to explain it. It's something that I thought was a whim and that I'd get over it. When I met you, I was so happy and…"

"Not happy enough to cut it off with your little milky-faced friend. You could even have exposed me to HIV, is that fair?"

"We've been tested, we're okay."

"I don't care about you or him. I don't care if you get HIV with a syphilis chaser just as long as I don't have it. Get out of here-now!" I screamed at him.

He tried reasoning with me but I didn't want to hear anything he had to say and went to his chest of drawers and began throwing his things onto the floor. He took as much as he could in an overnight case and a couple garbage bags and after trying to talk me again which I wouldn't do, he left.

~*~

I didn't leave the house for days. Apparently Alyn had been living a lifestyle that he'd kept a secret and I knew that it was not up to me to tell anyone. Besides I was too embarrassed. I knew people would find out and either feel sorry for me or wonder how I couldn't know. By the time I was able to venture out the first thing I did was file for a divorce. I left my job and my home and moved to another city.

I am trying to get on with my life, but it's hard. I haven't been able to establish a relationship with a man for fear of the lies. I am in therapy and its helping and I thank goodness that no children were born of the union between Alyn and me. It saddens me to think that somewhere out there, women are being lied to by their men about their sexual preferences. I am lucky, I am disease free, but how many others can say that? My heart grieves for them, and my tortured soul grieves for the loss of a man I truly loved with all my heart.

Tee for Two

"Girl, what are we doing out here?" my friend Doraleese
Harwell asked. "It's hotter than the tip end of the devil's…"
I threw her a warning look.

"I was gonna say tail," she said rolling her eyes at me.

"We're here to learn to play golf. It's a great toning
exercise and it also teaches strategy and patience."

"The only patience I have is wearing thin and the only
strategy I want to devise is how long it's gonna take me to get off
this hot ass field."

We were standing on the veranda of the *Reinfield
Country Club* gazing out over the lush greenery of the golf
paddock. In the distance I could see early morning golfers and
their caddies walking toward their next teeing off point.

"Just smell that fresh air Doraleese," I said.

"I'd much rather smell some Starbucks and a sticky bun,"
she said with surliness.

"This exercise is *because* of your out-of-control diet."
She ignored me with a flip of her middle finger and looked out
over the green.

"You think Tiger Woods ever comes here Kenna?"
I glanced sideways at her.

"No Dora, Tiger is busy in California right now with his
new girlfriend—you know, the woman he chose *after* his divorce
instead of you," I teased.

"Yeah I know and don't think I'm not mad about that
either." She sucked her teeth to emphasize her ire.
I glanced at my watch for the third time in the past fifteen
minutes. Our instructor was ten minutes late and that was
unacceptable in my book.

"I don't know why you're trippin'…" Dora said "Our
instructor is most likely some dried up, used up prune who has

seen his heyday come and go and now he's gonna teach us what he probably can't even remember,"

As if on cue the door behind us opened and *Mr. too-good-looking* in his khaki pants and light purple sports shirt walked in.

"Miss Jefferson, I'm Craig Bratton. If you'll follow me, I'll show you the club and we can get started."

*That was it? He wasn't going to offer any explanation as to why he was late? I wa*s plenty mad about how aloof he was being about his tardiness. After all, golf lessons weren't cheap and he should have been on time, or at least offered an explanation that would have satisfied me.

I looked at Dora, hoping for a little help, but I could see she was lost in the sea of his brown eyes with hazel flecks. She sauntered her bouncy hips over to him and extended her hand.

"I'm Doraleese Harwell Mr. Bratton-my close friends call me Dora." Her voice dripped with seductive offerings.

"Nice to meet you Miss Harwell."

He said her surname rigidly, taking her hand and shaking it. "Shall we go?"

Oh Hay-ell no! Did he just ignore me like a *P-Diddy groupie*? I was about a nano-second from expressing my dissatisfaction, but he had already turned and opened the door.

"Come on girl, the last time I saw thighs that strong was at the Fanadale winter wrestling smack-down," Dora whispered and pulled me along.

"I'm not interested in his thighs; I just want to learn how to play golf—and on a timely manner!" I said a little louder so he would catch it; as I let her tug me toward the door Craig was holding for us.

~*~

Finally we were on the green. It *was* hot and the sun was cooking us like country bacon on a cast iron skillet. Looking over at our instructor I noticed he managed to remain unfazed by the heat yet there I was standing a foot from him with sweat stains the size of Colorado under my pits. My hair—that I had carefully styled was hanging like a limp dishrag and I mentally cursed *MAC* make-up for lying about their waterproof-non-running Mascara.

"Now for the rules of the game...." Craig said leaning on his club.

"*Rules*? This boring ass game has rules?" Dora hissed at me.

"Apparently," I said.

Craig began his dissertation about greenery protocol and courteousness. I was trying to listen, but Dora wasn't the least bit interested.

"Well the only rule I want to know is what he likes and how he likes it," she whispered eyeing him lasciviously.

"Doraleese Harwell; I brought you here to help us be more focused, energetic and to get some much needed exercise." I whispered.

"I *am* focused, right on his butt cheeks and I'll just let him be responsible for my energy levels if he can handle a woman with my substantial attributes," she said cupping her breasts quickly.

"You're impossible." I laughed.

"Ladies, walk this way please..."

Craig led us to a mound of grass which was connected to a large kidney shaped sandy mass.

"Now this is the bane of every golfer's existence—the sand trap..." he began and explained how the choice and angle of the iron had to be consistent with being able to remove your ball from the sand, giving it enough momentum to proceed as close to the next putting hole as possible."

Well how hard could that be? I thought *it was only sand for goodness sake not molten lava.*

He must have noticed my expression and offered a sliver of a smile.

"Miss Jefferson, would you like to try it?"

"Sure," I said moving toward the teed ball with all the confidence of a WPGA superstar. I looked down at it then angled my butt out like I'd seen them do on television, wiggled it like they *never* did on television, then stopped to determine the distance over the mound and then made my shot. To my chagrin the ball sailed a mere two feet and landed even further into the sand with a dull flat thud. I looked back at Craig who was stoic but Dora was laughing her sides out.

He gestured at me to move further down into the sand.

"You mean go out there?" I pointed.

"The ball isn't going to come to you," he said.

I hesitated; my shoes were sinking into the sand.

"Of course if you like I could show you…" Craig said.

"No thanks!" I said and trudged my way over to the ball. But the golf gods liked to mess with people and were being playful because a foot from my shot I lost my footing and slid flat on my butt, my golf iron sailing three feet away from me. Dora was howling.

"Need some help?" Craig asked.

"No, I got this" and with as much dignity as I could muster I struggled to my feet, my hands covered in sand I brushed the sand from the back of my Bermuda shorts and went to retrieve my iron. I swung and missed that damned ball five different times. The one time I *did* manage to hit the darn thing, it shot up into the air along with a hail of sand and plopped right on my own head. I was beginning to hate this game. I looked at my two on-lookers and seeing them both trying to hold in a gut-wrenching laugh, I just picked the ball up and threw it out onto the green.

~*~

The lesson was three hours long, but I felt like I'd been at it all day. I knew that every bone in my body was going to be an aching mass of flesh the next day but I'd signed us up and paid for three months' worth of non-refundable lessons, so *not* taking advantage of the game was not an option. Before we left I excused myself and went to the ladies room to get some of the sand out of my shoes and the back of my legs.

When I went to the parking lot, I saw Craig and Dora standing by my BMW convertible, laughing it up like they were old friends. I went over and dropped my bag into the back seat.

"I hope you had an enjoyable afternoon Kenna," Craig said with an air of flattering familiarity.

"It's Miss Jefferson, and yes it was interesting." I said and got behind the wheel, signaling Dora to get in. I gave Craig a stingy polite smile then backed the car out the space and drove away.

~*~

The wind blew through my hair and the breeze cooled my warm body. We were about a block from her apartment when Dora spoke up.

"I'd say a week, maybe two?"

"For what?" I asked thumping my hand on the steering wheel to the music beat on the radio.

"Before he calls you or you call him?"

"I am not calling that egotistical, bag of wind?"
I drove on to the front of her building. She got out grabbing her *borrowed* bag of irons and slung it over her shoulder.

"McKenna honey, you are so dense sometimes that you can't even feel it when you've been knocked upside the head with cupid's cross-bow."

"You're insane, I'll call you later."
I snickered all the way home. How could my best friend think I would be even remotely interested in Craig Bratton. It was absurd.

That evening after a long soak in my tub, then smoothing Shea Butter all over my body, I climbed between my sateen sheets naked and waited for sleep to claim me. I dreamed—dreamed I was a naked island beauty waiting patiently for her lover to come and take her. Shadows of men passed in my mind, then a man exited the shadows, came forward and grabbed me. His kisses devoured me and at the moment of truth I awoke, startled by the realism and what I'd just dreamt. I felt the

moistness between my legs. Somehow, in my sleep I had climaxed. Was I going crazy? This was not me at all.
Dora called me every day wanting to know if I'd heard from Craig.

"Why should I? He's a golf instructor not A Mega-star from sports illustrated."

~*~

I had been working mad/crazy hours for weeks and it was all I could do to stop at the local market after work for a *Carb-Conscious* dinner and go home.

One Friday evening after a particularly grueling work week and steaming hot day, I stopped at the market for some soy milk and Captain Crunch cereal—one of my favorite easy meals. The store was relatively empty except for a few late shoppers like me. I got the milk and was on my way to the cereal aisle when I heard a woman's giggle. It wasn't your everyday *ha-ha* giggle, but one that said something was being done to her that she liked—a lot. Grabbing my box of cereal I backed up and hurried in the other direction. As I turned the corner toward the check-out, I saw him. It was Craig with a long legged mocha brown woman who was draped on him like cape. One of her bare legs was wrapped around his thigh as his hand held her by the curve of her tight trim waist. We saw each other at the same time, but I turned to go.

"McKenna!"
I kept walking. When had I give him permission to address me by my given name? I stopped, coerced a small, stingy smile and turned.

"Hello Mr. Bratton"
"It's Craig. I've been meaning to give you a call."
"Oh?" I said trying to maintain my nonchalant air.
"Yes, you left you Nine Iron at the club.
"I'm sure you're mistaken, if I'd left it I would have known."
"It's initialed, *K. Jefferson*, and they match the other clubs I saw you with."

It was mine all right. The clubs had belonged to my father, *Kendrick Jefferson*. I was stunned that I'd left one behind.

The woman he was with made a show of her boredom and kept flicking her tongue in and out of his ear while he pretended to bat her away playfully.

"I'll, um… well I…" why was I stammering?

"I can hold it until your next lesson, or if you need it before then, I can bring it by," He said swatting at the woman. She didn't like that. "Craaaaiggg!" she whined, "I'm hungry, and not for sushi or Captain crunch either."

Captain Crunch? I looked in his basket and among several items lay and a box of Captain Crunch cereal, the same size as I'd bought. He noticed mine too.

"Looks like we share similar tastes."

"I'll come by the club to get it tomorrow." I said too quickly.

"Sorry we're going to South Carolina for the weekend, we'll be getting an early start," the woman said with a note of irritation.

"How about say, next week?" Craig said.

"Will it be safe that long? It's kind of special," I said to him.

"As safe as a lover cradled in my arms," he said. Heat raced up my body at his suggestive remark and I hoped he hadn't noticed.

"Well then…" I said clearing my throat. "I guess I can't ask for more than that, enjoy your weekend." I barely glanced at the giggly amazon before turning and walking away.

I was mad and had no idea why. Seeing Craig with that woman somehow set my teeth on edge. She seemed so freaking needy, but she was a show stopper in the looks department. I hardly knew the man, why then did I feel so resentful?

I didn't feel like eating when I got home and I just put everything away and changed into a loose fitting pair of summer slacks and a sleeveless shell. Slipping into my comfort sandals which is another word for *out of shape and out of style shoes,*

grabbed my fanny pack and decided I'd go to LA CASE—
pronounced *LA-CAH-ZAY;* a downtown sidewalk café where I
could enjoy the evening breeze and a glass of Merlot.

It was crowded with people unwinding from a hellish
work week, tourists and locals but I managed to find a single
table close to the corner end. I ordered and was on my second sip
when a familiar voice spoke.

"It's not good to drink alone."

It was Craig. I turned to look up at him.

"Don't you have to be somewhere like packing for your
trip with Miss giggle-puss?"

"Oooh!" he said scrunching up his face, "Sounds like the
jealously bee has stung you."

"I don't think so," I guffawed.

Just then a waiter stopped. "Are you waiting for a table sir?"

"No thanks, I'll just sit right here, you can bring me some
mineral water with lime zest," Craig said pulling a chair from a
nearby table.

Did I invite him to sit with me?

"Right away Sir." And the waiter was off while Craig sat
down. It was then I noticed that he carried my father's golf club."

"You brought it!" I said reaching for it with relief and
excitement.

"It seemed important to you, I'd get it to you sooner than
later..." his voice was suddenly low and softer. "Or maybe so
you can practice up and surprise me at your next lesson."

"Don't flatter yourself and I can't be that bad!" I said
tucking the club safely out of the way.

I don't know why, but inside I was happy I was not alone, but
outwardly I just couldn't lose my sarcasm.

"Well let's just say won't be invited to any PGA tours
anytime soon," he grinned.

"Thanks for bringing the club, now if you don't mind I'd
really like to be alone."

"I don't think you want that at all. As a matter of fact I'm
sure of it."

"What are you an expert on my needs?"

"I'm just making an observation."

"Don't try you psych 101 on me because I do it all the time."

"Perhaps, but you have to admit I am charming and you might as well take advantage of my company."

By this time, my thin thread of patience strained and then broke. I leaned over so that no one else heard me.

"Listen Romeo, I'm not one of your giggly face stank ass girlfriends who fall out in the street the second you appear. And I'm not about to fall prey to whatever you think you have to offer—so you have a good night and a good trip." I reached into my wallet, extracted some bills and threw them on the table, got up and stalked away.

The first thing I did when I got home was undress and took a long hot then cool shower. I felt so much better and pulled on my Japanese silk robe, grabbed a bag of chips and a bottle of cherry seltzer then hunkered down on my living room floor to watch Lifetime television. This night was a full on marathon of *He-Done-Her-Wrong* series. But I couldn't concentrate remembering the conceited audacity of Craig earlier in the evening.

I was well into the drama of a man stalking his former wife when my doorbell rang.

Who the... I certainly wasn't expecting anyone. I got up and padded to the door and looked through the peep-hole. All I could see was the silver round head of my father's golf club. I opened the door and there was Craig leaning against the jamb.

"If I didn't know better I'd swear you keep leaving this just so I could bring it to you."

I grabbed for the club, but he yanked it out of my reach.

"The least you can do is invite me in for a *thank you* drink."

His eyes were smoky dark, his lips full and inviting. He rolled them in and out of his mouth as if he was contemplating something that would taste good. Everything that resembled sanity disappeared out of my head as I stepped aside to allow him to enter. He closed the door behind him, his eyes never leaving my face. Everything changed just then as an identifiable flutter began in my belly. With hands that seemed to belong to someone else I loosed the strap of my silk robe and let it fall to the floor. His eyes traveled down the length of me.

"Is that why you think I'm here?" he asked.

"It's why *I* want you here." I said.

I heard the golf club drop onto my thick carpet. Suddenly, his lips covered mine and sucked my tongue right into his mouth and my breath with it. In moments, he was tonguing and sucking my nipples pulling them until they were painfully taut and tender. I sucked in a breath when I heard the crackle of stiff cellophane then the unbuckling of his belt. Stopping only for a moment to place the condom on himself, he picked me up and impaled me on this rigid staff. I griped his arms, I wanted him, it was obvious to us both, but still the surprise of his entrance left me breathless.

Right there, mere feet inside my front door, Craig drove into me, pushing and pulling me up and down on him. His buttocks tensed and bunched as I gripped and kneaded them. He was so strong and a forceful lover as he pounded into my body. His grunts of pleasure only made me want more of him. He held me tight, pinching my skin as I continued to ride him. The only sound was my moans of pleasure and his grunts as he took me. He felt so food inside me as he rotated his hips and pulled down harder. I was holding onto his back and shoulder desperately trying to return the loving I was getting.

"Don't try and match me," he growled "Just feel it, enjoy it."

"You're not on your golf-green now, you don't have to show me how to do this," I hissed but never broke my ride.

I felt the tingle of my orgasm but there was no release for us as he pulled me off his stiff member and removed the rest of his clothes then laid me on my living room rug.

"The bedroom is just there." I pointed.

"The bedroom is for when I make love you. What I want from you now is something totally different."
And it was. It was primal, animalistic, groaning, grunting, biting and pushing. He pulled my legs up and rode me, then I urged him onto his back and I rode him. I felt so wanton as I ground myself down onto him, rotated my hips and threw back my head as I matched move for move. Every time I was close he stopped moving in me, interrupting release. I was whimpering now, a sure sign that I needed to come. He whispered in my ear and I clung to him and let go, pulsing my passion on his stiff rod. We stopped and started more than three times, finally ending in my bed for the finale. He spread my legs wide as he slid in slow then fast, teasing my clit with the tip of his penis. Twice he reached down and took some of my wetness onto find and licked it. It was so sexy and I wanted him to stay in me. He'd bring me to the brink then stop and then slide back to just to within inches of my desire.

"Please!" I begged.

"Not until you call my name."
That was too personal. What we were doing had nothing to do with affection.

"Say it!" he said tickling around inside me.
I shuddered and moved faster trying to force my own release, but he would not let me. I was in an agony of a pleasure that nearly brought me to tears and I was begging like I never did before.

"Please Craig, please." The words were soft and devoid of the harshness with which I'd spoken to him earlier.

"Tell me then, tell me what you want, "

"I want... I want..."
He pushed and rotated in me, hard pulling out then pushing in again. "Go on tell me, I can do this a long time."
I wanted him so bad, but I wasn't use to men taking such a charge in me.

"Is talking that is what keeps your dick hard?" I panted sarcastically.

"I have no trouble keeping myself ridged and ready."

"Well I want to come, but I don't have to, I can hold on just as long as you can."

"No you can't." he laughed," "I can make you come with words or just a touch if I want to."

"Then you need to take your best shot," I said climbing atop him and ground down on him.

He reached down and began to tease my clit, rolling it between his thumb and forefinger then pulled me down to whisper into my ear. True to his declaration he immediately made me gush my juice like it was from a seltzer spritzer.I collapsed on him; my heart beating like it was going to burst from my chest. He stroked my back gently and crooned, lulling me into peacefulness.

It was some time before I was able to roll off him, his penis slipping out of slowly. I didn't want to look at him and stared at the ceiling; this was all my doing; I had invited him inside my house and then my body. I didn't know what to say. Finally I summoned the energy to speak.

"I'm not like this, I'm a lot more....reserved," I tried to control my apologetic stammer.
He leaned over me.

"Do you think that's the kind of woman I want? Don't stress McKenna. We're just two people who recognize that we have a certain need."

"But..."

"That first day on the green and in the sand trap, it was hot and your perspirations mixed with your natural muskiness chose me even if you didn't know it."

"I have never done anything like this before. I swear."

"You don't have to convince or reassure me of anything, your husky need is like a she-wolf, sending a strong signal to her mate."

"What does this say...about me that is, "I asked despondently.

"It says..."

He leaned over to kiss me gently, "That we are two people who can admit to what we want and I want you—a lot."

"Yes but what does it all mean?"

"It means that I'm going to make love to you as much as you want and after… well we'll just see where it goes."

I wasn't looking for commitment, it was way too early for that, but he did have a point. He touched the raw nerve of my dormant sexuality and made want him like I never wanted anybody. Made me want to do things I had never thought about doing with anybody.

I opened my legs and pointed. "Think you can handle another go,"

"All you want every time you want,"

He moved over me. But I stopped him before he entered me. "What about Miss giggle-pants?"

"She's on her way to her sister's wedding in South Carolina, with her new date." And he kissed and slid into me simultaneously.

~*~

Two days later as Dora and I finished our workout, she squinted at me.

"Why are you humming like Scarlett O'Hara after Rhett took her up that staircase?"

When I didn't say anything her eyes nearly popped from her head as she nudged me.

"Mr.-Tiger-Woods-wanna-be! He's stop knockin' and started rockin'. Girl, you better give me some details or I'll beat you like a tin drum."

I gave her as much detail as warranted, keeping all the best parts to myself.

She chastised me with a wave of her chubby hand.

"Girl please, I know it was more than that because you're glowing like the New Year's crystal ball."

~*~

It's not about love for me and Craig, not yet anyway; but we've settled into a serious relationship level that is comfortable for us. Our hunger for each other almost overwhelming at times, but we also have a deep respect for one another.

On the six month anniversary of our getting together, Craig took me to a private golf club where he'd had flowers surround every hole and the sign above us that read, *TEE FOR TWO*.

Love is gaining on us like a hurricane and nether one of us is stepping out of the way.

The Drummond House Legend

Halloween was never my favorite holiday, but I was always a fan of a good Halloween costume party and my best friend Marie Drummond and her family gave the best ones ever. They were celebrating the annual tradition and the two hundredth anniversary of her family's heritage in Sutland Louisiana.

"I have an idea, why don't you come along Tami?" she asked me with excitement.
I was reluctant at first because I knew how serious the Drummonds took this particular holiday, and for me Halloween was really for kids, however playing dress up for night appealed to me. I had always read that Louisiana was a place filled with ghostly legends and local gris-gris lore but since I didn't believe in anything remotely ghostly supernatural, I found it only mildly entertaining. In my opinion, folklore was designed to frighten impressionable children or bilk money out of unsuspecting patrons looking for a way to commune with lost loved ones and I certainly didn't relish anyone possessing my body or swinging dead chickens over my head in order to make a believer out of me.

My new cookbook was in its second printing and in her effort to convince me to come along with her, Marie suggested that I might want to think about incorporating a book signing or at the very least obtain some new recipes while visiting her family home.

"Perhaps you can get my Grand mere or one of my *Tantes* to share some of famous and most secret recipes,"

That was enough convince me and the next thing I knew we were landing at the Louis Armstrong International Airport in Louisiana.

~*~

The Drummond house was situated on a hillock overlooking the Beau Reve River that spilled into the Mississippi. The house had been painstakingly restored to its historically accurate design and beauty and now served as an exclusive Bed and Breakfast—except for the week of All Hallows Eve, when the famous *Annual Drummond house Masquerade Ball* was held.

"We can rent costumes at Madame Tessle's. She has the best assortment—a little pricey but well worth it," Marie said with excitement.

"So are there going to be any eligible men at this shindig?" I asked.

"Girl yes. Everybody comes to the Halloween Ball at Drummond House, it's a ritual."

We went to the costume shop just before noon the next day and it was teeming with people looking for apparel for the various galas that were to be held throughout New Orleans on Halloween eve and night.

"Bon Jour Miss Drummond, your *Tante* informed me you were coming. I have a wonderful assortment set aside for you and your guest to choose from, "the heavily made up proprietress said leading us away from the crowd and to a back room.

There were several racks of dresses that ranged from gauzy-barely-there-see-through numbers to heavy billowing brocade dresses complete with bustier, bustles and hoops. Nothing appealed to me and I was about go back into the main store area when I saw a dress hanging on a hook at the far end of the room. It was deep mauve velvet with puffed sleeves and a double layer of lace at the wrists. The bodice boasted crisscrossing gray string that covered a white satin middle. On a shelf just above it was an ornate mask. I took it down and examined the exquisite workmanship of peacock feathers, sequins and pearls over the gold colored face piece. I don't know why but I suddenly knew this was the costume for me.

"I want to rent this." I called over to the saleswoman who was holding up a ridiculously wide dress against Marie. She shoved the dress she was holding into Marie's hands and hurried over to me.

"Where did you get that?" she asked staring at the mask.

"It was on the shelf above this dress."

"These are not for rent," the woman said abruptly snatching the mask from me and gently placed it back on the shelf.

I knew that hard sell ruse but didn't feel like haggling.

"Okay, how much? I'll buy it."

"They are not for sale."

"But I want…" The woman was adamant that is was not available for sale or rental and hurried back to Marie. I was miffed at her attitude and half-heartedly looked for something else, but nothing drew me as that dress and mask had. I strolled around the room looking for something that might appeal to me.

"It's no wonder she wouldn't let you have it. That dress has history."

A deep male voice brought me to attention. I turned and looked up into the dark sexy eyes and a skin tone that was the color of rich Brazilian coffee.

"What kind of history?" I asked but I really didn't care I just wanted to keep him talking in that sexy baritone voice.

"It's an exact replica of the dress worn by Cossette Bulae, a seamstress who worked at the Drummond House more than two hundred years ago."

I rolled my eyes, I knew I was about to get my first dose of ghostly folk tales and while I really was not interested I was enthralled by the storyteller.

"I guess that must mean something,"

"It does around here, but then you don't look like you're from around here."

"I'm not—Tamika Baines from New Jersey."

"Ahh yes. You're Marie's friend; she's spoken of you often."

I wanted to beat her ass into the next weekend because she hadn't told me a damned thing about this fine hunk of man.

"And you are?" I asked.

"Girard Vaneux." He said with a smile so bright I wanted to put on my shades and eighty level sunblock. I shook his extended hand.

"So, are you going to tell me about that dress Mr. Vaneux?"

"I'd love to over dinner tonight...if you're not busy and please call me Girard."

Marie came toward us, her arms filled with dresses, wigs and masks.

"Oh hey Girard, I see you've met my friend Tamika I call her Tami but she hates it."

"Yes, she enchanted me the moment I saw her."

"Girard is an obstetrician and an accomplished spoken word poet. We're hoping he will be reciting at the Ball. " She smiled with feigned sweetness.

"No need to ply your womanly charms on me, your *Grand'Mere* has promised me some of her famous roasted andouille if I recite, how could I refuse."

I noticed how he suddenly and easily he lapsed into a Creole Patois when speaking to Marie. She turned to me to explain the food they were talking about. "Andouille is a Cajun sausage seasoned with salt, cracked black pepper and garlic that is slowly smoked over pecan wood and sugar cane. And although it's not the healthiest thing to eat, it is delicious and his..." she said pointing to Girard, "favorite."

"I have asked your friend to dinner tonight, but she hasn't given me an answer."

There was a long pause and Marie nudged me in the side and grinned.

"Girl you better take him up on that because he doesn't ask too many of the local women out."

"That's not true, "he laughed. 'I've asked you out several times.

"Yeah, that's because you know I'm a safe bet since I'm hopelessly in love with your cousin Paul."
I was glad to hear that because Girard had without a doubt roused my interest.

"So how about that dinner?" he asked again.
When I hesitated, Marie spoke for me.

"You can pick her up at seven sharp, she'll be ready and she'll be beautiful."

"She won't have to work hard at that, "he said then kissed her on both cheeks and said his goodbyes.

~*~

I spent the early part of the evening getting ready for my date. I couldn't remember the last I primped and preened so much for a man. I must have changed three times and finally settled on a two piece dark green dress accented with a silver beaded necklace with matching earrings. I heard the sound of the front door chimes, then the soft shuffle of Katrine Drummond—Marie's Grandmother or *Grand'Mere* as she was called in Cajun Louisiana as she went to answer the door.

There was a light rap on my bedroom door and the maid entered carrying a large box which she placed on the bed and handed me embarrassingly large floral arrangement of purple wild irises and tiger lilies and the card read; *until tonight*, and it was signed *Girard.* On the box was a small note, I *convinced Madame Tessle to let me rent this for you. You will be look lovely in at the ball.* I untied the large orange bow from the oblong box and removed the top and gasped with delight when I saw the beautiful dress and mask from the shop.

~*~

Girard took me to a quaint bistro overlooking a large bay deep in Creole country. It was almost like I had been transported back in time from the décor to the wild yet hauntingly beautiful music. The food was both splendid and strange. Girard asked me if I preferred traditional; Creole or Cajun cuisine

"Is there a difference?"

He laughed aloud, "Spoken like a true non-Louisianan"

I wasn't offended but I was intrigued.

"Well…" he began, "In the eighteenth century New Orleans consisted of and was largely ruled by upper class French and Spanish decedents and as time went on it included native born slaves of African descent and free people of color.

"I'm not sure I understand how the Spanish influenced the city when it seems to have been French all along." I asked hoping I didn't sound stupid.

"*French Creole* defined someone of European ancestry that was born in the colony while *Louisiana Creoles* were labeled as being of mixed racial ancestry."

"I see, so each had their way cooking, it makes sense."

"It's actually a blend of various cultures; German, Caribbean, Native America, Portuguese—the whole enchilada."

"And I guess Spanish." I said laughing at his reference to *enchilada*. "Okay so there might not be that much of a difference between Creole and Cajun cooking?"

"To Louisianans, there is a huge difference, largely because some consider Creole food as a little more aristocratic."

"Ahh…" I said, "That age old class distinction."

"You have to remember that slaves prepared the food for the upper-classes and they were better able to obtain an array of exotic ingredients not available to the Cajun populace. Even when the same dishes were made there were differences."

"Like?"

"Creole Jambalaya for instance contains tomatoes but not in Cajun cuisine. Creole roux is made with butter and flour but Cajun roux is made with oil and flour."

I was excited by this information and vowed I would read more up on it as soon as I could. In the meantime I thought it would be best if I allow him to order for me.

Before long I was I was savoring the strong taste remoulade shrimp and a crawfish soufflé so light I thought it might float away before I could eat it.

I felt eyes on me as I ate and I glanced up and noticed Girard watching me, a smile creasing his lips.

"What?" I asked perplexed.

"You eat each mouthful as though you were trying to discern all the seasonings and flavors."

"Guilty as charged, you caught me!" I laughed in response.

I told him about my cookbooks and that I was hoping to come away from Louisiana with a few new condiments to compliment my own recipes, but not without acknowledgement of the region of course.

After a scrumptious dessert of creole bread pudding with a light caramel and whiskey sauce, he signaled the waiter then asked him to bring our aperitifs' out onto the portico.

"It was very nice of you to send the costume over," I said taking a seat on the lounge chair facing the bay.

"It was my pleasure. I know you will be beautiful in it."

"Thank you but are you going to tell me the history behind it?"

"Absolutely, then we shall see if you have the nerve to wear it to the ball."

"Please don't try and tell me it's cursed?" I giggled with delight.

His brow arched.

"To many of the people here it is no laughing matter, but it you'd rather not hear it then we will just enjoy the evening and our drinks," he saluted me with his glass.

"No, I'm sorry…" I said curtailing my mirth, "please go ahead."

"Well the story goes that in 1817 Cossette Bulae was a house maid at the Villa Lucro plantation and was indentured to the Drummond place when the Lucro's fell on hard times."

"Did something happen to her?" I asked trying to sound interested because I really didn't believe in fables and myths.

"She met and fell in love with Karl Courant a mulatto and *gens de couleur libre*—a free person of color, who resided at the Drummond house."

"Was he in love with her?" Now the story was becoming a little interesting.

"They say she was like the moon and stars to him and planned to be secretly wed. But his parents were adamantly against the idea because Cossette was… considerably darker and not at all what they wanted for their son. When they got wind of the impending nuptials they forbade Cossette to even speak to him informing her they were shipping him off to Paris where he was to meet his *true* bride.

"Oh dear, what about Karl didn't he object if he loved her so much?" I asked leaning closer to Girard.

"Instead, Karl's mother's concocted a feigned crisis with a complicit family member in the Carolina's and insisted Karl go an help out, hoping that she would be successful in moving Cossette to another household far away by the time he returned."

"How cruel."

"Thinking her beloved had betrayed her and had sailed to France; Cossette was understandably heartbroken and took sick. She sobbed for days clutching the mauve velvet dress she'd made to get married in. "

"Didn't' Karl come back?"

"Not for years and why is unclear, but every night in October—which was the month they had chosen to secretly wed—Cossette would don the dress and go out onto the balcony no matter what the weather until dawn; gazing out toward the sea as if willing her beloved to return.

"I've seen it," I said. "It's just above the ballroom, but I was told no one is allowed out there because of the weak railings."

"That's the excuse. They say it's haunted."

"Oh?" my brow rose with skepticism.

"They say that one October dawn a servant went up to close a banging shutter and she found Cossette's dress and shoes on the balcony landing. The servant thought that perhaps she had jumped; but when she looked over there was nothing—nothing except an eerie bone chilling sound carried on the wind that sounded like…crying"

"So I guess that's when the legend started," I said skeptically.

"I don't know, but people say that she can be heard weeping for Karl precisely at the witching hour every all hallows Eve—the night before Halloween to you. But of course that's just a myth." He chortled.

"I wonder what happened when Karl came back and didn't find Cossette?" now I was totally immersed in the tale.

"Folklore says that his mother told him that she had run off"

"Oh my,"

"What she hadn't told him was that Cossette's body had been found half submerged in a bog at the far end of a swamp where local fisherman ventured from time to time; nor did she tell him that she had Cossette's body buried in the slave grounds near the woods behind Drummond house."

"He never saw her again, how sad."

"Karl was beyond grief stricken and when the servant showed him the dress and slippers she'd found on the balcony, he cursed them and any replicas, vowing someday he and his beloved would be together."

"So you think because of the legend and the curse I won't wear the costume at the ball tomorrow night? It isn't the original after all."

"No but it is a dead on replica and people here take their curses very seriously," he said half-jokingly.

"Well you don't have to worry because I don't believe in ghosts, boogeymen or silly legends."

"But hopefully you do believe in romance, yes?" He asked in a voice that was as smooth as glacier ice. His eyes were chestnut brown pools of intense scrutiny, almost as though he was challenging me somehow.

It was a good thing he couldn't read my mind because I was
thinking of things along the lines a lot more decadent than spells
and curses. I knew it was too soon but I couldn't remember the
last time a man made me tingle the way Girard did, but I ignored
his question and changed the subject and asked, "So who are you
coming as?"

"It's a surprise," he winked.

"I can't wait," I said knowingly because I had an exact
idea who he was coming to the *bal masqué* as.

After we finished our drinks we strolled along the Rue St.
Massay riverbank and he entertained me with snippets of
Louisiana myths and traditions. When he brought me back to
Drummond house we talked on the porch for a little while as I
smiled and told him what a wonderful time I'd had. He leaned in
close and I closed my eyes waiting for the kiss, instead he
nuzzled my ear and whispered; ***bonsoir ma belle***—good night
my lovely one.

~*~

The ball was two days away and the house was in a
frenzy. I didn't want to be in the way so I kept busy by visiting
local eateries and talking to the chefs about recipies for my
book. Several of them were more than happy to share their
common favorites but it took a little more coaxing to get them to
part with some of thier more secret additives and condiments. Of
course I would much rather have spent the time with Girard but
he *was* a pediatrican afterall and it seemed that the single most
pastime in Sutland was *making* and *having* babies.

~*~

The Drummond household was bubbling with excitement
on the day of the Ball. I was amazed by how the place had been
completely transformed to resemble a habitat that had existed
two centuries before. I was a little disturbed at the sight of the
hired help dressed like servants at the big house as they would be
on an eighteenth century plantation. Seventy-five year old
Katrine Drummond with a mind sharp as someone half her age
approached me when she noticed my uneasiness. "Do not be

troubled by what you see my dear. This is all done to remind of us our past. We in no way would embrace those days of humiliation. I promise you will have a most enjoyable evening."

She left me calling out instructions to be sure and cordon off the upstairs balcony area so that no one ventures there by mistake. Girard called to find out how things were going and when he asked to speak to me, my heart soared at the sound of his voice.

The sun was setting and the brilliant hues cast colorful slanted shadows on the walls. Marie had told me earlier that it was customary for the house to slumber for an hour or so in order to be well rested for the evening's festivities. Being an East Coast work-a-holic I knew this particular ritual IPAD wasn't even remotely doable, but I didn't want the squeaky floors to disturb anyone so I got my IPAD and laid on the tufted chaise lounge and began to read the current reviews on the on-line version of *Gourmet Delight.*

~*~

It might have been the sound of the old air conditioning unit coming on that awakened me. I looked down at my IPAD; the screen was dark in sleep-mode and I knew I must have dozed off.

I got up, stretched then walked to the window and pulled back the drapes. It was completely dark out. Although I was refreshed I couldn't believe I had actually fallen asleep. *Must be the lazy Louisiana air*, I thought.

I noticed that someone had laid out the costume on the bed, along with the shoes, lace fan and the ornate mask. I went over and gently touched the velvet fabric and lacy sleeves. The workmanship was exquisite. I must have been in some deep sleep because I hadn't heard even a whisper of anyone coming into the room.

I went to shower then sat at the vanity mirror to apply my makeup. There was a knock on the door then Marie entered wearing a silk robe.

"Did you get some rest Tamika?"

"I sure did. I didn't think I was sleepy but I must have gone right off."

"It happens here all the time," she laughed. "Here let me do your hair."

And before I knew it she was brushing my hair and pulling it up into some kind of hairdo I would never have worn. She pulled some tendrils down the sides of my face with the rat-tail portion of a comb then surveyed her work.

"There! You're beautiful."

I had to admit it wasn't half bad and probably much more suitable for this kind of heat and especially if I intended to be dancing with Girard.

"Do you need me to help you get dressed? That's a lot of material there," she pointed to the frock on the bed.

"No I can manage you go on and get ready."

She blew me an air kiss and left.

I went to the bed and lifted the gown and instantly a brief moment of dizziness overcame me. For a moment I thought I heard a breathy sigh near my ear. As quickly as it had come the light-headedness passed. I glanced around the room. *Don't even try it, I don't believe in ghosts* I muttered then began to put on the dress. It seemed to have been made for me as the bodice molded itself to my breasts but it also seemed to hug me in the warmth of love *and* sadness at the same time. I slipped my foot into the black satin slippers, surprised that they fit perfectly. Girard had really done his homework.

It was eight 'o'clock and I could hear voices of guests that had begun to arrive. I took up the fan and the mask and went downstairs.

Dinner was served precisely nine with two hours after for dancing, drinking and enjoying conversation. The last hour leading up to Halloween—which was considered the witching hour and was reserved for when ghostly tales and locals legends were told. It was also, according to the program and much to my emotional glee was when Girard was to recite *Annabel Lee*, the haunting poem by Edgar Allen Poe.

The masks everyone wore were spectacular with intricate beading, large colorful plumage, lace and other vibrant materials. There was unending champagne, liquors and of course the local beverages of *Brandy milk punch, Creole Bloody Mary, Absinthe Frappe a*nd a flaming coffee concoction called *Café Brulot Diabolique.* I had never drank and danced so much in my life. As soon as I finished one dance someone would sweep me onto the dance floor where I was whirled around to the music until I was giddy with excitement. I had to admit this was the most fun I had had in since like—forever ago. A tall full-masked gentleman had whisked me onto the floor and we whirled around and around to the music and then with the softest almost imperceptible whisper in my ear, *"you are beautiful chere'"* I giggled with delight and was about to verbally unmask Girard when the gong of the tall grandfather clock sounded. The music stopped abruptly as did the dancers. With only the swish of ball gowns the people moved in unison toward the grand staircase and looked up. The tall man under the shadowed valance began to speak:

> *"It was many and many a year ago by the kingdom by the sea,*
> *that a maiden lived whom you may know by the name of Annabel Lee.*
> *And this maiden she lived with no other thought than to be loved by me."*

I looked to my left and wondered when Girard—my dance partner had left my side to do the much anticipated spoken word, but of course he was not there and I trained my eyes back to the speaker with a smile. *Damn he was good.* Oddly his voice was raspy but distorted and I was delighted with the simulated effect. The poem was long and haunting, beautifully done and I was caught in the magic of it.

"And so all the night tide, I lie down by the side
Of my darling my darling, my life and my bride
In here sepulcher there by the sea
In her Tomb by the sounding sea."

The deafening ovation snapped my attention away from the speaker as the crowd yelled and cried out for more. When I again looked up to where Girard had been reciting, it was empty. I grinned; these people certainly went all out with their pretend magical spectacle

Everyone went back to dancing, drinking and conversations and when Girard had not returned to my side, I took the opportunity to go find my mystery man.

Flushed with libation and dancing I went into library calling out his name softly, giggling and waiting for him to jump out and try to scare me to death. "Girard?" I called out giddily, but there was no answer. I searched almost every room downstairs but he was nowhere to be found and I was positive he was trying to give me as much a New Orleans Halloween Adventure as possible. I went upstairs and to the end of the hall near the stairs leading to the balcony. *He couldn't possibly be…* then I noticed the door was ajar and I smiled. Oh sure! Only *he* would give me a dead give-away-hint like this. I went inside. The room was pitch black but I knew Girard was there.

"Girard? What are you doing" I asked half laughing in the darkness.

"Waiting—for you."

With my hands out as if searching I moved forward until I touched a wall. Cool breath was on my neck as I was pushed against it and hands caressed me and touched me in the place that was now damp with need. I responded by pushing myself onto the exploring fingers.

"We can't," I said breathily.

I knew it was wrong, but there was something titillating about making love right then with a room full of people just downstairs.

"*Hush*," he whispered in the same raspy voice he'd used during the recital and I was surprised that he would go to these lengths to stay in character especially at a time like this. I was still up against the wall, but he pulled my bottom back and separated my legs, I didn't have on any underwear, after all who would know? The costume with its many layers was so full and hot. The pressure of his body pressed against me and I shoved a fist to my mouth to halt the gasp of pleasure as he rubbed a hand over my derriere. The air was dizzying and I was almost faint with desire. It was so decadent and I wanted more and opened my legs wider as an unspoken invitation. I waited with anticipation; my eyes shut tight willing him to do whatever he wanted to do. I reached down to touch myself, hoping he would understand and fill me. What happens to a woman when she wants a man so badly that she doesn't even care about consequences? I wanted Girard in me and opened my legs and leaned down with invitation. All I felt was his hands, his cool surgeon's hands caressing my face, my neck and my breasts. "Do it." I said. "Do it."

I don't know why I wanted it that way, but it just seemed to fit the mood. I moved back against him but he held me still. I clawed the wall with a desperate attempt not to scream out the exquisite yearning for what I wanted. I was still touching myself, waiting hoping that he would remove my hand and make love to me.

"*Love,*" I heard him rasp through my over indulged champagne haze. I wanted to kiss him and when I tried to turn and face him, he held me fast and I felt him, I felt him deep in me, pushing and filling me. My climax fast and strong I slid to the floor panting wildly. My gasping breath began to recede as my heartbeat slowed. *What just happened? Had I just allowed a man I hardly knew make love to me?* I was leaning against the wall in a heap and I reached back hoping Girard's strong hand would take mine, but there was nothing except warm air.

I got up unsteadily and turned. How odd, my dress was as it was and Girard was nowhere to be found. I wasn't sure I liked this game. To take me the way he had and then just leave like that?

I took a handkerchief from the lace cuff of my sleeve and dabbed away the tell-tale perspiration from my face and headed out the door. The hall was dim with the wall sconces turned down low but I a shadow disappearing up the steps to the balcony. *He shouldn't do that*, it wasn't safe, besides, I had something to say to him. I called out to him. "Girard wait!" But he didn't even turn around. I hurried after him and stopped short when I saw him standing on the rickety boards looking out into the distance.

"Girard you can't be up here, it's not safe." But he still hadn't turned around.
I moved a little closer, careful not to further aggravate the already stressed flooring. The air felt odd, like it was swirling when it really wasn't. *Was I suddenly afraid of heights or was I that drunk?* I shook my head to clear it.

"Girard?" I said once again.

"Come my love,"
He turned and it was *not* Girard, it was a handsome face but not the face of the man I thought had just made love to me. He held out a thin, seemingly transparent hand and moved toward me.
I screamed as darkness overtook me.

~*~

The strong smell of ammonia under my nose made me sit up coughing and pushing the horrid vial away.

"She's alright now," I heard someone say.
When I could focus I saw the concerned faces of Marie, Katrine and Girard.

"You gave us all quite a scare," he said smiling down at me.
My throat was hot and my voice raspy.

"You...you were on the balcony..." I stopped when I saw the look of complete puzzlement envelope his face. "It was right after you...after we..."

"I'm sorry Tamika, but I was at the hospital all night. Sarah Perreault's twins took their time making their debut. One of the babies was in distress and it was touch and go for a while but they're all doing fine now."

"But… but you all heard him," I looked from one face to another. "He spoke tonight, he recited Annabel Lee." I said frantically.

"No my dear, there was no recital, Paul—Girard's brother made the apologetic announcement is all. Girard arrived only moments ago. We heard a scream and it was he who found you out here on the balcony. "

Was I going crazy? "There was a man out there. I saw him!"

"What man?" Girard asked with a tinge of irritation in his tone.

"I thought it was you, I don't know…."
Everyone was silent and staring at me. "I swear I'm not crazy."

"Of course you aren't," Girard said slipping an arm around my waist. "But perhaps you've had a little too much Champagne."
Confused tears slid down my cheeks as I searched their faces for plausible explanations. I got up and smoothed the dress that now felt too constricting. I wanted nothing more than to get out of it and fast. "Maybe you're right; I do have a bit of a headache." I said and let them lead me from the terrace and into the dim room then to the door.

"Are you coming Grandmere?" Marie asked when she saw her Grandmother lag behind.

"You all go ahead I'll be along."
We left the room, but I hoped that I hadn't upset Katrine or ruined the party.

"Wait a moment; I want to apologize to your grandmother." I said and turned heading back to the door, Marie right on my heels.
I opened the door and as my eyes readjusted to the dimness of the room, I saw Katrine standing in front of a long red curtain on

the wall and she pulled it back slowly, uncovering a large portrait of a man—the same man I had seen on the terrace.

"Who..who is that?" I whispered to Marie.

"That is her great-great-grandfather, Karl Courant." Katrine hadn't heard us as we closed the door softly and continued on down hallway. The feeling of sexual fullness was gone now, *had it ever even been there*? I knew right then that I would never be able to explain what I had experienced or what I had seen without sounding crazy, but I knew I would never forget it. I looked down at the dress. Had the ghost of a man seeking his long dead love come to me because I wore an exact replica of her wedding dress? I didn't know but I hurried to my room and got out of it as soon as I could.

~*~

Two days later it was Girard who took me to the airport for my return home. As we sat in the waiting area I was usually quiet.

"So…" he said taking my hand. "Do you want to tell me what you think happened the other night, the night we…" he stopped and looked me in the eye.

"You were right; I must have had too much champagne. I never really was much of a drinker."

"Perhaps you'll tell me when you agree to let me visit you."

I stared at him with surprise and need. "You want to come East?" I said.

"I'd go to Mars to see you," he said huskily.

I was excited and told him that he should check his schedule and we could set something up. I was so happy to be sitting with him and I couldn't wait to until he came to be with me. He leaned in to kiss me just as the attendant said that my flight was boarding. He grinned and gave me a light peck on the nose.

"One of these days we won't be interrupted." He arose and took my carry-on bag to the shuttle door. I hugged him tight and before he let me go, he whispered in my ear.

"You're not the first to have seen *him*."

Then he let me go and handed me my bag. I smiled weakly and followed the other passengers into the airplane.

Sometimes people see what they want to see, other see what they need to. In my case it was probably a long dead love bringing together new love, peace and contentment.

Fleeing Lies

My past was staring at me once again. The white envelope with its neat script was a familiar identifier that had been haunting me for years.

"Mom! Where's my blue Knicks shirt?"
Tajahn, my precious rambunctious son was calling from upstairs. I quickly stuffed the unopened letter in my jean pocket and went to pull his favorite football jersey out of the dryer.

My husband Jeff was coming out of the small room we'd converted to an office for him smiled then reached out to grab me but I skipped out of his grasp and giggled.

"It's too early for that." I whispered.

"It's never too early." he caught me and dragged me into his arms. I felt him harden.

Even after all these years, he was still excited by my now ample body leaning into his.

"I don't have to be at the courthouse until noon, that should give us plenty of time if you can get our son out of here," he said nibbling my ear.
I had a million things to do, but everything left my head when I was in Jeff's arms. A heat overtook me that made me always want to get naked and spread myself for him, but now was not the time. I loosed myself from his embrace and turned to see Taj's standing in the doorway. I tossed the jersey at him. "You're going to be late." I said to him.

"I'm goin' I'm goin'" he winked at me and gave his father who was right behind me a knowing smile.

"Young man!" Jeff chastised jokingly, "you are too grown for your own good and you need to stay out of grown folks business."

Taj donned the jersey and grabbed his backpack.

"Grown folks need to keep their *business* in the right room. Don't y'all know I'm just am impressionable kid?" He laughed and kissed my cheek then ducked passed me as I swatted at the back of his head and hurried to the front door.

"You come home right after practice, ya hear?" Jeff called after him. The door slammed, but not before we heard a *"right-o pop!"*

I turned and looked at my handsome forty-five year old husband.

"And what were you saying Mr. Branson?" I smiled seductively.

"Come on in here and let me tell ya." He said pulling me into our bedroom.

Before I could breathe he was on his knees in front of me, his face buried under my skirt and pushing aside my panties. I held onto him as best I could because there was little prelude as he attacked the treasures of my flesh with his tongue. The moans that escaped me were loud and filled with satisfied pleasure. He could never get enough of me this way and lifted one of my legs and placed it over his shoulder to allow him even greater access to the places he liked best. I thought the walls of my body were going to cave in as he took every bit of love from me. The wet sounds always embarrassing to me was something he loved and urged him on. His moans of delight made me want to get naked and fast. I pushed him off me and tore my clothes off and let his hands play all over my naked flesh and literally tongued me back onto our bed.

By then I was panting from the heat that was consuming us.

"Deep my darling, I want you deep in me." My voice was a husky, panting whisper. I lifted my legs and opened them. The invitation was clear. Jeff disrobed as quickly as I had and leaned over me positioning himself for entrance.

"I love you Jaci. I love you more than anything in this world."

The first time we'd made love, he'd said those very same words and he's been saying them ever since. My body accepted him and made ready for his perfect and pronounced movements. He loved to tease and it made me push up to get more of him. He talked to me and smoothed my hair away from my face.

"You're so beautiful when we make love baby, I love the sheen on your face, your parted lips, your sweet breath as you inhale—I'm so lucky to have you my lovely lady."
Loving him was always a special experience and we'd done it in almost every way, but when he was gentle like this it made my love for him even greater.

Later as he lay resting with his arm crossed over his chest, I saw the barest hint of a satisfied smile. I got up quietly and retrieved my clothes. I decided to use Taj's shower as not to disturb my husband—my sweet lover.

After Jeff had gone to work where he oversaw family court for the County, I made a cup of coffee and fingered the edge of the white envelope I'd retrieved from my pocket. I knew what was in it, the same thing that had been in it for the last three years. I tore it open. It was just as I'd thought, only this time, there was no rambling letter, no pleading or idle threats. This time there was just an amount, and it shocked me. *Fifty thousand dollars*! I couldn't believe my eyes.
How did she assume we even had that kind of money? But like any blackmailer, she didn't care. *If you don't have it, then you'd better get it.* That's what the note *didn't* say, but I knew that's what it meant. I began to cry. How could I have allowed this to happen? To let it go on so long? I had to tell Jeff. *But what of Taj?* My wonderful, smart, funny son, what could I say to him? How could I tell him I was not his real mother?

Like a torrent of rain, the whole scene came rushing back to me. I had been twenty-four years old with a degree in Bio-Chemistry and teaching at one of the most notoriously understaffed, under-funded and worst schools in Ohio. I was idealistic and had hoped to make a difference, and while I tried to reach *all* of my students only few out of every twenty took a *real* interest in learning and it was those I gave my complete attention to. It didn't stop the others however, from coming to me for favors or to help them with a little money to buy food for their siblings or druggy parent. I admit it. I was a soft touch in those days.

I was delighted when I found out I had received a grant for a Master's program, but it meant I would have to go to Philadelphia for sixteen months. I hated to leave the students that I felt were benefiting from my teaching but I had to do what was right for me. I resigned from the school with pleadings from the superintendent that I would at least think about coming back after I received my Doctorate. I told him I would. I had spoken to my landlord about breaking my lease early and he was very kind and told me not to worry, that I had been an exemplary tenant and to take all the time I needed. What furnishings I didn't sell, I offered to the students to whom I knew had next to nothing and could use it. I was a little sad, but by the end of the month my apartment was pretty much empty and my car was being serviced for my drive to Philly.

On the night before I was ready to leave, I was boxing up some last minute items I'd intended taking with me when I received a frantic call. It was 10:30 and the voice was practically screaming in my ear. It was Regina Stanley, one of the worst girls in class—when she managed to even come to class that is. She was belligerent, crass but strikingly beautiful with a killer body. She was fascinated by the Hip-hop scene and was a local rap-artist groupie. None of their promises to put her in a video panned out and she was often caught up in the middle of one sexual scandal after another. I tried to talk to her about her activities but she didn't want to hear it and even accused me of being a *jealous old bitch*. After the first attempts of trying to find out why she missed so many days of school and received nothing but curt and even hostile responses, I just let it go and concentrated on the students who *did* want to learn. When she hadn't been in class for the last four months I went to check the school attendance roster but it too showed nothing but absenteeism. It took three weeks but I was finally able to get a truant officer to go to the address on her entrance papers to try and find her. He nonchalantly told me that he had gone but there was no answer. Although his response reeked of indifference and we had no funds to continue a more in depth investigation I had to assume that Regina had just dropped out.

But this particular night she sounded frantic and kept calling my name over and over into the phone. She was crying and sounded so scared I couldn't help it, I knew I had to go to her. It was all I could do to get the address out of her which was not the address we had on record and was in what had to be the worst section on the south-side.

When I entered the shabby building, I held my breath, as it had more than its share of disgusting cloying odors and the unsavory characters standing around chilled my blood. I wasn't at all surprised that Regina was staying in a place like this but I had to force myself to be brave.

I found the apartment number she had given me and when I knocked on the door a man of about twenty-five with a long jagged scar running down one cheek opened it. Fear tickled up my spine but I reigned in my dread and returned his sneering, hard gaze with one of my own.

"I'm here to see Regina."

He crooked his head back and I side-stepped him and headed in that direction.

When I entered the room, Regina was lying on a dirty mattress with bloody sheets. She was bathed in sweat and her fists were clenched as she beat against the bulge of her distended belly.

"Regina!" I screamed and ran to her and took hold of her hands.

"Stop it, what are doing?"

"It hurts; I have to get it out of me. Help me Miss Joseph! Please help me!"

The man reappeared and leaned nonchalantly against the door jamb. I looked back at him.

"She needs to go the hospital. Can you call 9-1-1?" I knew my tone had a disgusted slant that I couldn't disguise.

"We ain't going to no hospital," he said in an oily voice.

"But she's going to have your baby. She needs care," I nearly screamed at him.

"Don't know whose puppy that is. A lot of dogs rode that bitch."

I couldn't believe my ears.

"Well can you at least help me get her downstairs to my car?"

When he didn't move to assist me, I tried alone but Regina was too heavy and in too much pain. I tried again but she screamed and began double over to push. I had no idea what to do and could only rely on every *Grey's Anatomy* rerun episode I'd ever seen and hoped they were right.

Nature began taking its course and before I knew it, a new life was pushing itself into the world. I did what seemed to come to me almost naturally, like cleaning the baby's airways and knotting the umbilical cord. Only then did I examine the fat little boy with a head full of silky, dark hair. He was beautiful and when he curled his tiny fingers around my thumb, I nearly cried.

There was nothing to wrap him in but a dingy bath towel so I swaddled him as best I could and laid him next to Regina. She was weak and I went to the bathroom to get something clean her up with. The place was a barren pig sty but I was able to find a cloth which I rinsed over and over before I even approached her with it. All the while I was asking questions about her parents and how I could contact them, but by then she had already fallen into an exhausted sleep.

I spoke to the surly man still standing in the doorway.

"Can you go and get some infant pampers and maybe some milk? And maybe get something for Regina to eat." He stared at me like I had two heads.

"That stuff cost money," he said.

I reached into my shoulder bag, removed twenty dollars and held it out to him.

He took it and that was the last I saw of him or it.

When the baby became fretful I pressed the baby's mouth to his mother's breast and waited, hoping that he would know what to do and that Regina would let him. He attached that puckered little bud of a mouth onto her nipple and began to suckle. I blew out a breath of relief satisfied that he was getting the nourishment he needed. Regina awoke slightly but never looked at the baby.

"Where's Lonnie?" she asked.

"He's gone." I assumed she meant the man who had disappeared with my money. I was glad because I didn't like the way he looked at me and judging by the way he treated Regina she didn't need him either.

"Look Regina, I have to go find some things you need for the baby. Will you be all right until I get back?" She nodded and closed her eyes. The baby too had fallen into a satisfied sleep, still half sucking heartily at her breast.

~*~

I hurried downstairs and looked up and down the street trying to find a store that was open late. Two blocks later I found a Bodega and purchased necessities, including a couple of sandwiches and Gatorade for Regina. I hurried back and made my way to the apartment. The door was ajar and I figured Lonnie might have returned. I went in and set the packages down on the squalid table and went to the bedroom. It was empty except for a naked pecan-colored baby with jet black hair trembling on the rumpled bed. Every fiber of my being fought against the truth, that a girl who had just experienced the miracle of bringing a child into the world was gone and she probably wasn't coming back. But I waited. I waited four long hours with that child wrapped in whatever I could find to keep him warm, never putting him down for a second. I rocked him and fed him formula from the plastic bottle I'd bought. It was almost 4 a.m.

when I gathered myself and the child, enclosed him inside my coat and left the disgusting tenement.

~*~

I drove past the police station three times, but each time I did the baby whimpered and seemed to nuzzle closer to me, like he was telling me not to let him go. The third time I slowed as two uniformed officers came out of the precinct and looked at my car curiously. I looked down at the baby and drove away toward home.

There was no one around that time of morning as I entered my apartment and laid the baby on my bed, surrounding him with pillows and covering him with a bath towel.

As soon as I could the next morning I called the university and postponed my entrance to the Master's program for two weeks because I needed time to find Regina. But it was as though she had fallen off the face of the earth, and there was no one who knew or cared enough to offer any information about any family she might have had. Time was of the essence and I had to make decision. Should I leave the baby on the steps of a church? I knew if I went to the police there would be questions and they might even forbid me to leave and I couldn't afford to lose my grant. But more than anything the fat little boy whom I held and fed, looked up at me with trusting eyes and fell asleep in the my arms almost like he knew this was the place where he was loved. There was no mistake, he had stolen my heart like a seasoned pickpocket and there was no way I was going to allow him to become part of a system that moved children from one uncertain place to another.

I found a questionable pediatrician in the *hood* and told him that I had had the baby at home. I even produced a forged statement of *live birth* which is necessary when a child is not born in hospital or clinic. He signed it after accepting his three-hundred dollar fee and told me for another couple of hundred he'd produce a birth certificate with a raised seal from the registrant's office. I think he knew the baby wasn't mine all along. In retrospect I know what I *should* have done, but somehow my heart pulled me in another direction. I went to Philadelphia and I took the baby with me—the baby I named Tajahn—Taj for short.

~*~

Maybe it was angels looking after us because everything good fell into my lap. I found a small, neat, furnished apartment near the campus and the landlord told me of a woman who might be willing to take Taj during my school hours. Mrs. Welton was a widowed no-nonsense tight-lipped woman who melted like wax on a hot stove the moment I placed Taj in her arms.

"You go on and get your lesson, we'll be waiting right here when you get back," she said the first day I left him. I was in tears about leaving him because we hadn't been apart since the day he was born, but he was gurgling happily like he knew he was in the arms of safety.

Mrs. Welton didn't pry into my business and never asked me where Taj's father was. I had concocted a story in my brain that I offered anyone who asked. I simply told them that my baby's father died in Iraq. The war statistics was an everyday news occurrence so there was no reason for people *not* to believe me.

It was hard work, trying to keep up with the Master's Program and look after Taj but Miss Welton more than made up for it by keeping him on the nights I had to study late at the library or do field work. I missed him terribly and as soon as I could, I went and got my son. I graduated sixteen and half months later with honors, and was offered a position to teach at the University. I thought long and hard about it, because I did promise to go back to Ohio, but I knew I couldn't. What if Regina had returned? What if she came looking for me? What if she wanted her child back? I couldn't risk it so I took the job offer and began to make a new life for me and my son.

~*~

Taj was two when I met Jeff Branson. He was the night judge at traffic court then and I had gone with Taj in my arms to fight a violation that was no way my fault. My proof was that the stop sign that the officer said I passed was in fact not placed there until a later that week. The red-faced officer apologized but I knew his heart wasn't in it.

That next Saturday morning as I ran in the park with Taj in his jogging-stroller I turned at a bend in the path and almost ran into an oncoming runner. We both stopped. He peered at me.

"Another traffic mishap Mrs. Joseph is it?" It was Judge Branson.

"I'm sorry, I guess I got a little ambitious with my run today."

Taj was smiling up at us.

"Hey little man, whatcha got there?"

My son held out his teddy bear and gave the judge an earth moving smile. Sometimes that's all it takes, a smile and a sunny day to change your life. Jeff and I became friends and stayed that way for months. But hadn't taken me that long to realize I had fallen deeply in love with him.

The first time we made love, I had left Taj with Mrs. Welton and before I could finish preparing our meal, Jeff had me in his arms.

"What about dinner?" I asked breathlessly.

"Oh don't worry, I'm going to eat." His deep voice reverberated right through me. His hands, his face and his tongue were everywhere. He devoured me and since it had been so very long for me, I answered him in the only way I knew how.

Jeff asked me to marry him three months later. Without hesitation or thought I said yes. Less than two weeks after we got back from our honeymoon he filed papers to adopt my son. Things couldn't have been better. We bought lovely house with a large backyard for our child to play in and it was close enough to get back and forth to work easily. Life was good. I was teaching and things really began to move for Jeff who was considering an offer at a University in Arizona to head the Law Department at an embarrassingly high salary. He was interviewed on the local news and right after our family photo ran in the newspaper the letters started coming.

I knew they were from Regina even though they were unsigned. *Thank you for caring for my baby, but let's remember he is my baby,* it read. The words chilled me. I was the only mother Taj had ever known. What if she wanted him back? Why hadn't I told Jeff the truth about the boy he had given his prestigious family name to? *So many questions-so many lies.*

The letters were sporadic for a time, then started coming more often and then requests for money started. It wasn't much at first, but over time the amount increased. When I failed to send the money, the letters became threatening, *If I don't hear from you by…* I began to lose weight and my mind was always preoccupied with the notion that Regina could turn up at any time and wreck my life. Jeff noticed something was wrong, but he attributed it to the fact that we were still trying to decide about moving to Arizona, but I had already made up my mind.

"Let's just go Jeff. Let's get out of here." I said to him one night after dinner.

"Whoa baby what's the matter?" his face was full of concern.

"I'm just anxious to have my man start his new job in Arizona that's all," I lied.

"I haven't decided on that fully honey. I was waiting for the right time to tell you they're countering the offer at the Municipality. It would mean we wouldn't have to move out of state, I can get you your dream house in a great neighborhood and best of all Taj won't have to change schools or leave his friends."

I knew that if I pressed the matter it would only make things worse. I had a little money saved so I sent some of it to the Post Office Box that the letter had indicated. It wasn't nearly enough. A few weeks later a new and more threatening letter arrived. *How about if I make a little visit to your nice little home front?* The scratchy scrawl had read. I was frantic and tried to put it out of my mind. I began to send monetary installments out of my salary each month and that seemed to hold off anymore letters.

Months went by and I felt a small bit of relief and normalcy return to my life.

Jeff decided to stay in Philadelphia and we moved to a new house with a fantastic view. I was in heaven and Taj was almost giddy with joy when his father presented him with a gift on his fifth birthday.

"Okay son, this is a very special present. It's your responsibility, are we understanding one another?"

He looked puzzled but agreed. Opening the box, a Jack Russell Terrier leapt up and began licking his face. "Dad! A puppy, is he mine–my very own?"

"He's all yours son. But you have to make sure he's walked and fed and he'll be your best friend always."

The love on Jeff's face for Taj both warmed and filled my heart with sadness.

~*~

On Taj's seventh birthday he told us he wanted to go to "*Burnz*" the best Bar-B-Q place in town. We were more than happy to take him and he was all smiles when the staff sang happy birthday over a small cake and candles for him to blow out. I loved the way my son smiled when he was happy, it seemed to make everything right with the world. The place was crowded with parties and large groups of people enjoying a night out. A group of rather rowdy college kids were making their way out as we were paying the check to leave. I gazed out at them and thought for an instant I saw a familiar face.

"OW-Mom!" I realized I had gripped Taj's hand too tight. When I looked again the face was gone. I was being paranoid, I had to get a grip on myself. Soon after things began to happen all at once. The Dean asked if I'd represent the school at a seminar and dinner reception in California and I agreed, but Mrs. Welton informed us that she was selling her home and moving to Florida because she couldn't take the Pennsylvania winters anymore. We were all sad because Taj loved her so and she was the only one I trusted him with. I would have to tell the Dean he'd have to find someone else to go on the trip.

"Don't be silly, honey," Jeff said. "I can rearrange my schedule so I can pick him up. I'm perfectly capable of taking care of Taj by myself. Go and handle your business. The dean wouldn't have asked you to do it if he didn't have complete faith in the fact that you could handle it."

Reluctantly I went and it was the longest week of my life. All I wanted to do was get back home to my family. At the end of the week, I managed to get on an earlier flight and thought I would surprise my family with their favorite meal. When I arrived the house was relatively neat and orderly which surprised me with two men left to own devices. I half expected the kitchen to be a mess of take-out cartons and ice cream containers. At 4:30 Jeff came in and hugged me tight.

"You're home. Why didn't you call me, I'd have picked you up from the airport?"

"I wanted to surprise you," I said kissing him deeply.

"Well I have a surprise for you, and it's happening right now," He said and I felt him harden against my thigh.

"Oh no you don't, where's Taj?"

"It's Friday, he's got soccer practice until 5:30, which means we have time for a little *did-you-miss-me-sex.*"

"With whom?" I was always worried when Taj was out of my sight.

"Stop worrying he is in capable hands, and you know all the soccer moms are there."

He kissed me deeply and squeezed my breast. I had missed him. Jetlag and good lovemaking caused me to fall into an instant and deep sleep. I was awakened by the sound of my son's laughter and glanced at the clock. It was almost 7:30. I pulled on a robe and smoothed my hair back and padded into the bathroom. I washed up and went down to the kitchen where I heard my son's laughter.

"Mom!" he said when he saw me.

But my eyes were glued on the girl standing by the stove stirring something in a pot.

It was Regina, older, still beautiful, a great body and deceit behind her smiling eyes.

"Mrs. Branson, it's nice to finally meet you. Your husband has told me so much about you, I feel like I know you." The words held a hint of malicious syrupy sweetness. My legs were weak and I held on to the back of my son's chair to keep from fainting.

"You okay babe?" Jeff asked.

"Just a little tired from the trip, is all."

"This is Regina Stanley. She's been working part-time at the courthouse but looking for extra work. While you were away I had a couple of unexpected meetings and the clerk administrator suggested Regina look after Taj."

I couldn't believe it; he let a total stranger—at least to him, take care of our child? He was a Judge for fuck's sake!

"I was already at the office so we stayed until your husband finished with his meeting. We never even left the building did we big man."
She smiled at my son and my head was spinning; the devil was in my home.

"Yeah Mom, then after she and dad took me to play laser tag and she's real good too, but I got her on the hill, it was so much fun."

"I hope you don't mind, I told your husband I was good with kids, in fact I had one of my own—a boy, but I lost him." Her connotation held meaning for only me, as I looked from my son to my husband.
As if that wasn't enough, it only got worse when Jeff hit me yet another insane idea.

"Regina's about to lose her apartment, I told her I'd ask you if it was all right for her to stay here until she can find another place, we have plenty of room."
Regina's smile was sickening sweet as she faced me. "It would only be for a week or so. The owner wants the apartment for her daughter and new son-in-law. I have a prospect but I have to just wait until the landlord gets back to me," she said.

342

My brain was screaming *absolutely not*, but I didn't want to upset Taj.

"I'd love to be of whatever help I can while I'm here." She hurriedly added.

Every *Lifetime* Movie about letting another *well-meaning* woman into your home came rushing at me.

Jeff was beaming with the smile of the uninformed. "It would give you some much deserved relief honey; you wouldn't have to rush around all the time." He said.

"Yeah mom and maybe she can take me to the Laser rink again and I can get her behind the log pile," Taj interjected with that mischievously killer smile of his.

"We'll see." I said shakily, hating the way she looked at him with her eyes filled with maternal ownership.

She stayed for dinner and it was all I could do to get my food down with her sitting opposite me and smiling with knowledge that only the two of us knew about.

Later, in bed I managed to convince Jeff that it wouldn't be a good idea to have Regina stay with us. "Besides…" I said, "You know it's never a good idea to include another woman in a position of power in the home unless they look like Mrs. Doubtfire." I was trying to make a joke of it.

"Regina is baby… "He laughed, "Believe me you have nothing to worry in that area."

"Well in that case you won't mind if I don't have her taking care of *my baby*, and since I have nothing to worry about, why don't you just take care of *this* baby,"

I said and I took his hand and placed it between my opened legs which ended any any and all discussion about Regina.

A week later I got a call from her. "I don't have to live with you to be able to get my kid ya know?"

"You don't even want him." I hissed into the receiver.

"No I don't, but you do, so a little monetary compensation might be in order."

"How much compensation?"

"A hundred and fifty—large."

A hundred and fifty thousand dollars? The girl was insane, there was no way I could get that kind of money and I told her so.

"Then you best find a way because I'll be a thorn in your side for as long as it takes, and you know what? There are other people who would love to have a nice educated, well-mannered boy like Taj."

"You'd try and sell your own son?" I asked incredulously.

"You didn't have a problem paying for him," she sneered.

She was right. I gave her money to keep him. Everything was all wrong. I had to tell Jeff.

"Oh and if you're thinking about discussing our little arrangement with your hubby, I'll have no choice but to drop a tip on the news hotline. I can see the headlines now, *PROMINENT COURT OFFICIAL AND UNIVERSITY ALUMNI WIFE BUYS CHILD,* or worse, I can tell them how you stole him from me."

I didn't know what to do. I had to find a way to get her out of our lives.

~*~

I remembered how before we were married, my husband spent hours sharing some of his court stories with me over dinner or in bed after making love. The world was filled with unsavory characters willing to do anything for money or for the price of a fix. If I could find just one of those persons I just might be home free.

One night when Jeff had gone to his monthly poker night gathering I searched through some of his files until I found a name with information that just might be the type of person I needed—*Deacon Mapes*. His last known address was about fifteen miles away and in the seediest part of the Philly housing projects. I wrote down the phone number and address and stuck it in my purse. I called the number from my office and it took me three tries before Deacon Mapes got back to me. I explained briefly what I needed and he said that it would be better if I came to him.

I arranged for Taj to have a sleepover at one of his friend's house when Jeff was assisting at night court for another judge who had taken ill several days later. I called Deacon and told him I would be coming by.

Memories of Taj's birth came back to me when I entered the building. I rang the bell on the first floor. It was opened a scant inch or so and dark female eyes scanned me up and down. "I'm here to see Mr. Mapes."

The woman pursed her lips as she took in my stylish clothes and Gucci handbag.

"He said some woman was coming by. He said to tell you he was running late but he'll be here. You wanna wait?" She opened the door a little wider.
I didn't relish standing outside and I didn't know what he looked like, so I agreed. I entered the messy apartment. The woman shooed two kids off the couch then went to pick up a crying infant from a rickety bassinet. *So much poverty* I thought and this was Deacon's family living heavily in it. I knew then he was just the man I needed to do what I needed done and the money I'd give him would be a great help to them.

A half hour later a frighteningly tall, thin yet good looking man with small twist locks in his hair entered. He was smoking a joint, and to my confusion carried an armload of what looked like textbooks and plopped them on the table. *Probably something he stole in order to sell for drug money*, I thought meanly.
I got up. "I'm...."

"Let's talk outside." Then turned to the woman, "Yolanda, Gerald said he was bringing home some McDonalds for the kids," he said to her holding the door open for me.

I led him to my car which was parked in the middle of the block.

"Your wife is pretty." I said making small talk.

"She's my sister and I ain't got no wife and no kids, if you can believe that."

I noticed that there was intelligence about him but he was making a conscientious effort to talk with a street tinge.

"I see. Well um…. I have um…" now that I was here I had no idea how I was going to say what I'd come to say."

"You said you had a problem that you need to go away."

"Yes,"

"How?"

"Not killed or anything…" I said quickly "just… scared into leaving town and never coming back."

"Uh huh; and how much you willing to pay?"

"A thousand dollars?" I instantly knew I shouldn't have posed it as a question.

"Yeah, I can make it happen. Where's he stayin'?"

"It's a she," I corrected him.

"A woman? You want me to beat the hell out of a woman?"

"She's threatening my family—my son to be exact, I just need you to *convince* her that any continued interaction with us wouldn't wise or healthy."

He leaned against the car. "That kind of convincing is gonna cost a little more."

"How much more?" I asked.

"Two and a half large."

"And you'll make sure she leaves and won't come back?"

"Lady ain't nuthin' that sure except death and taxes, but I'm positive she'll get the message, just give me the address and I'll take care of it."

"When?" I asked.

"Couple of days maybe. What about the money?"

"I can give you a thousand now and the rest when I know she's gone, I'll bring it here," I said extracting a roll of bills.

"Deal!" he said accepting the wad of bills.

~*~

For the next twenty-four hours I was on pins and needles waiting for word from Deacon that Regina was out of my life forever. It was the beginning of the weekend so I arranged for Taj to have another sleep-over in case there was a problem when Deacon called on my cell.

Jeff called at 7:30 telling me that he needed me to pick him up at the courthouse.

"Are you okay? Where's your car."

"Can you just pick me up please?"

His voice was abrupt and I figured it was because of some case or other legal matter that had not gone according to the plan.

"Of course hon," I said. I turned off my cell phone in case Deacon called while I was with my husband and raced over. He was standing at the curb when I pulled up, his face a mask of what I thought was fatigue.

"I'll drive." He said sternly and opened the car door. Confused, I got out and went around and settled into the passenger seat. Gunning the motor, he peeled away from the curb and down the street in the opposite direction of home.

"Jeff? Where are we going?"

"I have to make a stop, but before we get there do you have anything you want to tell me?"
I almost melted into a pool of sweat. "About what?" I tried to play it off.

"I got a call today from someone who had been before my bench on more than one occasion. He said he wanted to talk to me, about you and our son."
A blinding headache suffused my brain. "Jeff I..." Before I knew it he pulled up in front of the very building where Deacon Mapes lived. Two men loitered near the stoop outside.
Jeff cut the engine, got out and came around pulled my door open and waited for me to get out. I wanted to explain, but his face was a mask that told me he didn't want to talk about anything just then. Together we walked to the steps.

"Wuzzup your honor," one of the men said and gave my husband *the brother* handshake.

"Go on in, no one's gonna bother your ride, I got this," the mans said.

My legs wouldn't work but Jeff took me by the arm firmly and ushered me in. We went to the door and Jeff knocked hard. Yolanda opened the door to let us in.

Deacon sat on a couch in the musty living room opposite a pouting Regina.

"Hey judge," Deacon said then cast his eyes over to me.

"Look Miz. Branson I'm sorry but this is whack. I had some of my
boys check you out and that's how I found out who you were."

"So you did what your kind do best, you threw in with her and now you want to hold me and my husband up for more money?" I sneered at him. He ignored my sarcasm.

"Those books you saw the other night? They're mine. I go to night school. I'm twelve credits from an engineering degree and it's all because of him," he said pointing to my husband. "He helped me get on the right road. If his family was in trouble I had to let him know."

I was weak and tears flooded my eyes. I knew I was about to lose everything.

"That don't change nuthin…" Regina chimed in. "Taj is my kid and she stole him," she said pointing at me.

My husband pulled out a sheaf of papers from his jacket pocket.

"I made a few calls to Ohio *and* New York. You've got quite a record young lady. Larceny, theft, possession, soliciting—says here you're a three time loser."

I saw her face pale as Jeff went almost nose to nose with her.

"You've upset my household, threatened my family. I can't have that. The best place for you is behind bars."

"On what fuckin' evidence?" she said.

"Letters and notes where you extorted money from my wife."

He looked over at me and I wanted to die right then and there.

"She can't prove nuthin. None of them letters have my name on em. They could be from anybody."

"So then what you're saying is that you *didn't* write them?" He was urging her to agree.

"Hell no! It was my man's idea. I don't want your snot-nosed brat."

"Then you won't mind signing this paper agreeing to that?" he said smoothly.

"What about them charges and shit?"

"I can't promise you'll never be caught, but it won't be because of anything I did or said as long as you keep your word and distance—as in out of this state." He held out the pen.

"Then I can go?" she looked at him tentatively.

"And never come back here—ever."
Regina leapt at the pen and scribbled her name in three places he'd indicated.

"If I ever see or hear from you or if you ever attempt to contact our son I'll have you thrown in jail so fast by time you get out there'll be no such thing as Medicare."

The girl grabbed the fake leather bag at her feet and went to the door. She looked back at me.

"He's a good kid. He's lucky to have you." And she was gone.
I sank to the sagging couch and cried.

"I gotta bolt Judge Branson, I have a test next week and I got to study."

"Thanks Deacon, for everything I won't forget this."

"You just be at my graduation like you promised that's all."

"With bells on," he said.
The next moments were a blur as I felt Jeff take my arm and lead me out of the apartment. Tears blinded me as he put me in the car.

At home he ran a bath for me and I soaked for an hour. When I came out, he handed me a cup of hot herb tea.

"Do you know how much I love you woman?"

Tears began to flow again.

"Jeff, I have to tell you about Taj"

"Regina told me everything—with a little coercion from Deacon."

"I don't want this to problem for you, we'll leave will, quietly. I will make sure none of this tarnishes you and I'll explain to Taj..."

"Woman don't you know I will walk through a wall of flames to protect you and Taj? I want your promise right now that there are no more secrets and you will always be with me. I promised him.

"And you have to promise to love me all your life because we have a son to raise and I can't do it or even live without you and him in my life. We can discuss what and when to tell Taj when the time is right."

"I'm so sorry darling—for everything." I cried. "And I think I owe Deacon an apology, I said a pretty mean thing to him."

"He understands. I'm just glad I was able to make a difference in that young man's life. Here, he said to give you this."

I took the envelope; it was every cent of the money I'd given him."

"I...I...guess we can save it for a graduation present for him," I sniffled. By then we were both tearful and Jeff was holding me. I was once again wrapped in the arms of love and safety and I knew I would never keep anything from my husband again.

Stolen money-Reclaimed Heart

I lived in a small town on a coastal island and was the plain Jane only child of parents who had made their living fishing and operated the *Fins and Claws*, the most popular seafood eatery on the island. Unfortunately, they were killed in a freak boating accident on my twenty-first birthday. I, of course inherited our small but comfortable house, the restaurant and surprising to me, an accidental death insurance policy worth just over three hundred thousand dollars.

I remember sitting stoically as Charles Wallisford, the only practicing attorney on the small island, read the will. His beautiful raven-haired daughter, Elise, who was also his *sometime* assistant, sat nearby with a pad perched on her knee. I remembered her from school because she had always been in one scrape after another and had one boy after the other. The rumor mill had it that the summer before we graduated from high school, she'd been sent away because she was pregnant. When she returned I figured her father decided the best thing for her was to keep her close and that meant letting her work alongside him.

"Well," Mr. Wallisford said as he folded the document up and placed it in a large brown envelope. "It appears your parents left you quite well off young lady. You might want to seek the aid of a financial advisor, however my immediate suggestion is that you separate the funds and place them in some good interest bearing mutual fund accounts until then."

But I didn't do that; I put the money in the bank and left it there. I had other things to think about. The summer season was upon me and that's when the restaurant did its best business. Now that

I was virtually alone, I had to get the menus ready, hire a seasonal chef and make sure I had enough help to accommodate the usual influx of off-Islanders for the duration of the summer.

News travels fast when you live in close community, and it wasn't long before everyone and anyone was giving me advice on what I should do with what they considered as my *windfall*. I knew there was no way Mr. Wallisford would betray a business confidence, so I figured it had to be Elise who spilled the beans. By the time the eighth person had stopped me to offer words of wisdom on my monetary situation, I had had enough. I walked away from the offender in a huff and literally bumped right into Tom Fallon. He was a seasonal and reclusive writer who had been coming to the island for as long as I could remember.

"Hi!" he said adjusting his glasses, "Look I wanted to tell you..." he started.
I cut him off before he could go any further.

"What? You want to tell me what to do with my fortune? Well I've had quite enough advice for one day and I don't need any more from you." I was fuming.
His left brow arched at an impossible angle as he stood there quietly taking my berating. "I was only going to mention that if you need some extra help at the restaurant, you might want to consider students from the university, they're always looking for work and they come cheap if you feed them too."
I felt as dumb as floating seaweed. I rubbed my brow.

"Look, I'm sorry; it's been a strange day. It seems everyone wants to give me advice about my money."

"Minding one's own business is not very popular in small towns."
His smile was incredible and I returned one that was just as brilliant—until I noticed the shiny gold bend on the third finger of his left hand. He was still wearing it, even though his wife had been dead for more than three years.

"Thanks for the information though, I'll post a notice in the library." I said and smiled again, then went on my way.

352

~*~

My mother had always done most of the cooking; she was an A-number one chef when it came to good old fashioned meals. She hardly measured, but eyeballed ingredients that made the meals perfect and almost impossible to duplicate. I was able to follow through with some of the simpler dishes, but when it came to her seafood soufflé or lobster Ravioli with shrimp sauce and especially her lobster bisque with saffron, I never could make it the way she had. When she had tried to explain it to me it sounded easy and I attempted them several times but I just couldn't get the ingredients right. I never tried them again even though they were the restaurant favorites. But now my father gone and me with a multitude of other assorted duties I knew I had to hire a chef *and* a good one. Sally Young, our regular waitress who had been with us for years; was ready to work as usual and I did end up hiring the two students as Tom had recommended. A cook of course, was another story and I was getting nervous.

I placed ads in all the culinary trade magazines and asked everyone I knew if they had any recommendations for a decent chef. A week before opening I was in panic mode because no one had answered any of the ads.

I was sitting in the small office in the back of the restaurant, trying to ward off a headache, racking my brain trying to think who I could ask to fill in until a fulltime replacement could be found; when I heard a tapping on the glass door. *What now*! I wondered.

I got up and opened the door a crack. The figure that stood there was tall and extremely muscular man with eyes so gray they looked like sea glass. His hair was short, thick and the color of wet sand. He wore a casual linen suit that hung in perfect folds and creases on his solid looking body.

"Can I help you?" I asked.

"The question is… can I help *you*?"

I looked at him questioningly and he held up a trade magazine where a big red circle was around one of the ads I'd placed.

"I'm here to apply for the chef's position."

He certainly didn't look like a chef to me—not with his bedroom eyes and beach-bum good looks.

I opened the door wider to let him in. He stepped inside and waited until I went to sit back behind the paper-strewn desk.

"Have a seat Mr....?" I motioned to the chair opposite me and waited for him to offer his name.

"Garrett Wade." He held out a strong, veiny hand.

I took it; mine was a sharp contrast in smallness against his larger strong one.

"Have you worked in a restaurant before Mr. Wade?"

"Several in fact."

"Do you have a resume?"

"Of course," he said holding up a packet.

"And I assume you've included references?"

He handed me and additional sheet of paper. I began to read quickly, trying desperately to hide my joy at his impressive culinary connections.

True, I'd never heard of any of the restaurants listed, but then I was rarely off the island so how could I know? I glanced up from the paper and looked at him.

"Is this it?" I said hoping nothing in my expression would give away my desperation.

"I've also worked in the homes of several prominent movie personalities on the West Coast, as well as foreign politicians stationed at embassies in and around Washington D.C."

He offered when I finished reading. It was *quite impressive.*

"Well I can assure you this job is in no way that glamorous. So I guess my question to you is, why would you want to work in such a small establishment? Your credentials prove you're more than capable of something more elite," I asked.

His lopsided grin was distracting and I pulled myself away from it as fast as I could.

"Famous people can be overly demanding and a bit on the neurotic side if you catch my drift. I guess I just got tired of the rat race."

"Well, this may not be Hollywood or anywhere near the Pentagon, but things *can* get a little hectic around here too—especially during the tourist season." I said desperately hoping I wasn't discouraging him.

"Still, I figure it can't be worse," He said with a broad smile, "and I could use a little small town peace and quiet."

"You won't say that when the main-landers get here with their kids, dogs and city noise," I chuckled.

"Does that mean I have the job?"
I stood up and smiled. "It means… you have a chance. I'd like to check your references, just a formality of course."

"Of course," he said.

"Where are you staying?"

"Not on this island. It's booked solid," he said with a sigh.

"It's always like that this time of year. How will I reach you?"

"My cell number is at the top of my resume."

"Okay then, thank you Mr. Wade I'll be in touch whichever way I decide."

"I'd appreciate that."
He smiled and headed for the door, then turned and looked back at me. "I make a mean seafood soufflé and a fruit trifle to die for."

"We're not all that fancy but our food is wholesome and plentiful," I said.

"Well I guess I'll be off and I hope to be hearing from you."

~*~

I didn't want to delude myself into thinking that I wasn't going to hire Garrett. In actuality I had little choice. No one else seemed to want the job and I was opening the restaurant in two weeks. I called one of Garrett's references, but all I got was a voicemail message so I left my information for a callback as soon as possible.

I worked well into the evening and by 10:00 I was exhausted. I straightened the desk as best I could and contemplated only briefly if I should sleep on the lumpy leather sofa. I decided against it, locked up the office and went home. I slept soundly that night, but in my dreams, two faces that I couldn't quite make out, danced around in my illusory subconscious.

I awoke the next morning and went to the office and placed a call to another one of Garrett Wade's references, again I got a voicemail and again I left my call-back information. I spent the rest of the day cleaning and reviewing the menus. I went to the local nursey and ordered some plants for the outside and I painted two of the wooden planters and railing. It was no wonder I was so tired and I knew I would need some help and fast. I arose at four a.m. the next morning so that I could be at the docks by five to place my seafood orders for the season. I knew most of the fishermen and they were familiar with my needs, but I wanted to make sure everything would be just as Mom and Dad would have wanted. On the way back to the restaurant office I stopped at the local deli where the waitress had a large container of my favorite latte ready for me. Deep in thought and trying to organize a hundred tasks in my head at once, I was about to take a sip of the hot coffee just as I got to the office door.

"Good morning!"

Startled, I jumped. The hot liquid spilling through the small slit of the container ran over the edge and scalding my fingers. I dropped the cup and began waving my hand around to cool it as I looked at cause of my accident. It was Garrett.

"Mr. Wade," I said shaking my burning fingers. "Did you forget something?"

"No, just thought I'd get a jump on the competition," he grinned.

"Well you certainly got a jump out of me." I pouted and unlocked the door. He followed behind me in and waited until I turned on the desk lamp.

"Here let me see that hand," he said moving to me, and before I knew it he had hold of it and was peering at my reddening fingers.

"You'd better run them under some cold water. It'll keep it from blistering."

"It's not that bad," I said jerking my hand away. His touch was burning me far more than the coffee had.

"Suit yourself, but I still think you ought to do it."

"So! What did you say you wanted?"

"The chef's job."

"I'm sorry but I haven't made my final decision yet." I don't think he even believed it. "Besides…" I continued, "I'm still waiting for a return call from your references."
His eyes slid over to the answering machine with and it's the blinking red light.

"That could be them,"
He was very sure of himself and I didn't know if I liked that. But it was the way his eyes roved over me that embarrassed me most. My hand seemed to move in slow motion as it moved to the answering machine button. I had one message. It was a female voice, professing that she was the manager at *La Masion* in New York and that she would be available to talk to me any time during the morning hours.

"Please have a seat Mr. Wade. This should only take a moment."
I dialed the number a female answered with the typical New York accent. She confirmed Garrett's employment at the prestigious eating emporium and gave rave reviews about his talent with beef and pork medallions.
When I hung up, I looked at him.

"Oh sure you can cook a cow, but how are you at shrimp bisque?" I laughed.
His eyes twinkled as he laughed with me. "I can cook anything you want, anyway you want it."

~*~

Perhaps I'd intended to give him the job all along, because the next thing I knew, we were going over menu plans and table arrangements. I told him I expected him to be at the restaurant no later than 7 a.m. each morning; earlier on weekends since those were our super busiest days.

"That may be a bit of a problem," he said with a grimace, "I can't get a room on the island, I'll have to get up at 4 a.m. just to ferry over."

I thought for a moment. If I hired him, his traveling woes might be a problem. We had a gardener's cottage on our property that had gone unused for a long time, but with some sprucing up it could be livable. I told him about it and his eyes lit up at prospect.

"I can have it ship shape in a day or so. It's not much but it's dry and comfortable." I said.

"That would be fine; I don't intend to spend a lot of time there anyway."

I wasn't sure what he meant by that, and I didn't the time to ponder it.

~*~

The restaurant opened on time to a slew of summer renters, weekend off-Islanders and of course our loyal locals. Garrett was a godsend. His cooking prowess was every bit as unique and wonderful as his credentials said they were. Sometimes after we'd closed I'd find him late at night in kitchen working on a new culinary concoction.

"Here, taste this." He'd hold a spoon out for me and my palate was treated to a delectable cream sauce or dessert. I tried telling him that we were a simple family seafood restaurant, but he insisted upon expanding our menu with *one-of-a-kind* dishes that not only won over the seasonal patrons, but some of the locals as well. Soon we were inundated with requests for more and more of the tasty dishes that he'd prepared.

One morning as I went to the wharf to order a new fish that Garrett had said he wanted to try I encountered Tom Fallon taking his usual sunrise walk.

"Good morning," he said with a shy smile.

"It is a beautiful morning isn't it?" I said lightly.

He shuffled a bit then looked at me with sable brown eyes.

"Look Mara, I never got a chance to tell you how sorry I was to hear about your parents. We didn't get off to a good start that day when you thought I was dipping my nose into your financial business."

My face suffused with color.

"No, it was me who was rude, but thanks. I'm sure I never got a chance to express my condolences for the loss of your wife. Please accept them now."

"Thanks." He said in a clipped tone and then changed the subject quickly. "So I guess you're here for the first catch-of-the-day?"

"Well something like that. Would you like to come along?"

"Sure. It'll be good to see exactly where my lunch or dinner might be coming from," he laughed.

We walked to the docks where the fishermen were sorting out baskets of crabs, clams, lobsters, flounder and other types of fish. I wasn't the only one up early and getting my order done but there were a specific few fisherman with whom my parents always dealt and I wasn't about to go against that. I asked about *Cobia* the new fish that Garrett wanted. It was touted as the new Tilapia but with more character and flavor. I chose the usual fish skillfully and carefully because Garrett insisted upon whole Bass and trout whereby he could filet them himself. I'd always paid the fisherman to do it in order to save time and I trusted them.

"Your restaurant seems to be doing quite well."

I was surprised he'd even noticed.

"It's my new chef; he works magic in the kitchen. I haven't seen you there in a while." I teased.

"Who can get in? Besides, I usually phone in my order and pick it up after the crowd has thinned."

"Tom, if you call me early in the day I'll make sure there's a table for you and your guests."

"That's nice of you, but there's only me."
He sounded so sad when he said that.

"You just give me a call and I will make sure you get in."

"That's nice of you; I just might take you up on it sometime."

After I finished making my selections, we said goodbye and he walked slowly away. I could see his heart was filled with sadness and that he still missed his wife very much.

Later that night after closing, I was almost too tired to stand but I still had work to do. I sat in the office going over the day's receipts, noticing that the restaurant was indeed doing quite well. I rubbed my tired eyes and yawned and laid my head on the desk for a moment. I must have dozed momentarily because the next thing I felt was hands—strong hands on my shoulders, kneading them gently. I sat up quickly and turned.

"You're still here Garrett. I thought you'd be gone by now."

"Just going over tomorrow's menu and looking over some new ones as usual. It looks like you've been burning the mid night oil yourself."
He was still massing my back and shoulder, I began to relax. In the single moment it took my aching muscles to unwind I felt the hands wander over my shoulders dangerously close to the rise of my breasts. I stiffened.

"Relax Mara. You're so tense. I could help with some of these details if you'd let me," Garrett said softly.

"I'm alright, I'm used to it," I said gathering up the money and papers on the desk.

I was acutely aware of his hands on me and the slow warmth that traveled up my body. Shaking off the comfortable lethargy that threatened to overtake me I stood up and his hands slid off my shoulders.

"Listen Mara, it's easy to see you're dead on your feet. Why don't you let me finish up here? I'll drop the money into the night box at the bank before I go home."
Garrett had been kind the past month and he was the reason the restaurant was doing better than it had ever done. But he was still a stranger so I decided to keep some things in my own hands.

"It's okay Garrett but thanks for the offer and for the massage. I'll take the bank pouch but if you don't mind locking up I'd sure appreciate it."
He agreed and I placed the day's receipts into the bank pouch and left, promising myself I'd sort through and file the stack of papers on the desk the following day.

I must have been over-tired because later after bits and pieces of naps, I was still unable to fall into a restful sleep. I reluctantly conceded that it might have been due to the tingling memory of Garrett's touch. I tossed, turned and beat my pillow into a pulp but it was no use I just couldn't sleep. Finally, I got up and contemplated making a cup of warm milk but I knew that urban legend remedy would never fix the reason I couldn't rest. I went out onto the back patio hoping the night air would lull me into some semblance of sleepiness. The salty scent of the sea was heavy and aromatic and the summer air was cooler than in the day. I fiddled with the wicker rocker and pulled a weed from a crack in the walkway. My eyes were drawn over the short distance to the gardener's cottage. The dim light shining in the window was a magnet and drew to toward it. The damp grass was cool on my bare feet as I moved to the lighted window and looked in through the parted gauzy curtains. Garrett lay on the bed, naked to the waist reading, a cigarette, burning in his left hand. The subtle glow of the small table lamp washed over his bare chest that shone like burnished gold—a testament that he enjoyed the beach, with strands of dark hair wending all the way down to where his jeans began. One long leg was propped up, as his eyes skimmed over the page.

Heat crept up my legs and a tremble began in my stomach. It was wrong of me to watch him like some sort of peeping tom and I quickly and carefully turned to sneak back to my house. Unfortunately, my cautious moves were rewarded with the sound of the clang of a rake that I bumped into causing it to fall against a garbage pail with a loud clattering din.

"Who's there?" Garrett called out.

I hurried toward my rear door, hoping to make it back inside before he saw me.

"Mara?"

I stopped dead in my tracks, my chest heaving with exertion and embarrassment." I turned and saw him hurrying toward me.

"What's wrong?" he asked with concern.

My mouth felt like it was filled with cotton and ashes as I tried to think of a lie.

"I—I thought I heard something. It must have been a raccoon or stray cat."

His eyes washed over me, almost looking right through my rather un-sexy cotton sleeping apparel. The cool night air breezed over me and I shivered. I felt my nipples stiffen and he noticed it instantly. He was standing so close to me I could feel the heat he radiated. His hand reached out and brushed a lock of my hair back behind my ear.

"There was no raccoon or cat was there Mara?" His voice was low and seductive.

"There was something..." I wanted to die of humiliation. He gently took my hand, pulling me close to his steely body. I gasped as I felt the urgency of a man in need.

"Garrett..."

"Shh!" he whispered then kissed any further words off my lips, all the while walking me back and into the cottage. He kicked the door shut and backed me to the bed and laid me down on it, his body covering mine. The lonely agony I had been feeling all my life, especially since the death of my parents slowly began to dissolve as the heat of his touch consumed me. The world ceased to exist as he whispered words of urging to me, telling me that everything was going to be all right and how much he desired me.

"I want you Mara. You must have felt it, otherwise why would you have come to me tonight."
With just those simple words, I offered up the gift of my most precious self, which he took gladly and roughly.

~*~

Afterwards, Garrett lit a cigarette and told me how wonderful it was. "It's going to be great Mara, you and me together."

The sex euphoria left me as the reality of what I'd just done hit me. While he felt wonderful inside me, I pushed away the thought that he was somehow disconnected from what we were doing. Hurriedly I donned my nightgown and stood up.

"Mara, what is it? Did I hurt you?" he said stubbing out his cigarette and reaching for me.

"This was a mistake Garrett. I'm sorry."
He looked dejected. "Why, because you took a little pleasure for yourself *or* because you might have to include someone else in your life? How is that bad?"

"You don't understand…" I began.

"I understand that we are both lonely and we need the company of someone who cares and I care about you Mara,"

My rational mind was telling me that with his looks and ego he'd never had a lonely day in his life, but the emotional sensation I was still feeling seemed to lead me in another direction.

"You can have anyone. I don't want to be some kind of pathetic project."

"I know you don't believe that Mara."

"Why not? You don't know me and I really don't know you."

"So you think I took advantage of you?"
His voice was low and filled with dejection.

"I don't think you meant to."

"I'm sorry if you feel that way but I can assure you right here and right now, it's not true. I wanted to make love to you."

"I'm just not the kind of woman that men normally…"

"That's bullshit!" He said cutting me of. "Look I understand your fear, a lot's happened to you. You're suddenly laden with all this responsibility, yet you don't want to accept any help."

"It's not that. It's just that I've had to do all this alone and now you've come and turned my world upside down and…"

"Don't let the fact that I have feelings for you get in the way of my willingness to take some of the burden off you. I'm here for you Mara, just let me help."

He helped me all right. He helped me out of my nightgown and right back into his bed.

"I'm just not sure about this." I said after another about of intense lovemaking. "I mean you're my employee for goodness sake."

He ran a finger slowly along my arm. "I know how you feel. It wasn't easy for me either, being so close yet unable to express how I feel about you."

He'd never given any indication that he felt anything toward me that wasn't work related. My head was spinning; it was all happening so fast.

"I need some time Garrett."

"Take all the time you need Mara. If you think it's right then you have to follow your heart," he said then kissed me tenderly. I dressed again and left the cottage and literally ran back to the house.

Much to my chagrin Garrett avoided me the next week. Whenever he needed to talk to me he did so in clipped professional tones and engaged me with cordial coolness. The more he stayed away from me, the more drawn to him I was.

~*~

Fins and Claws was closed on Mondays and usually that's when I did the books, employee salaries and other office duties that seemed to pile up by the minute.

But this particular Monday I couldn't concentrate and felt I had to try and patch things up with Garrett. The truth was, I missed him but I didn't want to seem too obvious.

I went down to the marina hoping to rent a skiff and surprise Garrett with a picnic on one of the smaller Islands in the cove. I went to the gardener's cottage, but he wasn't there. I knew there was only one place he could be, *in the kitchen in Fins and Claws, probably* trying out some new recipe.

As I approached my restaurant I saw a young woman hurrying with her back to me from the side entrance. I couldn't see her very well but she looked vaguely familiar.

I let myself in through the front door and walked back toward the kitchen. Just as I'd thought, Garrett was standing over the stove stirring something that smelled delectable.

"I knew you'd be here on your day off." I tried to sound cheery.

He gave me half-smile. "Just licking my wounds is all."

"Well I'd like to make it up to you, how about a picnic? I've rented a skiff, and it's a perfect day for it."

"I'm not much of a sailor, besides there's another little embarrassing situation."

"What's that?"

"I can't swim."

"No worries I'll get you a life jacket besides I can swim like a fish, if anything happens I'll save you." I joked.

He seemed skeptical but with a bit more of coaxing, he relented.

It was a warm sunny day and there were other sailors on the water, but Garrett was clearly uneasy on the skiff; even with his life jacket.

I moored in a tiny cove and we waded ashore. I laid out the blanket, the food and a bottle of red wine.

"It's nice here," he said.

"Yes it's one of my favorite places."

"So were you born on the island?"

"Actually I was. My parents inherited the house and the restaurant—which was originally a small mom and pop general store owned by my grandfather who got it from his relatives."

"The history goes quite a ways back. I was reading about it that night you came to the cabin."
I blushed at the remembrance. "It has and interesting past, especially about the high rate of deafness."

"Yeah, I read about that. They couldn't document the actual source, but it was believed to be the hereditary result of two centuries old inbreeding. Mixed marriages between deaf and hearing spouses comprised over sixty percent of all deaf marriages on the island in the late 19th century, higher than the mainland average of about twenty percent."

"My goodness, you did read about it."

"Well I couldn't work in community and not know anything about it now could I? What if a tourist asked me? I wouldn't want to look like a dunce."
I laughed appreciating the fact that he would take the time to read up on our local history.

We talked a long while and he made me laugh with his tales about some of his culinary disasters over the years.

"So I said to the guy... what do you mean it's burned, you did order blackened catfish. And he said, yeah but this is complete ash."

"And was it?" I was laughing so hard.

"It was drier than an army powder house; when he stuck his fork into it the damned thing collapsed into a cinder pile."
Tears were pouring down my cheeks with laughter. When I regained some semblance of composure he was looking at me and smiling.

"It's nice to see you laughing, you actually look happy."

"I guess it's this place, it does have a calming effect."

"I was hoping I had something to do with that,"
I was in his arms in a matter of moments and this time, I initiated our lovemaking and it instilled something in me that I knew had

been happening all along. I was falling in love with Garrett. By then end of the tourist season, he'd asked me to marry him.

~*~

I was walking on air. Everything was beautiful and I was looking forward to becoming Mrs. Garrett Wade.
Tom Fallon had returned after one of his extended excursions and I met up with him at the grocery store.

"Mara, it's good to see you."

"You too Tom; you've been off island for a while; it's a little odd seeing you here off-season."
He looked a little sheepish, almost like a little boy. "Yes. I was doing my usual jaunts, you know seeing other places and trying to build my courage up."

"For?"
He shuffled from foot to foot. "Well I might as well come out and say it. I was trying to summon the up the stones to see if you'd have dinner with me some evening. I mean now that the season is over, when you might have more time that is." He was rambling like a teenager.

"Tom." My face felt warm from the flush that covered it. "I'm... well I'm engaged."
The stunned look on his face quickly gave way to a disappointed smile as he looked at my ring-less finger. I quickly covered it, embarrassed that Garrett hadn't gotten around to giving me a ring.

"Oh. I didn't know. Who's the lucky man?"

"Garrett Wade." I said too loudly, then softer. "My chef."

"Uh huh."
The way he said that unnerved me.

"Seems a little quick doesn't it? I mean he's only been working for you since the season opened. How much do you know about him?"

"I know that I love him," I said with my chin stiff with obstinacy.
Tom's eyes bored into mine. "Then I guess that's what counts."

I could tell he didn't mean it. "Tom…"I began, but he quickly cut me off.

"I ought to get going. Good luck to you and Garrett." Before I could say another word he was gone.

~*~

Garrett and I were married in a small ceremony a month later. I wanted to get married in the Methodist church where I was christened and had attended all my life. But Garrett said he wasn't much for organized religion and when I asked him how we would raise our children when we had them, "We'll cross that bridge when we come to it darling, but whatever we choose it will be because it's what we both want."
So I let it go.

He wanted to go to Hawaii for our honeymoon—a treat for me since I'd never been anywhere so exotic.

"I got a great deal honey, but they need the entire amount to lock us in for the dates we requested, I'll reimburse you as soon as we get back and I transfer my accounts from them mainland."
I didn't give it a second thought as I over a blank check.

I was flabbergasted by the beauty of the big island, and even more so when we got to our destination at the exclusive Four Seasons in Maui at Wailea. Garrett was very attentive and together we enjoyed the breathtaking sites of rainforests and lava lands. He insisted I try traditional local fare and I must say that while I loved fish, I wasn't a fan of a pork dish called *laulau*, which is made with taro root leaves and baked for long hours in an underground rock oven.

We made love several times under the stars and once even under a waterfall and while the island was filled with beautiful women, Garrett only had eyes for me.
We spent two weeks there and while it was gorgeous and an experience of a lifetime, I was anxious to get back home.

It was still off season when we returned and we spent a good part of it laughing making love and with me trying to teach him about boating.

"I'm going to surprise you someday, I'm going to become so good at this, you'll be shocked," he said while we were out in the skiff one afternoon.

~*~

By the time we had been married six months Garrett had talked me into at *least* looking at plans for expanding the restaurant. In order to get the specs for renovation; he needed a few thousand dollars, which I gave him. Several weeks later he needed additional funds for surveyor and engineering fees. Also, it seemed that every day there was another box or crate being delivered with new silverware, dishes and cookware.

"It's for us honey. I want the restaurant to be a premiere showplace," he crooned to me when I questioned him.

"But Garrett *Fins and Claws* has always done well as it is. We don't need this extravagance."
He looked pained and sighed.

"Okay Mara. I understand. I'm just the chef. I can cook and stay in the background. It's clear that you hold the purse strings. I know what my position is."
He looked so sad. I went to him and encircled him in my arms. "Your position is as my husband and I love you."

"Then at least show it Mara. Let *me* be the man. Let me take care of you for once. Baby we really make this into something we can be proud of. Your parents would want that for you, *I* want it for you."
With those words, he did the very thing that always made me forget everything except the pleasure. We made love all that night and a good part of the morning. Just past noon, we were sitting in the bank and I was including his signature onto my personal and restaurant accounts.

Before I knew it we were again looking down the gun barrel of a seasonal opening. Oddly, Garrett had taken to spending a lot of time off the island telling me that he was looking into some investment deals that would triple our money in less than six months. I told him I wasn't interested and that I needed him here to help with the opening. Aside from everything else going on I was suddenly being harassed with a series of hang-ups both at home and at *Fins and Claws*.

Garrett had me going on one errand after another and it was hard keeping my head on straight; and still more and more boxes arrived at our home or the restaurant—many of them C.O.D. I was at my wits end on the day when one arrived and the total was over $1,500.00. I was fuming, but luckily I had just about that much in household petty cash.

Suffused with anger, I drove over to the restaurant to confront Garrett about his overspending. I could see the dark clouds building in the distance and I knew we were in for bad storm, possibly even a hurricane. I arrived at the restaurant and went to the back. As I approached I heard the distinct tinkle of a woman's laughter. I hurried to the door and snatched it open and saw Elise Wallisford sitting cross-legged on the leather couch opposite Garrett who was seated behind the desk. She leapt to her feet.

"Hey Mara, er I mean Mrs. Wade. There was a hint of sarcasm in her voice.

"Hi darling," Garrett said, "Ms. Wallisford came over to inquire about our catering services.

"What catering services?" I nearly hissed.

"Well um…" Elsie said, "I'm thinking about giving my dad a 65th birthday party. I'm kind of looking for a deal, I don't have a lot of money but I want it to be someplace he enjoys." I relaxed a little, after all, she had been on the couch and he was seated at the desk.

"Well I'm sure we can come up with something that will suit you Elise. We'll give you a call."

Elise got up. "Well then I guess I should get going that storm looks about ready to hit any time now."

"I'll get back to you on this as soon as possible." My husband said to her with an appreciative smile.

"Thank you very much Mr. Garrett." Her voice held a barely disguised tease.

After she'd left, I sat opposite him, something that made me uncomfortable because I was always in the *captain's* chair so to speak.

"Garrett, I have to talk to you about all this excess spending."

"Later baby, I have great news."

"What news?" I sighed, knowing that it was probably something that was going to cost me.

He smiled and waved a piece of paper at me.

"We are going into the premier restaurant and catering business."

"What?"

"Darling, this is a golden opportunity. I plan to hire a full staff and a Matre'D, new décor, the works. We're going to be an exclusive eating establishment, serving only the best reservation-only clientele."

I couldn't believe what I was hearing and my anger got the better of me.

"This restaurant is a *family* business," I yelled.

"Well I'm your family now," he screamed back at me, banging his fist down on the desk.

I tried to regain my composure. "Look Garrett, all I'm saying is that things are going too fast. You're changing everything I've ever been used to."

"Oh I get it, all I'm good for is cooking and staying in the background of *your family* kitchen. Well you know what? Perhaps I'm not suited for this life after all. Maybe you want to do it all, well you can have at it."

I watched in horror as he got up; grabbed his jacket and left with a slam of the door.

He didn't come home that night, or the next day.

The wind went from a sporadic bluster to a full-blown heavy gusting-rain-drenching downpour. I couldn't stay at home any longer and went to the restaurant but it was just as we'd left it, shut tight with a closed-for-renovations sign on the front door. I called home but Garrett didn't pick up. I checked the only hotel that was open this time of year, but they hadn't heard from him. I figured that maybe he'd taken the ferry and gone over to the mainland and there would be no telling when he'd get back with the impending storm. Two days later in y office I was at my wits end with worry and contemplated calling the police.

I was at my desk chewing my fingernails when I heard a rapping on the door. I leapt up and ran to open the door. It was Mr. Wallisford—Elise's father. He looked a hundred years old.

"He's gone isn't he?" Was all he said.

I was puzzled with his question, but his next statement hit me like a ton of bricks. "Elise is gone too."

"I don't understand. What has that…" I stopped and remembered the other day when I found them together laughing in my office. The same day we'd argued and he'd left.

Our suspicions were confirmed later when I went to the bank. I had been cleaned out. It had been done over time, starting almost immediately after I had put his name on the accounts. It was gone all of it.

As with any small town, the news spread like wildfire. Now the same people who had tried to give me advice about my money were now giggling behind their hands at my foolishness. I had just enough money left to pay all the debts Garrett had run up on the new items he'd ordered for what was to be the *New Fins and Claws*.

~*~

Six months later I was sitting at home alone and filled with despair. I had decided that I wouldn't open the restaurant, I was too ashamed. I didn't want see anyone, I just couldn't face people. The front door bell rang and I prayed it wasn't a latent delivery brought on by Garrett's spending extravagances or worse a bill collector with an invoice that hadn't been paid. I opened the door and stared into the dark eyes of Tom Fallon.

"I heard what happened, can I come in?"

I stepped aside and he entered. "Look!" I said, "If you're going to give me a lecture, forget it. Everything you're thinking about me right now I've already thought about myself. I was stupid and careless."

He stood back with surprise. "Okay, but that's not why I came."

"Well why did you come then?" I knew I was being confrontational.

"I wanted to see if you were alright."

"Do I look alright?"

"You look like you need a friend."

I gathered the worn blanket around me. A small smile creased his lips.

"Why don't you point me to the kitchen and I'll make us some coffee you look like you can use it," he said.

I let him follow me to the tricked out kitchen that Garrett had talked me into getting. Tom made coffee and I sat in a chair and watched him.

"Here you go," he said putting the steaming cup in front of me.

We talked well into the afternoon and by the time evening arrived I was on the verge of hysterical tears.

"What a fool I've been. I should have known someone like Garrett could never fall in love with me.

"That's not true and stop being so hard on yourself, He was a con man plain and simple. If it hadn't been you it probably would have been someone else."

I looked tearfully at Tom.

"Do you remember that day when you asked me if I knew what I was doing before I was married?

"Yep—but I shouldn't have."

"Did you suspect anything?" I asked.

He looked embarrassed for a moment. "No, not about Garrett, I didn't even know him. I was thinking more about myself.

"How so?"

"That perhaps it was time I started living again and I had hopes that—well…" his voice faded.

"Go on Tom." I said placing my hand on his arm.

"I'd hoped that you would… that maybe we could spend a little time together and get to know each other but you said you were engaged I knew I had lost my chance."

"Oh Tom I had no idea. I was stupid and blind."

He cleared his throat and stood up. "Well that's all in the past. So, have you thought about what your next steps are going to be?"

"I'm not sure. I have no idea where to begin."

"Do you still love him?"

I thought for only a moment before answering. "I'm not sure I ever did. I got it mixed up with infatuation, and completely misguided by the attention he was showering on me."

"Then we'll just have to take things one step at a time. And the first thing we have to do is go see Charles Wallisford."

"But Elise is his daughter; do you think he'll help us?"

"All we can do is try."

We went to see Charles and he was full of grief stricken apologies.

"Of course I'll help; I want to find my daughter."
~*~

It took almost a year, but we found Elise. She was two states away. The money was gone and so was Garrett and she was working in a sleazy strippers bar six hours a day to support her drug habit.

For a while Garrett was always two steps ahead of us and the near misses made me crazy. We caught up with him at a roadhouse in the next county where I had him served with divorce papers. At first, Garrett refused to sign me and demanded that I see him personally, so between Mr. Wallisford and help from the local police we threatened to have him prosecuted and tied up in court for years unless he signed the papers and he finally agreed but not before telling me that he never loved me and no one would care about a plain fish wife like me.
~*~

A little more than a year after my divorce was final; I became Mrs. Tom Fallon. It was a small-dignified affair and I didn't want an exotic honeymoon so we decided to stay right on our Island at a local Bed and Breakfast overlooking the water. Tom was the tender considerate lover I always dreamed of having, yet the deep urgency with the way he did it made me know that I had finally found my soul mate. By seasons end of the following year I was pregnant with twins and *Fins and Claws* was back to being the most popular family restaurant on the Island. My life had come full circle and my heart was filled with unimaginable joy and happiness.

Alone and Destitute

It's never good news when you answer the doorbell two a.m. in the morning and see two grim-faced policemen standing there. Their somber expressions told me something was terribly wrong.

"Mam…" one said as he looked at a small square notepad, then back at me, "Are you Cynthia Pearsall?"

"What's happened?" my voice was shaky.

"I'm afraid there's been an accident."

As though they too knew something was wrong my two-year-old twins Dana and Devon began to cry. That was all I heard before I felt my legs weakening and I began to sink to the floor.

That was a year ago. Mike, my husband of seven years had died in a boating accident off the New England Coast. It was deduced that there had been a fire on the small rented boat. The investigators said that he must have been trying to put the fire out when his clothes caught and he might have fallen or jumped into the water. The police report indicated from the debris that the engine blew and my husband might not have been far enough away to avoid the blast. It could have disoriented him or left him unconscious and he probably sank, drowned then was mostly likely washed out to sea.

"You wouldn't want to identify anything that would have been left of him even if he had been found," the investigator told me sorrowfully. All they found was a bit of jacket with traces of his blood. My husband—the loving father of my twins was gone.

~*~

Mike had always enjoyed fishing he said it relaxed him like nothing else. I'd gone with him many times before the twins were born and thank goodness we didn't this time or we might all be dead.

It was odd at the memorial service with nothing but a picture of him—the one where he'd been made salesman of the year at his job, but even worse, was the plaque on a granite stone bearing his name, birth and death dates over the empty grave.

Mike had been meticulous about handling all our finances and I knew that even though we no longer had him; I knew our twins and I would be secure until they were at least in high school and most likely college. What a shock it was to learn that we had no money and our lovely home had been re-mortgaged to the hilt without my knowledge. He had taken out insurance on himself, the kids and me, but when I presented the policies to the broker I was advised they had been cancelled a year after they'd been purchased. A sinking feeling gripped me as I forced myself to go through Mike's important papers, only to find there were no papers to go through. There were commodities brochures and meaningless clippings on penny stock trades, but that was about it.

Although I was filled with worry, it hadn't escaped my notice that no one from Mike's job had been to see me or even called. He'd worked there for a few years and he really loved it and what I'd heard from him, they adored him too. I made several calls, but each time I was told that Mr. Brailton—the District Director was unavailable. By Thursday when he still hadn't returned any of my calls, I packed up the twins and drove downtown.

I ignored the secretary's speech about not having an appointment and insisted upon seeing Mr. Brailton or I would raise enough hell to cause a scene worthy of a tabloid exclusive. When he finally came down, his face was stoic to the point of unfriendliness—odd considering Mike had been his best associate. His face softened when he looked at the twins squirming in my arms.

"Maybe we should go to my office Mrs. Pearsall."
Again a feeling of dread came over me. Once inside and with the
kids crawling on his expensive Aubusson carpet, he looked me
straight in the eye and told me the bad news.

"Mike hasn't worked here for more than six months."

"That's impossible!" I nearly shouted. "He left our home
every morning to come down here. He was your employee of the
year two years in a row for goodness sake."

The man looked puzzled. "No, he wasn't. As a matter of
fact, Mike was the worst investment we ever made. Oh he had
grand ideas, but he wanted too much too soon and he didn't want
to put in the effort it took to get there. We had to let him go."

"But…"

"I'm sorry you had to find out this way Mrs. Pearsall, but
there were other improprieties as well—some you are better off
not knowing."
But I insisted, nothing he said could hurt me anymore then the
things that had already happened. He told me that Mike had
embezzled a large sum of money and they did not pursue legal
action because he didn't want the company embroiled in an
embarrassing public scandal.

"We made a deal with him not to prosecute and if he
would pay back a good faith sum. He agreed, but he ever
followed through and then the accident happened. I'm sorry."

My face burned with embarrassment. Everyone knew
what my husband did and here I was demanding his due. With a
dry mouth and a lump in my throat I could hardly swallow over,
I retrieved my children and left the office.

Tears of confusion nearly blinded me as I drove home.
Mike never said a word about being out of work. *Where did he
go every day? And the money that paid the bills, was it from the
embezzlement?*
I soon found out that most of the bills in fact *hadn't* been paid.
When I got home and put my fretful twins down for a nap, I
pulled up our on-line banking service using the pin number for
our household account. It had exactly eight hundred dollars in it.

Making a trip to the bank the next day, I found that all other accounts for Mike and me had been closed all together. I had no idea what we were going to do.

~*~

By the end of the month, creditors were calling and threatening lawsuits. When I tried to tell them that I had never been contacted before, they informed me that they in fact had by mail to our Post office Box. *What post office Box?* I went to the post office and asked about it but the only information they gave me was that the box was full to capacity and that I should have the owner empty it as soon as possible. At home I searched for the key, but there wasn't one. Finally I took the death certificate over and after filling out a multitude of forms and fifty dollars to break to the lock, I was allowed access along with two bonded employees to witness it.

There it was, piles of unpaid bills from the electric and water companies, the bank and all sorts of places demanding payment along with copies of excuse letters Mike had written to stave them off.

It was all so crazy and I couldn't believe it was happening but I soon had to come to the serious realization that we could be homeless when the bank threatened foreclosure if the delinquent charges weren't paid.

~*~

When I look back on my life with Mike trying to make sense of it all, pieces of the puzzle began to fall into place. He never wanted me to continue on with my college education and in fact dissuaded me from working as soon as I became pregnant.

"I want you here at home raising our family. It's my job to take care of you my princess." That's what he'd always called me—*his princess.* How could I know that this royal person was about to be dethroned without so much as a shilling.

Mike had always kept to himself and by association I fell into the same pattern of seclusion. We had no dealings with our neighbors other than an occasional greeting, and never attended any parties or cookouts and never invited any of them over to our house either. Mike was an orphan with no siblings or even distant relatives to count on. I was an only child raised by an old maid aunt after my parents were killed in a senseless home invasion. She passed away a year after Mike and I married. I remembered how we argued about me going to her funeral after he'd found out that she had nothing of value and was in a nursing home when she passed away. He didn't want to *waste* the money on the trip.

"What's the difference? You haven't seen her since before we were married. She's gone now and I need you here with me princess."

But I insisted and he grudgingly relented. He made me pay for it by not speaking to me for an entire week after I'd returned and in fact had gone on a business trip and didn't call except the night he wanted me to pick him up at the airport. Afterwards, it was as though nothing had happened and he was back to being sweet, patient, soft-spoken man I'd married.

~*~

I began to panic when I had to go to the store to buy food and other necessary items for the twins. I'd never worried about money before, Mike always left a set amount for groceries and incidentals each week and always seemed like enough and I made it work. Now, even the generic brands seemed outrageous in price.

I was finally out of time. The bank sent a final notice and told me I had to vacate the premises within 90 days. I was down to my last $400.00 and I knew I had to do something. I had no babysitter so I couldn't go look for a job. Besides, what could I do after being out of the workforce for so long?

That Friday night, after the kids were asleep, I spent most of the night tagging items for the lawn sale the following morning. How many times had I seen Mike turn his nose up when he saw our neighbors having their yearly yard sales? *"They're just getting rid of their junk and people are buying it. It's disgraceful."*

I told him that it was good way to raise extra cash and sometimes one person's junk might be of good use to someone else.

"We don't have any junk Cindy. Nothing we have can even remotely be afforded by those cheapskate cretins."
I thought the statement a bit highbrow and the name calling offensive, and while I admit we did have top-of-the-line items in our home, the next day at the sale everything went for a mere pittance of its true worth. I sold the furniture and larger house items to an antiques dealer and I knew I was being cheated but there was nothing I could do, the rest I sold to a thrift store.

~*~

It was an early, dreary Sunday morning when everyone in the neighborhood would still be tucked warmly in their beds, that I collected the few bundles of clothes and necessary items that were left and put them in the trunk of my old Sedan. Thank goodness it was paid for and I owned it outright. I gathered the twins and although they slept through it, I cried like a baby when I placed them in their car seats and pulled out of the garage and left the only home they'd ever known. I could barely see through my tears as I left our comfortable little mid-western town and drove south with no idea where I was going.

By the time I reached Tennessee the money began to run out, primarily due to the fact that I had to have the brakes and radiator fixed on the old car. The kids were irritable from being confined in the car and I was snappish due to lack of sleep. It was 11:00 at night and there wasn't a soul on what would normally be a busy street in any other town. I was lucky enough to find an all-night gas *stop and go* where I was able to buy milk for the twins and a tasteless sandwich for myself. I asked the clerk if he knew of any accommodations and he told me there was a nice hotel downtown, but it didn't take long to find out it was well out of my price range. I drove on, but I was so tired I could hardly keep my eyes open. I drove until I saw a small, but high one-lane bridge. I looked around clandestinely and noticed there were hardly any cars going across it and there was no one around. I drove off the road and pulled the car underneath it and shut off the lights. The air was still with only the occasional sound of a night bird and the annoying buzz of flies and mosquitoes. I glanced back at the twins; they were fast asleep in their car seats. I didn't dare wake them to lay them down, nor did I have the strength. I pulled my legs up and postured myself uncomfortably in the front seat, too tired to think about what I was going to do next. I made sure that all the doors were locked and the windows in the front were opened just a crack.

I didn't think I'd be able to fall asleep, I just needed to rest a while, but the next thing I remember was the clumping sound of cars as they passed over the old bridge overhead. It was morning and the hot southern sun was already beaming through the cracks in the old bridge. I sat up and looked backward; the twins were awake but busy playing with their squeeze toys.

"Good morning darlings," I said to them. I was treated with the most precious and brightest smiles that warmed my heart and convinced me that I had to go on with the business of living, if not for me—for them.

Cranking up the car, it choked momentarily letting me know that it too was tired and wouldn't last very long. I pulled out from underneath the bridge and headed off the dirt road and into the morning traffic.

By the time I reached Atlanta, I had forty-three dollars left and I was in a panic. The kids were irritable and had been whimpering most of the morning. I pulled into a roadside diner and took them inside. Sitting in a booth, I was hard pressed to keep them from spilling the sugar and throwing the plastic salt and pepper shakers at one another.

"Well those are right cute little one's you got there, but they sure look like handful," a kind voice said.

"Thank you—and they are," I answered timidly looking up at the obese woman wearing a stained apron.

"You just hold on a sec, I have just the thing."

She left and a few seconds later returned with two large sheets of paper and several fat colorful crayons. She put them down in front of the twins who immediately took up the implements and began to scribble.

"Young'un's like to draw. I never saw a child who didn't love to make a mess on paper. Now, what can I get ya?" She poised her pen to her pad waiting.

"Oh I'm sorry," I said looking at the plastic covered menu hoping to find something inexpensive.
Suddenly, she leaned down and took it away. "Never you mind. I'll have Harry—that's my husband; fix you up something real good and something the kids will like too."

I didn't want her to know just how desperate I was, but I couldn't splurge my last few dollars, I had to make it last until I was at least able to find a job.

"A bowl of cereal for them. They can share it, and just some toast and a glass of water for me."
She stared at me a long time. "Alrighty, if that's what you want."

The kids were giggling and cooing and showing me their scribbled artwork and while I gave them all the attention I could, but I couldn't help but stare out of the window, my heart and mind filled with confusion and despair.

"Here we go!"
I was about to protest that she'd gotten the order wrong as she put down two bowls of cereal with banana's in front of the twins and juice boxes. She then set a full plate of eggs, bacon, home fries, toast a cup of coffee and a small glass of orange juice in front of me."

"There you go, cereal and toast. Oh I'll be back with your water in just a sec." She wrote something on her little pad, tore it off and plopped it face down on the table and waddled away.
With shaking hands I picked up the paper and almost cried when I saw the price. *One dollar Caledonia Diner Breakfast special*, it read.

When we finished eating, I took out three dollars and left it as tip then gathered up the twins. The woman was busy with a customer and I knew I would have bawled like a baby if she'd spoken to me. I was strapping the kids in their seats when she came wobbling out of the store.

"Hey! I think one of your young'un's dropped this."
It was Dana's stuffed bear.

"Thank you." I said. It didn't escape my notice that the three dollars I'd left as a tip was peeking out of the little bear's blue jean pocket. I wanted to protest but before I could say a word she interjected.

"So, ya'll visitin' kin folk around here?"
My hesitation was so long that she continued on. "Oh I see, you're just passin' through. Well if you think you might stay for the night I know a right nice place. It's clean, safe and cheap."

My heart pounded with anticipation. I would like nothing better than to have a nice hot soak in a real tub rather than a sponge bath in a gas station bathroom.

"We've been on the road for more than a week now. I guess the kids could use a bath and so could I for that matter." She peered at me closely. "Is everything all right honey?"

I didn't want to talk about my personal life and I started to get into the car. "Thanks for the breakfast, we have to get going."

She took hold of my arm gently. "You're right, it ain't none of my business, but the offer of a decent place to stay for the night still holds. Matter of fact, I got some time and can show you where it is. It ain't far."
I thought a few minutes, studying the woman's face. I couldn't see any mendacity, but I didn't want to get fooled by anyone or put my kids in peril. Sleeping in the front seat of the car had left my back stiff and achy and I didn't know how long the old sedan was going to last.

"Well…" I hesitated.

"I promise you and the young'un's will be right pleased—Harry!" she yelled back at the diner door.
A tall thin man came out rubbing his hands on his apron.

"I'll be right back. I'm taking the young Mrs. here over to Lula's."

He waved once and disappeared inside.

"Now you get on in and I'll tell you where to go." She opened the passenger side door and got in.

This was dangerous and I knew it. I hesitated again.

"Whatever been done to ya honey, there comes a time when ya have to start trusting people again," she said.

It was too soon, but I looked at my children and I decided with reservations, that I would start with her and got behind the wheel.

Her name was Caldonia Alice Maywood but she liked to be called Callie. She and her husband of twenty-five years, were born and raised in the small suburb of Atlanta and opened the Diner five years after they married. She was a fast talker and before I knew it I had learned a little more about her life than I really cared to know. Less than fifteen minutes later she directed me onto a long gravel driveway that ended in front of a large two-story house. I looked at her puzzled.

"Motels around here got more fleas than lazy field dog," she said getting out of the car. "This is my sister Lula's place, she can put you up for the night—Luuuula!" she yelled as she walked up to front steps. The screen door popped open and a thinner rendition of Callie emerged and stood on the porch with her hands on her hips.

"Brought some company. Smells mighty good in there." Callie glanced over at me and smiled. "Lula does all the bakin' for the diner."

I had gotten out and was standing by the car.

"Peach cobbler, but it ain't my best—not enough sugar this time." The woman scrunched her nose up and squinted over silver rimmed glasses at me.

"Don't pay her any mind, she's good and she knows it. She just likes hearin' it is all," Callie laughed.

"It smells wonderful," I said shyly.

"She also sells them to some of the small local food marts and all the *Busy-Bee* gas station chains.

I was impressed. Who would have thought an entrepreneur would be stuck way out in a country suburb.

"Howdy do," Lula finally smiled.

"Good morning," I said weakly.

"Come on down here Lu and help her in. She's got a pair of the cutest little *smoochie-poo's* you ever did see."
Lula's eyes seemed to light up as she hurried down the stairs. I opened the door to un-strap the twins.

"My word, they are just adorable. Will they come to me?" She held out her arms.
I knew they wouldn't. Their interaction with other people was minimal thanks to Mike. But to my amazement, Dana held out her chubby little arms and went right to the pleasant faced woman.

"You're a friendly little munchkin ain't ya? Ya'll come on in."
Callie took Devon while I retrieved our overnight bag from the trunk.
The house was large, cozy and while it wasn't air- conditioned there were ceiling fans moving in lazy rotation in every room. I followed the two women upstairs as they made ridiculous cooing noises to the twins who giggled with childish delight. She opened the door to nice room with a large four-poster bed.

"You can sleep here; the munchkins can have the room next door."

"Thank you but I'd rather have them with me. " I said anxiously. "There's plenty of room for all of us."

"Suit yourself," she said setting my little girl down. "The bathroom is right through there…" she pointed. "There's clean towels and plenty of soap. Make yourself at home."
Callie took the twins by the hand who were only too eager to follow her. "I'll take the little ones and bathe them in Lula's tub. That way, you can have a nice relaxing soak."
Hesitation again.

"They'll be all right honey, you just give me some clean clothes and they'll be right as spring rain in no time."

386

I opened the overnight bag and pulled out clean *Under-Roos* and two matching coveralls.

"I won't be long, if they give you any trouble just bring them in to me," I said as they led the children out.

"Don't you worry." Callie said as she was about to close the door.

"Hey wait! You didn't tell me how much..."

"We'll work that out when you get all nice and bathed." And she shut the door.

I couldn't believe I was so tired. Once I disrobed and lowered myself into the tub, my bones nearly screamed as the hot water began to loosen the tension. I scrubbed until my skin was raw, almost as though I was trying to get the stink of past few weeks off me. I could have stayed in that tub for the rest of the day, but I got out, dried off and pulled on my underclothes. I padded to the bed and sat down wearily. I could hear one of the women singing some silly child's tune and the distinct sound of Dana's giggle. I laid across the bed, intending to enjoy the peacefulness of the room and just relax. I closed my eyes for just a moment and that was all I remembered.

I awoke with a start and instantly knew what had awakened me. It was silence. There wasn't a sound except for chirping of crickets and the loud buzz of cicadas. The room was dark and what's more, it was dark outside. *How long had I slept?* I reached over to the nightstand and grabbed my watch. 8:30! I'd slept all day and well into the evening. I hurriedly pulled on a clean pair of jeans and a top. Running my hands through my hair I slipped my feet into my still dusty pair of shoes and went to the door. The dim hall light was little comfort to me. All I could think about was my children.

"Dana! Devon!" I yelled as I hurried toward the steps. Instantly, Lula's face appeared at the bottom.

"What's wrong honey, are you ailin?"

"Where are my children?" the words came out ungratefully harsh.

The woman came upstairs and took my hand and led me to a door. She opened it quietly and let me slip inside.

"Poor little dears. They played with *Bully* and *Tuck*-my two lop-eared hound dogs until they were plum tuckered out. They had a good dinner then I put them down. I expect they'll sleep right through the night."

I went to my twins who looked like angels sleeping together in the double bed. Lula had placed heavy chairs around the sides so they wouldn't fall off.

"I looked in on you and you were sleepin' so peaceful, I thought you wouldn't mind them being in here. You can take them in with you if you have a mind to."
I kissed each of my kids and tiptoed from the room. Shutting the door quietly, I looked at Lula.

"I'm sorry if I was rude. We've never been apart and I guess I was just a little nervous."

"Don't worry yourself another second about it. Come on downstairs, I left some chicken and dumpling in the warmer for you."

"Sounds wonderful, I could eat a horse." I said smiling at her.

"Well tomorrow I'll see what I can do, but tonight it's chicken," She grinned.
After eating more than I should, I insisted on washing my dishes. Lula brought out two tall glasses of lemonade and took them out onto the back screened in veranda.

"Come on sit a spell. It's peaceful this time of night and I love looking at the stars."
It was true. The sky was filled with thousands of bright, twinkling lights. She handed me a woven reed fan and indicated the rocker next to hers. There I was, twenty- eight-years-old, in the country sitting beside an old woman enjoying lemonade and I never felt more content.

~*~

After a perfect night's rest I was awakened by the squealing laughter of my son Devon. Glancing at my watch, I saw that it was 8:00 and I chastised myself for sleeping so late. I went to the window and looked down into the backyard and there was Callie cradling my son, tickling him mercilessly on his belly. Dana was sitting in the dirt in front of her, spooning it into a rubber bucket happily.

I packed our things and made sure that the bathroom was as neat as I'd found it, I made up the bed, then headed downstairs. The odors from the kitchen assailed my nostrils and set my stomach to grumbling.

"Well there you are, Sleep well honey?"

"Just wonderful"

"Sit yourself down then and have some breakfast. I have some…"

She rattled off a menu that would have put any diner to shame. I opted for eggs, toast, juice and coffee.

"Well I suppose you're right to turn down my buttermilk pancakes otherwise you'd be as big as Callie."

"Oh you should talk Lula, if it wasn't for your good cookin' I wouldn't be as round as I am," Callie said entering from the sliding screen door.

In spite of their barbs and quips, it was easy to see the siblings were completely devoted to one another.

Lula refused to allow me to help with the dishes and I knew I shouldn't prolong our departure any longer anyway.

"I guess we'd best get on the road. I um… have a some money and I want to give you a little something for you kindness."

A little something was an understatement as I reached for my purse, searching for my wallet.

Callie came over and sat down next to me.

"Do you have any idea where ya goin'?"

"I'm not sure. But I was wondering…" I hesitated.

"Maybe you know of a rooming house that takes kids, and not too expensive?"

"Rooming house my foot!" Lula shot up from leaning down by the oven, wiping her hands on the dishtowel that hung from her apron sash. "What's the matter with right here?"

"What?" I asked puzzled.

"I'm here all day pretty much by myself. I'd love the company."

I was astonished. These people didn't even know me.

"We haven't even settled our account for yesterday and last night," I said.

"We'll work something out and I'll just put it on your bill."

Something in the back of my mind told me she had no intention of ever doing that at all.

"What's more…" she went on. "I can watch the kids while you go looking for work."

"Or maybe you can help out in the diner, don't pay much, but tips are pretty good during the evening hours and weekends," Callie chimed in.

"She's not workin' at the diner. She needs to go downtown and get herself a *real* job. I bet you know all about them computers and such dontcha?" Lula asked me.

"Yes, I'm familiar with it, but I've been out of the work force for a while."

"Probably just like riding a bike. What say you start lookin' tomorrow? The kid's will be fine with me."

These were perfect strangers, yet they'd shown me nothing but kindness from the moment I met them. They both stared at me waiting for an answer.

"Well I guess I have to start trusting someone." I whispered, remembering the words Callie had said to me the day before.

"Good! It's settled then."

~*~

It wasn't until I was living in Lula's house for two months that I ventured to tell them my story. Callie wiped the tears from her eyes and said she couldn't imagine being a widow at such a young age, but to be left penniless with two young children was more than she wanted to think about.

Like everywhere, job's were scarce and my skills were lacking from nonuse. It was Lula's idea that I finish my education.

I had been studying Financial and Business Administration back before I met Mike and was within a year and a half of finishing when we decided to marry. But even community colleges weren't totally free and I had no money.

"Never you mind bout that..." Callie said picking up the phone. The next thing I knew two days later I was sitting in front of the Loan officer at the local bank, a few days after that a letter arrived advising me that my loan application had been approved. I didn't find out until later that an arrangement had been worked out with them by Callie and Lula.

I enrolled at the University and took on a full schedule. It was hard work, but I applied everything I had to learning all I could, as fast as I could. My professor was so impressed with my progress that I was assigned to work as a financial intern at the Valiant Hospital in Smyrna on my days off and some weekends.

"You'll be working for Eloise Huffington, she's a barracuda, but just stay out of her way and she won't give you any trouble," he said.

Eloise was the director at Valiant and from what I understood, a middle-aged *Daughter of the Confederacy* who came from money and didn't mix with anyone below her station professionally or personally if she could help it. She had buried one husband and was a three-time divorcee, but the office buzz was that she was currently engaged and was planning a huge wedding set for the end of the summer with a man nearly half her age.

~*~

My work at Valiant wasn't glamorous, mostly I had to scan multitudes of reports for monetary errors and proof the grants written by the elusive Miss Huffington. She might have been upper crust, but she couldn't write a grant to save her life and I spent a great deal of time correcting and rewriting many of her proposals and letters.

I'd been there for about two months when I dared to make some corrections and attach a memo with some ideas of my own about how to make a particular proposal better. I was rewarded with her equally stuffy personal assistant plopping it back on my little desk.

"Miss Huffington would like you to re-do this and send it out as she originally wrote it."

There were glaring mistakes and the figures didn't add up. I just couldn't put my name on the report as the examiner.

"I can't do that. It will look like I didn't proof it all and there *are* discrepancies." I said.

The assistant snatched it back and stalked off to the Dragon lady's office. Not more than five minutes later, she was at my desk.

"Miz. Pearsall is it? Is there a problem?"

The woman standing before me was short and a breath away from being over-weight but doing everything she could to try and hide it, and didn't have on one thing that cost under quite a few hundred dollars—from her too-snug Chanel suit, to her toe-pinching Prada shoes. Her makeup was impeccable, but couldn't hide the creeping crow's feet and laugh lines around her eyes and mouth. The large, gaudy dull diamond ring she wore was oddly out of sync with the rest of her other expensive jewelry.

"No Miss Huffington, I know how busy you are and sometimes when you're looking at rows and rows of numbers, things get missed. The figures I circled are items that I wasn't sure of that's why I put what I *thought* was the correct amount in the space next to yours, just in case you might want to check," I said trying to pacify the situation and make it sound like I was the one at fault and not her.

She snatched the paper and looked it. I saw her face blanche but she recovered nicely.

"Are you sure you didn't change my figures?"

"I assure you Miss Huffington I would never do such a thing." I controlled my anger, she knew she was wrong.

"All right, go with the new figures. Mail it out before you leave," she said before stalking off and leaving a vapor of expensive perfume.

Passing by her locked office at the end of the day, I vowed that my name would be emblazoned on copper nameplate attached to an office door just like hers someday. I had just put the documents in the mailroom and was heading to the door when I was almost knocked down.

"Oh Excuse me. I'm sorry—did I hurt you? Of course I hurt you—but don't worry, I'm a doctor I can fix it."
I looked up at the source of the rapid chattering, and I kept looking up, at the tall lanky, mountain of a man. I rubbed my sore arm.

"It's okay, I should have been paying more attention."

"I guess you just didn't expect a big old wall where there shouldn't be one," he joked, gesturing at his height, "Hi I'm Rueben Westlake—Surgeon." He said pointing to his black and white stenciled nametag.

"Cindy Pearsall—financial intern."

"Ahhh so you're the new wizard trainee everyone's talking about."

I blushed profusely. *People were talking about me?*

"I can't imagine what about." I said starting to walk again.

"Ellis Cummings—he's the chairman of the board said that you're worth more than your weight in gold."
I was about to burst with pride just hearing that.

"I bet it's not sitting right with ole Huffy though. She's quite used to being the big cheese around here," he indicated with a nod toward Eloise's office.

"I'm not looking to upset any apple carts and this is just an internship, I expect to find a real job by Fall."

"That's too bad." Reuben said softly. "Say, I was heading over to the cafeteria for a bite to eat. Care to join me?"

"Thanks but I need to finish up and get home to my kids." He was very handsome, but no way was I ready for anything that resembled a relationship.

"Oh," he said his smile fading.

~*~

I finished school with honors. My Professor was so proud of me and brought several guests and business acquaintances to the small celebration Callie, Harry and Lula had for me at the diner. One of them was Dr. Westlake.

"You should be very proud of yourself," he said. "I understand you've gotten job offers from several hospitals already."

"Yes, it's all pretty amazing. I can't believe how lucky I am."

Just then Devon waddled over raising his hands for me to pick him up. I introduced him to Rueben and the little minx literally flew into his lap.

"Here there little fella," his eyes were full of playfulness as he examined the toy truck my son held up to him.

A few minutes later Callie came over and retrieved him.

"Nice day outside, you young folks ought to be out enjoying it."

"Well I'm not so sure Mr. Pearsall would appreciate me taking his wife for a walk mam," Ruben said.

"Excuse me for telling your business," she said to me, then looked back at Ruben. "She's a widow and lonelier than a queen bee on the moon even if she won't admit it."

"She is!" Ruben's face lit up and sparkled. "I...I mean I'm sorry...about you being a widow, but glad that...well how about that walk?"

He was as tall and gangly as a teenager and just as shy, and he made me smile.

~*~

Ruben became a regular at the diner, first winning the heart of Callie, then Lula when she began inviting him to Sunday supper, then my twins. I thought it was time for me to find my own place but Lula wouldn't hear of it.

"You get yourself situated with a job first and then we'll talk about that," Lula snapped with loving maternal finality.I suspected she would miss the twins terribly if I left, and they adored her too. I didn't have the heart to separate them just yet. Although I had been asked to stay with Valiant, I didn't think it was right since Ruben worked there and we were sort of dating.

Several months later, I procured a job at Sunnyville Rehabilitation hospital. It was a premier treatment facility that had originally catered mostly to a precise and elite clientele, but Irving Benlow the Vice President, insisted that good rehabilitation care belonged to *everybody* and demanded that the facility accept regular patients as well.

When I arrived early that first morning, Mr. Benlow himself escorted me to my new office. It wasn't terribly big but it did have the same rich looking mahogany desk and deep purple plush chairs that I'd seen in the larger offices. But the best thing was my name, in large gold leaf letters attached to the door for anyone to see and that was a proud moment for me.

The next few weeks were hectic. I was at meetings everyday almost all day most of the time but I insisted on being done by five in order to be able to spend time with the twins. Under the loving care of *The Diner brigade* as I called them, my kids were happy and healthy and I hated to take them away when I finally found a small two-bedroom apartment closer to the city. I tried to give Lula my very first paycheck but she refused to take it.

"We gave a kindness, so you do a kindness. Someday someone might need *your* help and that's when you repay what you think we've done for you."

I hugged her tightly, she was like a mother to me and the kids had long ago started calling her *Grammy* to her and Callie's, absolute delight. Harry drove in every morning to bring the kids out to Lula's and sometimes she insisted that they spend the night which I agreed to when I knew I was too tired to give them the quality time they deserved.

Ruben and I had gotten close, and he knew my story. The first time we made love, I was as shy as a schoolgirl, but he was gentle and kind and as much as I fought it, I was falling for him.

My first work assignment was to prepare a procreation agreement for two floundering facilities. It was a bitter pill because one of them was Valiant. I wanted to discuss it with Ruben but I had been sworn to secrecy until all the negotiations had been worked out. The absorption of the facilities in question meant that there would be major changes including cutbacks and job reassignments. The entire process took ten months and by the time the new release manager called a press conference, word had already leaked out. I wasn't a bit surprised when I received a call from Eloise Huffington herself.

"Miss Pearsall? Did we miss each other when we were you at the Mayor's dinner a month ago..."
She knew darn well we didn't as I tried to ignore her usual condescending tone; even though she tried to mask it with her lilting southern drawl.

"No, Miss Huffington I wasn't invited to the mayor's gala, but we have met. I did an internship at your facility a year ago."

"Indeed? I don't seem to recall..."
She was lying and we both knew it.

"In any case..." she went on. "I'm giving a small supper at my little ole place in Alpharetta Saturday evening and I'm hoping you won't disappoint me by not coming."

"I'll have to check my calendar and get back to you."
I didn't have a darn thing to do Saturday night.

"Good! I look forward to hearing from you. If I haven't heard from you say... about five, I'll have my secretary... no I'll call you myself, would that be all right?"
I couldn't believe Eloise was sucking up to me.

"I'll give *you* a call," I said and hung up the phone.

Of course I would attend her little soiree, but I was going to make her sweat waiting for my answer.

~*~

Saturday night I arrived promptly at Eloise Huffington's *little ole place* that was actually a mansion, and judging from the grounds and what I could see of the land, she certainly wasn't shy about showing off the fact that her family came from money and lots of it.

I'd learned over the past few months that she had been just a figurehead at Valiant hospital because her name carried a lot of clout and that's what counted. All that was about to change and she knew it.

Her *small* dinner party guest list included no less than fifty of the most powerful people in the State, including three mayors two congressman and of course every high ranking law official for miles around. She complimented me outrageously over my choice of a simple black sheath, the borrowed strand of pearls from Lula and the small silk purse Callie had produced from her treasure chest. *"From my going out days,"* she'd said. Thankfully, Reuben wasn't there as he was watching over a seriously ill patient he'd operated on earlier, besides, our growing relationship wasn't exactly ready for public notice.

The banter during supper was light, but Eloise toyed with questions along the line of the impending acquisition. Dessert had just been served and I saw her talking clandestinely to one of her guests, when suddenly she looked up at me.

"Cynthia, I'm sure you won't keep us all in the dark about the new merger. Can't you give us just one or two lil ole hints about what's going to happen?" Her smile was sickeningly sweet.

"Now Eloise…" addressing her by her given name put even more outraged puff in her chest, but I just couldn't help myself. "You know that would be unethical. There will be a press conference on Monday, and you're invited."

"Can we safely say that Valiant has nothing to worry about?" she asked still digging for facts.

"I can safely say that Valiant will know when everyone else does."

The smile left her face and was replaced with a hard smirk.

"Looks like she ain't going to give up any secrets tonight Eloise—speaking of which, I hear tell you have a little secret of your own." A portly man said, whom I found out was the local Police Captain.

I saw her lower her head with fake shyness.

"Willard G. Pender I declare, you are a master at finding out the deepest of secrets. Too bad you couldn't get any information about the merger." She glanced at me.

"Come on Weezie old girl, tell us the news. If you don't I will?" he winked at her, but not before I saw her close her eyes in total disbelief that he'd dared call her by that awful nickname. A chorus of voices urged her to tell. She waved her silk napkin at them and smiled.

"Oh all right, if you just must know."

She stood up and her gold Lamé dress, which on a taller, thinner model would have been flattering but on her it bunched and pulled in all the wrong places.

"Ladies and gentleman, since only a few people can keep a secret in this town, I guess you all know I'm getting married!" There was thunderous applause.

"How many times does this make?" Willard guffawed over the din.

She threw him a murderous glance, then recovered nicely.

"That doesn't matter Willard, this time it's right."

"Well do we get to meet this mystery man? After all we have to make sure he's worthy of our dearest friend." Another guest called out.

"As a matter of fact I'm expecting him any moment. I was going to make the announcement while we enjoyed our brandy out on the veranda, but you all beat me to it."

There were hearty; as well as half veiled congratulations and I grinned inwardly as I watched her preen and hold court.

By the time we left the table and headed out to the candlelit veranda, it was close to 10:00 and I needed to check on the kids. I asked Eloise if I might use her phone.

"Of course dear, why don't you use the ones right there in the library." Eloise indicated an ornate paneled door.

Everyone had gathered around her once again congratulating her and asking her questions I assumed were about her beau. I grinned again as my mind ran through a gamut of the types of men she'd already had, and the one she was about to get. I entered the grand library, aghast at the size of it and the books there were shelved from floor to ceiling. I went to the large, neat desk and perched myself on it and dialed. Lula answered and told me that the kids were already asleep and were doing fine.

"No need to rush. Why don't you go on over and see that young man of yours?" she teased. I blushed. Although I knew she understood what was going on between Ruben and me I was still embarrassed.   I fiddled with the gold pen set as I listened to Lula give me all her own valid reasons why there was no need to come home so early. Absently, I took up the gilt-edged picture frame and turned it—sure that I was going to see a studio photograph of Eloise in one of her grand poses. But it wasn't Eloise.

My heart almost stopped, the voice on the other end began to fade as my mind tried to make my eyes believe what I was seeing. There staring at me were the same blue eyes that had captured my heart years ago, the same eyes that my children shared. I was looking at a picture of Michael Emerson Pearsall— my dead husband.

In a voice that sounded like someone else, I told Lula I'd call her back. I stared at that picture for what seemed like an eternity. It took that long for my eyes to notice the large familiar script that read, *WITH ALL MY LOVE-BILL.* I didn't even try to think that this was someone who merely *looked* like my husband; I'd spent too many years living with him, sleeping beside him. I knew it was him.

Anger consumed me. Why did he lie? Where had he been? Why hadn't he contacted us? I was filled with too much distrust to think he had amnesia and didn't remember us. He didn't *want* to remember us. I heard a knock on the door just as it was being opened.

"Everything all right Cynthia?" It was Eloise.
I hurriedly put the picture back and walked to the door. My bare arms prickled with goose bumps and I just wanted to get out of there.

"Yes—well no, one of the kids is running a temperature I think I'd better go."

"I'm sorry you have to leave so early. Maybe we can do lunch after that little ole press conference on Monday."

"That would be nice," I said hurrying away from her. I just needed to get out fast.
She was right behind me as I reached the door. I pulled it open— and there he stood, his hand poised to ring the bell. My heart was beating so hard I thought I was going to die. My knuckles ached from clutching my purse, as I looked up into the face of my husband who for a moment flinched, then looked right past me and held out his arms. Eloise rushed by me and went into them.

"Bill Coverlin" she admonished playfully, "You're late!"

"But I'm here darlin'." He kissed her hard on the mouth his eyes open, staring right at me.

"Honey, let me introduce you to Cynthia Pearsall, she's the new Director over at Sunnyville and quite a little fire-cracker as I hear it," Eloise gushed.

"A pleasure." The cad said holding out his large hand. There was no way I was going to touch him and there was certainly no way I was about to air my dirty laundry in front of some the most prestigious people in town.

"Thanks for a wonderful evening Eloise but I really must get home to my kids. They're all I have and I like to be with them as much as I can." The words came out as an accusing barb, and I knew Mike—or Bill as he was now being called, understood what I was saying. I left, barely able to drive myself to Lula's.

~*~

For the next two days I was a complete basket case. *How was it possible that Mike was alive and not contact us? How could he not want to see his children?* A million questions crashed around in my head and the worse thing was, I didn't know what to do.

It was days before I was able to talk to Reuben, and when he finally was able to reach me his concern was unabated.

"What's wrong Cindy? You seem so distracted, tell me please." Reuben's pleading voice, always so warm and comforting, now left me cold and distrusting.

"Nothing, I just have a lot of things on my mind—Look I really need to get back to work." I hung up the phone even before he was able to say good-bye.

I wasn't thinking only of myself, but of Eloise as well. In spite of her snootiness and self-centered behavior I surmised that she hadn't been lucky in her amorous dealings and the desperate look of relief on her face when she saw Mike at the door, made me think that she probably thought he was her last chance at happiness.

~*~

I barely got through the press conference on Monday, but I pulled myself together and after my speech I funneled my reserve strength and answered the rapid-fire questions about the merger. Afterwards, Eloise approached me.

"Well it looks like you've done very well for yourself. I don't suppose you'd like to hear some of my recommendations." She sounded a little desperate and I felt sorry for her.

"Of course Eloise, I value your input. As a matter of fact I was hoping you and I could get together sometime this week." She seemed genuinely shocked and pleased. What I really wanted to do was try and find a way to tell her about the charlatan she was about to marry.

"Why yes of course I'd love to, but I have to check my schedule. Why don't you give my office a call and set something up?"

I wanted to laugh, back to the same old grand dame, but I told her I would do just that, knowing in my heart that if I didn't, her secretary would be on the phone before I could pick up the receiver.

It was almost 5:30, I'd been in board meetings all day and although I was bone tired I still had a pile of documents to go through. A soft knock sounded on my door and I figured it was Janelle my new office assistant telling me she was about to leave. I was still pouring over papers when the door opened.

"You looked wonderful up there today Cyn. I was very proud of you."

It was Mike. The sound of his voice slid over my skin like an evil oil.

"What do you want?"

"To talk."

"The only thing we have to talk about is a divorce and back support for my kids."

"Look Cyn, I know you're upset…"

"Upset? Is that what you think I am? No Mike being upset was never part of this. There is no word for what I'm feeling."

"I know you hate me."

"Hate doesn't begin to cover it."

"Things got out of hand that's all. Everything was so overwhelming, I had to get out."

"*You* had to get out!" I snorted back a laugh. "You left us destitute. I had to sell everything we owned. My kids barely had food."

"I know and I'm sorry, look!" he started toward the desk. But I jumped up and backed away. I didn't want to be anywhere near him.

"Cyn, I was stupid I know that now. When I saw you up there today, looking so beautiful and talking to all those reporters, I—-well I knew I missed you. I want you back?"
I would have laughed but the sheer gall of his statement left me ill and unable to speak.

"What about Eloise?" I had to know what else was in his mind.

"That cow doesn't mean anything to me."

"I bet her money does?"

"Cyn we can have it all. If you'll keep quiet, I'll take care of the rest."
The man was truly mad.

"I want you out of my office right now. You no longer exist for me. The only thing I'll grant you is a quick and quiet divorce and you have to promise you'll leave town and never try to see us ever again."

"And if I don't?"

"Then all of Atlanta will know you for what you are—a liar a cheat and a deserter."

"What about my kids?"
It was the first time he'd even mentioned them. "What about them?"

"I have a right to see them."
I leaned over and placed both palms flat on the desk and glared at him.

"Just you try." My tone was even and cold, he knew I meant business. "Now get out."
He left and I was shaking as I took my seat. How dare he act like a deprived father when he'd left us out in the cold to fend for ourselves. There was no way I'd let him near my children. Selfish or not, I wasn't going to allow him to ease his conscious with my kids as his personal wailing wall.

My mind went to Eloise. She might not be the nicest person in the world but even she didn't deserve the pain Michael was about to inflict on her. I was thinking hard and fast but I had no idea what my next move should be.

"You should go to the police." Rueben said when I told him about my husband. His anger was so acute I thought he would try and find him and beat to within an inch of his life.

"I don't think that'll do much. He'll probably get Eloise to post bond before she even knows the whole truth about him," I said sadly.

"We've got do something."

He was right—but what?

~*~

The next few days were a blur of activity. I had a thousand things to do and Mike's emergence from the dead weighed heavily on me. Fortunately, he had the good grace to stay away from me but I did receive a few hang-ups throughout the day and I knew it was him.

I was sitting in my office when my assistant buzzed me.

"Miz Huffington is out here."

I winced before whispering back to her. *"It's, Miss Huffington to see you. Okay Janelle?"*

"Yeah okay, but she's out here."

I closed my eyes patiently. Training her to be a proper office assistant was going to take time. I'd recruited Janelle Spencer from the WORK FORCE program a few weeks after I'd gotten my job. She was a recovered addict who had been documented as being clean for more than three years and had been living in a shelter. Her obvious inadequacies aside, she had a sharp mind and was pretty well organized.   *"Comes from having very little and living in a cardboard box,"* she'd told me.

I went out to meet my visitor.

"Eloise," I sang, "What a nice surprise."

"Well I was downtown on business and thought I'd come on over and see if you were up for some lunch at the Halcyon Club. I was hoping you'd agree to look at some gowns I'm considering for my wedding."

I blanched. "How nice of you, but I'm positively up to my eyeballs with work, but if you have time I would like a moment with you."

She walked regally into my office, her Louis Vuitton clutch bag held close to her side.

"Wherever did you get that creature?" She gestured toward the door that Janelle had closed behind her.

"It's a long story." I ignored her distasteful frown when she mentioned my assistant.

"She really should do something about those long dragon nails, and that blouse she's wearing is not acceptable office attire." She flicked a non-existent piece of lint from her own silk shantung skirt.

"We're working on it. She's had a hard life; I'm giving her a chance."

"Don't they have organizations for that?"

I had to smile to myself. In truth, I believed that Eloise was so far removed from the real world that she had no idea what it was all about. But she was about to have it all come crashing down around her.

"Eloise I need to talk to you."

She came over and laid her soft, pudgy hand on mine.

"Why of course dear, anything I can do to help, why I'm right here."

She was such a phony, but an innocent one. I was about to begin my confession about her fiancé—the same man who was still married to me when her cell phone rang.

"Excuse me a moment will you dear?-Hello? Bill darling…"

I went to the window trying to give her some privacy, but inside I was fuming.

"What was that? Oh no not again," she said into the receiver, "Well this is awful short notice—I'll try and get to the bank before it closes and I'll have them wire the money right away. All right dear, I'll see you Saturday night." She snapped the cell closed and looked up at me.

"My fiancé is procuring some very valuable foreclosure property for a steal in Florida."

"Really?" I said probing for as much information as I could.

"Still, it's an awful lot of money, but then if you can't trust the man you're about to marry, who can you trust."
She laughed giddily, but I suspected the amount he'd asked for secretly rubbed her the wrong way. I went over and perched myself on the edge of my desk.

"Eloise, how well do you know your intended."

"That's an odd question," she said fidgeting with her purse. "Look, I know Bill's a few years younger than me, but that doesn't matter, not in this day and age."
I knew she was trying to convince herself. "Why people do it all the time," she ended stubbornly.

"It has nothing to do with age, Eloise…"

"My goodness look at the time. My dear, we can have our little talk at my soiree on Saturday. I promise I will make time for whatever you wanted to confide in me about, but right now I really must get going."

"But…"

"No ifs ands or buts, I expect you and your young man at my house at 8:00 sharp."
I really hadn't intended on going and even if I had, I wouldn't bring Rueben, but now I knew there was no way I couldn't attend. Too much was at stake.

"Of course I'll be there," I smiled with carefully masked sympathy.

~*~

After I picked up the kids at Lula's and got them home and bedded for the night, I wracked my brain as to what I was going to do. I begged off seeing Rueben when he insisted on coming over and made myself a cup of tea. I groaned thirty minutes later when the doorbell rang because I knew it was Reuben. He hadn't sounded like he was going to take no for an answer. I went to the door and foolishly opened it fully expecting to see his lopsided grin.

"Hello sweetheart."

It was my husband, devilishly handsome in expensive clothes I knew he could never afford and had to have been a gift from Eloise. I tried to close the door but he pushed against it.

"Now is that any way to greet the father of your children."

"Look, I don't care why you're here or what you want, I just want you gone."

"I don't think it has anything to do with what *you* want Cindy. But what I want and have a right, is to see my kids."

A headache raced full force from the back of my skull to my eyes.

"You gave up that right when you left us alone and hungry. They don't know you."

"Well why don't I just come in and re-acquaint myself, and while I'm here maybe we can get together the way we used to."

He flicked the collar of my blouse. I snatched away as though burned.

"I wouldn't let you touch me."

"I don't think you mean that. After all I am still *legally* your husband."

"You're supposed to be *legally* dead, but you're not are you? The only thing I want from you is out of here right now."

I hadn't wanted my neighbors to hear me, but I was so furious I was beyond caring. His smile was sordid as he grinned down on me.

"I can remember a time when you loved how I touched you. I can still hear your moans of pleasure while you writhed under me. I remember all those things we did and I remember you enjoying it immensely."

I thought I was going to be sick. Suddenly he grabbed me and began trying to kiss me. I pushed at him and tried to slap him, but he caught my hands, bringing his mouth closer once again.

"Stop it!" I hissed.
Suddenly he was snatched back and I heard a thud as he hit the
far wall of the hallway.

"I think the lady said no."

"Who the hell are you?" he said righting himself.

"I'm the man who *won't* beat the hell out of you if you
leave right now and the doctor who'll probably have to patch you
up if you don't."
It was Rueben, trying hard to hold his anger in check.
Michael grinned lecherously at me.

"Well I can see now why you haven't been missing me
Cindy."

"Get out of here Michael, just leave."

"Are you Okay?" Reuben said after showing Michael
roughly out and then ushered me to my couch.

"Yes I'm fine." I was just happy that the kids hadn't been
awakened by the disturbance.
I looked at him, then broke down. His arms, warm and
comforting slipped around me holding me gently.

"It's all right Cindy—it's okay honey."

"I'm so glad you're here. I thought I could do this alone,
but I can't. I don't know what to do."

"Don't worry; we'll get through this, together."

~*~

Now more than ever I didn't want to go to the Eloise
Huffington's Gala, but Saturday night at exactly 8:00 Rueben
and I stepped through her front door.

"Why Cynthia honey you're positively a vision in that
dress. Come on and let me get you and the good doctor
something to drink."
But before she could, she was whisked away by the Fire chief to
be introduced to a new business owner who had recently come to
town. I couldn't help myself, as I nervously scanned the room
looking for Michael. I found him standing before the large
fireplace, entertaining two young debutantes who were looking

adoringly up at him. I wasn't surprised. One thing I knew for sure was that he could charm the skin right off a rattlesnake.

An hour later I went into the library to call Lula about the kids. I was skittish about leaving them more than ever now that their father was back on the scene. As usual Lula assured me they were fine. I'd just hung up and was about to leave when Eloise entered the room.

"Cynthia, I was hoping to have a minute alone. Yesterday you wanted to talk to me. Well I'm all ears."
My hands grew sweaty and I tightened my fists unsure of where to begin. Before I knew it, words began to spew from my mouth.

"Eloise, Michael…" I hesitated; she wouldn't know him by that name. "Bill, is the father of my children."
Her face shriveled into a mass of incredulity.

"What?"

"He's my husband."
I could see the rise of her chest as her breathing increased.

"Are you mad Cynthia?" I understood that your husband was dead."

"I thought so too. You can imagine my surprise when I saw his picture in your office, then saw him that night, here at your house."
The silence that followed was the loudest sound I'd ever heard.

"It's not true." She held her head up high, but beads of perspiration had broken out over her face.

"It is. I'd give anything for it not to be, but he's a liar and a cheat. He left us with nothing and I'm sure he's scheming to do the same thing to you."

She was visibly shaken to the core, but fighting to maintain that old southern gentile quality of perseverance.

"You're lyin' and I'll prove it, we'll ask him. I'll just call him in here and he can confront your lies."
She wavered a moment and I thought she was about to faint.

"Let me get you a glass of water." I actually felt sorry for her.

"No, thank you." She waved me away. "I just need to throw some cool water on my face." She walked to the small powder room at the corner of the library and a second later I heard water running, then it stopped.

Maddening moments passed as I paced. The Library door opened and I turned and there stood Michael with an oily smile of confidence.

"I thought I saw you come in here."

"I was just leaving." My knuckles were tight on my purse as he barred my way.

"Now Cyn why do you want to be this way? That doctor fellow can't mean as much to you as I did."

"The only good thing that ever came out of you Michael Pearsall are my kids. They are all I live for and you do not exist for us."

I started to leave but he put his hand on my arms.

"Come Cindy, we could have it all you and me. We could live the way we always wanted to."

"On what? You don't have anything."

"I have plans?"

"Oh really, do those plans have anything to do with Eloise's money?"

"That old hag won't know what hit her. If you just give me a few months, we will be out of here before she can pick the cotton out of that sagging chin of hers."

"So you intend to just take her money and skip town, is that it?"

"Well, I will have to marry the old biddy, but it won't last. We'll be gone before I even have to share her bed—and believe me I don't want to ever have to do that again."

I hated him more than ever. "You're despicable." I shook free of him.

"Suit yourself. One way or the other I'll get the cash I want from ole moneybags and be out of here, and if you open your mouth I'll take my kids with me. You'll never find us Cindy… not ever."

"After everything you've already done, you dare threaten me with my own children?" I was shocked at his sheer nerve. I heard the soft squeak of the power-room door.

"Don't worry Cynthia; the only place he's going is to jail." Eloise stood in the doorway, regal and composed. Michael's face turned a pasty white. "Elly darlin'…"
But he knew he was caught.

"If you leave now Bill—Michael… or whatever your name is, I'll be happy to make your apologies."

"But…"

"This is an offer that will be made only once."

"She put me up to it." He pointed at me, "she was never satisfied with anything I ever did for her. "She devised this whole evil thing. But when I got to know you… Eloise honey I fell in love with you."
He looked down dejectedly. What an actor he was.

"You mean you fell in love with my money." Eloise swaggered confidently toward him. "I suggest you get yourself out of my sight as soon as you can."

"You can't mean that Eloise darlin…"
Her hard *Daughter-of-the-Revolution* glare caused him to take a step back, then ease toward the door.

"Well, I can see I'm no longer wanted here." And he hurried out.

"He'll find out that he'll be wanted in the only place that'll have him—jail." Eloise said with a grunt. She turned to me. "I guess you think I'm an old fool."

"No, I think we just both got fooled by a man who cared nothing about either of us, or his children."
She took a long look at me, then took my hand. "Thank you my dear, I know this couldn't have been easy for you."

"It was just as hard for you." I squeezed her hand.

"Well now that we have that fox out of our hen-house let's go join the party. I think we deserve a good time."

We walked out arm in arm for a moment then she excused herself and went over to whisper something to the police chief who then hurried off and out of the house.

~*~

Because of her ties with the press and everybody of any importance in town, Eloise managed to keep the scandal down to a minimum. Michael was picked up at the airport and brought back to stand trial for extortion, desertion and a host of other felonies I hadn't know about. After that, I heard that Eloise had closed up her house and was taking an extended vacation abroad.

Less than a year later, after I was granted a no-contest divorce, Rueben and I were married. It was a small affair with the reception held at the diner and included all the people I had grown to love—Callie and her husband, Lula and everyone who had embraced us with heartfelt friendship from the moment we'd arrived. My life was full, my children were safe and happy and I was hopelessly in love.

About the Author

2009 RWA/NYC Author of year and 2010 Mentor of the year, Patt gives praise to her late mother for encouraging her be what she wanted to be.

RWA the New York City Chapter, helped her to obtain valuable insight to the business, the INS the OUTS, pitfalls and of course the joy of that first acceptance.

Patt hosted a standing-room only workshop at the African American Slam Jam in 2004 and has spoken at libraries, book clubs and other forums to keep reading **FUN**damental.

Patt is currently retired from the Detective Bureau of the Somerset County Sheriff's Office and   lives in Hillsborough NJ with her husband and a very Hyper Rat Terrier named Jack.

R.I.P

Bailey

Patt invites reviews and comments on Amazon.com or at
Pattkal@yahoo.com

Made in the USA
Middletown, DE
25 March 2023

26815497R00235